Faith and the Pharisees

Sincere Critics Have Been Sincerely Wrong
About the Word of Faith Message

by
Ted Rouse

Dedication

Dedicated to all those who love our Lord Jesus Christ and have faith in the integrity of all of His Word. Special thanks to all the faithful men and women of God who, down through the ages, have stayed right with the scriptures of truth even when it wasn't popular with the religious society of their day.

Faith and the Pharisees

- Understanding satan's attack against God's message of Faith and Holy Ghost Revival.

- Correcting the critic's misunderstandings of the Faith Message.

- Learn the solid Biblical foundations of faith teaching and ministry.

- Experience victorious living through faith in the integrity of God's Word.

- Find out the truth about Job.

Copyright page

Faith and the Pharisees by Ted Rouse
Published by Insight Publishing Group
8801 S. Yale, Suite 410
Tulsa, OK 74137

This book or parts thereof may not be reproduced in any form, stored in a retrieval system or transmitted in any form by any means—electronic, mechanical, photocopy, recording or otherwise—without prior written permission of the publisher, except as provided by United States of America copyright law.

Unless otherwise noted, all Scripture quotations are from the King James Version of the Bible.

Copyright © 1999 by Ted Rouse
All rights reserved
ISBN: 1-890900-03-6
LOC: 99-95566

Reader Note: We hesitated to put in chapters as such, because to get the most from this book it is important to read it from beginning to end, beginning with the opening statements; line upon line, precept upon precept.

The Word, the Whole Word and Nothing but the Word.

Printed in the United States of America.

Contents

1. Faith and the Pharisees --------------------6
2. An Answer to the Critics of God's "Message of Faith"--------------------------17
3. Faith–Our Vital Link With God ------------33
4. What About the Word of Faith? ---------92
5. Prosperity and Health or Poverty and Sickness: Which Is God's Will?--------115
6. What About Job? ---------------------------143
7. Do Faith Teachers Deify Man and Teach We Are "god's" as the Critic States?-----155
8. What About Jesus Christ and the Atonement?----------------------------------175
9. Another Look at Prosperity ---------------206
10. Do Faith Teachers Teach Man Is Boss Over God?----------------------------------222
11. Faith In Faith or Faith In God? -----------252
12. Positive Confession Getting Rid of Corrupt Talk---------------------------------265
13. Another Look at God and His Sovereignty------------------------------------287
14. "A Different Gospel"---------------------314
15. The Holy Spirit Baptism ----------------332
16. The Biblical Evidence of the Baptism With the Holy Spirit---------------------348

Chapter 1

Faith and the Pharisees

"Thy Word is 'truth.'" This statement was spoken by the Lord Jesus Christ Himself concerning God's Word. The Word "truth" means the real facts. So then, the Scriptures contain the real facts about Christianity, what it is, what we are to believe and how we should live.

Jesus, in Matthew's Gospel, told His disciples to beware (be on guard, habitually on the alert) of the doctrine (theories or teachings) of the Pharisees and of the Sadducees. Who were the Pharisees and the Sadducees? What did they believe and how do these statements of Jesus apply to us today?

Very simply put, the Pharisees were those *religious leaders* in Judaism who put *their* religious opinions and *their* traditions on an equal level with God's Word itself (Mark 7:5-9, 13). The Sadducees were those who denied the resurrection and spiritual things (Acts 23:8), and they, like the Pharisees, wanted nothing to do with God's miraculous power, both groups saying it was of the devil (Acts 4:1-3; 5:15-18). For the most part, both groups were opposed to Christ's teaching and ministry. And they closed their eard to Him and His ministry because what He said and taught did not fit into their school of thought. They even went so far as to say that Jesus was a "deceiver" and that He had "a devil." Not only that, but they were the ones who finally stirred up the crowd, who, under their influence, yelled, "away with this man." By so doing, this religious system governed by men, was once again, ignorantly rejecting God's Word, which God sent to them just as each of these types of religious systems have done down through the ages (John 3:34; Acts 10:36-38; 13:46). Jesus was sent with the Word of God (John 1:1), and He truly was, and is, the fullest though the religious leaders had the scriptures that revealed these things, still they would have no part of Him. Even today, they still will not accept what Christ has revealed in the the Word about God, man's responsibilities, redemption, nor even the devil and his works (1 John 3:8), but rather they still choose to hold fast to what they want to believe about these things. Let it be understood that the true spirit of Christianity will always teach, do, and believe, the exact same things that were taught and done by Jesus and His disciples as is recorded in the Gospels, the Book of Acts and the Epistles (Matt 28:20; Mark 16:15-20). All later changes are forgeries (Jude 3).

When Christ came teaching the Word of God, this religious system governed by men withstood Him. The Pharisees main objective was to protect their religious system of beliefs that they had established, and to stop the multitudes from following Him by trying to make the people think that Christ's ministry was not of God but of the devil. Even so today, satan is intelligent enough to know that if He can get the leaders of religion *who control the beliefs of multitudes* to malign God's true work that God has raised up, and *make the people think* that God's true work and Word is of the devil, then he has accomplished his objective in stopping multitudes from hearing more of the truth. Satan knows many will listen to religious leaders even more so than to God's actual Word. And because Satan's objectives do not change and this tactic has been so successful in times past, we can expect that Satan, through misguided religious leaders, even today, will try to destroy any minister who really tries to follow Jesus' example, who believes in the integrity of *all* of God's Word, and has any degree of the power of the Holy Ghost operating or manifested in his, or her life or ministry. This very thing has happened during every revival of God's Word or Spirit in the earth in times past as history so clearly reveals, so there is no reason to think it is not, or will not, happen today.

In John 12:48-49, Jesus said: "He that *rejecteth Me*, and receiveth *not My words*, *hath one that judgeth Him: The Word* that *I have spoken*, the *same* shall judge him in the last day. For I have not spoken of Myself; but the Father which sent Me, He *GAVE ME A COMMANDMENT*, what I should *SAY*, and what I should *SPEAK*." "(emphasis added)." (see also 1 Corinthians 14:37-38) Jesus said, "If they have persecuted Me, they will persecute you. . . ." "If they have kept My Word, they will keep yours also. . . ."

When Jesus came, He found the religious leaders teaching things that weren't so from the beginning. They were teaching the people not the Word of God but rather their own traditions and opinions about it. They didn't stay with all that was written, but had made much of the Word of God of none effect by the things they said and taught, and yet *they thought* they were the keepers of the faith. No wonder the divine Word says, "beware of men," for religious men (thinking they are doing God a service) will "whip you (My disciples) in their places of worship" (Beck's translation in the Language of Today). Men will fight for what they, or their group believes, but not always for the Word of God or the faith that was once delivered to the saints (Jude 3).

So we can see then, if we do not want history to repeat itself in our day, ALL doctrine must be based clearly upon what the Scriptures *do say*, not on what they *don't say*. We are going to be judged on the basis of what *the Bible* actually does say and not by men's opinions concerning it, or by what any theological group or denomination's theory about it is. The Bible is God's truth and if anyone teaches otherwise, and not exactly what it says line for line, then he is not teaching truth in that area but his own opinion and is possibly found to be a "false teacher" (1 Pet. 2:1), or in the least, a sincere but misguided one. It is the Bible alone that God requires us to believe. We may not always understand it all intellectually, but we are commanded to believe it all (Heb. 11:3, 6). It is important then that we study God's Word with the intent to rightly divide it, and that we allow Scripture to interpret Scripture (2 Tim. 2:15; 2 Pet. 2:20-21), rather than interpret Scripture by what some man or some religious group or leader thinks. Christ's warning still stands, "Beware of the leaven (teachings) of the Pharisees," (religious leaders) for history has repeated itself in this area, time and again. As we look around, we can see that man's word and theology has gained the ascendancy once again over God's Word in much of Christendom, and this is the reason for the lack of faith and power in so many lives and in so many churches today. When Christ comes back, we can know that He will once again find religious men persecuting those who are carrying His Word, and these religious leaders of great influence will still be holding fast their traditions and labeling the real work of God, "the devil" (Matt. 12:22-24), just as was done with Jesus (John 15:20). History reveals the pattern.

In this book, we will clearly show you from the Scriptures God's plan for man and that there literally is an abundant life promised that Christ already purchased and that it is for all believers who will be obedient to the Word. We will further show you that not all believers have received this wonderful, Biblical message of faith in God. Why? Because of bad instruction, false accusations against it, disbelief, traditions of men and other obstacles. The remedy for all of this is the expounding of the truth of God's Word (Matt. 28:20; Mark 4:33-34), for truth is what opens a person's eyes (Ps.119:130). There is no other way a person can receive anything from God concerning redemption and its blessings, except through the truth of God's Word (John 15:7; Rom. 5:2). It will be found that redemption brings us full circle back around to the blessings man had before the fall, and that they are all to be received by faith (Rom. 5:2). Now, we do not say that what has been labeled the "faith message" contains all the truth on every subject in the Bible, but it is getting this foundation of understanding of what's really happening in the earth, that will help a Christian to become strong in faith, to be used more in the Kingdom of God, and to be a real blessing to others. God wants you to be victorious over the devil.

It is therefore necessary as we continue on, for each person to be open to the truth as it's revealed in God's Word, and not to block out the light of further truth by preconceived ideas or man-made theology. For men's ideas or theologies, religious though they may be, are not always mean that they are based on truth, and they can hinder rather than help, just as zeal for God also, if not based on a clear knowledge of the truth, can actually be destructive to God's work (Rom. 10:2; Gal. 1:13-14; Phil. 3:6). Jesus said to His disciples, the time will come when they that kill you *will think* that they are doing God a service. Jesus also said to some religious men that persecuted Him, "ye have not His (God's) Word abiding in you: for whom He hath sent, Him ye believe not" (John 5:38).

Many times, men who are religious in their zeal for God can actually be used of the devil to destroy the true work of God by verbally cutting down and attacking real God-called and God-anointed ministries and works, or even set out to destroy the church in what he thought was service to God as Paul did (Acts 9:1-3; Gal. 1:13). This is a fact of history that we must all take heed of (James 3:1), for we shall give an account to Him on that day for the things that we've done (Rom. 14:10-12). So we see then, that just because someone, or some group manifests zeal for God, it does not necessarily mean that all they believe in is the truth. Consider the Pharisees who were zealous of their man made religious doctrines, yet the impression they gave their many followers was that they were zealous for God and that they were defenders of "the faith."

It is necessary therefore for a person who desires truth to study the Word of God with the intent of rightly dividing the Word of Truth, but again this study *must not* be with preconceived ideas trying only to prove his or her point, for this clouds the mind (James 1:21).

Men, in trying to prove their point or the theological belief of the seminary they've come out of, will many times unintentionally twist the truth and bend it to fit their beliefs and the beliefs of those they have studied under. Anytime the Scriptures cannot be clearly seen and taken for exactly what they say, but people have a host of arguments as to why it's not for us today or why you can't take the Word at face value, you must beware, because to explain one thing away, means they will have to explain other things away in God's Word that confirm those Scriptures. So make sure you *read* for yourself what the Bible actually does say and stand on the side of truth, for it is not necessarily men's explanations of things that are the truth, but it is the Word of God that is truth! Realize then that most denominations and religious groups are run by *men*. They, or their group, are not God. Only God's written Word reveals the true facts of Christianity. Listen to what Jesus said in John 8:31-32, "Then said Jesus to those Jews which believed on Him, *If ye continue in My Word, then are ye My disciples indeed;* and ye shall know the truth and the truth shall make you free" (emphasis added).

If the Word is expounded in simplicity (Mark 12:37), and the Bible teacher *uses Scripture* to interpret Scripture, and it doesn't contradict other clear scriptures on the subject, it can be received. But if the Word is explained away, or there are clear Scriptures contrary to a person's teaching, then this is only the reasoning of men and should not be followed. There may be millions of explanations, but there is only one Bible and it is the Bible that has been given to mankind by God to reveal *the truth* (2 Tim. 2:15). Note too, that theologians will many times reject what their intellects cannot grasp, but realize man's intellect is limited while God's Word is unlimited; therefore in many places, God's Word can only be grasped by faith (Heb. 11:3; Mark 10:15).

Faith or Unbelief

It is really then a matter of faith or unbelief in the Word. How far does a person's *faith reach? How much of the Scripture* will he or his group really *believe?* This then is the real question and truly it is what almost all of the disagreements in Christendom are all about. People many times, thinking that they or their group have the corner on the market on God, fight others who believe certain areas of the Word that they don't believe. Scripture says, "according to *your faith* so be it done unto thee." God's truth, as it's revealed in His Word, is to be received on the basis of faith. A statement is true not because we can always understand it but because GOD SAID IT. But sad to say, millions of people in denominations and even in some born again churches, are basing their Christianity not strictly on God's Word, but on certain schools of theology and the opinions of religious men who will believe the Word of God only as far as they, themselves, have been taught. If they've been taught *by men* that certain parts of the scripture are no longer for us today, this then is what they teach to others. Jesus taught that a disciple will not rise above the one he submits to as his teacher. This applies to you, also. So make sure you're being taught *only* what the Word of God actually says and all of what it says.

Our faith then is to be based solely upon God's Word. If the Word of God clearly backs up someone's scriptural stand and teaching and it doesn't contradict the picture painted by the life, teaching and ministry of Christ, then you can follow that person's faith (John 14:6-10; Heb. 13:7-8). If certain scriptures have to be explained away, dispensationalized, or twisted to fit a particular belief while ignoring other clear scriptures on the subject, then that stand should not be followed. God has called every Christian to believe and obey the Word, the whole Word, and nothing but the Word, and it is the Word that will judge us in the last day, not men's opinions of it (John 12:48). You are responsible to follow a shepherd that instructs you from God's Word alone. Many in this day are preaching their opinions of the Word or something they were taught in some seminary rather than the Word itself, but scripture states, "preach the Word." Because people look upon someone as an authority on the scriptures they accept anything that's said by them or their religious group as though it were the truth when many times it may be contrary to scripture and contrary to the teachings of Christ. This is why Christ's Word says, "beware of men." "Beware of the leaven of the Pharisees." That is, beware of the religious leaders who add *their own* particular beliefs to their teachings and work to convince you to believe them.

Listen carefully therefore when you hear messages preached or when you read Christian literature. If you are cautious and prove all things by the Word as Paul said to do, you will be perceptive to that which is the Word and that which is mere opinion about the Word. In opinion, there is no substance, no power, but in the Word there is power and reality (Rom. 1:16). If you have a question about someone's teaching, go to your teacher and ask him for scripture. He should be able to show you clear scriptures on why he's saying what he's saying and it must not contradict other scriptures in the New Testament. If it does, or he can't give you scriptures, then you are following man and not God in that area.

It is absolutely necessary then in rightly dividing the Word that a person study it with an open mind and heart without preconceived ideas. It is very important that you read and believe what the Bible actually does say and put emphasis on that, for the scriptures reveal *the real faith* that was *once delivered to the saints*. Anyone who follows a blind leader will become blind themselves (Matt. 15:14-15). Isaiah once wrote, "If they speak not according *to this Word*, it is because there is no light in them" (Isa. 8:20). All things should be taken into consideration, looked upon and balanced properly with other scriptures on that subject and what will come forth will be the Word of Truth, the truth that sets men free (John 8:31-32), and gives to them the blessings of the Covenant (Acts 20:32), and victory over the devil (1 John 2:14). This is the truth that enables a person to live a life fully pleasing to God (Col. 1:10).

Faith Is the Key

Now faith is the key that unlocks all the unsearchable riches of Christ (Rom. 5:2). Faith is the avenue that men must take if they desire to walk in God's ways and enjoy God's intervention. (See Hebrews 11.) God, being a God of truth, requires that His people *believe* His Word. If we are going to walk with the miracle-working God of the Bible, faith is a necessity. Who could have reasoned out in their minds, *how* He would open the Red Sea; bring water out of a rock; rain manna down from Heaven; make the walls of Jericho to fall; feed the multitude with a little boy's basket of food; enable Peter to walk on water; raise the dead; heal through Paul's handkerchiefs, and so on. *No*, He doesn't require that we *understand* it all, but He does require that we *believe* His Word (Heb. 11:6; Matt. 4:4).

As far as a ministry, denomination or congregation believe God's Word, that is what He will do for them and no more. "*If* ye abide in Me, and My words abide in you, ye shall ask what ye will, and it shall be done unto you" (John 15:7). His only limitation in working in men's lives is either their lack of knowledge of Scripture or their unbelief in His Word (Ps. 78:41; Mark 6:1-6). He is held back from doing His mighty works many times in individual lives because of men's opinions, for opinions cause reasoning against His Word, and reasoning causes doubt and unbelief (Mark 2:8; Matt. 14:28-31), and unbelief will close the door on the blessings of God and the people will proceed no further in the things of God, for He will never work contrary to His own Word (Heb. 3:19; 4:2; Mark 7:13). A church's walk with God can go only as far as their faith in God's Word will take them (2 Cor. 5:7; Matt. 9:29), and this is governed by what they are being taught at that church or seminary (Rom. 10:17).

As we've mentioned before, Scripture states, "the disciple is not above his teacher" and again, "everyone that is taught shall be as his teacher." The important thing then is that whoever you consider to be your teacher should be teaching truth based on clear Scripture-teaching and pointing out to you what the Bible *does say*, and emphasizing that, and not emphasizing what the Bible *does not say*, nor ignoring other scriptures on the subject being discussed. He should never say such things as "tongues are of the devil," or "healing is not for today." No where in the Bible will you find a statement like that. Then where does it come from? It is a *man-made* addition and human theology. Jesus said the traditions of men make the Word of God of none effect (Mark 7). As it was in the past, so it is today.

Church, we have fallen into the same trap as Israel did by following its religious leaders who didn't stay with what is written. We've let others think and study for us and the church has, in many cases, followed blind leaders. Read the New Testament as though you've never read it before. Read it as though this Covenant is all for today, for it is (Matt. 28:20) and when you do, forget for a while all that men have taught you. Make the decision to believe the Word, *exactly* as it's written and then you will see the real truth (Ps. 119:130).

We must be like those in Berea who Scripture speaks of as noble (Acts 17:10-12):

– they received *"the Word"* with ALL READINESS OF MIND
– they *searched the Scriptures* daily whether those things were so
– *therefore* many of them believed (Rom. 10:17)

We can see a key here. We must approach a subject in God's Word with a readiness and openness of mind and then we must search the Scriptures and not our group's theology, to see whether or not certain teachings are so. This is all this author asks of you. Look up all scriptural references as needed if you question any of the statements made. If, by the end of the book you do not agree, be that as it may. You have a God-given right to believe any way you choose, but if you do receive what is being expounded from the Word, there awaits for you blessings from the Lord. Blessings that is, if you'll obey His Word and believe all His Gospel (Rom. 1:16).

As this Scripture from Luke 1:45 states concerning Mary, *"blessed is she that believed; for there shall be a performance of those things which were told her of the Lord"* (emphasis added).

And let us all follow the instructions of the Lord through Jude and "contend for *the faith* which was once delivered to the saints." Let us believe *everything* that's recorded in the "New Covenant" from Matthew through Revelation for this is the Covenant we are under, and there is only "one faith." "Let no man deceive you with vain words," saying this or that passed away. "Let God be true" and every *man* that contradicts Him, be a liar (Rom. 3:2-3).

And let us all continue to love, worship, and praise Jesus our Lord and Master, for He is Lord of Lords and King of Kings and it is He that is the "captain of our salvation." Let's follow Him and *His Word*, "That we henceforth be no more children, tossed to and fro, and carried about with every wind of doctrine, by the sleight of men, and cunning craftiness, whereby they lie in wait to deceive; But speaking the truth in love, may grow up into Him in all things, which is the head, even Christ" (Eph. 4:14-15). And remember, God's Word reveals the real facts about our faith and the true Spirit of Christianity. Let us believe and do everything that they believed and did for every real branch that shoots forth our of that same true vine, will produce the same teachings, fruit and manifestations of God's Spirit as did those first branches as recorded in the Book of Acts.

Note: The phrase *faith message* in this book means "the message of faith in God and His Word as it is revealed in the Bible."

The phrase *faith teacher* means "those who emphasize the integrity of God and all His Word (the Bible)."

The term *critic* refers especially to those critics that have written books to attack Holy Ghost revivals and God's message of faith.

Chapter 2

An Answer to the Critics of God's "Message of Faith"

Nearly all who have spoken out and written against what's been called the Faith message, have not even reverently hesitated to use the names of dedicated men of God, but rather, have attacked them with no mercy or Christian kindness whatsoever. But because we realize we are not wrestling with "flesh and blood," we will not name the critics, for this would not be Christlike. To help those searching for truth, we will simply point out in this book the many errors of the critics of God's message of faith and reveal that almost all of their accusations are wrong and Biblically unsound. If what they've written is what they actually believe, then they have not even begun to understand God's "message of faith" as it's revealed in the Bible.

The Word of Faith Which We Preach (Romans 10:8)

First of all, I will make this statement: What's been labeled by some as the "faith message" is not a new movement or message, but it is a return back to a simple living faith, in the integrity of God and His Word, believing in and doing the very things the early church believed in and did. It's one more thing that God, by His Spirit, has worked to restore back to the church since the time of the Reformation and the Dark Ages as will be clearly shown from the scriptures. Let us first see where the term "Word of Faith" or the term "Faith Message" comes from. Is it a new phrase or was it used to describe the Gospel message in Bible times? Paul wrote to the Christians in Rome, *"The Word is nigh thee, even in thy mouth and in thine heart that is the Word of Faith which we preach"* (Rom. 10:8).

Other translations say it this way: This is "the *message about faith* that we preach" (Goodspeed's American Translation). "*the Message of Faith* which we proclaim" (Twentieth Century New Testament); "it is the very *Word of Faith* which we preach. . . ." So Paul said, that the message he preached was a "message of faith" or more specifically he called it "the Word of Faith." *Faith*, he revealed, is not only directly revealed through one's actions, but it's also connected with believing God's Word in the heart and speaking it with the mouth. "That if thou shalt confess with thy mouth the Lord Jesus, and shalt believe in thine heart that God hath raised Him from the dead, thou shalt be saved" (Rom. 10:9). (See also verses 6-8.) Second Cor. 4:13 says, "We having the same spirit *of faith,* according as it is written, I believed, and therefore have I spoken; *we also believe, and therefore speak*." This, Paul said, is the very "Spirit of Faith." Faith speaks what it believes.

Listen also to these scriptures: "For *with the heart* men believe (God's Word) and obtain righteousness and *with the mouth* they make confession (of God's Word) and obtain salvation" (Weymouth, The New Testament in Modern Speech), (Rom. 10:10, emphasis added).

Paul wrote, "*The Word* is nigh thee even *in thy mouth* and *in thine heart*" (v. 8, emphasis added), that you may hear it and do it. It was the same in the Old Testament (Deut. 30:11-14). This message about faith then has much to do with believing God's Word in your heart, speaking it with your mouth and then being obedient to it (Rom. 1:5; James 1:22; Eph. 6:17; Rom. 10:10; John 15:7). "But without faith it is impossible to please him. . . (God)" (Heb. 11:6).

So then Paul's message, just like Jesus' message, was a "message of faith" – a message of faith in God and His Word (Mark 11:22-23). Just as Paul and Jesus received much persecution from satan and religion for proclaiming the living "Word of God" and the "Message of Faith" back then, so persecution is once again stirred up by the devil because ministers are once again teaching about having faith in the integrity of God and all of His Word. This has always been the case whenever and wherever God has unveiled more of His Word to men from Moses to Luther, from Finney to the present day. And no marvel for Jesus Himself said, "persecutions and afflictions" *will arise* because of the Word's sake, as satan comes to steal it; and religion, blinded by their own traditions, determines to stop it. In Mark's Gospel chapter 4:13-20 Jesus said unto them, "Know ye not this parable? And how then, will ye know all parables? The sower soweth the Word. And these are they by the wayside, where the word is sown; but when they have heard, *Satan cometh immediately and taketh away the Word* that was sown in their hearts. And these are they likewise, which are sown on stony ground; who, when they have heard the Word, immediately receive it with gladness; and have no root in themselves, and so endure but for a time: afterward *when affliction or persecution ariseth for the Word's sake* immediately they are offended. And these are they which are sown among thorns; such as hear the Word. And the cares of this world, and the deceitfulness of riches, and the lusts of other things entering in, choke the Word, and it becometh unfruitful. And these are they which are sown on good ground; such as hear the Word and receive it, and bring forth fruit, (results) some thirty fold, some sixty, and some an hundred" (emphasis added).

God has always willed that men have "faith in His Word" and that they obey it. His Word says, "But *without faith,* it is impossible to please Him. . ." (Heb. 11:6). While satan on the other hand from the time of Cain and Abel, has always worked to destroy and stop any real faith in the earth and has, as history has revealed, mainly done his work to stop it through religion and through zealously religious men who have had a temperament he could use. Is faith important? Let us understand that every man that God has ever used and worked through in the earth, has exercised faith from His heart in one way or another. . .there are *no* exceptions, and their faith was *always* expressed through what they said or what they did. (See Hebrews 11.) By faith Abel gave; By faith Enoch walked with God; by faith Noah worked for God; by faith Abraham obeyed; by faith Moses, Shadrach, David, Samuel, and others, cooperated with God and His plan, and confessed that they were strangers and pilgrims on the earth (Heb. 11:13.) It was by "faith" and faith alone, that all the elders (Old Testament saints) obtained a good report (Heb. 11:2). God's message then, always has been and always will be a "message of faith." Scripture says, "Man shall not live by bread alone, but by every Word that proceedeth out of the mouth of God," and if we are going to live by His Word and please Him, then we must "live by faith," believing in the integrity of all that His Word says (Rom. 1:17; 2 Cor. 5:7), and doing by faith what His "Word" says to do (Rom. 1:5; James 1:22). This is a *main* theme, not only of Paul's writings and of the other New Testament writers, but also of the present day "faith message."

Attacked by the Pharisees

Before we go on, let me explain some things about satan's tactics in attacking God's Word and the "Message of Faith." As we've stated, Satan's methods have not changed over the centuries. One of the main ways satan has always used to malign God's messengers who have carried His Word, is through religion. The supposedly orthodox religious leaders of Jesus' day, said such things concerning Christ as "He hath a devil," "He is Beelzebub" or He's doing miracles by "the prince of the devils," and it was, for the most part, not the people of the world, but the religious leaders who attacked Christ the most and falsely accused Him. One time, the Pharisees came tempting Him with dishonest motives trying only to catch Him in His words, that they might twist what He said. "Then went the Pharisees and took counsel how they might entangle Him in His talk" (Matt. 22:15). In the next few verses, they went to Him and lied, trying to trick Him into saying certain things, that they might manipulate what He said and turn the people against Him. Men are basically the same today as in days gone by and the methods of the modern day Pharisees have not changed. For the same, blinding religious spirit that hindered the Pharisees from hearing and believing Christ's message of faith in that day, also hinders people today (John 5:38; 8:43). People are just as protective of their religious beliefs today as in times past. And just as there are men of God moving in faith and in God's power today, so also brethren, the Pharisee spirit too, is still alive among us, and Christ's warning still stands; "beware of the leaven (teachings) of the Pharisees" (religious leaders) and recognize them for what they truly are. As we continue, please notice in the scriptures used, where all of Christ's persecution came from. God's revelation is abundantly clear.

"Now the *chief priests*, and *elders, and all the council SOUGHT FALSE WITNESS against Jesus* (The Word, John 1:1) to put Him to death. . ." (Matt. 26:59-68). At first they found none, but after *their diligent search*, "At the last came two false witnesses" (v. 6).

People, especially religious men, who are bound and blinded by their own theological beliefs, will see only what they are looking for as they search to prove that their theology is right and what others believe is wrong. The sad part is they will dishonestly twist and use whatever they can, true or not, to make their point, all in the name of religion. "Likewise also, the chief priests (the most well known leaders of religion) *mocking Him, with the scribes and elders* said, He saved others; Himself He cannot save. If He be the King of Israel, let Him now come down from the cross and we will believe Him. He trusted in God, let Him deliver Him now, if He will have Him: for He said, I am the Son of God. The thieves also, which were crucified with Him, cast the same in his teeth" (Matt. 27:41-44, emphasis added).

Notice how they mocked Christ saying, "He saved others, Himself He cannot save." "He trusted in God; let Him deliver Him now *if He will have Him*; for He said, 'I am the Son of God.'" They knew not what was going on, but attacked the very Messiah they professed to be waiting for. *It was religion then, that persuaded the people* to turn against Christ and His Word, and to crucify Him, all in the name of defending religion. It was not the unbelievers so much, but those who professed to believe in the God of the Bible that did so. Sadly, the majority of the people sided in with the Pharisees, the thieves on the cross and with the Herodians, all the time *thinking* they were doing God a service. Instead of checking things out with God's Word, they listened to men rather than to God, proving to us that the majority is not always right. History has proven when it comes to the things of

God, the majority is usually wrong. If Moses whom God raised up to lead the people, would have listened to the majority, they would have gone back to Egypt. And remember Joshua and Caleb were the only ones of their entire generation that entered into the Promised Land, while the others could not enter in because of their unbelief (Heb. 3:19; 4:1-5). One thing about this religious spirit that the majority of men seem to follow is the sarcastic, mocking attitude which it has when confronted with truth, which is not consistent with the spirit of Christ, but is seen constantly in the writings of the critics of the "Faith Message."

The religious leaders of Christ's day hated God's healing power because it was foreign to them, and they disliked His not keeping their traditions. "And they watched Him whether He would *heal* Him on the Sabbath day; that they *might accuse Him*" (Mark 3:2, emphasis added). When Jesus then healed the man in Mark 3:6, scripture says, ". . .the *Pharisees* went forth and straightway took counsel with the Herodians against Him, how they might destroy Him."

"And *the scribes* which came down from Jerusalem *said*, He hath Beelzebub and by the prince of the devils, casteth He out devils" (Mark 3:22). We see then how the religious leaders of Christ's day refused to believe in the present day "power of God," but they did believe the devil had power. Is it not the same today? For some strange reason, there are some religious leaders who have "faith" in the devil's power as being present today, but not in God's power. Yet the very New Testament that the critics profess to defend, teaches us not only to believe in the power of God (Acts 1:8; 4:33; 6:7), but that we are to turn away from those who have a *"form"* of godliness, but deny the power (in the Greek, it means "the miraculous power") of God (1 Tim. 3:5; 1 Cor. 4:20). Religion controlled by the minds of men, *always has and always will* reason away the present day "power of God." It has always criticized God's power and it has done so in every generation. It too has always been the greatest persecutor of all of the men of God who have ever moved out in strong faith in ages past. Think about it. Look at the history of revivals and you'll recognize that this is so. Can you not see the pattern? Make sure then, that you don't get caught up in it with them, or you may be found to be in the group that is fighting and speaking out against God and His servants.

Jesus rebuked the Pharisees and showed the fallacy of their reasoning saying, "How can satan cast out satan?" explaining that for Him to be doing these miracles by satan's power is not possible. He then proceeded to warn the religious leaders that if they continued to attribute the power of the Holy Spirit to an unclean spirit, they were in danger of committing an unforgivable sin. Because they said, "He hath an unclean spirit" (Mark 3:30). This same sin can most certainly be committed today and the warning is clear.

Because men haven't changed and human nature is the same, you can most assuredly expect a certain category of top religious "leaders" to do and say the same type of things today as the Pharisees, in order to protect their positions and theological beliefs. If you are discerning, you will know who the Pharisees of today are, for "by their fruits, ye shall know them." What they produce is suspicion of men of God, division among the body of Christ and a denial of the plain, written Word of God. While at the same time they profess to be defending it. There is a very close parallel between the misled religious leaders of the past and those of today. "And *the Pharisees* came forth, and began to question with Him, seeking of Him a sign from Heaven, tempting Him" (Mark 8:11, emphasis added).

Today also, they say to Spirit-filled believers, "show me a sign;" or "physician, heal thyself," but even as in Christ's day, when many signs and wonders were happening around them, they refused to see what was taking place right before their eyes. Having eyes they saw not and ears they heard not, neither did their heart understand.

Man-made Religion Fears the Message of Faith

Some religious leaders of our day, fear the message of faith, for it does not agree with their tradition or religious beliefs. If the "Word of Faith" is right, then most of what they believe and have been teaching the people is all wrong. I'm sure the Pharisees of Christ's day, thought they were right, and even thought it justifiable to twist the things Christ said, malign Him and falsely accuse Him in order to protect what they considered the faith. Their traditions (man-made doctrines and beliefs) had made most of God's Word of none effect in the lives of the people who listened to them and there was very little, if any, real faith being exercised by them. So much so, that Jesus was moved to say "when the Son of man comes, will He find faith on the earth?" It's obvious religion will always be here, so he did not say, "Will He find religious organizations on the earth," but *"faith!"* The two are not necessarily synonymous. One thing the Pharisees did have was a lot of scriptures taken out of context, a lot of tradition, and crafty ways of trying to trick Christ, and twist what He said. Many of the religious leaders do precisely the same thing with the "Word of Christ" today (2 Pet. 2:1). They give their opinions, teach their theology, say certain parts of the New Testament have passed away, and so on. Do they really take it for *exactly* what it says? No! Instead, they still "teach for doctrines, the commandments of men. . . ." For anything that says something contrary to the written Word, is either a doctrine and commandment of men, or a doctrine of devils (1 Tim. 4:1).

When Jesus brought to those of His day the real Covenant that they had in Scripture all the time (Rom. 15:8), and preached it as God's living Word and message for today, multitudes believed in it and were healed and set free supernaturally in this life by God's power, (Scripture reveals that God has always been here in every age to supernaturally help His people through His Word and power), but the religious leaders who were locked into their own theological systems of beliefs, didn't comprehend it nor did they perceive the power of God. Instead, the religious leaders wanted to throw Christ over a cliff (Luke 4:23-30), and said that the people who listened to Him are "cursed." The Pharisees could only say such things as "we know God spoke to Moses, but as for this fellow, we know not from whence he is" (John 9:29).

These same critics of today, if living in Moses' day, would not have believed Moses heard from God either, nor would they have followed the miracle working Jesus of the Bible. Religion has always looked back to the heroes of faith of the past and put them on pedestals, and has professed to side with them (Matt. 23:29-33), yet refuses to see God at work in a miraculous way today and instead works to malign and destroy anyone in the present time through whom God works in such a way. Know this, that if the men of faith whom God used in times past were here today, the present-day critics would attack them also. Why is this? They have no real faith in God's present day intervention and power as is revealed in God's Word. They have made theology out of this living Covenant that God has given to mankind. In Christ's day, critics rejected the miracle working power of the Holy Spirit, but they constantly affirmed they believed that the devil had power, saying Christ's miracles were done by the devil. Even now the present-day critics presume God's miraculous power no longer operates, but was only for past generations. Therefore, we see and hear similar things by those following modernistic theologies: "miracles are past;" "the day of divine healing is over;" "the gifts of the Spirit are not for us today." In so saying, they deny the very Word and Gospel they profess to contend. For all of these things are promised to us in the church age in God's Word and Gospel (Acts 1:8; Matt. 28:20; 1 Cor. 12). The apostle Paul, in his Gospel said, that men's faith should "not stand in the wisdom of men, but in the power of God" (1 Cor. 2:5). "And He (Jesus) charged them (His disciples) saying, Take heed, beware of the leaven of the Pharisees, (religious leaders) and of the leaven of Herod" (Mark 8:15). Notice that Jesus spoke this to His followers and remember His "truth endureth forever." It is still relevant brethren, for His followers today. Have you not discerned who the Pharisees of today are? They are the ones who will add to or take away from God's Word and substitute their own religious theories of how things are instead. They will, as the Pharisees of old, deny the power of God but yet believe the devil has power to do things. Will you also, as people have done in times past, allow them to persuade you to attack the very Word of God, its message and its messengers that God Himself, has raised up and sent to help you?

"But where unto shall I liken this generation? It is like unto children sitting in the markets and calling unto their fellows and saying, We have piped unto you and ye have not danced; we have mourned unto you and ye have not lamented. For John came neither eating nor drinking, *and they* (the religious leaders) say, He hath a devil. The Son of man came eating and drinking, and they say, Behold a man gluttonous, and a winebibber, a friend of publicans and sinners. But wisdom is justified of her children" (Matt. 11:16-19). Remember, this was supposedly orthodox acceptable religion that said such things.

"Then answered one of the lawyers and said unto Him, Master, thus saying Thou reproachest us also? And He said, Woe unto you also ye lawyers, for ye lade men with burdens grievous to be borne, and ye yourselves touch not the burdens with one of your fingers. Woe unto you, for ye build the sepulchers of the prophets, and your fathers killed them. Truly ye bear witness that ye allow the deeds of your fathers: for they indeed killed them, and ye build their sepulchers. Therefore also, said the wisdom of God, *I will send them prophets and apostles and some of them they (the religious leaders) shall slay and persecute;* that the blood of all the prophets, which was shed from the foundation of the world, may be required of this generation; from the blood of Abel unto the blood of Zacharias, which perished between the altar and the temple: verily I say unto you, It shall be required of this generation. Woe unto you lawyers, (religious leaders) for ye have taken away the key of knowledge *ye entered not in yourselves, and them that were entering in ye hindered.* And as He said these things unto them, *the scribes and the Pharisees* began to urge Him vehemently, and to provoke Him to speak of many things; laying wait for Him and seeking to catch something out of His mouth, *that they might accuse Him*" (Luke 11:45-54, emphasis added). (See also Matthew 23.) None of the multitudes who followed the religious leaders of Jesus' day wanted to believe that they were deceived by the leaders of religion, but they were. The Pharisees negated much of God's Word, then added a lot of high sounding words, their own traditions (Mark 7:13), great intellectual, religious arguments, and carnal reasonings (Luke 5:21), but it helped no one in their daily walk with God. On the contrary, it only caused division among the people concerning Christ, His Word, and His message of faith. When they were through with the people, they had "made the Word of God of none effect" through their traditions and had taken away from the people the "key of Knowledge" (Luke 11:52). They entered not in themselves; and those that were entering, Jesus said, they hindered. No one could "live by faith" and confidently act on God's Word after the Pharisees were through with them. And so it is today.

What's more, the religious leaders of Jesus' day could not comprehend any of the bold statements Jesus made (Luke 4:20-22), and said what Christ spoke were "blasphemies." You can expect then the same kinds of things to come out of the mouths of modern-day Pharisees, because human nature is still the same. Another time they got so upset that someone was healed that the Bible says, "They were filled with madness" (Luke 6:11).

Luke 19:37-39 says, "And when He was come nigh, even now at the descent of the Mount of Olives, the whole multitude of *the disciples began to rejoice and praise God with a loud voice for all the mighty works that they had seen.*"

While the Pharisees on the other hand, got upset and angered. "And He taught daily in the temple. But *the chief priests and the scribes and the chief of the people sought to destroy Him*, and could not find what they might do: for all the people were very attentive to hear Him" (Luke 19:47-48).

One more thing this religious spirit does not like, is crowds of people shouting and praising God with a loud voice—crying and thanking the Lord when miracles happen. The Pharisees just staunchly stand on the sideline and say, "that's not God healing the people, that's the devil." "Look at those people shouting so loudly and praising God; they are all deceived." Again, isn't it strange how they always believed the devil had power to do things in their day, but not God? Is it not the same today? There are religious critics today who constantly label the gifts of the Holy Spirit and God's healing power as "occultic," "metaphysical," "demonic." Has not modern theology taken away from the people the (living) Lord, and they (many church people) "know not where they have laid Him." They have hidden the Lord and the reality of this Blood Covenant in a maze of made up theological statements, rather than preaching the simple pure Word of God. Over and over again, the divine Word reveals that it was the heads of religion who attacked Christ and God's Word the most. Is not God's message abundantly clear about this? Should we not then pay very close attention to this clear warning and check out everything anyone says, with the Bible, especially with the New Testament? We need to prove all things, regardless of what label men have or what large religious group they may be the head of (1 Thess. 5:21). For we are warned in Scripture, *"Let no man deceive you."*

Luke 20:1-2: "And it came to pass, that on one of those days, *as He taught the people* in the temple, *and preached the Gospel, the chief priests and the scribes came upon Him with the elders*, and spake unto Him, saying, Tell us, by what authority doest Thou these things? Or who is He that gave Thee this authority?"

After all, they reasoned, He never sat in their big, theological seminaries, nor did any of His disciples have degrees from them. The Pharisees therefore claimed that Jesus and His apostles were "ignorant and unlearned men" (Acts 4:13); (John 7:15-17). Do they not do and say the same things today? But note that Jesus never did go to any of the big theological seminaries of His day to get disciples, but rather to ordinary people such as: fishermen, doctors, tax collectors, and so on. Those were the ones He called and anointed with His power. The Pharisees and Sadducees were so rigid and blinded by their own religious beliefs to accept change and the message Christ gave that He could not use them. While the Pharisees stood by and accused the disciples, calling them ignorant men and deceivers, those same disciples went forth with the Gospel message in the power of God and turned multitudes to the Lord (Mark 16:20).

Religion Counterfeits Bible Christianity

There are multitudes of men today that have gone through

seminaries and, sad but true, some of those seminaries have "made them twofold more a child of hell than themselves." They come forth from some of those places trained to attack anything that even resembles living faith in God saying miracles have ceased; tongues have passed away; it's not the devil anymore making people sick, it's God (Acts 10:38); and many such like things they do, contrary to God's own written Word. They convince the people who trust in their doubting words that what *they say* is what God's Word says (Rom. 16:18). Yet, anytime someone steps out in real faith on God's Word, they tell the people, "You can't believe that;" "God won't do that;" "Don't listen to them;" "Don't expect that;" "That's passed away;" "You're not who the Bible says you are, you cannot do that;" "God's not your puppet, so don't expect Him to answer prayer." No wonder Jesus asked, "When the Son of man comes, will He find faith on the earth?" For religion that counterfeits Christianity is one of real Bible faith's worst enemies (2 Pet. 2:1). Religion governed by men's minds, is a wolf in sheep's clothing (2 Cor. 11:13-15) and it has kept multitudes from being born again; filled with the Holy Spirit; healed; delivered and blessed by God's power. Make sure then that you and your faith do not get devoured by it.

Hebrews 4:2 says, "For unto us was the Gospel preached, as well as unto them: *but the Word preached did not profit them*, not being mixed with faith in them that heard it." As for us, we will believe it all.

Luke 20:20: "And they watched Him and sent forth spies which should feign themselves just men, *that they might take hold of His words* so that they might deliver Him unto the power and authority of the governor."

In Galatians 2:4 Paul wrote, "And that because of false brethren unawares brought in, who came in privily to spy out our liberty which we have in Christ Jesus, that they might bring us into bondage."

Are not these religious men crafty sometimes? They came disguised as someone who wanted to learn, but yet they really came to spy, and to collect any information they could use, which they could use to twist, accuse, and attack. (See also Luke 22:1-5.) This, sadly, is so concerning some even today who believe their ministry is to criticize. And *the rulers* "derided Him" calling Him (Jesus) a "deceiver" and said He "is mad."

John 7:47-49 says, Then answered them *the Pharisees*, "are ye also deceived? *Have any of the rulers or of the Pharisees believed on Him*? But this people who knoweth not the law is cursed." They will say even today, that anyone following the Word just as it's written, or Word preachers are cursed saying, "We don't believe that way do we?" And, "You know we are the heads of big religious organizations, aren't we? So we must be right." But it is really they, like the Pharisees of old, who do not know the Word and are wrong. How cleverly satan works. He uses people's good religious intentions, and their lack of knowledge to get them to attack the very thing they think they are defending (Acts 9:1-3; Rom. 10:2). But in many cases they are not really defending God's Word at all or "the faith that was once delivered to the saints," but rather, their own theology. Please try and grasp hold of this and you'll see what is really happening (Eph. 1:15-19).

John 8:42-43 says, "Jesus said unto them, (that claimed God was their Father but hated Him), If God were your Father, ye would love Me: for I proceeded forth and came from God; neither came I of Myself, but He sent Me. Why do ye not understand My speech? Even because ye cannot hear My Word."

"And ye have not His Word abiding in you: for whom He hath sent, Him ye believe not" (John 5:38). "The Pharisees therefore said unto Him, Thou bearest record of thyself; thy record is not true" (John 8:13).

All you need to do is to look at the Book of Acts and you'll see that the Pharisees constantly made false accusations against Christ's disciples calling them "ignorant and unlearned men." "They threatened them," "set up false witnesses" and twisted what they said; they stirred up men "of the baser sort" tried to turn the people against them, and tried to get them to stop doing miracles in the name of Jesus. (See Acts 4:1-17; 5:12-18; Acts 6:8-15; Acts 8:1-3; 9:1-2; 14:1-2) But no marvel, for Jesus said to His followers in John 15:20, "Remember the word that I said unto you. The servant is not greater than his lord. If they (the religious leaders who know not the Scriptures nor the power of God) have persecuted Me, they will also persecute you, if they have kept My saying, they will keep yours also." He also said, the time will come when they that kill you will think they are doing God a "service." The modern-day critics of God's message of faith fall into this very category and know it not, as we shall clearly point out. It is an historical fact that anytime there is, or has been, a move of God and more of God's truth uncovered, religion will rise up against it.

So brethren, beware of the leaven of the Pharisees (religious men that are in high positions) who, coming clothed as righteous men and defenders of the faith, but yet try and keep you in unbelief and from "walking by faith." They will try and discourage you from believing *all* of God's Word just as it's written and from speaking in agreement with God's Word (Eph. 6:17). They will try and keep you from believing God will do all that He said He would do. Instead, they will try and persuade you to believe their theology and tell you that much of God's Word has passed away. Since the time of Cain, religion has always attacked those who walked by faith. Cain had his altar, an offering, claimed he believed in the same God as Abel, but he really didn't believe God's Word at all and so set up things his own religious way. Instead of following the Word, (like much of religion after him), he listened to the wicked one, and persecuted and finally killed his brother (Heb. 11:4; 1 John 3:12-14). There has always been a conflict between those who believe God is "I AM"– the God of the now–and accept God's Word at face value, and those who believe God could only, or would only, do supernatural things in times past, which takes little or no actual faith. Do you want to hear the real "Word of Faith" message that we preach? The message of faith in the absolute integrity of God's Word?

Then let us share with you God's message of faith. It proclaims as the apostle Paul did, "The Word is nigh thee even in thy mouth and in thine heart, that is the Word of Faith which we preach" (Rom. 10:8). "For it is believing in the heart that makes a man righteous before God and it is stating his belief by his own mouth that confirms his salvation" (Rom. 10:10, Phillips Translation). And it is an obedience to God that springs from a heart of faith, which is the way of the New Covenant (Rom. 1:5; 2 Cor. 5:7; Acts 6:7).

Chapter 3

Faith–Our Vital Link With God

Faith. It is our vital link with the unseen God (Heb. 11:27). Jesus said, "According to *your faith* be it unto you" (Matt. 9:29). *"Believe ye* that I am able to do this?" (v. 28). "Go thy way and *as thou* hast believed, so be it done unto thee " (Matt. 8:13).

". . . All things are possible *to him* that believeth" (Mark 9:23). "Daughter, *'thy faith'* hath made thee whole."

The Scripture speaks of the "Word of Faith" (Rom. 10:8, 17). "The law of faith" (Rom. 3:27); "the walk of faith" (2 Cor. 5:7); the "spirit of faith" which speaks what it believes (2 Cor. 4:13). It says the just shall "live by faith." That the "victory that overcometh the world" is by faith (1 John 5:4).

Jesus called "faith" one of the weightier matters, which should be taught (Matt. 23:23). The Bible reveals that faith in God can make you whole (Mark 5:34); clothe you (Matt. 6:30); bring deliverance from evil spirits (Matt. 15:28); bring things to pass in your life (Mark 11:23); ward off all the devil's attacks (Eph. 6:16). He finds faith coming out of people's mouths (Matt. 8:8-10; Rom. 10:9-10; 2 Cor. 4:13). He sees it in their actions (Matt. 9:2). It can bring divine healing to others (Acts 3:16); it releases God's power (Acts 6:5, 8); and purifies people's hearts (Acts 15:9).

We are saved by grace through faith (Eph. 2:8); we continue on by faith (Col. 1:23); we resist the devil with faith (Eph. 6:16; 1 Pet. 5:8-9), and work for God by faith (1 Thess. 1:11). We must mix faith with God's Word to benefit from it (Heb. 4:2).

Faith can remove mountains (Matt. 17:20); enable a person to be used by God to do signs and wonders (Acts 6:8) and to win many to the Lord (Acts 11:24). Faith can grow (2 Thess. 1:3), and through it we understand (Heb. 11:3). Faith moves people to give sacrificial offerings to God (Heb. 11:4); to walk with and please God (Heb. 11:5); to prepare themselves before judgment comes (Heb. 11:7); we are heirs of righteousness by faith (Heb. 11:7). It moves people to obey God (Heb. 11:8); enables them to receive God's miracle working power (Gal. 3:5; Heb.11:11). It moves people to speak of things yet unseen (Heb. 11:21-22); to confess things (Heb. 11:13; 10:23; Rom. 10:9, 10). It moves people to act (Heb. 11:23); to refuse things not in agreement with God (Heb. 11:24-25); to see by the Word the reward of serving God (Heb. 11:26); it enables us to see Him who is invisible (Heb.11:27); to keep God's orders (Heb. 11:28); to do things not logical to the carnal mind (Heb. 11:30).

It brings answered prayer (James 1:6-7). Through faith, people have with God's intervention, "subdued kingdoms; wrought righteousness; obtained promises; stopped the mouths of lions; quenched the violence of fire; escaped the edge of the sword; out of weakness were made strong; waxed valiant in fight; turned to flight the armies of the aliens; women received their dead raised back to life again. . . " (Heb. 11:33-34). Others, by faith, were enabled to endure torture, for they had faith in a better resurrection—deliverance; and Scripture says, we are to be followers of others' faith (Heb. 13:7), and follow them who through faith and patience inherit the promises (Heb. 6:12). Is this not truly then all a "faith message?"

So we are not supposed to be against those who are strong in faith and seeing God's power and provision manifest, but rather, we are to be followers of them. We are to "ask in faith" (James 1:6), to show our faith by our actions (James 2:18). They all "received a good report through faith. . ." (Heb. 11:31). The prayer of faith will bring healing to the sick (James 5:14-15). "According to your faith it will be done unto you" (Matt. 9:29), and so on. Faith has found that God is the same in every generation. These Scriptures are sufficient to know that "the message of faith" is an all important message, which was from the beginning when God first created man on the earth and always will be, for without a person exercising faith from the heart in God's Word (Rom. 10:10), the Bible says, "it is impossible to please God" (Heb. 11:6). Mark 6:5-6 says, "And He *could there do no* mighty work, save that He laid His hands upon a few sick folk and healed them. And He marveled because of *their unbelief*." The fact is, unbelief in Christ's Word and message is still the main obstacle that hinders Him from working in the lives of so many people today. "So we see that they could not enter in because of unbelief" (Heb. 3:19). While faith in God's Word, on the other hand, opens the door for God to work in a person's life. (See Rom. 5:2; 1 Pet. 1:5; Eph. 1:19; Eph. 2:8-9.)

When God created man in the beginning, it was God's design that man use His free will to "live by the Word of God," that man "walk by faith" trusting in his Creator, and in what his Creator said. It is the same now; all Scripture is given by inspiration of God (2 Tim. 3:16-17), and God will work in the lives of those that accept it as it is in truth, the Word of God (1 Thess. 2:13), but it will not profit those who in any area of the Word, refuse to mix faith with it. As a free moral agent, you are free to believe what you want (Heb. 4:2). He will not change your doctrine (2 Tim. 2:15). Jesus has provided deliverance from the fall and all its effects in every area of our lives (Gal. 3:13-14), but only those who use their liberty of will to believe and obey all of His Gospel will benefit fully from it (1 Tim. 4:10; Rom. 1:16; 2 Pet. 1:3-4).

We have seen numerous scriptures about the vital importance of faith. Let us now look at a basic brief overview of the Word message concerning what happened and why faith is necessary before we proceed into the rest of this book and deal with the critic's false accusations. We believe your eyes will be opened to see that God has raised up this strong message of faith in God's Word and restored it once again to the church so that the body of Christ might live victoriously over the enemy and bring many into the Kingdom. But the devil has also, as usual, put up a strong resistance coming through religion to "steal the Word" just as he has done every time the Word has gone forth in ages past (Mark 4:13-14). Just as he used Saul's religious zeal but lack of knowledge to persecute the church then, so he now uses men today of like character to attack the real faith that was once delivered to the saints. In order to refute the errors of the critics, it is necessary to give you numerous scriptures to prove by the

Word that the faith message is and has always been God's message. To be most benefitted, please look up the scriptures and believe what they say. Here then, is the real "message of faith" *that we preach*. I speak from what I've seen and learned in the faith message for the past two decades.

The Message of Faith That We Preach

In the beginning, God created the Heavens and the earth. It is by His will and for His pleasure that they exist and were created (Gen. 1:1; Rev. 4:11). Let's see how God creates. Scripture reveals that God created the heavens and the earth by His spoken Word. "By the Word of the Lord were the heavens made" (Ps. 33:6). "The worlds were framed by the Word of God" (Heb. 11:3), and "By the Word of God the heavens were of old." Hundreds of times God spoke things in Scripture that came to pass. God said, "Let there be light and there was light." God said, "Let the waters under Heaven be gathered together unto one place and let the dry land appear and it was so. . ." (Gen. 1). The apostle Paul said, God "quickeneth the dead and *calleth* those things which be not as though they were" (Rom. 4:17). One translation puts it like this: He "calls things into existence the things that do not exist" (Revised Standard Version). The Lord said, "So shall My Word be that goeth forth out of My mouth: it shall not return unto Me void, but it shall accomplish that which I please and it shall prosper in the thing whereto I sent it" (Isa. 55:10-11).

This then, is *how* God creates, as almost every Bible commentary also agrees. This is revealed to be the very essence of the "spirit of faith," which believes and therefore speaks (2 Cor. 4:13; Mark 11:23). It is not that God exercises faith in something outside of Himself, but that faith, like the love of God, the long suffering of God, and the joy of the Lord, is an attribute of God Himself. It is simply the way that He, as a person, does things. Now according to the Scripture, He not only creates this way, but He also "upholds all things by the Word of His power" (Heb. 1:3). So just as He is a God of love (1 John 4:8, 16), He is also a God of faith and His Word is the source of life and of all things everywhere.

To believe His Word, obey it, and speak in agreement with it (Rom. 10:8), is to walk in agreement with Him and be blessed. To live and speak contrary to it is to go contrary to the "law of life" and "Word of faith," which will greatly hinder His working in a person's life for He will never operate contrary to His own Word (John 15:7). Therefore, He will not perform *His Word* in the lives of those who use their liberty of will to disbelieve His Word or go contrary to Him either willingly or because of ignorance (Hosea 4:6; John 8:31-32). He has only promised to confirm His own Word that abides in us (John 15:7; Jer. 1:12; Heb. 4:2). So God spoke and it was done. He commanded and it stood fast (Ps. 33:6-9; Hosea 4:6).

Before there was matter and spiritual creation, God was. Now He had no place to go and get eternal substance from in order to mold into shape and form, the planets, stars, moons, mountains, trees, living creatures, and so on, so all things and all life came forth out of the very being of God Himself. In Colossians it says, "for by Him were *all things* created, that are in Heaven and that are in earth, *visible and invisible*" (Col. 1:16).

The word *created* means to "bring into being from nothing, to cause to exist, to bring it forth." He brought it all forth from Himself by speaking it into existence. He said in Ezekiel 12:25, "I am the Lord: I will speak, and the Word that I shall speak shall come to pass. . . " (Ps. 33:6; 2 Pet.3:5-7). Peter said, "By the Word of God the Heavens were of old. . . ." Just think of the tremendous ability of Almighty God. We're talking about millions and millions of miles of universe, millions of stars and numerous planets. Scripture reveals He not only created them all, but He knows each star by name. John 1:3 says, "All things were made by Him and without Him was not anything made that was made." *Everything* came into existence through Him (Goodspeed's American Translation). "Through Him *all things came into being*" (Twentieth Century New Testament).

God first created the invisible creation, the angels and other spiritual things, and He then created this natural, physical world and universe. The natural world has similar looking things in it as Heaven and the spirit world does. In the spirit realm in Heaven, there are such things as trees, rivers, houses, gates, activities, animals, people, and so on (See the Book of Revelation.) (Rev. 1:10-11; John 4:23-24)

So after the spiritual, God then created the natural planets, stars, sun, moon, and the earth and made it a habitable place. Isaiah 45:18 tells us, "For thus saith the Lord, that created (brought into existence) the Heavens; God Himself, that formed the earth and made it; He hath established it, He created it not in vain, He formed it to be inhabited: I am the Lord; and there is none else." God created the plants, flowers, grass and many different kinds of fruit trees by His spoken word, "And God said, let the earth bring forth grass, the herb yielding seed, and the fruit tree yielding fruit after his kind, whose seed is in itself, upon the earth and it was so, and the earth brought forth grass, and herb yielding seed after his kind and the tree yielding fruit, whose seed was in itself after his kind, and God saw that it was good" (Gen. 1:11-12).

But before there was a tree, or even a seed, there was only the Word of God. Jesus said, "the seed is the Word of God" (Luke 8:11). So again, His Word is the original seed of everything. It all began as His Word. God then proceeded to create the living creatures forming their bodies out of the dust of the ground (Gen. 2:19), and giving them life. Before the foundation of the world, God had purposed a family of sons and daughters. "And (I) will be a Father unto you, and ye shall be My sons and daughters, saith the Lord Almighty" (2 Cor. 6:18). First John 3:2 says, "Beloved, now are we the sons of God, and it doth not yet appear what we shall be: but we know that when He shall appear, we shall be like Him, for we shall see Him as He is." "For this cause I bow my knees unto the Father of our Lord Jesus Christ, of whom the whole *family* in Heaven and earth is named" (Eph. 2:19; Rom. 8:29; Eph. 3:14-15; Eph. 1:4-5). He willed to bring many sons and daughters to glory (Heb. 2:10), but willed them to be created in such a way that they too, like Himself, had liberty of will (Gen. 2:7).

God Creates Man

God said in Genesis 1:26-27, "Let us make man in our image, after our likeness: and *let them have dominion* over the fish of the sea, and over the fowl of the air, and over the cattle and *over all the earth,* and over every creeping thing that creepeth upon the earth. So God created man *in His own image,* in the image of God created He him; male and female created He them."

We've seen then that God created Adam in His own image and likeness, after the similitude of God (James 3:9). *Similitude* means, "likeness in appearance; a portrait; likeness in qualities." Adam was a created "son of God" (Luke 3:38). He was created so much in the image and likeness of God's only begotten Son that Scripture calls Him, "the figure of Him who was to come" (Rom. 5:14). "And Adam foreshadows the One to come" (Twentieth Century New Testament). "Now Adam is a type of Him who was to come" (Mon) a type that is of God's own eternal Son . (Figure means, "shape; form; appearance; a representation.") He resembled God's own eternal Son so much, that God's Son could, some four thousand years later, come down to the earth in the likeness of men, become a man, and tabernacle among us (Heb. 2:14-17; Phil. 2:5-7; 1 Tim. 2:5). Not only that, but although Christ is divine, He will yet remain a man forever (1 Tim. 2:5; Heb. 10:12). (See also Romans 8:29.)

Let's continue. Now God created man with a free will, a being with a spiritual nature, and also a natural side to his nature, a being that had the authority and responsibility given to him by God to choose. He could choose to obey or disobey His Creator. (See Deuteronomy 30:15-19.) The choice was his and this freedom was by God's own design.

God then said, concerning Adam and Eve whom He created *"let them have dominion* over the fish of the sea. . .and over all the earth. . ." (Gen. 1:26, 28). *Dominion* means, "sovereign authority; the power to direct, control, use and dispose of at pleasure; the power of governing; independent control." This too, was God's will.

So Adam, unlike the angels, had a physical side to His nature and unlike the animals, he had a spiritual side. He was a unique being created by God, not to be a robot, a pet, or a slave, but a son. Someone whom God could walk, talk and fellowship with in the ages to come (Gen. 3:8-9; Rev. 21:3; Eph. 2:7).

The Word also reveals that mankind was to be a help meet for His Son (Eph. 5:29-32). A bride who would *willingly* enter into Covenant with Him, submit to Him, and reign with Him forever (Rev. 22:5-6). Now God, by His own sovereign choice, gave Adam authority over all the earth, but only for a certain allotted time period, and God determined that at the end of this time period, a day of judgment would be set when all men who ever lived, would have to give an account of themselves and their lives to God (Rom. 14:12; Rev. 20:11-15). But God also sovereignly determined that for the time now being, that is, during this time period in which the earth would be given to man, that He would not interfere or intervene in the lives of individual free moral agents, unless they willingly called upon Him from their heart (Rom. 10:13; Gen. 4:26), acted on His Word (James 1:22-25), or were prayed for by others (Eph. 1:15-19).

Psalm 115:16 says, "The Heaven, even the heavens are the Lord's, *but the earth hath He given* to the children of men." So it was determined, that men would be coworkers together with God in the earth (1 Cor. 3:9). That men could, through faith and prayer, beseech God for His aid, could talk to and fellowship with God, and cooperate with Him (Heb. 11:5) Men, if they so desired, could ignore and refuse God and His will (Eccl. 12:13-14). "And the Lord God, *commanded the man*, saying, Of every tree of the garden thou mayest freely eat, but of the tree of the knowledge of good and evil, *thou shalt not eat* of it, for in the day that thou eatest thereof, thou shalt surely die" (Gen. 2:16-17). In literal Hebrew it says, "in dying thou shalt die." Here God speaks of a two-fold death. The first type of death is spiritual, and this is being alienated from the life of God; a life that made him God conscious (Eph. 4:17-18; 1 John 5:11-12; John 17:3). Loss of this life is also called in Scripture, being "dead in trespasses and sins" (Eph. 2:1). It is a spiritual separation from the Father God because of the works and sins of the flesh (Hab. 1:13; Gal. 5:19-21; Rom. 8:3; Isa. 59:2).

Sinful flesh then, causes a veil between man and God (Gen. 6:2). To paraphrase it, God told Adam, if you sin and use your will to disbelieve Me, disobey My Word, and follow satan, if you choose the lust of the flesh, the lust of the eyes and the pride of life, you and I will be separated (1 John 2:15-17) and a veil will come between us (Isa. 59:2).

This same principle is also seen in Hebrews 3:12-14 where Paul, in speaking to the Hebrew Christians who had been restored back to a relationship with God through Christ's redemptive work said,"Take heed, brethren, lest there be in any of you an evil heart of unbelief, *in departing from the living God* (and returning back to follow satan). But exhort one another daily, while it is called today, *lest any of you be hardened through the deceitfulness of sin.* For we are made partakers of Christ, *if* we hold the beginning of our confidence (in God and His Word) steadfast unto the end" (Col. 1:22-23). Now if a Christian sins it doesn't automatically sever his relationship with God, only his fellowship. But if he persists in sin without repentance it will eventually sear his conscience, harden his heart, and deceive him into making a decision of his will to once again *live* for sin and satan rather than for God, and it will cause him to make shipwreck of his *faith* (1 Tim. 1:19). So we see that the free will of man is still involved. Men who are brethren, who once used their will to repent and submit to Jesus' Lordship, can still use their will to later depart from God, go back to a life of rebellion and fleshly sin (James 4:4), and choose, once again, to love and serve this present, sinful world rather than God (1 John 2:15; 2 Tim. 4:10; 2 Peter 2:20-21), or if they so choose they can stay with God. "Therefore, brethren, we are debtors, not to the flesh, to live after the flesh. For if ye live after the flesh, ye shall (eventually) die (Jude 12-13): but if ye through the Spirit do mortify the deeds of the body, ye shall live" (Rom. 8:12-13; 1 Tim. 6:11-12). Men can also, like the prodigal son, use their "will" to return back to the Father once again after they've gone astray. Thank God He will graciously accept them back by grace if they do so. "Brethren, *if any of you* do err from the truth, and one convert him; Let him know, that he which converteth the sinner (the brother that's gone astray) from the error of his way shall save *a soul* from death, and shall hide a multitude of sins" (James 5:19-20). (See also Ezek. 18:20; 1 Pet. 2:25; Luke 15:18; Rom. 11:22.)

The will is always in the position where it can choose or reject what grace offers and has provided. The will is always free. God has provided the cleansing power of the blood of Jesus so that if we are willing to confess our sins He's faithful and just to forgive us of our sins and cleanse us from all unrighteousness (1 John 1:9). The heart then stays sensitive to God. Satan, on the other hand, works to recapture the will (1 Thess. 3:5).

When Adam went astray, he died to God and there was no blood of Jesus at that time to cleanse him from his sin. But now, thank God, we have the blood of Jesus available to us. So the first type of death was spiritual; it was a separation from God because of the sin of treason; this means a breach of faith (Eph. 2:1). Now the second type of death God spoke of is physical (the unnatural separation of the man from his body). Adam disobeyed God and died as God had said. This spiritual veil and separation took place "on the day" Adam ate of the tree thereof, just as God warned, but physically he did not die and become separated from his body until over nine hundred years later (Gen. 2:17; Gen. 5:5). Both separations were unnatural and both came because of sin (1 Cor. 15:26).

Before the World Was

Now before this world, or man was ever created, God foresaw the entrance of sin into the world because of making free moral agents, so the plan of a redeemer was established in the counsel of God's own will (Eph. 1:11). "Who hath saved us and called us with an holy calling, not according to our works, but according to His own purpose and grace, which was *given us in Christ Jesus before the world began*" (2 Tim. 1:9). Before mankind ever sinned, grace provided a plan of forgiveness and restoration for all (Mark 16:15).

Eph. 1:4: "According as He hath chosen us *in Him before the foundation of the world*, that we should be holy and without blame before Him in love." Notice it's "in Him" that people are accepted in God's sight. And anyone who calls on the name of the Lord enters into Him and is accepted by grace. This is God's plan. "For whosoever shall call upon the name of the Lord shall be saved" (Rom. 10:13). Jesus said, "I am the door: by Me if *any man* enter in, he shall be saved, and shall go in and out, and find pasture" (John 10:9). It was God's choice then, to establish this plan *in His Son* before man was ever created. A plan to restore men to holiness *in Christ* while retaining their liberty of will. In Christ, He provided a way for sinners to be cleansed of sin and as we've said, this plan was made before the foundation of the world.

First Corinthians 2:7 says: "But we speak the wisdom of God in a mystery, even the hidden wisdom which God ordained *before the world* unto our glory."

First Peter 1:18-20: "For as much as ye know that ye were not redeemed with corruptible things, as silver and gold, from your vain conversation received by tradition from your fathers, but with the precious blood of Christ, as of a lamb without blemish and without spot. *Who verily was foreordained before the foundation of the world*, but was manifest in these last times for you." It's not that any specific individual is foreordained or predestined, for all human wills are free (Mark 16:15), but Christ was predestined to come as the Lamb of God and pay the penalty of sin for all men (John 1:29; Heb. 2:9; 1 John 2:2). That *just as Eve was taken from Adam's side. . .* to be his help meet, so also Christ, the last Adam, would come to take a bride, a help meet, which would be taken from those who would willingly receive Him, accept His saving work, enter "into Him," and become bone of His bone and flesh of His flesh (Eph. 5:30-32). And He would cleanse this bride with His own blood (Rev. 1:5-6) that flowed *from His side*. "But one of the soldiers with a spear pierced His side and forthwith came there out blood and water" (John 19:34).

He came then to enter into an eternal (marriage) covenant with people who would choose to receive Him and *want to* be with

Him forever (2 Cor. 11:2; Rev. 7:4; John 1:12). "The next day, John seeth Jesus coming unto him, and saith, Behold the Lamb of God, which taketh away the sin of the world" (John 1:29). God then, simply chose in His eternal predestined plan to adopt into Christ all sinners who would use their wills to receive Jesus as Lord and these He chose to make His sons (John 1:10-12; Rev. 13:8; Heb. 2:9; Rom. 3:23). And now in God's plan, "whosoever will" can return and enter "into Christ" and be saved because in Him is life (Heb. 2:9; John 1:4; Rom. 10:9; 10:13; 2 Pet. 3:9). Paul said that we all were "by nature children of wrath even as others." But the Bible further says, "but as many as received Him, *to them* gave He power *to become* the sons of God" (John 1:12; 1 John 2:2).

Adam and Eve, in their innocent state were a picture of Christ and the church and were here by God's sovereign choice. By His will and determinate counsel He turned the earth over to them, and told them, "Be fruitful and multiply: have dominion over the earth and subdue it." He then placed Adam and Eve in the garden to keep it and dress it. "To work it and to watch it" (Gen. 2:15, Septuagint translation).

The Serpent

Now the serpent (the devil) was more subtle than any beast of the field that the Lord God had made.... And coming into the garden he said to the woman, "Yea hath God said ye shall not eat of every tree of the garden?" She reasoned with the serpent and the old serpent (the devil--the deceiver of the world) (Rev. 12:9), said unto the woman, "ye shall not surely die...." "For God doth know that in the day ye eat thereof, then your eyes shall be opened, and ye shall be as gods, knowing good and evil" (Gen. 3:5). But satan knew they were already created in the image and likeness of God and so he hated them. But sadly, Eve reasoned with the devil. Any time satan can get people to reason against God's Word, believe it's passed away or that God's Word won't be fulfilled as God said, satan then has them in those areas under the power of unbelief and they then become blinded and deceived (Rev. 12:9; 2 Cor. 4:3-4). (This is why we must beware of the leaven of religious leaders.) What you believe affects the way you see things (Matt. 6:21-24). "And when the woman saw that the tree was good for food, and that it was pleasant to the eyes, and a tree to be desired to make one wise, she took of the fruit thereof, and did eat, and gave also unto her husband with her, and he did eat" (Gen. 3:6).

Notice, Adam was right there with her. And the Bible says, "Adam was not deceived." "Adam was not fooled by the serpent" (Kenneth Taylor's Living Letters), (1 Tim. 2:14). He was totally responsible for the decision and actions he took, for the Bible says, "Wherefore, as by one man sin entered into the world and death by sin; and so death passed upon all men, for that all have sinned" (Rom. 5:12). "Therefore to him that knoweth to do good, and doeth it not, to him it is sin" (James 4:17). The Bible says Adam sinned, therefore he knew.

Have you ever wondered why that serpent (the devil) was in the garden in the first place? Or why he was permitted to be there? God gave Adam authority and told him to subdue the earth. *Subdue* means "conquer with superior power; overcome any enemies" (Gen. 1:25) If Adam was not deceived as the Scripture says, then he knew that there was an enemy. He knew who the serpent was. . . (at least he knew it according to God's Word for if he was not deceived, God must have then told him about the devil).

Because of the promise of greater things and under persuasion of his wife (Gen. 3:6), Adam willed to believe and act on the devil's word rather than God's Word. Of his own free will, he ate forbidden fruit contrary to God's Word, and when he acted on what satan said, he became subordinate to the devil. Death entered the world and satan, who by nature is no god, became the "god of this world" Adam unwittingly chose to have the devil lord it over him and his posterity, and by this act of treason God was shut out of his life, in much the same way it is with unbelievers today, who "walk according to the course of this world, according to the prince of the power of the air" (2 Cor. 4:3-4; Rom. 5:12; Heb. 2:14; Eph. 2:2). Scripture says they also are "without God in this world" (Eph. 2:12).

We know, according to the Bible, that sinners must use their wills to turn from satan, repent, and accept the Lord willingly back into their lives and hearts (Gal. 4:6). For *"as many as received Him*, to them gave He power *to become* the sons of God, even to them that believe on His name" (John 1:12). So let us realize that satan, by Adam's act of treason, gained entrance into his life, and gained a certain degree of authority over Adam's offspring (seed) because of his willful disobedience. Satan then became the spiritual stepfather, so to speak, of the human race. Unless we make a decision to serve God, we are locked into Adam, our forefather's, decision. This is why Jesus said, "Ye are of your father, the devil" (John 8:44), and Paul wrote that we were all "children of wrath by nature," just as the rest of mankind is (Eph. 2:3). (See also 1 John 3:8-11; Rom.10:13.) And so, *by Adam's choice* and disobedience, satan became temporarily the "god of this world" as Paul also reveals in 2 Cor. 4:3-4: "But if our Gospel be hid, it is hid to them that are lost: in whom the *god of this world* hath blinded the minds of them which believe not, lest the light of the glorious Gospel of Christ, who is the image of God, should shine unto them."

In Luke 4:5-6, it speaks of satan tempting Christ when He was here as the Son of man thousands of years later, "And the devil, taking Him up into an high mountain, showed unto Him *all the kingdoms of the world in a moment of time*. And the devil said unto Him, All this power (authority) *will I give thee*, and the glory of them: *for that is delivered unto me,* and to whomsoever *I will*, I give it." Jesus recognizing that satan had this temporal position, called satan "the prince of this world" (John 14:30). So the enemy of God and man acquired legal entrance into the earth through Adam's transgression (Rom. 5:12; Heb.2:14).

A Mystery Unveiled

Now let me show you something about why the serpent was even permitted by God to continue in his course of action and be in the garden of Eden after his own fall. First of all, because he also is a free moral agent with a certain allotted time frame to do as he chooses just as mankind does (Isa. 14:12-13). In Revelation 20:1-3

John says, "And I saw an angel come down from Heaven, having the key of the bottomless pit and a great chain in his hand. And he laid hold on the dragon, that old serpent, which is the devil, and satan, and bound him a thousand years. (Lucifer's time for him being free to act as a free moral agent here temporarily ends. His doom is certain.) And (the angel) cast him into the bottomless pit and shut him up and set a seal upon him, that he should deceive the nations no more, till the thousand years should be fulfilled and after that *he must be loosed a little season."*

Notice, it says he "MUST BE LOOSED a little season." Why? To give the natural people who are born and live natural lives during the millennium, the opportunity to exercise their free wills. They MUST *be given the right to choose or their will is not really free*–God's Word or satan's word–life or death, blessing or cursing, good or evil, Jesus or satan. The choice is man's (Deut. 30:19). So it was necessary, according to God's plan, that Adam be given the freedom and right to choose good or evil, God or satan, and so it was then and is even now (James 4:4; 1 John 2:15-17). Let us not also depart from God because of satan's promises of sinful, selfish, worldly pleasures, but let us remain faithful.

Let me point something to help us understand redemption. Eve, a type of the church, sinned. Adam could have been the savior of the body (Eph. 5:22-23). He could have stayed with the Word as the head of his house and asked for her forgiveness (Num. 30), but instead, he sinned and *by one man* sin entered into the world and death by sin (Rom. 5:12). The responsibility was on him not her at that present time, but he failed to do his part and yielded also to satan at the tree of knowledge. Now the people Christ created to be His help meet, also sinned. If He was ever to have a bride, a help meet, He, the *last Adam*, would have to go to the tree of Calvary and pay the full penalty for sin and suffer the full consequences and effects of sin that His bride deserved if she was ever to be clean and white again and be totally free (Rev. 1:5-6). The debt could not be just partially paid, so the picture is clear. Christ, the *last Adam* could only clear: man by full payment. Look up these redemptive terms, "ransom" and "redeem," and it will help you to understand what I am saying here (Matt. 1:21).

Satan's Will and Man's Will

Now just because satan gained entrance into this world, and Paul called him the "god of this world," he is still, by no means, an equal opposite to God, but just a created being. As we've seen, it will only take an angel who was also created by God to cast him (satan) into the pit (Rev. 20). Before man was ever created, Lucifer (an angel, a created being) of his own will, with no one to tempt him, chose to rebel against God even though he lived in God's very presence, saw God and knew Him intimately. He persuaded some of the angels and other beings, now known as demons, to also use their wills to rebel with him (Luke 11:24). And he is still working through deception to get other free moral agents (people) to reject God and to follow him. "How art thou fallen from Heaven, O lucifer, son of the morning; how art thou cut down to the ground, which didst weaken the nations? For thou hast said in thine heart, I will ascend into Heaven, *I will* exalt my throne above the stars of God: *I will sit* also upon the mount of the congregation, in the sides of the north: *I will* ascend above the heights of the clouds; *I will* be like the most High" (Isa. 14:12-14). He chose his course and because he was created also with liberty of will, God is allowing him to continue on in his ways for a certain allotted time period until the day of the Lord (Ezek. 28:13-15), just as he is doing with mankind.

As it is with every free moral agent, men must also be given the opportunity to exercise their wills and choose between God and satan. God's Word of Truth or satan's lies, right or wrong, good or evil. If they are not given the choice, then they are not free to choose.

In Deuteronomy 30:15-19, God says through Moses, "See, I have set before thee this day, life and good, and death and evil, in that I command thee this day to love the Lord thy God, to walk in His ways, and to keep His commandments and His statutes, and His judgments, that thou mayest live and multiply, and the Lord thy God shall bless thee in the land whither thou goest to possess it. *But if thine heart turn away*, so that thou wilt not hear, but shalt be drawn away, *and worship other gods*, and serve them. I denounce unto you this day, that ye shall surely perish, and that ye shall not prolong your days upon the land, whither thou passest over Jordan to go to possess it. I call Heaven and earth to record this day against you, that I have set before you life and death, blessing and cursing, *therefore, choose* life, that both thou and thy seed may live."

To choose life, one has to choose to will to believe God and His Word and obey Him. In other words, you must choose to make God your God. Whomever you obey is your God and master (Heb. 5:9; Rom. 6:16; Luke 6:46).

From the time Adam and Eve exercised their wills to side in with satan's lie, satan became as Jesus said, "the prince of this world" (John 14:30), or as Paul wrote "the god of this world" (2 Cor. 4:3-4), but only for the period of time originally given to man. This temporal reign is all that he gained (Rev. 12:12) but after that point in time, it was determined beforehand that God's Son would first come to get His bride, at the rapture of the church (1 Thess. 4:15-18), then come back to the earth at a set time with the church and put down all rebellion in this part of God's creation. The saints (His bride) would then rule with Him on earth for one thousand years, over the natural people still alive here (Rev. 5:10). "Then cometh the end, (after the millennium) when He (Christ) shall have delivered up the kingdom to God, even the Father; when he shall have put down all rule and all authority and power. For he must reign, till He hath put all enemies under His feet. The last enemy that shall be destroyed is death. And when all things shall be subdued unto Him, then shall the Son also Himself, be subject unto Him that put all things under Him, that God may be all in all" (1 Cor. 15:24-26, 28). The church (His bride), the redeemed of the Lord, He'd forever have with Himself the eternal helpmeet He desired. So the final result is that God is, and always has been, in ultimate control and God knows the end of all things (Acts 15:18). But until that time actually occurs, satan has a legal right to be here, and do what he wills, and men also are given during this time period, the right to choose whom they will serve, whether it be God, the source of all good, or satan, who is the source of evil and sin (1 John 3:8). And so the battle continues between right and wrong, between faith and unbelief.

At the dawn of human history, satan gained entrance into this world and all that was good (Gen. 1:31) began to deteriorate. Death, pain, poverty, murder, crime, misery, and sorrow, entered the world all of which is contrary to the will of God, who wills all things to be "on earth even as it is in Heaven" (Matt. 6:10; James 1:16-17). But the thief has not ceased to kill, steal and destroy God's creation, since the time that he gained entrance here (John 10:10). And all of his works are contrary to God's will (1 John 3:8). Now no man has to stay under the devil's authority, for each person can use their own free will, repent and turn to God, calling on the name of the Lord, and God will intervene and save them (Rom. 10:13). Scripture says that God "commands all men everywhere to repent." So it is that God created men, empowered them with the freedom of choice, and turned the earth for this certain allotted time period over to mankind. It is in this sense that we say that God is on the outside of people's lives, desiring to enter in and yet He has chosen not to intervene in the earth, in the lives of people unless they use their wills to search for Him, call on His name, pray, or act on *His Word* (Jer. 29:13; Matt. 6:8; James 4:2).

None of this makes God a failure, as many critics imply, for God Himself is the One who set it up this way. And God, through foreknowledge, foresaw evil entering the universe by the decisions of free moral agents, so worked out a plan to counteract it and even use it as long as it's here. In His plan to create free moral agents, He also allowed satan to take his own course, because he too was, and is, a free moral agent who was given a certain allotted time. But yet as we've shown, the time for his judgment is also set, just as it also is for man (Rev. 12:12; 20:10). The day of the Lord will come. Now, it is always God's will that people choose Him, His Word, obedience, peace, health, prosperity, righteousness, and abundant life. The choice is theirs to believe either His Word or satan's lies. This is why Christ said, "According to your faith, so be it unto you." That is according (in proportion) to how much you use your free will to believe God and His Word and obey it, so it will be done unto you, or, for that matter, how much you believe the devil and do what he says to do (Eph. 4:27; John 15:7). We must all, as Paul wrote, "fight the good fight of faith" and strive to stay true to God's Word.

This is the battle we are engaged in (2 Cor.10:3-5). God knew that by creating free moral agents, some would choose to do evil, would listen to the devil and persecute those who chose righteousness and faith in God, so He worked out a plan in the counsel of His own will. If people, religion, or devils persecuted you for your faith, you could receive eternal blessings for handling it according to God's will (Matt. 5:1-12). So negative circumstances and persecutions although they are not God's will, can turn out for your benefit, if in the midst of them, you do what God's Word says to do. *For those who will be faithful and obey God in the midst of persecution or devil brought trials*, because you're following the Lord you will receive reward in the age to come (2 Cor. 4:17; James 1:12; Matt. 5:10-12). Now it's not the trial that brings reward, but how you handle it. Some will go through trials and receive no reward, while others will. And if in the midst of them, they *will* believe and obey God fully, God will give them victory all the time, every time, in their life, over the devil and trials (Deut. 28:1, 7; 2 Cor. 2:14). Not only that but you'll receive reward for overcoming satan's tricks and enticements, and in that sense, Paul said *these light afflictions that come against us*, which are but for a moment, *can actually "work for us*, a far more exceeding and eternal weight of glory."* (See 2 Corinthians 4:16-18.) So what the devil means for evil can actually work for us, *but only* if we handle things God's way (1 Pet. 3:9; James 1:12). Oh, the depth of the wisdom of God!

God's Will Be Done on Earth as It Is In Heaven

Nowhere in God's Word does it say God wills you to be poor, defeated, sick, oppressed, fearful, in sin, or any other such thing; but rather, He wants His will to be done on earth EVEN AS it is done in Heaven. You are to agree with God, have His Word abiding in you, speak according to it and overcome the wicked one. ". . . ye are strong young men, and the Word of God abideth in you, and ye have overcome the wicked one" (1 John 2:14). "And they overcame him by the blood of the Lamb, and by the word of their testimony" (Rev. 12:11).

"And take the helmet of salvation, and the sword of the Spirit, which is the Word of God" (Eph. 6:17).

We are to overcome the enemy in every arena of life and do so by faith in God's Word (1 John 5:4). In proportion to how much you believe God's Word of life and obey it, is how much of the abundant life that was lost in Eden is restored back to you (Rom. 1:16; Matt. 4:4; John 10:10).

So then, we say that God has foreknowledge, and has an over all eternal plan to have sons and daughters that will come to pass, which neither devil, man, nor angel can stop (Rev. 12:9-10). And we teach that God has chosen during this time period, to deal with men on the basis of their conformity to His Word by their own free wills and if people will diligently hearken unto Him, they'll be blessed coming in and going out, as He has said. Listen now, to the Lord in Deut. 28:1-14, "And it shall come to pass, *if thou* shalt hearken diligently unto the voice of the Lord thy God, *to observe and to do* all His commandments which I command thee this day, that the Lord thy God will set thee on high above all nations of the earth: and all these blessings shall come on thee, and overtake thee, if thou shalt hearken unto the voice of the Lord thy God, blessed shalt thou be in the city, and blessed shalt thou be in the field. Blessed shall be thy fruit of thy body and the fruit of thy ground, and the fruit of thy cattle, the increase of thy kine, and the flocks of thy sheep. Blessed shall be thy basket and thy store. Blessed shalt thou be when thou comest in and blessed shalt thou be when thou goest out. The Lord shall cause thine enemies that rise up against thee to be smitten before thy face: they shall come out against thee one way, and flee before thee seven ways. The Lord shall command the blessings upon thee in thy storehouses, and in all that thou settest thine hand unto; and He shall bless thee in the land which the Lord thy God giveth thee. The Lord shall establish thee an holy people unto Himself, as He hath sworn unto thee, *if thou* shalt keep the commandments of the Lord thy

God, and walk in His ways. And all people of the earth shall see that thou are called by the name of the Lord: and they shall be afraid of thee. And the Lord shall make thee plenteous in goods, in the fruit of thy body, and in the fruit of thy cattle, and in the fruit of thy ground, in the land which the Lord sware unto thy fathers to give thee. The Lord shall open unto thee His good treasure, the Heaven to give the rain unto thy land in his season, and to bless all the work of thine hand: and thou shalt lend unto many nations, and thou shalt not borrow. And the Lord shall make thee the head and not the tail, and thou shalt be above only and thou shalt not be beneath; *if that thou hearken* unto the commandments of the Lord thy God, which I command thee this day, to observe and to do them."

This then, is God's will for you and it is abundant life. He commands us to choose to obey Him, just as He commanded Adam (Gen. 2:16-17.) In John 10:10 Jesus said, "the thief cometh not but for to steal, and to kill, and to destroy: I am come that they (mankind) might have life, and that they might have it more abundantly." And Jesus is called "the Word" (John 1:1; 3:34). The Word then came to give you the abundant life God intended for man in the beginning. "And thou shalt not go aside from any of the words which I command thee this day, to the right hand, or to the left, to go after other gods to serve them. But it shall come to pass, if thou wilt not hearken unto the voice of the Lord thy God, to observe to do all His commandments and His statutes, which I command thee this day; that all these curses shall come upon thee, and overtake thee."

So if people choose then to listen to satan, act on his lies, and obey him, then all of these curses shall come upon them and their offspring and overcome them (Deut. 28:16-88). For God's righteous decree is that the wicked one can rule over the wicked, or over those that refuse to believe in, speak according to, or act on, God's Word (1 Cor. 10:10; Deut. 30:11-14), for they are then acting in agreement with the devil (1 Pet. 5:8-9). It's man's choice (Eph. 4:27; Deut. 5:29). Please note though, there can also be, as in Job's case, those who are destroyed by satan because of lack of a knowledge of God's truth (Hosea 4:6; John 8:31-32). They may consent ignorantly to his working but it is still consent, nonetheless. But be assured, John 10:10 is the dividing line. "The thief cometh not but for to steal, and to kill and to destroy. I (the Word) am come that they might have life and have it more abundantly." (See also James 1:16-17.)

Scripture says, "the curse causeless shall not come" (Prov. 26:2). What then brings it? What can open the door to it to defeat a person? First of all, Adam opened the door of this world to untold sorrows and storms of life, then also a person's own sin, unbelief, lack of knowledge, wrong teaching, parent's or ancestor's sins, believing traditions of men rather than God's Word, disobedience, self-will, giving place to the devil, failing to do the Word or speak in agreement with it and other such like things, can cause people to fall in defeat when the storms of life come. But regardless of what it is that moves people to use their wills, victory or failure, depends on them. "According to *your faith* be it unto you." You don't have to stay defeated if you'll learn and believe the real "Gospel." In Matthew 7:24-29 Jesus says, "Therefore, whosoever heareth these sayings of Mine, and doeth them, I will liken him unto a wise man, which built his house upon a rock: and the rain descended, and the floods came, and the winds blew, and beat upon that house; *and it fell not*, for it was founded upon a rock. And whosoever heareth these sayings of mine, and doeth them not, shall be likened unto a foolish man, which built his house upon the sand, and the rain descended and the floods came, and the winds blew and beat upon that house and it fell, and great was the fall of it. And it came to pass, when Jesus had ended these sayings, the people were astonished at His doctrine, for He taught them as one having authority, and not as the scribes." People can choose then to believe or not believe His Words; to act on them or not (James 1:22). (Notice that just because you hear His Word does not mean that you're exempt from all the storms of life.) But if you obey Him, you'll be kept from many of them (Prov. 6:20-23; Ps. 17:4), and overcome the rest of them (Prov. 1:33), after you fight the good fight of faith.

So because of man's free moral agency, God will not work on behalf of a man unless that man or someone else acts on His Word or prays in faith (Heb. 11:6). Satan also seeks to get people to exercise their wills, but he works to get them to live and speak contrary to God's Word and truth (1 Cor. 10:10; Proverbs 18:21). Now satan (as in the beginning with Adam and Eve), works to persuade people to go contrary to God's Word through temptations, deceptions, lies, creating imaginations, false religious ideas, and such like things, and if they yield, he then has their consent to work in their lives (2 Cor. 10:3-5; Eph. 2:2-3), while God gives man His Word of Truth, and sends out His messengers (Mark 16:15; John 3:34; Ps. 107:20; 1 Thess. 2:13).

Noah and Abraham

Let us now continue. After the fall, God promised a redeemer whom He called "woman's seed" (Gen. 3:15), and after this, Adam and Eve had two sons. One, (Abel) who was a man of faith and had faith in God's Word; the other, (Cain) was religious in his own way but was not a person of faith. And satan, seeking to destroy faith in God on earth, moved Cain to kill Abel (Heb. 11:4; 1 John 3:11-19). For he feared the promised "seed" that God said would come, and he knew it had to be one who believed God. After this, there's not much mention of faith for many years, and then in Enoch's generation, Enoch walked with God and he was the "only one" that pleased God by faith in the earth at that time so God took him (Heb. 11:5). As time passed, the earth later became so over spread with evil, that the thoughts of man's heart was "only evil continually" (Gen. 6:5; 11-12).

And when God saw the extent of men's evil, it "grieved God" and repented Him that he had ever made man on the earth (Gen. 6:5-6). Then God found and spoke to Noah, *a man who had faith* in God (Gen. 6:9). Again, although there were probably many religious people in the earth, Noah's family was the "only" family that had real faith in God on the earth at that time and lived for God), (Gen. 6:9-12), and God told Noah He would destroy man on the earth with a flood. By faith (in God's Word), "Noah being warned of God of things not seen as yet, moved with fear, prepared an ark to the saving of his house, *by the which he condemned the world*, and became heir of righteousness *which is by faith*" (Heb. 11:7). And the "longsuffering of God waited in the days of Noah, (for men to repent) while the ark was a preparing" (1 Peter 3:20). Noah, Peter said, was a "*preacher* of righteousness" (2 Peter 2:5). But because the people of Noah's day refused Noah's preaching and refused to repent, God, through Noah, brought in a flood upon the world of the ungodly.

We can be sure that as Noah preached, he warned and declared what God would do. God worked through Noah's mouth in the earth, just as He did through the mouths of all of His many prophets in the Scriptures. ". . .which God hath *spoken by the mouth* of all His holy prophets *since the world began*" (Acts 3:21). It was through these holy men of God in the earth, that God brought judgments. For remember, "the earth hath He given to the children of men." So both satan and God are now presently working through man in the earth. Think about it and you'll know this is so (1 Kings 18:36-39). "Now all this was done that it might be fulfilled which was spoken OF THE LORD BY THE PROPHET. . ." (Matt. 1:22). God always then, works in and through willing men of faith during this six thousand or so year time period He has given to man (Mark 16:20). And there are numerous other Scriptures that prove this point (Heb. 1:1). (See also 2 Kings 18:36-39; Exodus 3:11-12; John 3:2; Acts 5:12; Mark 16:20; James 5:17-18; Matt. 9:37-38.)

After the flood men multiplied and the world once again went astray following after satan. Faith in God diminished until God, the Searcher of the hearts, found another man named Abram. Later, the Lord again appeared to Abram and in Genesis 17:1-4.

"And when Abram was ninety years old and nine, the Lord appeared to Abram, and said unto him, I am the Almighty God, walk before Me and be thou perfect. And I will make My Covenant between Me and thee, and will multiply thee exceedingly. And Abram fell on his face, and God talked with him saying, As for Me, behold, My Covenant is with thee and thou shalt be a father of many nations."

Notice in verse 4, God said, "AS FOR ME" not "as for you"

this is what you must do. God couldn't force him, for Abraham had a free will. God will not ever go contrary to His own Word or plan. And God told him, *if he would keep His covenant*, that He would be a God unto him and his seed after him. Wasn't He already his God? No! Satan had become the "god of this world" because of Adam's act of treason.

But as we've said, Abraham's will also was free. He could choose for Himself God the Creator as his God and reject satan (the god of this world) if he so desired. He did not have to stay locked into his forefather's, Adam decision, just as you and I do not have to stay locked into our father's lifestyles or decisions. The Gospel of a promised redeemer and redemption was revealed to Abraham (Gal. 3:8), and it was told him that through him "the seed" would come to save mankind if he'd obey God's voice (Gal. 3:16). Now listen: and ". . .Abraham *believed God* (believed His Word) and it was accounted to him for righteousness. . . ." A righteousness that is by faith. He used his "will" to *believe and obey God* (Heb. 11:8). That's faith (Gal. 3:6).

Faith and obedience to faith is the open door God needs to work in a person's life. For faith moves a person to walk in agreement with the unchangeable God (Amos 3:3; 2 Cor. 5:7; Rom. 1:5). God then became known as the "God of Abraham" as they entered into a covenant together. Abraham and his wife, Sarah, had a miracle child in their old age *because they believed God. . ."* (Rom. 4:17-21; Heb. 11:11), and again it was all *by faith* (Eph. 1:19; Matt. 16:19). Time passed and God later told Abraham to offer up his only son Isaac on the altar (Gen. 22). *"By faith* Abraham, when he was tried, offered up Isaac, and he that had received the promises offered up his only begotten son, of whom it was said, that in Isaac shall thy seed be called, *accounting that God was able to raise him up even from the dead*, from whence also he received him in a figure" (Heb. 11:17-19). Notice that it was "by faith." According to this Scripture then, Abraham had "resurrection faith;" He believed God could raise the dead. God had promised the blessings through Isaac, so he believed that even if he slew him, God would have to raise him up, even from the dead in order to fulfill His promise. Notice that Abraham said to those who went with them to make the sacrifice that, "I and the lad (Isaac) will go yonder and worship and come again to you" (Genesis 22:5). That was his faith talking.)

Faith then, is not limited to reason, but believes God can and will do whatever His Word says He will do (Rom. 10:9). If people could only see that it always has been and always will be a FAITH MESSAGE! Faith in God's Word is the only thing that pleases Him and opens up the door for His working, while unbelief shuts Him out (Heb. 11:6). From Adam until now, this is what God has desired, and can you not see how evil it is for the traditions and theologies of men to make the Word of God of none effect. God, at the last moment, provided a ram, which represented Christ, for the sacrifice instead of Abraham's son. This was in response to Abraham's faith *who said* to his son, "God will provide Himself a lamb for a burnt offering. . . ." Note also what is said to him in Genesis 22, "And the angel of the Lord called unto Abraham out of Heaven the second time, and said, By myself have I sworn, saith the Lord, for *because 'thou' hast done this thing*, and hast not withheld thy son, thine only son, that in blessing I will bless thee and in multiplying, I will multiply thy seed as the stars of the Heaven, and as the sand which is upon the sea shore, and *thy seed shall possess the gate of his enemies*, and in thy seed shall *all the nations* of the earth be blessed, *because thou hast obeyed My voice*" (Gen. 22:15-18).

Now God had a free moral agent in the earth, who by faith, offered up his own son on the altar and had obeyed God's Word. So on behalf of the Covenant cut with Abraham in the earth, God could now, during this time period given to man, offer up on the altar of the cross His only begotten Son whom He loved. And for this reason God said, "ALL THE NATIONS OF THE EARTH shall be blessed; BECAUSE 'THOU' hast obeyed My voice" (v. 18). The critic of the faith message says God is sovereign; He doesn't need anyone; He could have done it without Abraham obeying Him. The critic says if He needed Abraham's obedience, then He's not Almighty. This is how ignorant some men are of the way God works in His dealings with mankind.

Abraham had believed God's Word and obeyed it and because of Abraham's obedience, God blessed him with gold, servants, cattle and so on. Through Abraham there then, came forth the Israelite nation (Gen. 18:17-18). And with it, a clearer revelation of God back into the earth. God later spoke many things through the Jewish prophets, concerning the coming Savior, (the details of His life and ministry were clearly portrayed) and many great faith achievements took place by these people who were in Covenant with God, as recorded in Hebrews 11. Regardless of what satan threw at them to stop them many times using the ungodly, God always caused His people to have the victory, but only when they BELIEVED HIS WORD and obeyed Him (Heb. 11:6). There was always a remnant who did believe.

God later worked with Moses, with Elijah, and with the other prophets. They chose to obey Him, and cooperate with Him, and He spoke to them what He willed, and they prayed for it or acted on it, and God responded to their faith in His Word and brought forth the results (Exod. 14:13-16, 21; 1 Kings 18:36-39). They were God's open door in the earth. But God did not work apart from man (1 Cor. 3:6-9). Someone, somewhere, has to be praying or acting on His Word. John Wesley once said, "It seems to me, that God can do nothing in the earth except a man ask Him." His observation is true (Matt. 16:19). Let me ask this, if He could, at this present time, do anything just because He's Almighty God, why then doesn't He? Why let innocent babies suffer? Why not stop all the pain and accidents? Why are even animals born crippled and sick only to become prey and suffer? Why do some of His own people get in car wrecks, get divorced, and are destroyed for a lack of knowledge? Why are there backsliders? Why do people die and go to hell? *We know* these things are not His will and we know this according to what He said in His own Word (John 10:10; 1 John 3:8). So while He *could* have controlled everything, He has *choosen* not to because He's given man a free will (2 Pet. 3:9; Rev. 20:11-13).

The Truth About Romans 8:28

Some will take Rom. 8:28 out of context and try and say *everything* that's happening in the earth is all working together for the good. But that is a "man-made theology" or doctrines made up by devils. Whenever there is responsibility put on man to believe and obey God, these people want to escape the responsibility of having to believe God's Word and to speak it and do it as God said (Deut. 30:14; Rom. 10:8), so they twist what is written and take it out of context. They shout the excuse "God is sovereign" and so they do nothing God said to do. That does not glorify God in the least. Remember, Jesus said, victory comes "according to YOUR FAITH" (Matt. 9:29), not according to His faith. Rom. 8:28 does not say everything the devil does will work out for a person's good. Some are deceived by the devil and go to hell. Then it sure didn't work out for their good. Christian families, many times, are destroyed; children are beaten, and so on. This is never God's will and is not working for good but for evil! So there is a multitude of things that happen to people and even Christians, which are nothing more than the devil coming to "kill, steal and destroy." Christian's should be taught how to believe God and resist the devil and his works "steadfast in the faith" (1 Pet. 5:8-9). But sadly, in many cases, they are wrongly taught that these evil things are all from the hand of God, and they believe another of the serpent's lies and accusations against God. This is one of the real problems in the body of Christ.

Know ye not that we are still in a warfare (2 Cor. 10:3-5)? That there still is a serpent who deceives the world and much of his work is through religion and the things taught by religious men? He knows people have a spiritual tendency towards God and so He works to twist God's Word and pervert it and make these perversions sound reasonable (See 2 Corinthians 11:3.) God orders us all to "prove all things and hold fast to that which is good."

The Bible says, "This is the victory that overcomes the world, even our faith" (1 John 5:4). It's only when we, as free moral agents, choose to believe God's Word over satan's lies, deceptions, etc., and act on it, and are persistent in it that God has the liberty to work in our lives and change things and turn situations around. (See John 15:7; Matt. 7:24-29.) This is the only time things will turn around and work out for our good. Again, this is because of the liberty God gave the human will. This will become more clear later. But for the present time, we see that mankind can do what they will to do, and believe what they want to believe and God will not directly interfere with their present activities unless they or someone else prays for them or preaches the truth to them (2 Chron. 7:14). But the day of the Lord is coming.

Escape Theology

Let me give you an example of what I mean when I say, "Escape Theology." The reason people have to make up a theology that says, "God wants you sick," or "He's" sending the evil trials to teach "you," is because they have *no faith* in God's Word to believe what God said about praying the prayer of faith for the sick for them to be healed (James 5:14-15). They are either ignorant or refuse to believe what God said to do about overcoming, such as resisting the devil "steadfast in the faith," or "taking the shield of faith wherewith ye shall be able to quench all the fiery darts of the wicked one." They have no or little faith in the dozens and dozens of Scriptures and promises of God that reveal God wants you healed and blessed and that He desires His will to be done on earth even as it is in Heaven. So to make an excuse for their lack of faith, they teach people all manner of nonsense in the name of theology, saying such things as, "this passed away;" "that doesn't happen anymore;" "it's not for today;" "God is sovereign;" or "it was only for the apostles." These phrases and modern day traditions of men are nothing more than the excuses of unbelief, they are *not* Scripture.

Concerning healing, James simply said *to the church* in James 5:14-15: "Is any sick among you? Let him call for *the elders* of the church; and let them pray over him, anointing him with oil in the name of the Lord, and the *prayer of faith shall save the sick, and the Lord shall raise him up*, and if he have committed sins, they shall be forgiven him." God wants His people free from the works of the devil (Acts 10:38).

"For no man ever yet hated his own flesh: but nourisheth and cherisheth it, even as the Lord the church: for we are members of His body, of His flesh and of His bones. For this cause shall a man leave his father and mother and shall be joined unto his wife and they two shall be one flesh. This is a great mystery: but I speak concerning Christ and the church" (Eph. 1:9). He wants His bride taken care of. He wants her protected against the cruel criminal satan, who's a thief and a robber. Jesus has left us the authority of His name, the power of His Spirit, a supernatural prayer language, the gifts of the Spirit, so we can defeat the enemy (Luke 10:19). But religion blinded by the enemy doesn't believe it. They just have excuses such as, "It passed away;" "The days of miracles are over;" "We don't believe that way." Anything God set in the church to help His Son's bride against the enemy, the critics want to remove, and they then tell people the bridegroom wants His bride sick, poor, defeated, and that this is the work of God, and then they attack anyone who tries to teach Christ's bride the truth. Woe to them! But again brethren, that's nothing more than unbelief in God's Word.

Can you not see that this is what the Bible calls a "form of godliness, THAT DENIES THE POWER," and are we wrong if we believe all "*the faith*" that was once delivered to the saints Jude 3? Is this not what Jude said to contend for? Religion in every age, has always denied the "power of God" and refused to believe in it, for satan fears a recurrence of the Book of Acts type of Christianity (2 Tim. 3:5). So then, these men who teach God's power is passed away, do not really know what's happening in the earth. Concerning God's will that we be blessed in this life, all one needs to do is look at Deut. 28:1-14; John 10:10; 2 Pet. 1:1-4; Eph. 1:3; Phil. 4:19; Mark 11:24; Rom. 8:31-32. For that matter, the whole Bible declares it.

Dear reader, if you learn anything from this book, please learn to stay with what is *actually written, and forget all that*

"Escape Theology," which takes any and all of the blame off satan and man and points the finger at God, and saying it's all happening, good or bad, because of His sovereign choice. *Over four thousand times* in Scripture God tells man to choose, repent, turn, act, pray, obey, believe, and then He will perform His Word (John 11:40; Luke 1:45). Need He say it more than this to get His point across?

Remember that phrase *"Escape Theology."* And whenever any one layman or preacher tells you God won't do something He said He would, or you can't have what He said you can, or that part of the New Testament Gospel has passed away, you can be sure that that's nothing more than religious unbelief and they are *making up* a "theology" that takes the responsibility off of themselves to have any faith for real results (Mark 5:34). And so the serpent is still at work behind the scenes (Luke 22:52-53). It's a whole lot easier for them to say "God is sovereign" or "it passed away" like the Pharisees of old, than to fight the good fight of faith and believe what's actually written and act on it in the face of contrary circumstances. What's really happening many times is people are ignorantly taught to submit to the devil and someone unwisely says, "the will of the Lord be done." Let's get back to God's Word and stop dishonoring God by implying it's not the way He says it is. "Let God be true and every man a liar." Is this not why He gave us the Bible?

Romans 3:3-4 says, "For what if some did not believe? Shall their unbelief make *the faith of God* without effect? God forbid: yea, let God be true, but every man a liar; as it is written. That thou mightest be justified in thy sayings and mightest overcome when thou are judged." (See John 12:48.) But beware, lest when you think you're following God, you're really following the doctrines of men (Mark 7:7). Check out all that's said by anyone with the written Word of God and stay with the Bible regardless of any man's label, title, position or name. Even having many followers or a large church means nothing in itself. There are multitudes in numerous religions following many different kinds of beliefs. In other words, stick with exactly what God has said in the Bible, and you'll overcome when you are judged.

Paul, in Romans 1:16 wrote, "For I am not ashamed of the Gospel of Christ: for *it is* the power of God unto salvation *to every one that believeth*, to the Jew first, and also to the Greek." So yes, God is sovereign, but He sovereignly chose it to be this way. **MAN MUST BELIEVE GOD OVER SATAN.**

As time passed, the prophets being moved by the Holy Ghost (2 Peter 1:20-21), spoke God's Word (Heb. 1:1). And through them, a clear picture was painted of the coming Messiah so that people could recognize Him by God's Word when He came. (See Isaiah 7:14; Micah 5:2.)

Then when the fullness of time came, God *sent forth* His Son, who is also called "the Word" (Gal. 4:4), to be born of a woman. God had said in Gen. 3:15: "And I will put enmity between thee (the serpent) and the woman, and between thy seed and *her seed*; it shall bruise thy head, and thou shalt bruise his heal."

Isaiah wrote, "Therefore, the Lord, Himself, shall give you a sign: behold *a virgin shall conceive* and bear a son, and shall call His name Immanuel" (7:14). Now where did the virgin get the "seed" from, for it to be called "woman's seed"? We'll see she received God's Word by *"faith"* and that this was "the seed."

God gave Abraham and Sarah a child by His "word of promise." "Of His own will He begat us with His Word of Truth" (James 1:18). We have been "born again of incorruptible seed" by the Word of God, which liveth and abideth forever (1 Pet. 1:23).

The original seed He placed within every living thing, began as "His Word." He spoke in Gen. 1:11-12 : "*And God said*, Let the earth bring forth grass, the herb yielding seed, and the fruit tree yielding fruit after his kind, whose seed is in itself, upon the earth and it was so. And the earth brought forth grass and herb yielding seed after his kind, and the tree yielding fruit, whose seed was in itself, after his kind, and God saw that it was good." So we see it was God's Word that brought into existence the first plants and seeds in the plants and Jesus said, "the seed is the Word of God" (Luke 8:11). God's Word is the original seed of everything.So the angel Gabriel was then sent from God unto a city of Galilee named Nazareth *to a virgin. . .*and the virgin's name was Mary (Luke 1:26-45).

The angel bringing to her the Word and the promise of God told her, "Thou shalt conceive in thy womb and bring forth a son, and shalt call His name Jesus." Then Mary said unto the angel, "How shall this be, seeing I know not a man?" (Knowing that a seed was necessary.) And the angel answered and said unto her, *"The Holy Ghost shall come upon thee and the power of the highest shall over shadow thee:* therefore also, that holy thing which shall be born of thee shall be called the Son of God."

Then the angel told her of her cousin Elizabeth's miracle conception in her old age (v. 36), which came to pass also because of God's Word. And in verse 37 said, "For with God nothing shall be impossible." "And Mary said, Behold the handmaid of the Lord; *be it unto me according to Thy word* (v. 38). And the angel departed from her." God's will and Mary's will had agreed. So where as Eve reasoned away and disbelieved God's Word, Mary believed God's Word and accepted by faith that such a miraculous event, beyond all natural reason would happen, and later Elizabeth, her cousin, filled with the Holy Ghost, prophesied under the Spirit's influence to her saying. . . verse 45: ". . . *blessed is she that believed,* for there shall be a performance of those things which were told her from the Lord."

So then Jesus, although He existed in eternity with God, yet in His humanity, was born of the Word and of the Spirit (Matt. 1:18-20). And "the Word became flesh and dwelt amongst us" (John 1:14). Surely, if the same critics of living faith today were alive when these things were first reported, they, too, would have sided in with the Pharisees and mocked this also. Realize this.

His Body therefore, did come directly from the seed of the Word (Heb. 10:5). And when Mary accepted it by faith, God did the miracle. "And the Word became flesh and dwelt amongst us" (John 1:14; Gal. 3:5-7).

Now God could not have just done it through Mary just because He's sovereign or just because He willed to...no, His Word is forever settled in Heaven and He will not alter what's gone out of His mouth. With Him there is no shadow of turning. He created people with living souls and gave the earth temporarily to men and once done, it was necessary that He deal with each person accordingly. So Mary also had a free will and thank God she believed and obeyed. In this same sense, God wills all men to be saved (2 Pet. 3:9), but contrary to His will, not all will be, but only those who use their wills and agree with Him and His Word and accept His Son (Rom. 10:9-10; 1 Tim. 4:10). Again, can you not see through this that it's all a "message of faith"? In the Bible, when results came it has always been that free moral agents have believed God's Word and cooperated with Him. It was then that there came supernatural interventions of God in the earth during this time period given to men. (Acts 17:26; Heb. 11) This is the case from the beginning and is so even to this day; from Genesis to Revelation it's the same (Rev. 22:17).

God's Son Came to Earth as Man

Hebrews 10:5 says, "A body hast Thou prepared Me..." So Christ the Lord was born into the earth as a man (1 Cor. 15:47). This then is what gave Him certain rights here as a man, seeing the earth for this time period, was turned over to men (Ps. 115:16). Jesus said, "Verily, verily, I say unto you, He that entereth not by the door into the sheepfold, but climbeth up some other way, the same is a thief and a robber. But he that entereth in by the door, is the shepherd of the sheep" (John 10:1-2). Paraphrasing it He said, that He came in through the door into this world, which is through a woman and was born here. He did not climb in some other way as the thief and robber (satan) did, through deception (John 10:1-5). So again, by being born here, He had rights as a man to cooperate with the Father and therefore referred to himself as "the Son of man" on numerous occasions. Now because His body did not come from Adam's seed, He was in no way, subject to the "god of this world." He said, "The prince of this world cometh and hath nothing in Me" (John 14:30). He had come *in the likeness* of sinful flesh

(Rom. 8:3), but yet He did not have sinful flesh, for His flesh came directly from God's Word (John 1:14).

Scripture says, He was found in fashion as a man and "made in the likeness of men" (Phil. 2:7-8). That He was limited in all points like you and I (Heb. 2:17), yet by nature He remained divinity. Divine, but yet man. The things He did here on the earth in His earthly ministry, He did *as a man* anointed with the Holy Spirit, as He, Himself, declared (Luke 4:14-21). (See also Matthew 4:3-4; Acts 10:38; John 5:30.) In this way, as a man, He could "leave us an example that we should follow in His steps" (1 Pet. 2:21), and He further said that the works He did, we could do also (John 14:12), but only in proportion to how much we believe God's Word and live as He lived (Mark 16:17; Matt. 9:29). And as the Father sent Him out into the world, even so, He sends us out to do the same things (John 17:14-18).

It was as the Son of man that He set the multitudes free from satan's works (Acts 10:38), for as we've pointed out from Scripture, the earth during this time period, was given to man (Ps. 115:16). He said to His disciples, "Whom do people say that I, the *Son of man am?*" (Matt. 16:13) His dependence in the days of His flesh to do miracles and bring supernatural blessing to people, was totally dependent upon the Father, anointing Him with the Holy Ghost (Acts 7:56; 10:38; Luke 4:17-18; 6:12; Heb. 5:7; Matt. 8:20). Through this anointing for ministry, He did all of His miracles. He said, "The Son can do nothing of Himself" (John 5:19-20). But He said He did it all by the power of the Spirit of God who anointed Him (Matt. 12:28; Luke 4:18-19). He later told His disciples to wait until they also were equipped with the same power to do the same things, that they also, as men of God, might continue His work in the Church Age which was to come and destroy the works of the devil (Acts 1:4-5, 8; Mark 16:15-20; Acts 4:33; Acts 6:7). But He said in order to do this, they must believe (Mark 16:17-18). Some today though, teach God wills the works of the devil to be in your life. That God wants you sick, poor, fearful, and defeated, for some mysterious reason. How far much of the church has gotten from what is actually written. Should we not, dear brethren, go by what is "actually written?" Is this not why He's given to us His written Word?

Now Jesus' earthly life *as a man,* was filled with miracles (John 21:25), angelic visitations (John 1:47-51), gifts of the Spirit, being led by the Spirit, healing anointings (Luke 4:40). He cast out many devils, He lived as a man who's life was full of God's intervention, the only perfect man that ever lived, fully believing in and fully cooperating with the Father (John 5:17). He showed us that we are to strive to be like Him (Luke 6:40). But today when one follows Jesus in this way to any extent and cooperates with the Holy Spirit, some religious men write books to attack that person. My brethren, these things ought not be. When Jesus was here as a man, He operated in "the power of God" and He always had His needs supernaturally met and every Christian has the "power of God" operating in his life to some degree (1 Pet. 1:5). Will these critics attack all Christians?

When Jesus needed tax money, He told Peter to go fishing and that the first fish he caught would have a coin in it's mouth, with enough value to pay for both Peter's and Jesus' taxes. (This was supernatural.) Through God's intervention and multiplication of food, He fed five thousand to fifteen thousand people a few times. His life was full of supernatural deliverance's from troubled situations, and full of miracle working power. He knew how, as a man, to cooperate with His Father God and walk fully in the light of the written Word. He said concerning Himself when confronting the devil, "It is written, MAN shall not live by bread alone, but by every word that proceedeth out of the mouth of God" (Matthew 4:4). Jesus, in His earthly life, also demonstrated the power of words that was originally given to men, and told us to believe that when we speak, results could also come through us (Mark 11:23). Jesus taught that man is to operate in faith the same way as God also does by speaking, for man was created in the image and likeness of God. The critic says God doesn't have faith. But to that person we say, not only does the Bible speak of the "faith of God" (Rom. 3:3-4; Gal. 2:20), it also speaks of the love of God, the longsuffering of God, the peace of God, and so on. How could God deal to us "the measure of faith" (Rom. 12:3), if He didn't have any?

The God Kind of Faith

Forgive me for shifting the subject here for a little while, but let's see something about the God kind of faith and see that God wants men, whom He created in His image, to be imitators of Himself (Eph. 5:1). We've already seen that God speaks and things come into existence.

Listen now to what Jesus taught His disciples. Mark 11:12-14: "And on the morrow, when they were come from Bethany, He was hungry, and seeing a fig tree afar off having leaves, He came, if haply He might find anything thereon, and when He came to it, He found nothing but leaves, for the time of figs was not yet. And Jesus answered and *said unto it,* No man eat fruit of thee hereafter for ever. *And His disciples heard it.*" Mark 11:20-23: "And in the morning as they passed by, they saw the fig tree dried up from the roots. And Peter calling to remembrance, saith unto Him, Master, behold the fig tree which Thou cursedst, is withered away. And Jesus answering saith unto them, Have faith in God (or as the margin says, "Have the faith of God," or the "God kind of faith"). For verily I say unto you, (here it is), that *whosoever shall say* unto this mountain, be thou removed and be thou cast into the sea, and shall not doubt in his heart, but *shall believe* that those things which he saith, shall come to pass, *he shall have whatsoever he saith.*"

So we see that Jesus, the Son of man, imitating His Father's way of doing things, affected an inanimate object with words and told His disciples they could do the same things (Matt. 17:20). Not only that but Jesus cast out devils with words, healed the sick with words, calmed the waves with words, stilled the winds with words. He said the words He spoke were "spirit and life," while others were speaking words of death (1 Cor. 10:10; Prov. 18:21; James 3:1-6), and remember, He was the "Son of man." He knew words could open the door to the devil or defeat the devil. Listen to Him as He says, "it is written," "it is written," "it is written," to the devil to drive the devil away (Matt. 4:4, 7, 10; Rev. 12:11), and His

Word tells us to do the same thing and take "the sword" through which the Spirit works, which is the Word of God. We are to resist the devil with God's Word in our mouths (Rev. 12:11; 2:16; Isa. 59:20-21; Rev. 2:16; 1 Pet. 5:8-9; Eph. 6:17). He also taught us that words were like seeds, which produce a harvest (Mark 4:14; Luke 8:11; Prov. 18:20), revealing that the good seed is the Word of God and that this is what we are to speak in agreement with.

"As for Me, this is My Covenant with them, saith the Lord, My Spirit that is upon thee, and My words which I have put in thy mouth, shall not depart out of thy mouth, nor out of the mouth of thy seed, not out of the mouth of thy seed's seed, saith the Lord, from henceforth and forever" (Isa. 59:21).

His Word further teaches us to hold fast our confession of faith, without wavering (Heb. 10:23), and to have His words abiding in us (John 15:7). So then, your words do set much of the course of your life. James wrote by inspiration of God, "My brethren, be not many masters, knowing that we shall receive the greater condemnation. For in many things we offend all. If any man offend not in word, the same is a perfect man, and able also to bridle the whole body. Behold, we *put bits in the horses mouths*, that they may obey us: and *we turn* about their whole body. Behold, also the ships, which though they be so great, and are driven of fierce winds, *yet are they turned* about with a very small helm. Whithersoever the governor listeth. *Even so, the tongue* is a little member, and boasteth great things. Behold, how great a matter a little fire kindleth, and the tongue is a fire, a world of iniquity, so is the tongue among our members, that it defileth the whole body, and *setteth on fire the course of nature:* and it is set on fire of hell" (James 3:1-6).

Your words set on fire the course of your life, and your words are the fruit of what's in your heart. They affect your life (Matt. 12:33-37; James 1:26). They establish your boundaries (Job 22:28). Faith is released through words (Mark 11:23; Matt. 8:8, 10, 16, 17:20; Rom. 10:9-10; 2 Cor. 4:13). Your life, according to the Bible, will be satisfied by the words you speak (Prov. 18:20; Matt. 12:34-37). Let me encourage you to read the Book of Proverbs and meditate on it concerning what is said about the mouth, words, tongue, and lips, and it will prove this point for any honest person.)

We say nothing new when we say and teach these things, but say only what the Bible instructs us. And if some do not believe it, that's something they must live with. But for us, we will continue on with the Word. Now Christ faced satan's temptations as a man (Matt. 4:3-4). He was tempted in all points like us, yet without sin (Heb. 5:8-9; 7:24-26). Jesus Christ, who had come as the last Adam and the second man, overcame where the first Adam had failed (1 Cor. 15:45-47). The first Adam yielded to satan but the last Adam wouldn't. Whereas, the first Adam used his will to disobey God and His Word, the last Adam said, "Not My will, but Thine be done" and stayed with the "Word."

The Ministry of Healing

The first Adam yielded to the serpent at the tree of knowledge of good and evil and brought death. The last Adam yielded to God and His Word to be obedient even unto death, at the tree of Calvary to give us life once again (1 Pet. 2:24; Phil. 2:5-11). Jesus had demonstrated for three years of ministry, the real will of His Father by healing, delivering, forgiving and setting free the multitudes from the works of the devil and showed us what results could come through faith in God. And *His ministry is an example to everyone else whom He would call into the ministry* to be His disciple and a laborer in His Kingdom. Let's take a look at His ministry and see God's will in action. This will show us what we are to believe and do for He is "the Truth." And truth never changes. Heb. 13:8 says, "Jesus Christ the same yesterday, today and forever."

Luke 4:40-41 says, "Now when the sun was setting, all they that had any sick with divers diseases brought them unto Him, and He *laid His hands on every one of them*, and healed them. And *devils* also came out of many, (of the sick and diseased people), crying out and saying, Thou art Christ, the Son of God. And He rebuking them suffered them not to speak: for they knew that He was Christ." Note that devils caused the diseases.

Matthew 8:16 says, "When the even was come, they brought unto Him many that were possessed with devils, and *He cast out the spirits with His Word and healed all that were sick.*" This was done with the authority that originally was given to Adam (Ps. 8:4, 6; Gen. 1:26; Luke 10:17-19). So remember, that although Jesus was divine, He operated in the earth as a man who cooperated with God (John 14:10; 15:24). "And Jesus went about all Galilee, teaching in their synagogues, and preaching the Gospel of the Kingdom and healing all manner of sickness and all manner of disease among the people. And His fame went throughout all Syria, and they brought unto Him all sick people that were taken with divers diseases and torments, and those which were possessed with devils, and those that had the palsy, and He healed them" (Matt. 4:23-24).

"And when He had called unto him, His twelve disciples, *He gave them power* against unclean spirits to cast them out, and to heal all manner of sickness and all manner of disease" (vs. 7-8), and He said unto them, "And as ye go, preach saying, the Kingdom of Heaven is at hand. Heal the sick, cleanse the lepers, raise the dead, cast out devils, freely ye have received, freely give" (Matt. 10:1, 7-8). This is still His will today and what all His followers should now be teaching and doing. (Heb. 13:8; Matt. 28:20).

In Luke 13:10-13, 16 it is recorded, "And He was teaching in one of the synagogues on the Sabbath. And behold, there was a woman which had *a spirit* of infirmity eighteen years, and was bowed together, and could in no wise, lift up herself. And when Jesus saw her, He called her to Him and said unto her, Woman, thou art loosed from thine infirmity, and He laid His hands on her and immediately she was made straight, and glorified God." In verse 16 Jesus said, "And ought not this woman, being a daughter of Abraham, *whom satan hath bound,* lo, these eighteen years, be loosed from this bond on the Sabbath day?" Have you been taught it's satan who binds people with sickness and disease? If not, why not? It was not God's will that she be bound. He had no purpose in it. He did not will it and didn't do it to perfect her character. He didn't send the devil to bind her so that it would work out for her good. He sent His Son Jesus to destroy the works of the devil and set her free.

"And He said unto them, Go ye into all the world, and preach the Gospel to every creature. He that believeth and is baptized shall be saved, but he that believeth not, shall be damned. *And these signs shall follow them that believe, in My name shall they cast out devils*, they shall speak with new tongues, they shall take up serpents and if they drink any deadly thing, it shall not hurt them, *they shall lay hands on the sick, and they shall recover*" (Mark 16:15-18). Has your teacher instructed you to cast out devils, to speak in tongues, and to lay hands on the sick as well as preach the Gospel? Have you been instructed that "The thief cometh not, but for to steal, and to kill, and to destroy," but that Jesus came "that mankind might have life, and that they might have it more abundantly"?

And that "For this purpose the Son of God was manifest, to destroy *the works of the devil*" (1 John 3:8). If not, you may be being taught a "different gospel" (2 Cor. 11:4). Peter summarized the ministry of Christ in his message to Cornelius and his household in Acts 10:38 when he said, "How *God anointed Jesus of Nazareth with the Holy Ghost and with power, who went about doing good and healing all that were oppressed of the devil*, for God was with Him." Here it shows *they all* were oppressed by the "DEVIL." It was God who had sent Jesus to heal them (John 6:38). Jesus then, was a revelation of God's will and what He did was God's will expressed. He said, "If you've seen Me, you've seen the Father." He's the express image of the invisible God. It is clear to anyone who will take God's Word for what it says, that God doesn't will any person to be sick or mentally oppressed, but rather all suffering comes directly or indirectly from the work of the devil.

Jesus Dies for Our Sins

After instructing His disciples concerning these things, and teaching them to believe God's Word for results, the time came for Him to die for the sins of the world (1 Tim. 1:15). Jesus went to the garden of Gethsemane and there He prayed; and knowing what was facing Him, He sweat, as it were, great drops of blood (Luke 22:42). He said, "Father, if Thou be willing, remove this cup from Me, nevertheless, not My will, but Thine be done" (Luke 22:42). It was not just the physical death that caused Him to sweat great drops of blood. If that were the case, why don't others who also face physical death sweat blood? No, He knew He faced much more than just the physical torture. Jesus knew that He would be facing all the consequences of sin and all the wrath due sin in order for men to go free. He knew He had to taste death and all that it included (Heb. 2:9) in order for us to legally be blessed with all spiritual blessings (Eph. 1:3). Satan then filled Judas Iscariot's heart to betray Him and he, in turn, instructed the *chief priests* as to how and when to take Christ. And so at the planned time, the religious leaders went to apprehend Him in the garden where He was praying. "Then Jesus said unto *the chief priests and captains of the temple, and the elders,* which were come to Him, Be ye come out as against a thief, with swords and staves? When I was daily with you in the temple, ye stretched forth no hands against Me, but *this is your hour and the power of darkness*" (Luke 22:52-53). Notice He said, this is "the power of darkness." So, Jesus yielded Himself into the hands of sinners and to the power of darkness, which means satan and his kingdom, in order to deliver us from the power of darkness (Col. 1:13). It was the moment that God spoke of when satan, (the old serpent), would strike His heal and death would temporarily have dominion over Him (Rom. 6:9; Heb. 2:9, 14; Gen. 3:15).

But little did the serpent know his own head would end up being crushed in the process (1 Cor. 2:8). That is, his power over men because of sin would be destroyed and he'd lose the keys (authority) of death and hell. Losing authority over every man that would accept Jesus' redemptive work. Heb. 2:14 says, "For as much then as the children are partakers of flesh and blood, He, (Christ), also Himself, likewise took part of the same, *that* through death, *He might destroy him that had the power of death,* that is, the devil." So His work was not only to pay sin's penalty in the sight of God, but also, on the other hand, to set people free from satan's legal hold on them which he gained at the fall through sin (John 8:44; Eph. 2:2-3; 1 John 3:10; Col. 1:13). Jesus had come to conquer death and hell by allowing satan who had the authority of death to kill Him and open the door for Him to enter that realm. God's realm is life, satan's is death and when satan killed Christ, Christ legally entered the realm of death with one purpose to conquer it.

Concerning the way God planned to set mankind free, 1 Corinthians 2:8 says, "Which none of the princes of this world knew, for had they known it, they would not have crucified the Lord of glory." It was demonic powers that stirred the religious leaders and the people to crucify Christ, and so in that sense, "they" had Him crucified. "For we wrestle not against flesh and blood, but against principalities, against powers, against the rulers of the darkness of this world, against spiritual wickedness in high places" (Eph. 6:12). (See also John 12:31-32.)

So by wicked hands, Christ was crucified and slain (Acts 2:23). *Religious men* yielding ignorantly to the wicked one as Cain did, nailed Christ to the cross (1 John 3:11-12). On that cross, Jesus–God's holy, eternal Son–*bore our sins in His own body* on the tree (1 Pet. 2:24). He bore the curse of sin for us (Gal. 3:13-14), and as our sin was laid on Him (Isa. 53:6), Jesus cried out, "Father, into Thy hands I commend (commit) My Spirit." His statement was a statement of trust that God would not leave His soul in hell, but raise Him from the dead. "Who in the days of His flesh, when He had offered up prayers and supplications with strong crying and tears unto Him that was able to save Him from death, and was heard in that He feared" (Heb. 5:7). Rotherham translation says, He cried out "unto Him that was able *to save Him out of death.*" As He bore *our* sin, a veil, caused by our sin in His flesh, came between Him and His Father and they were separated (Isa. 59:2; Heb. 10:20; Rom. 8:3). He who knew no sin, God made to be sin for us that we might be made the righteousness of God in Him (2 Cor. 5:21). And Jesus cried out on the tree, "My God, My God, why hast Thou forsaken (in the Greek, "abandoned") Me?" (Matt. 27:46). Christ was tasting death and its sting for every man. "But we see Jesus, who was made a little lower than the angels for the suffering of death, crowned with glory and honor, that He, by the grace of God, should taste death for every man" (Heb. 2:9).

Jesus, who by nature, remained the Holy Son of God, on the cross took our sin into His own body and suffered as a man (1 Pet. 2:24). It was the just suffering for the unjust, but yet He experienced the consequences of being forsaken, just as the sinner does. (Just as Adam did at the other tree.) Again Paul wrote, "He who knew no sin was made to be sin for us, that we might be made the righteousness of God in Him" (2 Cor. 5:21). Now He could not literally become sin, but He was dealt with in the same way God would have to deal with sin in order for Him to be able to put away sin by the sacrifice of Himself (Hab. 1:13).

Jesus in John 3:14 said, "And as Moses lifted up the serpent in the wilderness, even so must the *Son of man* be lifted up." Sin is the serpent's venom, so to speak. It's what gives satan authority over a man, for sin causes God to withdraw and gives satan place (Isa. 59:2; Mark 15:34; Heb. 5:7-8). There on the cross, Jesus, the Holy Son of God, hung as the Son of man and took our sin (the serpent's venom) unto Himself, into His own body.

It was then as He said, *the hour* when darkness would rule. For a little while then, satan, who had the power (dominion) of death (Heb. 2:14), did have dominion over Him (Rom. 6:9), but it was to be short lived. For it was not possible that *death*–satan's power–(Heb. 2:14), could hold Him (Acts 2:24). Now darkness covered the land. First He was separated from the Father because of "our" sin. (The same thing that happened to the first Adam as a consequence of sin.) Then Jesus died physically. This happened when His spirit was released from His body (James 2:26), "Jesus when He had cried again with a loud voice, yielded up the ghost" His spirit (Matt. 27:50). Jesus then went down into hell. As He said, in Matthew 12:40: "For as Jonah was three days and three nights in the whale's belly: *so shall* the '*Son of man' be three days and three nights in the heart* (core; center) *of the earth.*" The Bible clearly reveals that Jesus went down to hell. Christ said through prophecy, "My flesh shall rest in hope because Thou wilt not leave (in the Greek, "abandon," "forsake") My soul (Isa. 53:10), in hell, neither wilt Thou suffer Thine Holy One to see corruption" (Acts 2:26-27). Peter preached that David being a prophet, saw this before and spoke, "of the resurrection of Christ, that His soul was not left (in the Greek, "abandoned," "forsaken") in hell, neither did His flesh see corruption." Christ went where you and I as sinners, would have had to go. Through death He'd destroy Him that had the power of death, and through going to hell for us He'd also obtain the keys of hell and free us so that the gates of hell would lose its power over us and not prevail against the church (Matt. 16:18; Rev. 1:17-18). Satan blinded by hate ignorantly let Him into his realm of death and hell. Paul quoted Scripture about Christ defeating death and hell in 1 Corinthians 15:55-57 when he wrote, "Oh death, where is thy sting? O grave, where is thy victory" (v. 55)? The word for grave here in verse 55 is the word Hades which translated in English is "hell." Some try to make the Word "Hades" fit their theology and say Hades is not to be translated "hell." If it is not, then there is no such place called hell for the word *hell* comes only from the Greek word "Hades." But God's Word, history and conscience testifies that there is a hell. According to God's Word, "Hades," as is used in the New Testament, is always translated "hell," a place of torment. Listen to Jesus,

"And it came to pass, that the beggar died, and was carried by the angels into Abraham's bosom: the rich man also died, and was buried; and *in hell* (Hades) he lift up his eyes, *being in torments*, and seeth Abraham afar off, and Lazarus in his bosom. And he cried and said, Father Abraham, have mercy on me, and send Lazarus that he may dip the tip of his finger in water and cool my tongue; for *I am tormented in this flame*" (Luke 16:22). The word hell here again is "Hades," and as we can see, it is a place of torment. Did Jesus know what He was talking about? Of course He did.

Now let's see a glimpse of what happened to Jesus by cross referencing 1 Corinthians 15:55 and Hosea 13:14. Here it is: "I (the Messiah) will ransom them (sinners), *from the power* of the grave; *I will redeem them from death, O death, I be thy plagues*; O grave, (hell, as Paul revealed), *I will be thy destruction*, repentance shall be hid from mine eyes." Jesus became a curse *for us* (Gal.3:13). Now notice also that once sinners go there they can try and repent, but it's too late. Repentance is hid from the Lord's eyes. "Now is the day of salvation; now is the accepted time" (Heb. 9:27; 1 Cor. 6:2).

Satan doesn't want you to believe what Christ suffered for you. He doesn't want you to realize the awful price Jesus had to pay to redeem you from the curse when He became "a curse for us" (Gal.3:13). He who loves you, bore the curse and suffered for you, so that He'd not have to say to you later, "depart ye cursed into everlasting fire" (Matt. 25:41; Isa. 53:10-11).

Satan constantly works to belittle anything Jesus has done. There are some who want to diminish the awful sufferings that Christ had to endure for us, but believe them not. For Jonah, Jesus said, was a type of His sufferings; and for three days and three nights, Jonah prayed to God out of the fish's belly (Jon. 2:1). In verses 2 and 3, it says: "*out of the belly of hell* cried I and Thou heardest my voice. . . . Thou hast *cast me INTO the deep*." This is a type of *the deep* where Christ was *raised* from (Rom. 10:7), and where demons dreaded. "The floods compassed me about; all thy billows and thy waves (judgments) passed over me" (Isa. 53:10). Jonah 2:4, "then I said, I am cast out of thy sight; yet I will look again toward Thy holy temple." (See Acts 2:26-28.) Jonah 2:5-6, "Weeds were wrapped about my head. . . . I went down to the bottoms of the mountains." "The earth *with her bars* was about me forever" (Matt. 16:18). It is obvious this could not be a type of paradise as some have taught.

"Yet thou hast *brought up* my life *from corruption*." (in Hebrews it means the pit) Verse 7: "When my soul fainted within me, I remembered *the Lord*, and my prayer came in unto Thee, into Thine holy temple." Verse 10: "And the Lord spake unto the fish, and it vomited out Jonah upon the dry land."

So Christ went into the deep (Romans 10:7), and into hell (Acts 2:24-32), where He suffered what sinful men would have had to suffer (Luke 16:19-26). After he paid in full the penalty and suffered all of the consequences of sin, He was raised up again from *the deep*, (the pit) as Paul said. The Word "deep" in Romans 10:7 where Christ was raised from, is the same Greek word as *bottomless pit* in Revelation. In all probability, He was raised up out of that place by God speaking to hell to release Him from the pains of death (Acts 2:24), just as *He spoke* to the fish to release Jonah in response to Jonah's prayer.

Do we have further evidence that such a thing could happen? First of all, we've shown that God always uses His Word to do things (Gen. 1:3; Isa. 55:10-11; Ps. 53:6, 9; 107:20; Ezek. 12:25). We know by Scripture, *that Jesus spoke* to Lazarus to "come forth" and his spirit came again from Abraham's bosom, which was in the earth, back up into his body (John 11:39-44). We know that *Jesus spoke* to the dead girl and her "spirit came again" into her body. . . . We know that God spoke to John and Ezekiel and immediately they were in the spirit. John was *caught up* to Heaven (Rev. 4:1-2), as soon as the voice spoke. The Bible says that Jesus will descend from Heaven "with a shout" and the whole church will be "caught up" to meet Him in the clouds in the air (1 Thess. 4:16-18), and the dead in Christ shall rise.

In John 5:28-29, Jesus said, "Marvel not at this, for the hour is coming, in the which, all that are in the graves *shall hear His voice, and shall come forth*, they that have done good, unto the resurrection of life, and they that have done evil, unto the resurrection of damnation."

Notice, they will *hear His voice and come forth*. "And the sea gave up the dead which were in it; and death and hell delivered up the dead which were in them: and they were judged every man according to their works" (Rev. 20:13). So God spoke and it was done. He answered Christ's prayer of Hebrews 5:7. Concerning Christ Scripture says, "Whom God hath raised up, having loosed the pains of death, because it was not possible that He should be holden of it" (Acts 2:24). When did He raise Him up and loose Him from the pains of death? According to God's Word, it was *after* three days and three nights that He was raised. So *His soul*, which was the offering for sin (Isa. 53:10), was not abandoned in hell, neither did His flesh see corruption (John 10:11, 17), (Acts 2:31). Some have presumed wrongly that He went to Heaven immediately after He died. But the Scriptures *do not say He came down* from paradise (or Heaven) after three days, but was *raised up* from the deep, (the pit), and that He was not abandoned in hell (Rom. 10:7; Acts 2:27-31). This is what the Bible actually does say. When He was raised as victor, He also had with Him, the keys of *death and hell* (Rev. 1:17-18), the serpent's power was destroyed, and now "the gates of hell cannot prevail against the church." The church is His bride and it includes anyone who accepts Jesus and His saving work and enters into Covenant with Him (Matt. 16:18). It was *after three days, that He ascended to the Father* for He told Mary, on the morning of His resurrection, *"Touch Me not, for I am not yet ascended to My Father*, but go to My brethren and say unto them, *I ascend* unto My Father and your Father, and to My God and your God" (John 20:17).

Jesus then, ascended to His Father, went into the Heavenly Holy of Holies, "with His own blood" (Heb. 9:12-24), which is the blood "*of the sacrifice*," the blood "of *the sin offering*" as it's stated in the Word of the Lord, to appear in the presence *of* God *for us* (Heb. 9:24), and the New Covenant then went into effect. It was at this time He obtained eternal redemption for us (Heb. 9:11-12), and the New Testament was finished. The old was finished at the cross.

The Blood then, which represents all the death and suffering of the sinner's substitute, was accepted and eternal redemption was made available to man. When God accepted the blood of the spotless Lamb, it was a sealed Covenant. The New Covenant went into effect. Let me also point this out. In light of these Scriptures, it is obvious that when Jesus said, "it is finished," on the cross, He was not speaking of the New Covenant as some have erroneously thought, but of the Old. Further evidence are the scriptures such as Romans 5:10, which states, ". . .we were reconciled to God *by the death* of His Son." At the time He said "it is finished," He hadn't even died yet. Romans 4:25 says He was "raised for our justification," and, His resurrection too, has an all important part to play in our redemption. Yet when He said, "it is finished," He hadn't been raised yet for without a death first there can be no resurrection. There are yet many more scriptures to point this out, much of which will be covered in more detail in the pages and chapters to come. It is sufficient now, for us to know that it was three days after His crucifixion that He ascended into Heaven with His own blood to obtain eternal redemption for us (Heb. 9:11-12). Then He sat down because His work was finished. The New Covenant had gone into effect. "For where a testament is, *there must also of necessity, be the death of* the testator. For a testament is of force *after* men are dead: *otherwise, it is of no strength at all while the testator liveth*" (Heb. 9:16-17). So we see, the New Covenant couldn't have gone into effect until after His death. That is, not while He was still alive and speaking on the cross.

Now satan does not want anyone to believe in the love that Jesus and the Father have for man; that the Lord would suffer the full consequences of sin to pay the ransom and redeem man from all of sin's debt. He paid it all for His bride, that He would not have to abide in eternity alone (John 12:23-32; Isa. 53:10-11). Some renounce the fact that Christ went to hell or the deep (pit), even though the Word says He did. They will reject the many clear passages and accept an obscure passage and try to prove their point. This is always the case with those who refuse to believe all that is written. The difference between "Word" teachers and those bound by their own religious beliefs is that we take God's Word for exactly what it says. If we can't understand it, we accept it by faith; we don't reason it away like they do, and because of that, they persecute God's message of faith.

Identified With Christ

Now the Bible reveals that we were identified *with Christ*. It says we were "*crucified with Christ*" (Gal. 2:20). We died *with Him* (Rom. 6:8); we were buried *with Him*" (Rom. 6:4; Col. 2:12); we were then *quickened together with Him* (made alive spiritually together), (Eph. 2:5) and raised up with Him (Eph. 2:6). First the spiritual resurrection out of our death of trespasses and sins, and then in the time to come, He will change our vile bodies to be made like unto His glorious body (Phil. 3:21). Both resurrections out of death come through His redemptive work.

His experience of dying to sin; being under death's dominion (Rom. 6:9); being quickened, that is, made alive by the glory of the Father (Rom. 6:4), also becomes ours, when we, by faith, accept Him and what He's done. He identified Himself with us so that we could identify ourselves with Him. For when we accept Him, we become members of His body and His experience through faith, is then transmitted to us (Col. 2:12). Therefore because He lives, we live also.

Jesus Tasted Death and Its Sting

Let's look at some other interesting things here. Notice what Paul says in Col. 2:11-12: That Christ came to free us from the "sins of the flesh," and then Paul goes on to say, "You also *are* risen with Him" (notice this is present tense), (v. 12). Whatever kind of resurrection this is he speaks of, to this Colossian church, it was not physical for *they had not yet been raised physically*. He then says, and you being "dead in your sins" (though physically alive) God hath "*made you alive," together with Him* (Eph. 2:5). His experience becomes ours by faith. He did it for us that we might be freed from our state of death. This has to be speaking of being spiritually quickened or made alive, for it is present tense and it has already occurred to the born again born-again believer. His resurrection out of death has provided for our resurrections, spiritual and physical, as is obvious by these passages, but later, we will receive our resurrection bodies. So again, the quickening Paul spoke of in that passage is not a physical, but a spiritual quickening. Paul said to the people at the Colosse's church, "*you hath He made alive together with Him.*" (past tense) Surely He wasn't telling them He had already given them their resurrection bodies, but rather, He made them alive spiritually together *with Him*. And (1 Cor. 15:21-22, 45) when Jesus was reunited with His Father, you too, that accept His work, are reunited and reconciled to God by His finished work (Heb. 13:20-21). After His resurrection, "Jesus saith unto Mary, Touch Me not; for I am not yet ascended to My Father: but go to My brethren and say unto them, I ascend unto My Father, and your Father; and to My God, and your God" (John 20:17). Note also this interesting Scripture passage that records the words of Paul.

"And we declare unto you glad tidings, how that the promise which was made unto the fathers, God hath fulfilled the same unto us their children, in that *He hath raised up Jesus again; as it is also written in the second psalm, Thou art My Son, this day have I begotten Thee*" (Acts 13:32-33).

Notice this next passage of Scripture: "And from Jesus Christ, who is the faithful witness, and *the first begotten of the dead*, and the prince of the kings of the earth. Unto Him that loved us, and washed us from our sins in His own blood" (Rev. 1:5).

Well, praise God, the blood of Christ can now remove the sins of the flesh and when one turns to the Lord for cleansing, the veil is removed between man and God, and union with the Lord occurs once again (2 Cor. 3:15-18; Heb. 10:19-22). (See also John 12:23-27; Eph. 3:20.)

Jesus had to suffer the full consequences of sin and be forsaken in order to remove the spiritual veil caused by sin and reconcile us to God (Heb. 7:25). He had to go through it all for it all to be legally removed from us (Matt. 27:46), He had to go to hell, so we would not have to go there (Acts 2:27, 31). He had to die physically so we could have a resurrection body (Matt. 27:50). He had to suffer God's wrath to deliver us from the wrath to come (1 Thess. 1:10). He had to enter our condition and, for awhile, be made a little lower than the angels for the suffering of death (Heb. 2:9). During that period, He had to be under death's dominion to deliver us from satan and His power (Heb. 2:14; Col. 1:13; Rom. 6:9). He had to yield Himself to the power of darkness (Gen. 3:15; Luke 22:53), to deliver us from the authority of darkness (Col. 1:13). He had to be in a body to experience the consequences of sinful flesh. Those who refuse to believe Jesus really and truly suffered these things for us are the ones who belittle the work of Christ. The last Adam had to undo *all* that the first Adam had brought into the world. The faith message simply magnifies the truth of what Jesus has done and worships and praises Him for it.

At the very least, I hope you can see how wrong it is for the so-called "Christian critics" to attack other Christians who are born again and love the Lord simply because they believe these scriptures. What is so awful about believing God's Word?

Christ's Precious Cleansing Blood

Now His blood, as we said, is the "blood *of the sacrifice*," the "blood *of the sin offering*," the blood "*of the Covenant*." It now represents all Jesus did for us and we believe that the power of redemption is "in the blood." Every drop of that precious blood speaks out of the sacrifice that has been made, that the ransom is met and justice is satisfied (Heb. 12:24).

In the Old Testament, the Spotless Lamb was slain, His blood poured out, then He had to be "burned with fire," which represents the judgment due sin, and after that they took the blood of the sin offering," "the blood of the sacrifice" and brought it unto the Holy of Holies. Then the people were sprinkled with the Blood of the Covenant (Heb. 9:19-20). Sin had been judged.

The blood is directly connected with the death and sufferings of Christ: *His soul* being the offering for sin. "Thou shalt make His (Jesus') 'soul' an offering for sin" (Isa. 53:10). The word for life in John 10:17 is "soul." "Therefore doth My Father love Me because I lay down My life (soul), that I might take it again." The fact is His soul went to hell as He said (Acts 2:24-31). Then Scripture says in Romans 4:25: "Who was delivered for our offences, and was raised again for our justification."

Notice again that *when He was raised*, then, and only then, were we justified. *That's when justification was made available to us. Only then* could we be raised; only then we could be justified, for His work was then completed. Paul then said when He was quickened (made alive), we also were "with Him." All that was left to do was to bring the blood of the sacrifice into the Heavenly Holy of Holies, to seal the Covenant. Romans 5:10 says, "We were reconciled to God by *the death of His Son*, and are *now* saved *by His life*." Because He experienced death but now lives (Rev. 1:18), we who were dead in sin, can now accept Him and live again, too, spiritually and physically, "because I live, ye shall live also" (John 5:26-27; 14:19).

Adam lost life first spiritually and then physically. We are restored by the last Adam first, spiritually and later, physically, and so death in all its forms will be swallowed up in victory. We could not be quickened and come alive to God now unless Christ had entered all realms of death and conquered them for us. When we believe in our hearts God raised Him from the dead, we, by faith, partake of His resurrection first spiritually and then physically (Rom. 10:9).

So we see His death, life, and resurrection all have a part also to play in it and the blood truly represents it all. We now put faith in all that His blood can do for us and as we've said, the power of redemption is "in the blood." Revelation 1:5-6 reveals that because of what Christ has accomplished, it can now wash away sin. Ephesians 1:7 says we now have, "redemption through His blood." His blood can cleanse the conscience (Heb. 9:14); Give us boldness to enter the holiest (Heb. 10:19); His life and *all He did for us* is represented in the blood. When God accepted Jesus' blood, when He carried it as High Priest into the heavenlies, the New Covenant became a settled fact (Heb. 9:11-12). It was the blood of God, of divinity, that established this New Covenant (Acts 20:28). But we also believe all the other scriptures about His "life," resurrection and death, as also being necessary for redemption to take place. So *we* leave nothing out as the critic does. But again, to emphasize our stand, we do believe that He suffered such things for us, and that the power of redemption is now in His blood.

We were reconciled to God by the blood of His cross and through entering death He conquered death and He conquered him that had the power of death over us, that is, the devil, and by going to hell, He conquered it for us and obtained its keys. The Amplified version says, we shall now be saved"through His resurrection life." Williams' translation says, we will "be saved through His new life." When He was raised with resurrection life those who accept Him are now also raised (with resurrection life) from *their death* of trespasses and sins, which caused them to be alienated and forsaken of God, they now enter into newness of life (Rom. 6:4), and will, in time, also have a resurrected body like His (Phil. 3:21; Rom. 8:29).

Therefore, Jesus is truly, as scripture says, "the firstborn among many brethren" (Rom. 8:29); "the firstborn from the dead" (Col. 1:18); "the first begotten of the dead" (Rev. 1:5). (Lazarus and others were raised from the dead before this, not born from the dead.) How did this all occur?

God can do exceedingly and abundantly above all we can ask or think. All we need to do is read it, believe it and stand in awe. "But we see Jesus, Who was made a little lower than the angels for the suffering of death, crowned with glory and honor, that He, by the grace of God, should taste death for every man. For it became Him, for whom are all things, and by whom are all things, in bringing many sons unto glory, to make the captain of their salvation, perfect through sufferings. For both He that sanctifieth and they who are sanctified are all of one, for which cause He is not ashamed to call them brethren" (Heb. 2:9-11). He willed to go through this for us that we, as His inheritance and bride, might live with Him forever, and He did it this way so that He, Himself, could be *the* FIRST to rise again from the dead, that as the scripture says, "in all things He might have preeminence" (Col. 1:18). Not only the firstborn of all creation, but also now the firstborn from the dead and head over the new creation and its beginning. If you cannot understand what He went through for you as the Son of man, don't change it. Don't nullify Scripture; just believe it.

Now through all this, He remained the Holy Son of God, for He was "declared to be the Son of God with power by His resurrection from the dead" (Rom. 1:4). So then what scriptures reveal He suffered, He really did suffer and it was all necessary for man to truly be free to retain liberty of will and for God's righteousness to be fully satisfied.

Because He redeemed us from the curse and made grace available to us, we can now, if we will believe and turn to Him, be born again, be filled with His Spirit and use the authority of His name (Luke 10:17-19; Mark 16:15-18). We can now, in proportion to our faith, cast out devils and heal the sick. We can believe He will supply all of our needs (Phil. 4:19); we can have answered prayer *for anything* that we ask which is not contrary to a good and godly life (1 John 3:20; 5:14-15). We can have dominion over sin (Rom. 6:14). We can operate in the gifts of the Holy Spirit (1 Cor. 12:1-8); speak in tongues (in prayer) (1 Cor. 14:2, 4, 14; Acts 2:4; Jude 20). We can be in health (3 John 2; 1 Pet. 2:24; Gal. 3:13-14), and the gates of hell shall not prevail against us.

Faith gives us access into all of His wonderful grace, and redemption brings us full circle back around by making available to us that which man had in the beginning before the fall, most especially the wonderful relationship we have with our Lord. Yet as Adam did, we also have an adversary whom we must resist "steadfast in the faith" (1 Pet. 5:8-9). And this adversary, the devil, constantly tries to get Christians to speak and do things contrary to God's Word, and to believe the wrong things, so that he can get their consent of ignorance and continue to "steal, kill and destroy" things in their lives.

In view of the fact that Christ paid for our total redemption to free us from sin, sickness and the authority of darkness, can you now see how awful it is then for religion to lead God's people wrong and say God put that disease or evil trial on you to teach you, to humble you, or to perfect you (James 1:13, 16-17)? They are teaching Christ's people to put themselves into the hands of the devil saying that it will all work out for their good and that it's God's will. Yet our Covenant says we must take the shield of faith, and the sword of the Spirit, (speaking as Jesus did with the written Word), and resist the devil and his works, steadfast in the faith. It is our faith in God's written Word that will bring results and enable us to overcome the wicked one (1 John 2:14). Let's then, do all to stand and as Paul said, "stand therefore" against this enemy of man, and let's resist the curse from which we've been redeemed, for only satan wants you to suffer, be fearful, be sick, poor, defeated, and have destroyed homes. Never blame God for these things (James 1:16-17).

Forget the "Escape Theology" made up by religion, that seeks to escape responsibility for having to have faith. They dispensationalize things, nullify God's Word, and dishonor the Lord. They reject the Word that they may keep their own traditions. Recognize all that for what it truly is, "unbelief." Let's get back to the real blueprint, back to the Bible and the Book of Acts, which reveals the real church the way the Lord established it. Without the power of the Holy Spirit, the name of Jesus and the Word of God, the miracles, the divine healing and casting out of devils, the church of Acts would have been a powerless organization.

There are numerous large organizations, religious and secular, that are built without the Holy Spirit being involved. A large church doesn't necessarily mean God is in it (2 Tim. 4:1-4). Jesus said, "These signs will follow *them that believe. In My name* shall they cast out devils; they shall speak with new tongues. . .they shall lay hands on the sick and they shall recover." We see these signs of the church in the Book of Acts and still see these signs to varying degrees wherever true believers gather today. Let us then, get back to what's actually written, or we are liable to be running in the wrong direction. God is who the Bible says He is; He will do what the Bible says He will do; we can have what the Bible says we can have; we can do what the Bible says we can do; we are who the Bible says we are! Jesus said, it's the Word that will judge us in the last day. You will not be able to get by with saying, "but my teacher or pastor said." For God only goes by His own Word and judgment will be according to what is written. Adam blamed the woman for his sin. Eve blamed the serpent but yet they still suffered the consequence of going contrary to God's Word. God's Word repeatedly says, "Let no man deceive you" and "the Word *that I have spoken*, the same shall judge him in the last day" (John 12:48). So stay with the Word.

First John 5:4 says, "For whatsoever is born of God, overcometh the world, and this is the victory that overcometh the world, even our faith." Our faith should be word for word what is written in the New Testament. Do not let the serpent get you to believe any of it has passed away (1 Pet. 1:24-25).

So as we continue, you will see and understand that the message of faith is based solidly on the integrity of God's Word. And we will answer the criticism of those who in unbelief, malign God's message of faith and victory. We will then look at the scriptures and expose the errors of "the critics," "the skeptics," and those "bound by tradition." And yet we do it in love, wanting only for these people also to see the truth (Acts 26:18), and to escape the snares of the wicked one (1 John 2:14), who has some of them fighting against God and His Word thinking they are doing God a service.

God's Plan Condensed

In James 5:16-18 the Word says: "Confess your faults one to another, and pray *one for another, that ye may be healed.* The effectual, fervent prayer of a righteous man availeth much. Elias was a man subject to like passions as we are, and *he prayed earnestly that it might not rain, and it rained not on the earth* by the space of three years and six months. And *he prayed again, and the Heaven gave rain*, and the earth brought forth her fruit."

Elijah prayed; God did the miracle. Moses lifted up the rod and God parted the Red Sea. The Church of Acts prayed (Acts 4:29-33), and God answered with miracles.

From Genesis to Revelation, it is clearly revealed that God is always seeking a man, apprehending a man, leading a man, to cooperate with Him, and using a man as the channel of His working in the earth. Mark 16:20 says, "And they went forth and preached everywhere, the Lord working *with them*, confirming the Word with signs following."

First Corinthians 3:9 says, "For we are laborers together with God: ye are God's husbandry, ye are God's building" (John 3:1-2). When God created man, He made man in His own image and likeness, (so much so that His own Son could later come in "the likeness of men," (Phil. 2:7). As we've seen, Adam was the type, the picture of the Son of man, to come (Rom. 5:14).

So God, in His sovereign choice, willed to create free moral agents from which there would come a bride; a help meet for His Son, and for an allotted time period God gave man total authority in the earth (Gen. 1:26; Ps. 115:16), so much so, that during this time of man's reign Scripture says, God "sought for a man" to stand in the gap (Ezek. 22:30). He tells us to pray His "will be done on earth even as it is in Heaven," to ask of Him, "rain in the time of the latter rain," *to pray* that "laborers would be sent into the harvest," and there are hundreds of other things He told us to do to cooperate with Him that He might bring His will to pass in the earth.

Mark 16:15 and 2 Corinthians 5:18-19 further show us that He's depending on us. Where He can find a man who will believe Him, obey Him, and act on His Word, He works through that man in the earth in proportion to that man's faith. He worked through Noah to preach righteousness then to bring the flood (2 Pet. 2:5; Heb. 11:7); and through Elijah to bring fire down from Heaven (1 Kings 18:36-38); and He worked with Moses to divide the Red Sea (Exod. 14:15-16). It is His power but man was, and is, His point of contact in the earth and He willed it to be so. Yet He set certain boundaries according to His own will (Acts 17:26). Now "according to your faith," in His Word, so it shall be done *unto you* as Jesus said in Matthew 9:29. Why? Because you're a free moral agent. Both God and satan endeavor to influence men to use their will to believe them. God brings truth to man through His Word while satan brings deception and lies and works through this world and false religion to draw men away from God (1 John 2:15; Eph. 2:2; Rev. 12:9).

Now satan is no match for God. Satan is like a speck of dust compared to the great Mount Everest, or a drop of water compared to the mighty ocean. There is no comparison at all in wisdom, power, or anything else between God and satan. Although to some it seems as though satan is almost as powerful as God, yet it is only because both God and satan are mainly working presently through man in the earth, and not many people will believe God fully and act on His Word as Christ did when He was here as "the son of man." Satan has sown a host of traditions telling people, "you can't believe God will do that, He's sovereign." "God won't answer all your prayers, even if you do believe, He's not your puppet, He's not your mastercard," and he accuses God of numerous evils. All this is designed to ridicule and stop God's people from operating in faith on God's Word and to thereby hinder God's real working and power in the earth, in the lives of people. The other thing he does attack is anyone who has the power of the Holy Ghost upon him.

It's up to you to side with God's Word and with what's actually written, and not with the attacks and excuses of the critics. Under the disguise of honoring God, these people actually advance the work of satan for if people hear such unscriptural sentences and implications as these which are taught by the critics and some religious leaders, they will not have any confidence or boldness to believe God and act on His Word. So they never use their wills to agree with God, and thereby they limit the Holy One of Israel and ignorantly submit to the devil. Instead of being strong in faith, they are weak through what they've been taught. In view of the fact that God has told men to choose, act, do, repent, believe, pray, obey, and have faith, over four thousand times in Scripture, let us accept *the truth* that man is a free moral agent, and that God deals with, helps and blesses men on earth on the basis of their conformity to His Word or through the prayers of others. Again, "According to *your* faith be it unto you. . . " (Matt. 9:29).

The Bible is a book revealing that man must "fight the good fight of faith" and live by God's Word to please God (Heb.11:6; Matt. 4:4), and also to overcome the wicked one (1 John 2:14; James 1:22).

Chapter 4

What About the Word of Faith?

"The Faith Message"
Here Is an Answer for the Critics

Some have made it their personal crusade to attack dedicated Christian ministers that have been bringing back to the church a clear message of faith in God. While a few extremes may exist by those who don't yet have a clear picture of how things are, so do extremes exist within all denominations, especially with eternal securityists who say and teach many things contrary to God's written Word, and with the critics themselves, as we will clearly point out. In this chapter we will speak about, as the critic calls it, the so-called controversial "faith message," and see whether it really is what the critics make it out to be, or if it is, in truth, the Bible revealed message of faith in God.

Q. *What is the Faith Message?*
A. "But what saith it? The Word is nigh thee, even in thy mouth and in thy heart: that is, *the Word of faith which we preach.*" It has been called the "Faith Message" because of the emphasis on faith in the integrity of God's living Word. Faith teachers believe that the New Testament is a real covenant, as it declares itself to be, given to us by Almighty God: that it can be taken literally, and that if God's conditions are met and faith exercised, then a Christian can, and will, reap the benefit of the fulfillment of the promises and provisions of the Covenant providing that he is also living right in the sight of God. The Faith Message further believes that "God is no respecter of persons" (Acts 10:34). What He's done for one, He will do for another. He responds to everyone equally, on the basis of their conformity to His Word and Gospel (Rom. 1:16; 1 Pet. 1:17; Acts 10:34). And we also believe as Paul preached, it's

not just faith but "obedience to the faith" (Rom. 1:5). In other words, it's faith that moves a person to live obedient to God. See in Hebrews 11 how faith *moved people* to give to God; walk with God; work for God; obey God, and keep His ordinances.

Q. *Do faith teachers only emphasize faith and blessings?*
A. No, the main focus for any Christian, is, or should be, the preaching of the Gospel of salvation to others who don't know the Savior, which is in itself, a message of faith, but realize this: Faith teachers are mostly called by God to teach those who are already believers (Eph. 4:8-11). Holy living, walking in love, and numerous other Biblical topics are also taught. But faith is emphasized at times, because faith is involved with every one of these areas in our Christian life. Christians definitely need to be taught how to walk and live by faith, for their pleasing God, walking in victory, and their usefulness in the Kingdom depends on it (Heb. 11:6; 1 John 5:4; 2 Thess. 1:11).

So every pastor, teacher, evangelist, prophet or apostle should be as Jesus was, a teacher of faith. Look at these vital Scriptures:
"The just shall *live* by faith" (Rom. 1:17)
"We walk by *faith"* (2 Cor. 5:7)
"Christ dwells in our hearts *by faith*" (Eph. 3:17)
"Purifying their hearts *by faith"* (Acts 15:9)
"Without *faith* it's impossible to please Him" (Heb. 11:6)
"According to *your faith*, be it done unto you" (Matt. 9:29).
"If *thou* canst *believe* all things are possible *to him* that believeth" (Mark 9:23).

By faith, Abel offered a more excellent sacrifice to God. By faith, Noah worked; Abraham obeyed and Sarah received strength from God. The Bible says that "through faith they subdued kingdoms; wrought righteousness; obtained promises; stopped the mouths of lions; quenched the violence of fire; escaped the edge of the sword; out of weakness were made strong; waxed valiant in fight women received their dead raised to life again." It was God's power, but their faith.

Historic Christianity has its roots in the New Testament, in *"the faith* that was once delivered to the saints." So we must look then to the Word of God and to its teaching to see what the early church did, and what they believed and taught about salvation, the blessings and promises of God, divine healing, tongues, gifts of the Holy Spirit, holy living, visions, and faith, to see the real truth concerning our redemption. We are to observe all these things even unto the end of the age (Matt. 28:20). We simply say, put full faith in the Word of God and all it reveals about these things.

To find out what really is Christianity, we must go back to what is actually written. Back to that first branch that grew out of the True Vine and see what fruit and results the church of Acts produced. Not saying this or that passed away, as some groups do or as the critics do, for to do so would be to preach "a different gospel" than Paul and the early church did, and we are warned against that (Gal. 1:8).

We, in love, want to clearly show you the errors of those who have attacked this Biblical "message of faith in God," and distort what's said in the Faith Message. If you only read their books, which are written with a critical eye against God's message of faith and under the influence of a spirit of religion and suspicion, you will think the "Word of Faith which we preach" (Rom. 10:8), is saying many things it's not. It is not the "Faith Message" that is wrong, but their misunderstanding of it and of man's free will. In their attacks, the critics use such words as: visualize, consciousness, reincarnation, and so on and refer these things to the Faith Message, not because the Faith Message teaches these things, but because of their constant involvement in attacking cults, and their lack of knowledge of God's Word and power. They do exactly the same things the Pharisees of old did. They do error, not knowing the Scriptures *nor the power of God* (Matt. 22:29). Most of the critics do not believe the areas of the New Testament that teach us to be led by the Spirit; they don't believe in the gifts of the Spirit or the *prayer of faith* for the sick, even though it's New Testament Christianity and is written in the Word of the Lord. Some of the so-called Christian research institutes designed to attack cults have become a misguided product of their own environment, going to the extreme in their attacks, actually thinking everything they say is true, and *all* supernatural occurrences are of the devil, regardless of what the Word of God says. They "think" they know all that's in God's Word, and know all of His Spirit's operations, and because of their being a self-appointed critic and judge, they not only come against the real cults, but also in their ignorance, they come against many of their Christian brethren that are moving out in strong faith and destroying the works of the devil. Mr. Critic, *what if* there are men of God in the earth that *do know* more than you about God's Word and Spirit? Is it not wise to check things out with the written Word? Another tactic critics of the Word of Faith use is to ridiculously exaggerate what's said with the intent to sway people to think that what is preached in the faith movement is according to their ridiculous, taken–out–of–context exaggerations. This tactic of religion is not new. If the Word of Faith preached what the critics say it did, neither would I believe it, but it doesn't; it simply preaches the Word.

But no marvel, for even satan himself comes as an angel of light clothed in religion, and is always seeking to "steal the Word" and stop any progress the church makes. Remember, it was the supposed orthodox religious leaders of Jesus' day that attacked Christ the most, and they knew not what they did. Is there not a parallel today? Now I also realize like Saul (Paul), *their intentions* may be good but it is with some of them as it was with him, that they have "zeal without knowledge" and while they think they are doing God a service, they are really yielding to the enemy and destroying God's work (James 3:1).

These modernists are like the Pharisees of old who could not understand Christ and His message, fearing therefore that the people of their synagogues would follow Him; the religious leaders said that Christ had a devil and that He was Beelzebub. These men of like mind attack things they don't understand, ignorantly ridiculing the work of the Holy Spirit and the message of faith in God, which the Holy Spirit has *restored* to the church. Friend, these people are attacking others *in their ignorance, for believing more of the Bible than they do*. Is that right? May God have mercy on them for the damage and division *they've caused* in the body of Christ by hindering Christians from learning to live by faith. By all their theological reasonings and high sounding arguments, they have taken from God's people "the key of knowledge" entering not in themselves and hindering those who would have, if only given the true Word. Faith ministers have been given a certain message for the body of Christ; we realize other ministries are also called to do certain other things. Why don't we all just obey God and stick with His Word?

Let us continue on, and instead of digging into a bunch of metaphysical quotes like the critics of the faith movement do, let us stick right with what God's Word actually says. We will now deal with areas of the faith movement they attack, and because they go over and over and re-emphasize their views in their books and articles, we also, in this book, will repeat ourselves to emphasize the truth. Let's now deal with their attacks.

Do words affect our lives and things around us? Does our holding fast our confession of faith have anything to do with our victory in Christ?

The critics say no. Those who attack the message of faith say that speaking God's Word and teaching Christians the effect of Words is not scriptural, but metaphysical! But what does God's Word say? Jesus said in Mark 11:23: "For verily I say unto you, that *whosoever shall say* unto this mountain, be thou removed and be thou cast into the sea, and shall not doubt in his heart, but shall *believe* that those things which he *saith, shall come to pass, he shall have whatsoever he saith.*" And notice in verse 14, *Jesus actually spoke to a tree and it withered away.* This was His demonstration on the effects words can have on things and He said it works for *"whosoever."* Paul wrote in 2 Corinthians 4:13: "We having *the same spirit of faith*, according as it is written, I believed, and therefore have I spoken, we also believe and therefore speak." The very spirit of Faith then has to do with believing and speaking. Romans 10:6 says, "faith speaketh," and believe in Proverbs 18:21, which reveals, "Death and life are *in the power of the tongue*, and they that love it shall eat the fruit thereof."

Paul wrote in Ephesians 6:17: "And take the helmet of salvation, and the sword of the Spirit, which is the Word of God." It is the sword which the Spirit uses. "Repent; or else I will come unto thee quickly, and will fight against them with the sword of My mouth" (Rev. 2:16).

Hebrews 10:23 states: "Let us hold fast the profession (confession) of our faith without wavering, (for He is faithful that promised)."

Isaiah 59:21: *"As for Me, this is My Covenant with them*, saith the Lord, My Spirit that is upon thee, and *My Words which I have put in thy mouth, shall not depart out of thy mouth, nor out of the mouth of thy seed, nor out of the mouth of thy seed's seed, saith the Lord*, from henceforth and forever." God anoints men to speak His Word (Acts 1:8). In Matthew 4:4 Jesus said, "It is written," and He overcame the devil. James, the Lord's brother, referred to your tongue as being the rudder of your ship, (or life) teaching us that whatever way you turn it, is the direction your life will take (James 3:2-6). Jesus further said that men will give an account of every idle word they have spoken and that "by thy words thou shalt be justified and by thy words thou shalt be condemned" (Matt. 12:37).

So speaking in agreement with God's Word is not copied from metaphysics as the critics say in their ignorance, but rather, satan has gotten his followers to steal and copy the principles of God's Word and pervert them, for He knows more than the critics do, that God created man in His own image and likeness. Satan is not a creator but a copier. Remember, the faith message only tells you to do what "God's Word actually says." If God says, "Take the Sword of the Spirit which is the Word of God" (Eph. 6:17), and say, " it is written" like Christ did, then that's what's said and taught by faith teachers. We only say what the Bible says about these things, but the critic still attacks, regardless. What about the things Jesus and Paul taught then about words and faith? Is their teaching also metaphysical because the critics can not grasp it? Dozens of times in Scripture God shows us our words have a tremendous effect on our lives. Your words also reveal what's in your heart, just as the critic's do his (Matt. 12:33-34). We will further point out more about words as we go on. But it is shown by these Scriptures that the critic does not know the difference between the Bible and metaphysics. All we ask, is that you believe what is actually written in God's Word (Prov. 18:20-21).

Are All Present-Day Supernatural Acts of Satan?

Some Christian critics think that anything supernatural today has got to be the devil. They don't believe in the present day power of the Holy Spirit. How ridiculous for some to think so. Certainly we must prove all things by God's Word and hold fast to that which is good, but let's look in the Word at the supernatural that happened in the ministry of Christ, the apostles, and especially, the church of the Book of Acts, which is our blueprint, for there we see many manifestations of the Holy Spirit.

First of all, Christianity revolves around supernatural interventions and workings of God. From the angelic visitations to Mary; the supernatural birth of Christ, His miracles, walking on water, Christ calming the winds and waves by speaking to them; His casting devils out of people by His Word, His supernatural receiving words of knowledge from the Holy Spirit, divine healing, being led by the Spirit, supernatural anointings to minister, and so on. And many of these same things occurred in the lives of His disciples in the Book of Acts. Now these are not things contrary to the written Word, but are recorded in the New Testament, and are things that took place through Christ and the lives of His followers. Surely God is still God and His miracles are as much for us today as ever (1 Cor. 12). Some say, miracles have passed away. But we say, for miracles to pass away, God would have to pass away too, and He won't. A new birth is a miracle; answered prayer is a miracle, (surely no one would deny answered prayer); the cleansing with the blood of Jesus is a miracle. Let's see other New Testament Gospel experiences and we'll see what is included in the "real Gospel" they preached.

Stephen had a vision of Christ; Peter fell into a trance; Paul had a visitation from the Lord and was caught up to paradise;

Philip was translated by the Spirit from town to town. People were healed even as Peter's shadow passed by; there were angelic visitations; Paul said he would come to visions and revelations of the Lord; healings took place as the Gospel was preached; they were led by the Spirit of God; cast out devils; the Spirit spoke to them; they spoke in tongues and prophesied; gifts of the Spirit were in operation; the supernatural power of God worked through them and their hands; Paul's handkerchiefs were laid on the sick and they were healed and delivered of evil spirits; Peter spoke of supernatural dreams and visions by the Spirit. Paul spoke of discerning of spirits, gifts of healing, workings of miracles, signs and wonders.

Brethren, we are in the age of the Holy Ghost, the Miracle Worker. This is New Testament Christianity. This is all a part of the Gospel, but much of the church is like Israel and its religious leaders who went into unbelief and became blind to what's written. And if you follow blind leaders, Jesus said, you too would become as blind as your teacher. "And He spake a parable unto them, Can the blind lead the blind? Shall they not both fall into the ditch? The disciple is not above his master: but every one that is perfect, shall be as his master" (Luke 6:39-40). Always remember you won't not rise above your teacher or what he teaches. All of the above workings of God, are a part of the Gospel and Paul said, "if any man preach any other gospel unto you, than that ye have received let him be accursed" (Gal. 1:6-8). How odd it would be for there to be no supernatural working or manifestation of the Holy Spirit in the church, when the Word reveals we are in the age of the Holy Ghost and tells us that He will manifest (1 Cor. 12:1-11). So look at the Book of Acts and the Epistles. Here is the real picture of the real church. Don't let those who in unbelief say these things have passed away persuade you, for they that are such have the "form of Godliness, but deny the power," and from such, the Scripture says, turn away. Under the guise of truth, don't let modernists get you to deny the plain, written Word of God. Most of these critics have also denied the baptism with the Holy Spirit, as it's revealed in Scripture, and the Biblical scriptural evidence of speaking in tongues. It's because they deny these parts of God's Word that they cannot comprehend the supernatural workings or manifestations of the indwelling Spirit as is revealed in the Book of Acts. But to the Spirit-filled believer, these things make perfect sense. There is little, if any, of the workings or manifestations of the Spirit in the critics' ministries, but they do have great intellectual arguments and reasonings against the Holy Ghost and His manifestations, which operations of the Spirit work through those who have yielded themselves over to the will of God and believe God's Word (Acts 1:4-5, 8). (See also 1 Corinthians 2:1-5.)

For just as a few may have gone too extreme on one side of the road, these critics are too far over in the ditch on the other side, so much so that even those who have a well-balanced, solid teaching ministry of God's Word and believe in the gifts and operations of the Holy Spirit as is revealed in God's Word, are attacked by these critics as heretics, when most of the time the critics are the heretics who are seducing people away from God's truth, all in the name of defending truth. And people believing them are led astray from the plain, written Word of God. Let us be wise enough to go to the written Word and see what it actually says and then agree with it. Then you're on solid ground. Your victory in life now, and your eternity depends on it. Remember this: The same serpent who said to Eve, "Is it really so what God hath said?" is still at work in the world today (2 Cor. 11:3).

Are There Miracles and Miracles of Healing Today?

Some of these critics attack the Spirit's work by denying the Holy Spirit's ability to heal through His people today. But Jesus said in John 14:12, "Verily, verily I say unto you, he *that believeth* on Me, *the works that I do, shall he do also*. . . ." And again, Jesus said in His great commission to the church concerning the Church Age, "These signs *shall follow them that believe*. In My name shall they cast out devils, they shall speak with new tongues. . .they shall lay hands on the sick and they shall recover" (Mark 16:17-18).

Dare any man negate, or weaken, the words of the Son of God? Jesus clearly revealed signs that would point to what He considered believers, but with a stroke of a theological pen a man says, "it passed away." Who gave him the right to change the Word of God? We are strongly warned against doing that (Deut. 4:2; Rev. 22:18). The critics over look the many thousands of sincere Christians who will testify that they've been healed or set free of things by the power of God, to search for someone who didn't receive and report on them. By doing so, they seek to deny the very words and promises of Christ and reject any reports as to Christ's faithfulness. This is the lopsided type of investigation that goes on many times by these men. Are they really searching for truth or trying, in religious pride, to build their own reputation as a "defender of the faith?" Sadly, some of them are very much like the secular media in the way they report things.

What Does God's Word Say?

In every commission Christ ever gave, He told them not only to preach the Gospel, but also to heal the sick and cast out devils. Just look up *every time* He sent people forth and you will see that this is so. In His great commission to the church, He told His disciples to "teach ALL nations." Teaching them "to observe *all things whatsoever* I have commanded *you even unto the end of the world.*" (Matt. 28:18-20) We are to observe all things, This is the actual Word that is given by God to all of Christ's disciples throughout the Church Age, unto the end of the world. In His great commission, He told them, these signs *shall follow them that believe* (Mark 16:17-18).

Are these signs accompanying the critics? Do they pray for the sick and cast out devils? Do they speak with tongues? If not, why not? Who's right—Jesus or man? It is evident these things were manifested through the church in the Book of Acts and are there as an example to us. There are millions of Christians who have experienced these things in this present time. Let me ask this question: Why would God want sickness and disease, which is the work of the devil, to remain on the body of Christ (Christ's bride) when about two thousand years ago, He sent Christ out to destroy those "works of the devil"? Acts 10:38 says, "How God anointed Jesus of Nazareth with the Holy Ghost and with power: Who went about doing good, and *healing all that were oppressed of the devil*; for God was with Him."

This reveals that the multitudes of people whom Christ healed under His ministry were sick and diseased because of the DEVIL'S oppression. Jesus further cast out blind devils, deaf spirits, dumb spirits and spirits of sickness and disease (Luke 4:40-41; 6:17-19; Matt. 12:22). *And the Word* now commands us to pray the prayer of faith for the sick also, that they may be raised up by the Lord (James 5:14-15).

It is obvious from the Scripture that sickness and disease is a curse, and that satan is the one making people sick. Wouldn't God have made healing available to us in this new and better Covenant seeing that even under the Old Covenant David said that God, "forgiveth all our iniquities and healeth all our diseases" (Ps. 103:1-3)?

Some of these critics, in order to nullify God's promises and provisions say things such as, "God gave us medical science now." If that's so, what about the last 1950 years, before our present day medical technology, and why are there more sick people now than ever before? And it's a known fact that many doctors just experiment to find a cure. . .so why then would God give us something not as good as the Holy Spirit's healing power which healed them all? And did not Christ say *when He sent forth His disciples to heal*, "Freely you have received, *'freely give?'*" Does medical science "freely give?" In some places if you don't have the money then neither will they help you. Others will say, "God has a purpose for the disease." Ok then, why go to a doctor and try to have it removed? Would that not then be trying to stop the will of God? Let it finish its course, then when God is through with you, He will sovereignly remove it, if such is the case. But regardless of people's theology, they all try to be cured and get rid of disease and sickness through every natural means as quickly as possible. It's obvious then, that such is not the case for Jesus was manifest to destroy the works of the devil and *whenever* He had opportunity and they believed, He healed them ALL to fulfill the will of His Father (John 6:38; Matt. 4:23-24; 8:16-17; Luke 4:40; 6:17-19; Acts 10:38). Listen to Jesus after He set a woman free of a curved spine. . ."ought not this woman, being a daughter of Abraham whom *satan hath bound* lo these eighteen years, be loosed from this bondage on the Sabbath day" (Luke 13:16)? Can it be any more clear? This is God's real Word, the real Gospel. To preach otherwise is to preach a "different gospel." Why believe ye the critics?

Who Is Jesus? The Critics Say That the Message of Faith Demotes Him to a Mere Man. Let Us Now See What the Faith Message Really Says About Jesus

First of all, He is the One we worship as Lord. He is the Son of the living God; the Savior of the world; the Word who was with God in the beginning; the eternal Son; Creator; Redeemer; friend.

Some of these critics in not looking at both the deity and humanity of Jesus, have taken statements certain faith teachers have said about Jesus when He was here in the days of His flesh, found in fashion as a man (Phil. 2:7-8); made in all things like His brethren (Heb. 2:17); having come in the likeness of men (Phil. 2:7); and said this is what people in the faith movement say about Jesus. That He's just a man, like you and I. No more, no less. But this is not the case. If you'll continue to read or hear what is actually said by most faith teachers, you'll find out their worship services are directed to praise and worship both the Father God and the Lord Jesus Christ. It is very evident then, that they do recognize Him as Lord, Savior, Master, Redeemer, Creator and as the unique holy, divine Son of God so they could not be saying what the critics are saying they are. But again, things are taken out of context and twisted, which ironically, is the same thing they claim faith teachers have done. "Therefore thou art inexcusable, O man, whosoever thou art that judgest: for wherein thou judgest another, thou condemnest thyself; for thou that judgest doest the same things" (Rom. 2:1). But more on this later.

Is the Holy Spirit Baptism and Tongues Necessary In Understanding the Present-Day Supernatural Work of the Holy Spirit?

Yes, and we will make this abundantly clear through scripture in a later chapter on the Holy Spirit Baptism (Acts 1:4-5; Acts 2:4; 1 Cor. 14:2, 14).

Does the Faith Movement Teach That Men Are Little gods?

No, but it does teach that through the new birth we have become as John the Apostle said, "the sons of God" and as the Father God Himself has said, "ye shall by My sons and My daughters, saith the Lord" (2 Cor. 6:18). It is true that man was created in the image and likeness of God, so much so that God's own Son could later partake of human flesh, come in the "likeness of men" (Phil. 2:7), and now be called "the Son of man" (Dan. 7:9-14; 1 Tim. 2:5). But He is eternal, the Creator and we are forever the creatures, taken from the dust of the earth, living by the breath of God. So we are not deity, but are grafted into the True Vine and are now partakers of God's divine nature (2 Pet. 1:4). But without God working in and through us, we are helpless human beings who in and of ourselves do not even have power over devils and fallen angels in (Luke 10:17; Acts 19:13-16). But as we submit to God, the Holy Spirit can work through us and the devil will flee (James 4:7). So it is not taught that we are divine gods. There is only one true God (John 17:3), and none besides Him (Isa. 44:6). "But as many as received Him, (Christ), to them gave He power to become the sons of God" (John 1:12).

Does the Faith Movement Demote God to the Place of a Servant as the Critics Say?

Certainly not. We know the critic says this because faith teachers confidently teach God is faithful to His Word and will fulfill it, when we believe it and meet *His* conditions. It is understood that God is Almighty God and we are to respect Him, we are to fear Him, tremble at His Word, obey Him, love Him, and worship Him.

But it is He who taught us to "pray His will be done on earth even as it is done in Heaven." He told us to believe and do His Word and we would be blessed (James 1:25).

Of course, we know you cannot move God to do something He does not will to do, but He has promised, "all things whatsoever you ask for in prayer *believing, you shall receive*," and again, in Mark 11:24 He says, "Therefore, I say unto you, *what things soever ye desire*, when ye pray, *believe* that ye receive them, and ye shall have them," and what He has promised, He is also willing to do. Is it wrong to boldly believe that God will do what His Word says He will do? Does this mean we demote Him to the place of a servant? Is it wrong for a child to believe his parents will do what they say they will do? No, and God answering prayer does not make Him a servant any more than you blessing your children with the things you promised, makes you their servant (Matt. 7:11). Faith in His Word and promises is what pleases and honors Him, and He will fulfill His promises to those who believe His Word for He is the faithful, Covenant keeping God. This is what's taught and this is what the critic has a problem with. To the critic we say, if someone is not living right in God's sight and believing His Word, they won't receive from Him anyway, so don't worry that a person might get from God what God is not willing to give (1 John 3:22). "For the Lord God is a sun and shield: the Lord will give grace and glory: no good thing will He withhold *from them that walk uprightly*" (Ps. 84:11).

Does the Faith Movement Claim That Satan Is God or Equal With God as the Critic Says?

Absolutely not. Satan is not almighty, he's merely a fallen archangel, and in the Book of Revelation, it will only take one angel of God to cast him into the bottomless pit (Rev. 20:1-3).

Paul the Apostle did, call him the "god of this world." John said the "whole world lieth in the wicked one." Jesus, too, called him the prince and ruler of this world. He temporarily gained this position and entrance into this world through Adam's sin. Remember, the Bible says, "The Heaven of Heaven's is the Lord's, but the earth He has given to the children of men" (Ps. 115:16). In Luke 4, satan in his temptations, showed Christ all the kingdoms of this world in a moment of time and said to him, "All this power will I give thee, and the glory of them: for that *is delivered unto me*; and to whomsoever I will, I give it." He gained this position when Adam committed treason.

So for those who refuse to have God the Creator rule over them, they end up indirectly worshipping him who is by nature no god at all but is called "god" because people are following and serving him in their ignorance, rather than the only true God. So then satan is not by nature a god, but a corrupt, perverted fallen angel and is no more equal with God than a drop of water is to the mighty ocean.

What About the Atonement? What Happened? What Did Christ Suffer?

Someone once said that the faith movement teaches that Jesus was recreated on the cross, from divine to demonic. This shows you how far off some of these critics' thinking is. How could He be re-created if He never was created? On the cross, Christ, the Son of God, bore our sins in His own body on the tree (1 Pet. 2:24).

When this occurred a veil caused by our sin, came over Him and the Father judicially withdrew His presence from Him. Christ was willing to die for us, "the just for the unjust." When this happened and our sin caused a veil between Him and His Father, Jesus cried out, "My God, My God, why has thou forsaken (abandoned in the Greek) Me?" As one preacher puts it, "Jesus was not mistaken when He said He was forsaken."

Now satan did not conquer Jesus at the cross as one critic ignorantly claims that faith teachers teach, but Jesus willingly yielded Himself into the hands of sinners and was by wicked hands, crucified and slain for a divine purpose, after the counsel of God's own will (Acts 2:23-24). This was determined beforehand to be done by the determinate counsel and foreknowledge of God to redeem and deliver man from satan and the other consequences of sin. God therefore would permit it. (See John 19:11.) Now that these people did yield to the powers of darkness who had moved them to do this, the Scriptures do declare in Luke 22:53 that Jesus said, "this is your hour and the power of darkness." But Christ clearly expressed that no man or devil could take His life from Him (John 10), but that He laid it down for the sheep, according to the will of His Father (Gal. 1:4).

He did it so that by entering into the realm of death for us, He might conquer it, rise victorious over it and destroy him who had the power of death, that is, the devil (Heb. 2:14; Rev. 1:17-18).

Now although Christ yielded Himself into the hands of sinners to be put to death, He knew He would pay sin's penalty, conquer all of man's ancient foes, and rise again from the dead on the third day. Let me explain something.

The Bible states that Jesus came in the likeness of sinful flesh to condemn sin in the flesh (Rom. 8:3). Jesus had to have a body of flesh and blood in order to experience the consequences and effects of sinful flesh and pay its penalty. As He bore our sin in His own body, our sin in His flesh caused a veil (1 Pet. 2:24; Heb. 10:20; Gal. 5:19-20), and He was alienated from the Father;

forsaken (abandoned) by God, as He put it, and then He died physically. After that He went to hell as the scriptures testify. In Rom. 10:7: Paul writes, "Who shall *descend into the deep*, that is, *to raise Christ again* from the dead?" The word *deep* here is the same Greek word as "bottomless pit" (used in Revelation 20:1), and is always used of those who are under judgment. Remember, the demons pleaded with Him not to send them into the "deep," so surely that wasn't paradise they were afraid of. I say this because many of the critics try and place Jesus up in paradise during the three days and nights (2 Cor. 12:4). But these lower parts of the earth where Christ had to go first, were prisons. "Now that He ascended, what is it but that He also *descended first* into the lower parts of the earth" (Eph. 4:9). (See Revelation 20:7.) This is where He was three days and nights. Let's look also at Acts 2 and listen to Peter as he preached his message on the day of Pentecost, speaking the prophetically recorded words of Christ as He speaks to God the Father, "Thou wilt not *leave* (abandon; forsake in the Greek) My soul in hell, neither wilt thou suffer Thine Holy One to see corruption. He (David) seeing this before (it happened) spoke of the resurrection of Christ that His soul was not *left* (forsaken; abandoned in the Greek) in hell, neither did His flesh see corruption" (Acts 2:24-31). Again, the words *leave* and *left* here in this passage are the same Greek words Christ used when He said, "My God, My God, why hast Thou *forsaken* Me?"

Now Jesus was not a sinner in hell, but the Holy, righteous Son of God, paying the full penalty of our sins. Then Scripture says, that after three days, God raised Christ up and "loosed Him from the pains of death" for it was not possible that He should be held by it (Acts 2:24).

With the penalty paid for and Christ having put away sin by the sacrifice of Himself, the Spirit of God raised Him again from the dead (Rom. 1:4; 6:4; 8:11). He was raised when justification was made available for us. "Who was delivered for our offenses, and was raised again for our justification" (Rom. 4:25).

Some want to remove from Christ His sufferings. They say Jesus did not go to hell, as the Bible says. They say He was not "forsaken" as the scriptures teach, but He merely died physically and then went to Heaven, and that was it. But Jesus Himself said where He was, by the Spirit of prophecy. Where then was He for three days and three nights? In hell. This is what the Bible *actually does say*. Don't let yourself be convinced by men's arguments, which deny what's plainly written (Col. 2:8). Jonah in the whales belly (See Matthew 12:40), was a type of Christ's sufferings, as Christ Himself, testified. And Jonah said, concerning his experience, "the earth with her bars was about me forever," and "out of the belly of hell I cried and Thou heard my voice." Let me ask this also--what of all the burnt offerings? For after the sins of Israel were pronounced on the Lamb, it had to die; its blood be poured out *and then* it was burned with fire. Is it not obvious God's judgment on sin is eternal fire? The fact of the matter is that those who come out against and refuse to believe in all the sufferings of Christ may possibly be the ones who are denying His atonement. For IF it was all finished at the cross as the critic says, what then does His resurrection have to do with anything? Will the critics deny the part that the Resurrection of Christ plays in our redemption (Rom. 4:25; 1 Cor. 15:12-17)? If the New Covenant was finished on the cross, then we could be saved whether Christ was raised or not, but Paul, in the above Scriptures, says this is not so. He said if Christ be not raised, we are yet in our sins. As a matter of fact, if it was finished before Christ even died, as the critics teach, what of all the many scriptures that teach His death to sin had a major part to play in our redemption?

He either went to hell or He did not. The scriptures say He did. What do you say? As for us, we can only side in with the plain Word of God. Are we wrong for believing what the Bible actually says? He then, according to Scripture, went to hell, where you deserved to go, so that you could go to Heaven where He deserves to go. He had to pay the full ransom price (1 Tim. 2:6). He had to suffer every single aspect of the curse that came because of sin to redeem you from all of the curse. If He did not suffer it and pay for it all, then there are still some things that you will have to suffer, for the debt then has not been fully paid. But, thank God, it has been "paid in full."

Know this also: the word *hell* (Hades) is always used in the New Testament for "a place of suffering" (Luke 16:13), and it is always used in connection with death which is also declared to be an enemy (1 Cor. 15:26; Heb.2:14). If you refuse to use the New Testament word Hades as "hell," like the critics do whenever it's convenient for them, then there is no hell. Rather those who do so by twisting the meaning of the word Hades are saying that there is no hell mentioned in the New Testament. This is merely their desperate grasp to make these Scriptures fit into their man-made theology and deny the sufferings of Christ, just like they deny healing, the Holy Spirit baptism, and other things written in God's Word. And what of the *two evil spirits called "death" and "hell"* (Hades) in the Book of Revelation (Rev. 6:8)? Christ further said, the gates of hell (Hades) would not prevail against the church, and when Christ arose, He told John that He had the keys of hell (Hades) and of death (Rev. 1:17-18).

As stated, Hades and death are always connected and are always the enemy of man in Scripture. Hades is not anywhere in the New Testament a place where saints went, but rather where sinners went. It is not just a place of departed spirits, but a place where sinners now go after physical death, and are tormented as was the rich man in Luke's Gospel.

Are we saying Christ was a sinner? By no means, for He is the Holy Son of God, who went to where sinners would have to go. He did it in order that through tasting death and its sting in all of its workings, He could then overcome it and conquer it for us and become the head of a new body of people; a people whom He redeemed and received for Himself. Having paid the full price of the consequences of sin and having put away sin completely by the sacrifice of Himself, there is no sting left in it for us (1 Cor. 15:55). On the one hand, He had to satisfy the claims of justice. On the other hand, He had to conquer satan, who had the power of death and deliver us legally from his authority (Heb. 2:14), and also from the gates of hell. Thank God, because Christ redeemed us from *all* of the curse, we can now be blessed with "all spiritual blessings in Heavenly places in Christ" (Eph. 1:3), and because He paid the ransom, we are delivered from all the authority of darkness (Col. 1:13).

There is much more we could say about this, but space and time prevent us. Hopefully, this has clarified the stand of most faith teachers. One critic says, *"faith teachers say Jesus was reincarnated in hell"* That's ridiculous! This is no more than the same tactics the Pharisees used against Jesus Himself, making false accusations. (See also Acts 6:8-15.)

In two decades of being involved in the faith ministry, I've never taught nor heard anyone teach, such a thing. This again shows us that some of them belonging to those so-called Christian research places have their minds filled with such phrases because their Christianity is centered around studying cult and occult material. The focus of their lives and that which their Christianity is centered around, is nothing but fighting and quarreling with people. What has probably happened to some of them is that they have yielded to a spirit of suspicion that works on their minds as it did on Paul's (Saul), to destroy the church. thinking that they are doing God a service. They are a product of their own environment. Now we don't necessarily question their motives or the good they may have attempted to do or have done in some areas, but rather we question their knowledge of the Scriptures and of the power of God.

So again, I've never heard, and I'm sure *no one else* of the faith movement has either heard or taught the statement that either Jesus was ever reincarnated. Where do these men get these things from? I'm sure from the devil himself–the accuser of the brethren.

Now what about faith? Is it a magic want? Do words have anything to do with faith? Are there certain faith formulas? Do faith preachers emphasize faith in God? Are words connected some how to faith? The critic implies we think faith is a magic wand but that's only his opinion.

Jesus answers some of these questions about faith. Turn again to Mark 11:23: "Verily, verily *I say unto you that whosoever shall say* to this mountain be thou removed and be thou cast into the sea and shall not doubt in his heart but *shall believe* that *those things* which *he saith shall come to pass*, he shall *have whatsoever he saith."*

The critic says, "to think you can bring things to pass by speaking words is occultic." He implies it's magic. Mr. Critic, will you say Jesus was lying about this? Will you say He was metaphysical or occultic? Why won't these critics believe the words of Jesus? Listen to Jesus again speak concerning faith and believing God for "things." "Therefore, I say unto you, *'What things' soever you desire* when you pray, believe you receive them and you *shall have them"* (Mark 11:24).

Is Jesus, then, into "name it and claim it"? That is what the critics would say. Please realize that the term "name it and claim it" is just a phrase the devil mockingly coined to hinder Christians from learning how to operate in faith and receive actual answered prayer. Satan doesn't want you associating with anyone who has learned how to walk in faith and please God. This is the real reason for these mocking phrases he's made up. Jesus here, simply teaches you to "let your requests be made known to God." *Name it* and believe ye receive it. *Claim it* by faith and you shall have it. Christ further taught *"all things* whatsoever you ask in prayer believing, ye shall receive." And, Mr. Critic, what about Paul who says, "hold fast to your confession of faith without wavering," and you'll thereby obtain the promise, or "we believe and therefore speak" and also, "take the sword of the Spirit which is the Word of God." "For with the heart men believe (God's Word) and obtain righteousness (right standing with God) and with the mouth they make confession (of God's Word) and obtain salvation" (Weymouth translation, The New Testament in Modern Speech), (Rom. 10:10).

"For it is believing in the heart (God's Word) that makes a man righteous before God and it is stating his belief by his own mouth that confirms his salvation. . ." (The New Testament in Modern English, by Phillips).

Scripture says, "The Word (your salvation; deliverance; healing; protection), is near thee, even in thy mouth and in thine heart" (Ps. 107:20).

And Paul said that this is what the message of faith is centered around. It is the message about faith that he preached. (See 2 Corinthians 4:13.)

We could go on and on. It is up to you, dear reader, to believe God's Word, regardless of what some of these critics say, who, in some cases, are directly following in the paths of the Pharisees and Sadducees. These Pharisees and Sadducees are still among us today, and they know not the ways of faith. But none of them want to believe that this is the actual category they fall under. History seems to repeat itself, for man hasn't changed.

It is obvious Jesus believed that words had an affect. He cast out spirits with His words, healed the sick with words; stopped the raging sea and wind with words; spoke to a fig tree and it withered away, and said men would give an account of every idle word they've spoken on the day of judgment. He taught us to pray and use words in agreement with His Word (John 15:7), and then inspired James to write that your tongue is like the bit in the horses mouth and the rudder on the ship, whatever way you turn it, is the way your life will go (James 3).

Are faith teachers wrong for teaching people these long neglected truths from God's Word? And then some self-deceived man has the nerve to come along and call this Biblical teaching "cultic." Brethren, let's believe the Bible. It is the critic who needs to come back to the Word. Just because it's something in the Word he has not learned, he calls it "occultic." Shame on him.

In Hebrews 11 it says that the elders obtained a good report by faith. This means they believed God's Word and acted on what it said. Were they wrong for doing so? Are we wrong for believing more of the Word than the skeptics? When the centurion spoke, Jesus said, "I've not found such *great faith*, no, not in all Israel." Where did He find it? Coming out of that man's mouth (2 Cor. 4:13).

Faith is still directly connected with what people say today, for out of the abundance of the heart the mouth speaketh. "With the heart man believeth and *with the mouth confession is made unto salvation*" (Rom. 10:10). The effect of words is revealed throughout the Scriptures. And yes, all of our faith is faith in God and His Word. For further proof, see these Scriptures: 1 Cor. 10:10; Isa. 57:19; Dan. 10:12; Prov. 10:14; 11:9, 11; 12:6, 14; 13:2-3. "A man's belly shall be satisfied with the fruit of his mouth; and with the increase of his lips shall he be filled. Death and life are in the power of the tongue: and they that love it shall eat the fruit thereof" (Prov. 18:20-21). Need we say more? These are not mere formulas, this is a part of the Word of God!

Chapter 5

Prosperity and Health or Poverty and Sickness: Which Is God's Will?

What About Prosperity? Does God Want You to Prosper?

Certainly people can understand that poverty is not a blessing, but rather it is recorded in Deuteronomy 28 as a part of the curse. God, all through the Bible, blessed those that lived right, did His will, and believed in His Covenant. He said, no good thing will He withhold from them that walk uprightly. And Jesus said, "According to *your faith* so it shall be done unto you" (Matt. 9:29).

Psalm 112:1-3 says, "Praise ye the Lord. Blessed is the man that feareth the Lord, that delighteth greatly in His commandments. His seed shall be mighty upon earth, the generation of the upright shall be blessed. *"Wealth and riches shall be in his house and his righteousness endureth forever."*

Ecclesiastes 5:19 tells us, "Every man also *to whom God hath given riches and wealth* and hath given him power to eat thereof, and to take his portion, and to rejoice in his labor, *this is the gift of God."* Paul said we are to lay up in store (for God's work) as "God hath prospered" us (1 Cor. 16:2).

Many times these men that say they are against the prosperity message have nice cars big homes and take long vacations. One of the leading critics of prosperity as it's revealed in God's Word, has written a book against faith and prosperity, but yet he has a home worth about seven hundred thousand dollars. He drives new cars and has big accounts. They are prospering, but want others to stay poor. One critic has received tens of thousands of dollars for a book written against his brethren, when he had originally agreed to put money obtained through writing books back into his ministry. Shame on him (Rom. 2:1). Now I realize that although the Lord has pleasure in the prosperity of His servants, and He has blessed His people down through the ages, yet we are told to let our "moderation be known to all men;" "to be temperate in all things," so as not to become a stumbling block to the world (Matt. 17:24-27). God is not against you having a nice home, a good job, and being plenteous in goods as His Word says, but He is against all covetousness and you being a stumbling block because of extreme extravagance (Rom. 14:21).

Faith teachers do not really teach Jesus lived in luxury, as the critic says they do, although some may have felt they needed to go to some extreme in their teaching to get their point across, which may not have been the wisest thing for them to do. Yet Jesus did have all of His needs met. Supernaturally, He fed five thousand men plus women and children, (anyone who's had to pay for a wedding would know how much that would cost), He fed and took care of those who were with them; He had a treasury (Luke 8:4); sent His disciples out to *buy meat*; paid His taxes with a coin taken from a fishes mouth; turned water to wine; filled the fishing boats with fish, and so on. So when there was need, it was supernaturally supplied. He revealed then God's willingness to supply men's needs (Phil. 4:19). He said, "If you've seen Me, you've seen the Father." The first part of chapter 28 of Deuteronomy reveals God's blessings to those who obey His Word and *do according to all that is written* therein. (vs. 1-6):

"And it shall come to pass, if thou shalt hearken diligently unto the voice of the LORD thy God, *to observe and to do all His commandments* which I command thee this day, that the LORD thy God will set thee on high above all nations of the earth: *and all these blessings shall come on thee, and overtake thee*, if thou shalt hearken unto the voice of the Lord thy God. Blessed shalt thou be in the city, and blessed shalt thou be in the field, blessed shall be the fruit of thy body, and the fruit of thy ground, and the fruit of thy cattle, the increase of thy kine, and the flocks of thy sheep. Blessed shall be thy basket and thy store. Blessed shalt thou be when thou comest in and blessed shalt thou be when thou goest out. . ." (See Josh. 1:7-8.)

The Bible says, "all the promises of God in Him are yes and amen." If you then are in Christ, all of God's promises including these in Deuteronomy 28 belong to you. (See 2 Cor. 1:19-20.) "Christ hath redeemed us from the curse of the law, being made a curse for us: for it is written, cursed is every one that hangeth on a tree: that the blessing of Abraham might come on the Gentiles through Jesus Christ; that we might receive the promise of the Spirit through faith. Brethren, I speak after the manner of men; though it be but a man's covenant, yet if it be confirmed, no man disannulleth, or addeth thereto. Now to Abraham and his seed *were the promises made.* He saith not, and to seeds, as of many; but as of one, and to thy seed, which is Christ. . . . And if ye be Christ's, then are ye Abraham's seed, and heirs according to the promise" (Gal. 3:13-16, 29).

God did not create poverty, but it came as a result of the fall. It is not His perfect will for you. We understand that being born again is being spiritually rich and that this is the greatest of all blessings, but it is obvious if you study the Bible at all, there are certain things you can do such as tithe, give to the poor, promote the Gospel with your money, which will bring God's financial blessing on you. (See Luke 6:38; Galatians 6:7; 2 Corinthians 9:6-8.)

Another thing that should be noted is that many of the large faith ministries, send out tens of thousands, or even hundreds of thousands of dollars consistently to overseas Gospel outreaches, which bring the message of salvation to multitudes in other countries. Would they be doing this if they were not men of God? But the critics would never let you know this. Do the critic's ministries do as much for salvation ministries? If not, what gives them the right to criticize those who are seeing many times more people saved and healed than they? Before you believe the worst about well known faith teachers, do look at their fruit (1 Cor. 13:4-6). In 3 John 2 it says, "Beloved, I wish above all things that thou mayest prosper and be in health, even as thy soul prospereth."

"But thou shalt remember the Lord thy God, *for it is He that giveth thee power to get wealth*, that He may establish (confirm) His Covenant which He sware unto thy fathers, as it is this day" (Deut. 8:18).

Psalm 105:37: *"He brought them forth also with silver and gold*: and there was not one feeble person among their tribes."

Matthew 6:33: "But seek ye first the Kingdom of God and His righteousness, and all these *things shall be added unto you.*"

Deuteronomy 28:11-12: "And *the Lord shall make thee plenteous in goods*, in the fruit of thy body and in the fruit of thy cattle, and in the fruit of thy ground, in the land which the Lord sware unto thy fathers to give thee. The Lord shall open unto thee His good treasure, the Heaven to give the rain unto thy land in His season and to bless all the work of thine hand: and thou shalt lend unto many nations, and thou shalt not borrow."

Ps. 35:27: "Let them shout for joy, and be glad, that favor My righteous cause: yea, let them say continually, Let *the Lord* be magnified, which *hath pleasure in the prosperity of His servant.*"

Proverbs 10:22: *"The blessing of the Lord, it maketh rich*, and He addeth no sorrow with it."

Seems to me that God wants His people to prosper. Stay with the Word; don't sit in the seat of the "scornful" who scorn, ridicule and talk against these things that God has put in His Word to help His people. "Blessed is the man that walkest not in the counsel of the ungodly, nor standeth in the way of sinners, nor sitteth in the seat of the scornful. But His delight is in the law of the Lord; and in His law doth he meditate day and night. And he shall be like a tree planted by the rivers of water, that bringeth forth his fruit in his season; his leaf also shall not wither, *and whatsoever he doeth shall prosper*" (Ps. 1:1-3).

But always remember that the greatest riches anyone could ever have is not financial, but a relationship with Jesus, the Son of God.

What About Sickness? Where Does it Come From?

One critic does not believe we should pray in faith for healing but should pray, "If it be Thy will." Who's right here?

One time they say, "healing is passed away," then they say we should pray "if it be thy will to heal." It seems they cannot make up their minds. Can we receive healing from God? Should we pray, "if it be thy will concerning this," even though Jesus has clearly revealed it is His will? Do we pray "if it be thy will save me?" No, of course not. Why? Because we know His will. How do we know it? It's revealed in His Word. Well then, let's look to Jesus and His Word on this topic of sickness and divine healing to find out His will. First of all, it's obvious sickness is from the devil.

Matthew 8:16 : "When the even was come, they brought unto Him many that were possessed with devils: and He cast out the spirits with His Word, and healed all that were sick."

Luke 4:40-41: "Now when the sun was setting, all they that had *any sick with divers diseases brought* them *unto Him*; and He laid His hands on every one of them, and healed them. *And devils came out of many*, crying out, and saying, Thou art Christ the Son of God. And He rebuking them suffered them not to speak; for they knew that He was Christ." Notice, devils came out of the sick and diseased that were brought to Him.

Matthew 12:22: "Then was brought unto Him *one possessed with a devil, blind, and dumb*: and He healed him, insomuch that the blind and dumb both spake and saw."

Luke 13:16: "And ought not this woman, being a daughter of Abraham, *whom satan hath bound*, lo, these eighteen years, be loosed from this bond on the Sabbath day?"

Acts 10:38: "How God anointed Jesus of Nazareth with the Holy

Ghost and with power: who went about doing good, and healing *all that were oppressed of the devil*; for God was with Him."

Again, we could probably give dozens more scriptures that reveal sickness is a work of the devil, but more of this later. What we can say now is that we know by the Word that "the Son of God was manifested to destroy *the works* of the devil," and He had come not to do His own will, but "the will of Him who sent Him." So God's will was that people be healed and set free from satan's works and this has always been God's will (James 1:16-17; Gen. 1:31). If God wanted people sick, why does His Word say He sent Jesus to "destroy the works of the devil?" Has He whom Scripture says never changes, now changed His mind?

One author who writes against the "Faith Message," implies that it is a cruel thing to teach people your body's freedom has been bought with a price (1 Cor. 6:20), or that you are redeemed from the curse of the law, which curse included sickness and disease. He says that it's wrong to tell people God wants them healed. Is that cruel? Is not Jesus Christ, "the same yesterday, today and forever?" Why would He will the "evil diseases" of satan on us, (His bride), when He came to give us life and life more abundantly (John 10:10)? Does not the Scripture say, "For no man ever yet hated his own flesh; but nourisheth and cherisheth it, even as the Lord the church: For we are members of His body, of His flesh, and of His bones" (Eph. 5:29-30)? Remember, we are to love our wives and demonstrate it, "even as also Christ loved the church." So it is not us, but the critic who is cruel for telling people God put sickness on them, or wills it on His Son's bride. Oh, the subtlety of the serpent!

Then the critic implies that there is no connection at all between sin and sickness, and he says to say so is to be cruel. Let us answer this with the Word.

If someone was living like the devil, sin may very well have opened the door to their sickness. "Fools because of their transgression, and because of their iniquities, are afflicted" (Ps. 107:17). Sin, in Adam's case, opened the door for death, as the Scripture states. Romans 5:12:

"Wherefore, as by one man sin entered into the world, and *death by sin*; and so death passed upon all men, for that all have sinned." And satan, who is the one who had the power of death (Heb.2:14), entered this world through sin (Luke 4:5-6). After Jesus healed a man, He said, "go and *sin no more lest a worse thing come upon thee*." Evidently sin, in this man's case, brought sickness the first time and could bring it again even worse. Now faith teachers do not teach that sickness always only comes as a direct result of someone's personal sin. But that sin can and does *truly give place* to the devil. It is clear to anyone who knows their Bible (Eph. 4:27). God's people on the other hand, can *also* be destroyed, Scripture says, "for a lack of knowledge" (Hos. 4:6), or by listening to teaching like the critic's, which says God wants you sick and oppressed. First he says God makes people sick and thereby attributes the work of the devil to God (Acts 10:38). Then he says it's cruel to teach people God wills to heal you. Who's side is he on?

Sicknesses can also cleave to a person because of not resisting the devil (James 4:7), and not fighting the good fight of faith, or not being fully persuaded concerning God's will (Rom. 4:17-21; Heb. 11:1). Sickness, too, can just be an attack of demons (Acts 10:38), for "the thief cometh not but for to kill, to steal, and destroy," and we are, Scripture says, to "resist him steadfast in the faith," and take the "shield of faith" to stop the attacks of the enemy (Eph. 6:16). If we don't, it could take its natural course just as it does with the sinner. So what is really wrong is to teach people that God wants them sick; that He put it on them, or that He willed it. This makes people bitter towards God. This is what's cruel (James 1:16-17). But to try and help them see how faith in God's provision can be used to resist the devil's tactics, is not cruel.

It is obvious to me after looking at some of the books of the critics, that they understand very little about the victorious life of faith that Jesus came to bring, and know very little about where sickness comes from and why. And so they continue to hold fast to their traditions and make the Word of God of none effect (Mark 7:13).

One critic attacks a minister and takes a partial quote out

of context and says, "one of our bestselling 'evangelical' authors writes 'Never, ever, ever, go to the Lord and say, If it be thy will. . . . Don't allow such faith destroying words to be spoken from your mouth.'" Well, it's taken out of its setting again, just as the Pharisees did, and its meaning is twisted. The statement, if left complete and in its setting, is correct. I'm sure that the preacher the critic is criticizing, was talking about where the will of God is clearly revealed in His Word, we are not to say, "If it be thy will." For that would be dishonoring to God.

But the critic in his dishonest way of journalism, does what the secular press does and pulls things out of their setting, so the meaning is changed in order to get those who have never read any of the "faith books" to think all faith teachers are teaching what he says they are. But that is not so, for he has already proven he doesn't even know what is being preached. It's obvious he doesn't know, understand or perceive at all, the simplest principles of the Bible's message of faith in God and His Word. If he did, he wouldn't be fighting it.

He implies that if we don't say, "IF it be Thy will," we take away from God's sovereignty. The fact of the matter is, if we say, "if it be Thy will" when His will is clearly spelled out in His Word, then we are dishonoring God and calling Him a liar (1 John 5:9-10; Heb. 11:6). Any honest being can be taken at his word. Do we have to question God, whether His Word is so or not and say, "IF?" Now it is OK to say, "IF it be Thy will" where His will is not clearly written out in His Word, such as "If it's your will, I will take that job, move to that city, or join that church." That's OK but to say it in connection with His promises or revealed facts in the Bible is unbelief trying to look like humility. To say "if" when God's Word and will are clearly revealed, is not respecting God's sovereignty, but disrespecting God's integrity.

Again, this is further proof that these critics know little about rightly dividing the Word. They want you, (the bride of Christ), to remain poor, sick, questioning and frightened, while the faith message brings you God's message of faith and hope showing you that through faith in God, you can overcome the devil, have abundant life and please God by being obedient to the faith (Rom. 1:5). They will cite certain cases they've searched the world over for, to imply the message of faith in God's Word is wrong. Then they completely ignore the testimony of teeming thousands of Christians who will testify that their life is now closer to God, and that they have been healed, delivered and set free to the glory of God, because of learning to walk by faith. Truly, as John the Apostle said, "faith is the victory that overcomes the world." We will stay with our Father's Word.

How Is Faith Released?

Is it a law? Can faith be released through words? Does God use words to do things?

Again, the critic attacks the Bible's teaching on faith. He implies that speaking words has nothing to do with our lives or with faith. But let's see what the scriptures actually do teach. Does God use faith and words to create?

Hebrews 11:3: "Through faith we understand that *the worlds were framed by the Word of God, so that things which are seen were not made of things which do appear.*"

Psalm 33:6: "*By the Word of the Lord were the Heavens made*, and all the host of them by the breath of His mouth."

Isaiah 55:10-11: "For as the rain cometh down, and the snow from Heaven, and returneth not thither, but watereth the earth, and maketh it bring forth and bud, that it may give seed to the sower, and bread to the eater, *so shall My Word be that goeth forth out of My mouth, it shall not return unto Me void, but it shall accomplish that which I please, and it shall prosper in the thing whereto I sent it.*"

Romans 4:17: "(As it is written, I have made thee a father of many nations) before him whom he believed, *even God, who quickeneth the dead, and calleth those things which be not as though they were.*"

Genesis 1:3: *"And God said, Let there be light, and there was light."*

Hebrews 1:3: "Who being the brightness of His glory, and the express image of His person, *and upholding all things by the Word of His power*, when He had, by Himself, purged our sins, sat down on the right hand of the Majesty on high." (See also Ezek. 12:25.)

    One might say, yes, but that is how God releases faith and operates, not man. If that's so, what about Jesus' teaching on faith in Mark 11:23? "For verily I say unto you, that *whosoever shall say* unto this mountain, be thou removed and be thou cast into the sea; and shall not doubt in his heart, *but shall believe that those things which he saith* shall come to pass; *he shall have whatsoever he saith.*" "Whosoever" includes you me.

    Where did Jesus find faith in connection with the centurion? In Matthew 8 after the centurion said, "Speak the Word only and my servant shall be healed," Jesus said, "I've not *found such great faith*, no not in all of Israel." Where did He find it? Coming out of that man's mouth. Second Corinthians 4:13 says: "We, having *the same* spirit of faith, according as it is written, I believed, and therefore have I spoken; *we also believe, and therefore speak.*" And look at Proverbs 18:21: "Death and life are in the power of the tongue, and they that love it shall eat the fruit thereof." The very message of faith that Paul preached, is directly connected to putting God's Word of faith in your mouth and heart. "But what saith it? (What does faith say? v. 6). The Word is nigh thee, even in thy mouth, and in thy heart: that is, the Word of Faith, which we preach" (Rom. 10:8). (See also vs. 6-10.) Here are some things from Scripture about words. God says people's words are stout against Him; the angel came for Daniel's words; Paul wrote, "hold fast your confession of faith without wavering;" "neither *murmur ye* as some of them did and were destroyed of the destroyer;" "Thou art snared by the words of thy mouth;" the tongue; "setteth on fire the course of nature;" "by thy words thou shalt be justified, by thy words thou shalt be condemned." and "He cast out the spirits WITH HIS WORD;" "the WORDS I speak unto you they are spirit and they are life;" "moving his lips he bringeth evil to pass." Jesus spoke "Lazarus come forth" and he that was dead came forth;" Jesus spoke to diseases, the winds and waves, and they obeyed His words. He said, "Whosoever shall 'SAY'" and doubt not, he shall "have whatsoever he saith."

"As surely as you've spoken in my ears, "that will I do unto you." "I create the fruit of the lips." "If thou shalt *confess with thy mouth* the Lord Jesus and believe in thine heart God has raised Him from the dead, thou shalt be saved." "Take the Sword of the Spirit, which is the Word of God." According to Isaiah 59, this is the Covenant God made with the church. "My Spirit that is upon thee and *My words* which I have put *in thy mouth, shall not depart out of thy mouth* nor out of the mouth of thy seed, nor out of the mouth of thy seed's seed, saith the Lord, from henceforth even forever." And *God said*, "Let there be light and there was light;" "and He is upholding all things by the 'word of His power;'" "He sent His Word to heal them;" "A fool's mouth is his destruction. . . ." "How can ye being evil speak good things." "The mouth of a righteous man is a tree of life." A man shall be satisfied with good by the fruit of his mouth," (by what he's saying). "Every tree is known by it's own fruit." That is, by the words they are speaking, we can pinpoint exactly what they really believe, and where their faith is at and so can God (Matt. 12:33-37). "Whoso keepeth his tongue and mouth, keepeth his soul from troubles." Set a watch (guard) O Lord, before my mouth: Keep the door of my lips." "Suffer not thy mouth to cause thy flesh to sin." These are just a few of the hundreds of scriptures on words.

Now even though the critic cannot see how destructive to faith even his own words are, it is clear if we believe the Bible we can see our words are very important to our lives, our walk of faith, and to God. For him to say it's occultic to believe your words have any effect in your life or upon your faith, is to reveal his ignorance of the scriptures and of life in general, for words have started wars, destroyed homes, captured nations, or blessed multitudes. It shows that although he is very intellectual, he doesn't even know the difference between Bible faith and the occult. Sad to say, Christians spend God's money to buy such books that will negatively affect their faith in God and cause division in the body of Christ. Come on brethren, let's get back to the Bible. Jesus said, "Out of the abundance of the heart the mouth speaks." Some of the critics have studied so much occult material, it has warped their whole view of Christianity, and so now many times when they speak, they create fear and suspicion in others. The Bible says, "preach the Word." Jesus further said, "If you abide in Me AND MY WORDS abide in you, ask what ye will and it shall be DONE unto thee" (John 15:7). Our whole existence revolves around words.

In saying that words are not important he also denies the words of Christ, for faith teaching only says what Jesus actually taught about words. But the critic would never directly speak against Jesus, even though Jesus said the same things faith teachers do, for to do so, he himself would be labeled a heretic. Who's right then—Jesus or the critics? Of course, Jesus is right, and so is whoever sides in with the Bible and the words and teachings of Christ (1 Tim. 6:3-4).

The critic ridicules God, using His Word and faith to create. Can he not read? Some of these so-called Christian research institutes get so wrapped up in studying how satan counterfeits God, they fail to recognize that if there's a "counterfeit," there must be a "real." Sure, satan attempts to use real spiritual laws and principles, but to use them contrary to God's will and purposes, and yes, there are certain spiritual laws just as God also created numerous natural laws. There are laws that govern physics, chemistry, mathematics, gravity, electricity. The authority to use words and being created in such a way by God that our words do have a certain amount of affect in our lives and to a degree, the things around us originate with God, not with satan. So God says in His Word, "Take the sword of the Spirit, which is the Word of God." That means put God's Word in your mouth and say what is written (Matt. 4:3-4; Eph. 6:17).

Dear Mr. Critic, let me ask this question. What is the original substance of all things? Where did everything come from when "In the beginning" there was only God? There was no outside eternal material substance from which God made things. Where did God get the substance of things hoped for? We must let God reveal it for none of us were back there in the beginning.

Hebrews 11:3: "Through faith we understand that the worlds were *framed by the Word of God*, so that *things which are seen were not made of things which do appear.*" "Now *faith is the substance of things hoped for,* the evidence of things not seen" (Heb. 11:1).

Psalm 33:6: *"By the Word of the Lord* were the Heavens made; and all the host of them by the breath of His mouth." "In the beginning was the Word. . . ." Genesis 1:3: "And God said, Let there be light: and there was light."

Romans 4:17: (As it is written, I have made thee a father of many nations,) before him whom he believed, even God, who quickeneth the dead, and calleth those things which be not as though they were." Romans 3 speaks of the "faith of God."

But the critic's mind, cannot comprehend that God has used His Word and His faith to create all things as the Scriptures reveal, so again he ridicules anyone who believes God's clear revelation.

He implies faith is nothing, that faith is not needed and that contrary to Jesus' teaching, God will even answer prayers without faith. He ridicules those who believe as Jesus taught and therefore ask confidently in faith, implying that if God responds and watches over His Word to perform it because someone's obeying Him and believing it, that God is then "demoted to the status of a mere bellhop who blindly responds to the beck and call of formulas uttered by the faithful."

This man should be under some good pastor, studying the Word of God and trying to rightly divide it, not leading an organization that supposedly represents all of Christianity. Let us choose to believe Jesus. If He said, "speak it," then do it. If He said, "be a doer of the Word," do it. If He said, "believe you receive it when you pray," do that. If His Word says, "hold fast your confession of faith without wavering, for He is faithful who promised," then let us teach people to hold fast their confession, it's that simple. (See Matthew 7:24-29.) He wouldn't have told us to do it if it were not necessary. If the Lord has told us to do certain things, then it's useless to pray about them. Let's do what He said to do, this is the solution, and let us then pray about we are to pray about.

One criticized Reverend Kenneth Hagin's book, *How To Write Your Own Ticket With God*, and cuts it down even though it's all scriptural. The critic says confidently in his ignorance, "It couldn't possibly have come from God."

Here's the four things he attacks:
1) *"the saying of it"*-- He implies saying it has nothing to do with it. Again, what did Jesus say in Mark 11:23? He said, "believe" and "say." And remember the woman with the issue of blood who in Mark 5 *said*, "If I can but touch His clothes, I shall be made whole," *and* she was.

2) *"the doing of it"*-- The critic claims you don't have to do what is written, and ridicules Reverend Hagin where Hagin says, "Your actions defeat you or put you over." James said, "But be ye doers of the Word, and not hearers only, deceiving your own selves" (James 1:22). Will he ridicule James also? *"The woman pressed through the crowd."*

3) *"receiving it"*-- Mark 11:24: Jesus said, "What THINGS SOEVER you desire when you pray, *believe you receive it* and you shall have it." The critic says, that's nothing "but name it and claim it."

4) the *"telling it to others"*-- Jesus said, "Go thy way and tell what great things the Lord hath done for thee." So then there is nothing unscriptural about these four points in brother Hagin's book.

But yet in his conclusion the critic says, how then can Jesus have revealed this to Reverend Hagin?" Can't the critic read the Word? Doesn't he understand English? Doesn't he know, "Jesus Christ is the same yesterday, today and forever?" How then, Mr.

Critic, are people to get their prayers answered if not to obey Jesus? You offer criticism but no solution, no Scripture. The critic ignorantly really does little more than mock Scripture and promote unbelief in these areas. He speaks boldly and ignorantly of the things that he understands not.

Jesus said to the woman in the Mark 5 situation who did these steps, "daughter be of good cheer, *'THY FAITH'* hath made thee whole." Jesus recognized it as faith, do you? Christ's power, but her faith. There you have it, from the Word of the Master Himself.

It would do you good, dear reader, to go with an open mind to the "faith books" that have been criticized and be like those in Berea who *searched the Scriptures* to find out whether or not these things were so, rather than read a book full of criticism by someone who spends three quarters of their time researching occult and cult material. "The simple believeth every word: but the prudent man looketh well to his going" (Prov. 14:15). The New English Bible translation reads it like this, "A simple man believes every word he hears; a clever man understands the need of proof." Believe exactly what the Bible says. This is your proof.

Hear what is really said by faith teachers, and then in the light of the Word, judge for yourself. You will see that many of the things the critics claim faith people are saying, they are not even saying. And in the other areas also you will see that faith teachers who simply teach the "Word," are for the most part, right, while the critics are absolutely wrong and confused about faith and Christian living. No where in the Scripture, does it say He (Jesus) gave "some apostles, some prophets, some evangelists, pastors, teachers, (and some Christian research institutes or critics) for the perfecting of the saints."

In light of the Word, it is evident that some of these organizations are raised up *by men* whose intentions have been good but because they've not been anointed to stand in the office of a teacher, their discernment therefore of truth is all off. They may have great intellectual ability and be good at using words, but they are sheep trying to be shepherds or perhaps they are men called of God, but are trying to minister without the "baptism with the Holy Ghost," when Christ said not to (Acts 1:4-8). He told them to "wait" and they ran. The label men have given themselves means nothing if God didn't put them in that position (1 Cor. 12:18, 28). They that are such, should really be sitting in some good Holy Ghost-filled congregation somewhere, being taught to be a soul winner, or some other useful area. To put yourself in a ministerial position in Christ's body when He didn't set you there, is a dangerous thing because of the souls you're responsible for influencing. Realize this, the scientists that teach evolution also use great intellectual arguments and convincing theories, so much so, that they've persuaded most of the world to believe a lie. So is the power of intellectual argument. But let us stay with the simplicity of *"the Word of Truth"* (2 Cor. 11:3).

One critic claims that present-day healing is wrong because faith teachers say, "you can lose your healing." What did Jesus say? He healed a man and told him, "sin no more *lest a worse thing* come upon thee" (Luke 11:24). It is then possible according to these Scriptures that a man could be delivered from disease or evil spirits and his last state be *worse* than his first, if he doesn't continue to walk with the Lord and believe. (See also 2 Peter 2:20-21.)

The critic's statement is equivalent to someone saying, "if you're saved from sin you could never sin anymore." We know better (1 John 2:1). So then Jesus Himself believed a person could be healed, but then later have an even *worse thing* come upon him if he got back into sin. Healing is received by faith and kept by faith. The same devil that brought it the first time, can bring it again if a person has not learned to resist him steadfast in the faith. The demon may flee at the preacher's faith (Luke 10:17), but then deceive the person that was healed into accepting it back (1 Pet. 5:8-9).

The critic is also against faith teachers taking quotes from other faith teachers, but Scripture says, "Remember them which have the rule over you, who have spoken unto you the Word of God: *WHOSE FAITH FOLLOW* considering the end of their conversation" (Heb. 13:7). Paul said, "follow me as I follow Christ." He also said, "teach faithful men who shall be able to teach others also," and be "followers of them who through faith and patience inherit the promises" (Heb. 6:12). We do not just swallow everything—hook, line and sinker—because another said it, but rather prove all things and hold fast to God's Word. Do those who listen to the critic do the same (Matt. 15:12-14)? We always encourage everyone to check out all things with the Bible and to STAY with the Bible. All faith teachers are not identical, just as there are probably many Baptist preachers who are extreme and out of the main flow of the Baptist denomination. Should we go find every statement they've ever made, pull them out of context, make partial quotes and then write a book saying the whole Baptist movement is of the devil? Of course not, they are our brothers in Christ. But if we used the tactics of these critics, we could attack anyone, anywhere and make them look bad. But we refuse to use such worldly methods against any of our brethren, but choose rather to walk in love and prove all things by the Word.

Now faith is not the only area taught by faith teachers, but also soul winning, holy living, obedience to God, righteousness, giving to God, family life, healing, and living lives that please God. But faith, as we have seen in Hebrews 11 is what moves people in all these areas.

Again, by faith Abel offered to God; by faith Enoch walked with God; by faith Noah worked; by faith Abraham obeyed; by faith Sarah herself received strength; *by faith Joseph spoke* concerning his bones; by faith Moses kept the Passover; by faith they passed through the Red Sea; by faith the walls of Jericho fell down; by faith they wrought righteousness; obtained promises; out of weakness were made strong; woman received their dead raised to life again. They all walked by faith and not by sight, and they spoke what they believed. They heard God's Word and chose to have "faith in God," and responded to life accordingly even when to do so seemed unreasonable and out of the main flow of everyone else. And all down through the ages as we can see by Hebrews 11,

God was pleased with, and miraculously intervened in, the lives of those who believed. Why would He stop now?

Every person that ever did anything for God was moved by faith. Is faith then important? Did Jesus emphasize a message of faith? We know He was a teacher. Was He then, a "faith teacher?" Let us listen to His own words as He instructed people, "*If thou canst believe*, all things are possible to him that believeth." "According to *your faith* be it unto you." "Daughter, *thy faith* hath made thee whole." "*He that believeth* on Me, the works that I do shall ye do also." These signs shall follow *them that believe*, "in My Name they shall cast out devils, they shall speak with new tongues. . .they shall lay hands on the sick and they shall recover. . . ." "Go thy way *as thou hast believed* so it shall be done unto thee. "*Believe ye* that I am able to do this." In His own home-town He "*could there do no mighty works*" and He marvels because of "*their unbelief.*" "O thou of little faith, wherefore didst *thou doubt?*" "O ye of little faith, *why reason ye.*" "If *you have faith* and doubt not, you shall *not only do this* which is done to the fig tree, BUT ALSO IF YE SHALL SAY unto this mountain, be thou removed and be thou cast into the sea; IT SHALL BE DONE. And (in addition to this) ALL THINGS whatsoever ye shall ask in prayer, *believing*, ye shall receive" (Matt. 21:21-22). If Jesus' message could be labeled anything, it could be labeled a "message of faith," or a "faith message." And Jesus, the Bible says, is the "author and finisher of our faith," and "left us an example" that we should follow in His steps.

Paul revealed it's a message that starts with faith and ends with faith (Rom. 1:16-17). Faith first and faith last. And what else then are you going to do in prayer but name it (what you want) and claim it (in prayer) in Jesus' name? Jesus is the one who taught it in Mark 11:24 and Matthew 21:22. That is not a strange or evil thing as some imply, and concerning this, faith teachers have only taught the Word, they did not coin this phrase "name it and claim it," to mock Jesus' teaching. Those who have ridiculed the promises of God did, but really have, in their ignorance, stated a truth in doing so. Finally! (1 John 5:14-15).

And it was Jesus who said, "...verily I say into YOU IF YE have faith as a grain of mustard seed, *ye shall SAY* unto this mountain, remove hence to yonder place, and NOTHING shall be impossible *UNTO YOU*" (Matt. 17:20). Believing in the heart and speaking with the mouth is the number one way to exercise and release faith, as God's Word clearly teaches (2 Cor. 4:13; Rom. 10:10; 12:3; Mark 11:23).

Will the critic also criticize Jesus for emphasizing faith and the effects of words? No, because it's a lot safer for him to attack Jesus' followers, and sell books to those who haven't been taught these truths (John 15:20). Jesus taught that along with judgment and mercy, faith was one of the weightier matters (Matt. 23:23). A person must use their God-given free will to believe. This and this alone, taps them into the provision God has made for people in redemption. "By whom *we have access by faith into this grace* wherein we stand, and rejoice in hope of the glory of God" (Rom. 5:2).

Here are some more scriptures concerning this.
"Go thy way, *thy faith* hath made thee whole..." (Matt. 9:22).
Jesus saith unto them *"have faith in God"* (Mark 11:22).
"Where is *your faith?"* (Luke 8:25).
"Thy faith hath saved thee" (Luke 7:50).
Stephen *a man "full of faith'* and the Holy Ghost did great signs and wonders among the people" (Acts 6:5).
Paul perceiving *"he had faith* to be healed..." (Acts 14:9).
"The just shall live *by faith*" (Rom. 1:17).
"For *we walk by faith* and not by sight" (2 Cor. 5:7).
"We having the same *spirit of faith* according as it is written, I believed, and therefore have I spoken. WE ALSO BELIEVE and therefore SPEAK" (2 Cor. 4:13).

Not only these Scriptures but *over 225 times faith is mentioned in the New Testament alone*. This does not even include the words "believe," or words such as "believeth," "believed," and so on, which are also spoken of hundreds of times.

What other subject is mentioned so much in the New

Testament? Faith teachers emphasize faith because God, by His Spirit, emphasized it in His Word as a vitally important part of every area of our Christian walk, and if we have the same Spirit, He will lead us also to teach it and put emphasis on it just as He has done in the scriptures.

Are we wrong for doing so? Those who practically never teach their listeners about living by faith, are the ones who bring these accusations, while we only want to help God's people understand these important truths that they might more fully cooperate with God. Romans 10:17 says, "So then faith cometh by hearing and hearing by the Word of God." Everything we do for God, everything we receive from God, must be by faith. For "without faith it is impossible to please Him. . ." (Heb.11:6). If Christians then don't understand how to walk by faith, or perceive God's requirement for us to live by faith, they will miss out on much that God has provided for them in this life. Not only that, but they will not be able to cooperate with God effectively without the understanding of how to operate in faith in God's Word. And then religion comes along and makes up theologies mocking the need of faith and making up reasons as to why God's people are suffering according to the will of God. Dear fellow belever, you've been redeemed from the curse that came because of sin. Believe therefore the "Good News;" have faith in God.

Some of these critics who come against people who teach faith are high on intellectualism, but little on faith. Heb. 4:2 reveals God's Word will not profit you at all unless you mix faith with it. So why listen to their unbelief when the Bible is here to fill you with faith (Acts 6:8)? So again we say as Paul also said in Romans 10:8: "But what saith it? (What does faith say? v. 6). The Word is nigh thee, even in thy mouth, and in thy heart, that is, the Word of faith, which we preach." First it goes in your mouth then in your heart (Mark 4:13-15). This is the message about faith that He preached.

Some even go so far as the Pharisees of old and claim if there is any supernatural manifestations of the Holy Spirit, that it is the devil or sorcery, or metaphysics, not realizing they are getting close to attributing the works of the Holy Spirit to the works of the devil, the sin of which if persisted in there is no forgiveness. This sin can take place today.

Remember, satan copies God. God does not copy satan. Some of these critics are so steeped in hunting cults, that all they see in their imagination is "cult." When there's things taught right from God's Word that they haven't seen or don't understand, or they don't agree with, they then become upset and yell "cult." They say any visions, hearing the voice of the Holy Spirit, gifts of the Spirit and other things revealed in God's Word, are really occultic.

Sad to say, satan knows more about God's ways than some of these men in these areas, and he has deceived them into reasoning against God's Word, and made them think they are doing God a service by attacking anointed men of God whom God has raised up to teach these Biblical truths to the Body of Christ. The critics are the real stumbling blocks, who, in their ignorance, are being used as the devil's pawns as was Saul of Tarsus, while he was yet in his ignorance (Acts 9:1-3; 1 Tim. 1:12-13; Gal. 1:13-14).

Sure, satan gets people in the occult to learn about words through which they release curses, and this gives demons some permission to operate. Proverbs 16:30 says, "moving his lips he bringeth evil to pass." So yes, there is the negative side of things going on, but that doesn't do away with the truth of God's Word. The reason it even works to a small degree in the negatives is because of the way God created man; satan knows this. That's the very reason why he gets people in the occult to do it.

Now Jesus taught us to speak to "our mountain." To take the sword of the Holy Spirit, which is God's Word and put it in our mouths so that He can work through us. The Bible says, God "creates the fruit of the lips," "hold fast your confession of faith without wavering," "we believe and therefore speak." The Bible says, God "calls things that are not as though they are" and they come into being. And God said, "let us make man in our image after our likeness and let them have dominion;" "be imitators of God as dear children." So there is the "real." Critics, wake up.

Just because a person finds a counterfeit twenty-dollar bill, doesn't mean that every real twenty-dollar bill should be tossed out because it looks like the counterfeit. The real will spend. The real was first. Satan copies God, not vice versa.

"And the Lord spake unto Moses and unto Aaron saying, When Pharaoh shall speak unto you saying, Show a miracle for you: then thou shalt say unto Aaron, Take thy rod, and cast it before Pharaoh, and it shall become a serpent. And Moses and Aaron went in unto Pharaoh and they did so as the Lord had commanded: and Aaron cast down his rod before Pharaoh, and before his servants, and it became a serpent. Then Pharaoh also called the wise men and the sorcerers: now the magicians of Egypt, *they also did in like manner* with their enchantments. For they cast down every man his rod, and they became serpents: *but Aaron's rod swallowed up their rods*" (Exod. 7:8-12). They can try and copy, but they will never win.

The critic speaks and says "faith teachers think they can control God." Do we? Of course not. What he doesn't realize is that it's not a matter of controlling God, it's a matter of God watching over "His Word to perform it" and being pleased with faith (Heb. 11:6). "God is not a man that He should lie; neither the son of man that He should repent: hath He said, and shall He not do it? Or hath He spoken, and shall He not make it good" (Num. 23:19)? This we do believe. If God said it, He is faithful (Heb. 11:11). So confidently saying in faith that God will do something when He promised to do it is not controlling God, but believing God's promise. There is a world of a difference.

God is the one, who in His sovereign choice, chose to give man dominion in the earth for a certain period of time, and determined He would not interfere with the lives of free moral agents unless they, of their own free wills, called upon Him, believed Him, or obeyed what His Word said to do. But once they believe and they obey Him, He is totally committed to His part of the

Covenant, for He "watches over His Word to perform it" (John 15:7). Let me ask this: does the repentant sinner control God when he calls upon His name (Rom. 10:13)? Will God respond to every sincere, repentant sinner that cries out on the name of the Lord? Yes. Why? Because He's a faithful, Covenant-keeping God, and He's no respecter of persons and so He watches over His Word to perform it. Are they then, controlling God? No, God is responding to faith in their hearts. It's always His will to do so (James 1:17; 2 Pet. 3:9). God then, responds because He wills to do so, because He is pleased *whenever* a person believes Him and He's totally committed to His own Word. It's "forever settled in Heaven." Faith teachers realize that you can never make God do something He doesn't will to do, but you can hinder Him from doing what He wills to do by unbelief.

Mark 6:5-6: "And *He could* there *do no mighty work*, save that He laid His hands upon a few sick folk, and healed them. And He marveled because of *their unbelief.* And He went round about the villages teaching" (Heb. 4:2).

And again Scripture says, "They limited the Holy One of Israel." Not because they could control God, but because as free moral agents, they limited what He wanted to do to help them by unbelief. Even though he led them forth out of Egypt with silver and gold, with not one feeble among them; (Ps. 105:37), yet "we see that they could not enter in (to the Promised Land) because of unbelief" (Heb. 3:19). Is it not so that God "wills all men to be saved?" Yes, but yet people are perishing every day without being saved. Are men then overriding the will of God and controlling Him? No. His will says one thing that He desires for men, but yet a man must also use his will and submit to God for God's will to come to pass in that person's life (John 5:6). So man is not really, in this sense, overriding the will of God, because God, Himself, is the one who made them free moral agents. God's desire then for a man is not always fulfilled in that man's life. If that were so all would be saved and come to the full knowledge of the truth (1 Tim. 2:4).

Does the fact that God responds to faith make Him a bellhop and give us a puny view of God as one critic says? No, for we realize He is Almighty God, Creator of the Heavens, the earth and the sea and all that in them is. But if God emphasizes in His instructions to us such things as faith, obedience, the effect of words, casting down imaginations, speaking to our mountains, gifts of the Spirit, visions, and tongues we are intelligent enough to believe He knows more about it than we do, so by faith we respond to life how He tells us to. Is it wrong to take God literally for what He says? We believe He's totally honest and true to His Word (2 Tim. 3:16). The ones who have a modernistic *"Escape Theology"* say it's all passed away and therefore, we don't need to have faith for any of these things. It's all so convenient to just say "it all passed away." This is *the big excuse* for unbelief and its close associate is "God is sovereign." So we will take literally the scriptures on holy living, obedience, keeping His commandments (1 John 5:3), staying separate from the ungodly world system (1 John 2:15-17), and we also will believe all He said about faith and the Holy Spirit's power.

The critic is upset because a preacher implies God needs our prayers, and our cooperation; that He searches for a "man" to "stand in the gap" during this time period He has given to man. The critic implies that God is sovereign and doesn't need our cooperation at all. If He doesn't need prayer, why pray? Why doesn't He just save everyone then and fill them with His truth, for this is what He wills (1 Tim. 2:4)?

Why did He instruct us "to *pray His will* be done on earth, even as it is in Heaven"? Were those just empty words? He also said, "Pray ye that the Lord of the harvest would send laborers into the harvest." Why then doesn't He just send them without us asking if that's His will? Why does He through James say, "Ye have not because ye ask not?" Does He want you to have good things? Undoubtedly yes, but His Word says He gives good things to them that "ask Him." Why ask? Why doesn't He just give them? For He knows what you have "need of before ye ask Him." The reason is very clear, it's because we are free moral agents with free wills, created that way by God and therefore your will is the doorway into your life. Scripture says, "Whosoever will let him come." Jesus said, "Wilt thou be made whole?"

Scripture says, "The Heaven of Heavens is the Lord's, but the earth *He has given* to the children of men" (Ps.115:16). If God doesn't need our prayers as the critic implies, why then did He search for "a man" to stand in the gap? Why did He tell us to pray and call us "coworkers" with Himself? Now remember, all things are working according to how He set things up, so He's in ultimate control. So we do not belittle Him by saying boldly that He will respond to our prayers, when He promised to do so (1 John 5:14-15), but rather, we honor Him (1 Sam. 17:43-47; Gen. 12:3). If He's chosen to give man this kind of dominion and authority on the earth for a certain time period, and then chose to have a certain day in which He would judge men, that's up to Him. But to say God didn't give man this dominion in the earth when God said He did, is to call God a liar and neglect our duties and responsibilities. To say that God will not keep His Word like He said He would, is unbelief. And to say "God is sovereign" so he can therefore go contrary to His own written Word is to say His "perfect law of liberty" and Word of Truth does not endure forever; that God changes and He's unfaithful (James 1:16-17).

Now realize, faith teachers do teach God is omniscient, omnipotent, omnipresent. He's the great Creator. He is everything the Bible says He is. Nowhere have I ever heard a faith preacher saying God is *nothing but* a faith being as the critic says faith teachers do. The Bible reveals that God does do things by faith and "without faith it is impossible to please Him." This we know is true, according to His own Word.

But again the critic says, "but God doesn't have faith, nor does He do things by faith." But again, what do the Holy Scriptures say? Romans 4:17, "God who quickens the dead and calleth those things that be not as though they were." Is that not faith? Listen once again to this next Scripture: "We having *the same spirit of faith*, according as it is written, I believed, and therefore have I spoken; we also *believe* and therefore *speak*" (2 Cor. 4:13).

Genesis 1:3: "and God said, 'Let there be light' and there was light." That then, is the very "Spirit of Faith." It's what faith is all about. Believing and speaking (Romans 10:8, 10).

Hebrews 11:3: "Through faith we understand that the worlds were framed by the Word of God, so that things which are seen were not made of things which do appear."

Hebrews 1:3: "upholding all things by the Word of His power."

Psalm 33:6-9: "By the Word of the Lord were the Heavens made, and all the host of them by the breath of His mouth, He gathered the waters of the sea together as an heap, He layeth up the depth in storehouses. Let all the earth fear the Lord, let all the inhabitants of the world stand in awe of Him, for *He spake, and it was done, He commanded and it stood fast.*"

The critic is very critical about someone saying God is a faith God. Now only He knows what His interpretation of that is, but as far as faith teachers go, it is no different than saying as John the Apostle said, "God is love." We know John was describing an attribute of God and do not accuse John of teaching that God is an impersonal force of love who people can manipulate through spiritual laws.

The critic says that God did not use faith to create the world, but the Bible says, through faith we understand that "The worlds were framed by the Word of God." "By the Word of the Lord were the Heavens made." "He spoke and it was done, He commanded and it stood fast." Again, this is the very nature of faith. It is further revealed in Scripture over and over again, that faith is released through words, and the Bible does speak of the "faith of God" (Rom. 3:3), and the faith of the Son of God (Gal. 2:20); and says *He* dealt to us "the measure of faith" (Rom. 12:3).

Romans 10:10: "*For with the heart* man believeth unto righteousness; and *with the mouth* confession is made unto salvation." This Paul said, is the message of faith which he preached (Rom. 10:8). In Romans 10:6, Paul said, "faith speaketh."

The critic thinks that because we say Almighty God can believe and speak anything into existence, that we are saying God is an impersonal, metaphysical God. He fears that by faith teachers saying God can speak things into existence, and that He does these things by knowledge and understanding (Prov. 3:19-20), that faith teachers are saying that God is limited by His own laws and therefore, He is no God at all. Why does he continually refuse to believe God's Word? Because he is so full of reading about satan's counterfeits that he has been duped into believing satan would never imitate God in this area, and is now used by satan as Saul was, to attack the very faith he thinks he is defending. God is who He is. He does things the way He does things. This does not stop Him from being God. Again, let's believe the Bible just the way it is written. If we cannot understand it all, we can at least believe it all. This is all we ask, that people believe God's written Word. Let us pray for these critics, that their eyes may be opened, lest they become accountable for doing even more damage to the body of Christ (James 3:1).

Now it's obvious to anyone who studies God's Word that God does work only in certain ways and can't just sovereignly do anything. He is limited by truth, for it is "impossible for Him to lie." He is limited by light, for it's impossible for Him to walk in darkness (I John 1:5). He will not do unrighteousness, have respect of persons, or judge wickedly, nor can a person please Him without faith. Hebrews 11:6: "For without faith IT IS IMPOSSIBLE to please God."

Is He then, as the critic says, "a prisoner of impersonal laws" because of not going contrary to righteousness? So then it is seen that He does work within the boundaries of His own will. His ways are perfect, therefore, He will not operate according to what's imperfect. If you must say that these are limitations, so be it but God is still Almighty God.

Let it be known that faith teachers are totally dedicated to worshipping the God of Heaven as Creator, as Almighty God, and when we speak of faith, it is faith in His Word, believing that we can do what His Word says we can, believing we can be who His Word says we can be, and believing everything God has so clearly revealed about Himself. Nothing more, nothing less (Deut. 4:2). If Jesus said, "*All things whatsoever* ye ask in prayer *believing*, ye shall receive" (Matt. 21:22), we will take Him at His Word, knowing that consecration to His will is of first importance, and it's taken for granted that the praying one is also living for the will of God.

The critic complains, if that's what Jesus said, then Jesus is nothing more than "a Mastercard that allows you to charge to your heart's content." Is it not obvious He refuses to believe either God or Jesus, the Son of God, calling them both liars, saying God will not do what He said He would do?

Again Jesus said, "According to YOUR FAITH BE IT UNTO YOU." But the critic argues with this also saying it is not so. The critic turns and points to someone's experience in a book, to prove God's Word is not so. Shame on him!

Chapter 6

What About Job?

The Critic Believes God Opened the Door For the Devil to Attack Him

First of all, Job was a man of God who served God and walked in all the light he had. The Bible commends, "the patience of Job," but does not include him in Hebrews 11 on men of faith. We do not belittle Job, nor anyone who is doing what they know to serve God. But this does not take away from the fact that good people can be "destroyed for a lack of knowledge" (Hos. 4:6).

Who is the destroyer? Satan. Jesus said in John 10:10, "The thief cometh not but for to steal, and to kill *and to destroy. . .*" The Bible says Jesus "went about doing good and healing *all that were oppressed of the devil*" (Acts 10:38). And "for this purpose was the Son of God manifested, to *destroy the works* of the devil" (1 John 3:8).

Therefore Jesus, according to the will of His Father (John 6:38), set people free from satan's works by "healing all manner of sickness and all manner of disease among the people." He "cast out the spirits with His Word and healed all that were sick" (Matt. 8:16). He cast out blind devils, deaf spirits, dumb spirits, spirits of diseases. "Now when the sun was setting, all they that had any sick with divers diseases brought them unto Him; and He laid hands on every one of them, and healed them; and *devils also came out of many,* crying out, and saying, Thou art Christ the Son of God. And He rebuking them suffered them not to speak: for they knew that He was Christ" (Luke 4:40-41). They knew He was the Son of God in His divine nature and questioned Him as to how He could be casting them out during this time given to men, ". . .art Thou come hither to torment us *before the time*" (Matt.8:29). But He wasn't doing it at that time as God, but as "the Son of man" (Rev. 12:12). Jesus in one place said, "I have authority to execute judgment because I am the Son of man."

Remember, the people brought to Jesus were diseased people and devils came out of many of them, so these devils caused the diseases, but Jesus healed them all. Here is the perfect will of God in action. Jesus said, "if you've seen Me, you've seen the Father." Now remember, He is "no respecter of persons" (Acts 10:34). He is the same *yesterday,* today and forever. God neither contradicts Himself, nor changes.

Now back to Job's situation. Scripture tells us the things that were written beforehand, were written for our learning. But we need to look at things in the light of the clearer revelation of the New Testament and then put it all together, then we will see God's lessons, and let us also realize that everything we teach needs to agree with the life, teaching, and ministry of the Lord Jesus Christ (1 Tim. 6:3-4; John 8:12; 14:6). For if we've seen Him, we've seen the true and unchangeable will of God in action.

The critic is upset, because a preacher tells us never, in these kinds of situations, say, "the Lord giveth and the Lord taketh away," for the preacher said that Job said that and not God. What the preacher said is true. Remember, we are to do as the Father God said when He said, "this is My beloved Son, *hear Him*." (See also 1 Timothy 6:3-4; Acts 3:22-23.) Let's then listen again to His Son and we'll see things clearly. Jesus said, "The thief cometh not but for to steal, to kill and to destroy" (John 10:10). Well now, we can see through Jesus' teaching that it was the devil who came against Job to kill, steal, and destroy.

It wasn't "the Lord giveth and the Lord taketh away." It was the Lord who gave and the devil who came to kill, steal and destroy. Now there is a difference between God saying something and God recording that a man said something. . . . It is true Job said it, just as the Pharisees and Sadducees also are recorded in Scripture. but it doesn't mean all they said was truth. It has to be judged in the light of the rest of God's Word and in the light of what Jesus taught and did (Acts 3:22-23). This, evidently, the critic has not yet figured out.

It is true, Job did not charge God with wrong doing in the opening chapters, but neither did he understand what was happening or why, as he himself declares. So it wasn't that Job was an evil sinner, a wrong doer and therefore, deserved the calamities, as the critic implies faith teachers say, but rather, it was his lack of knowledge of God's truth that brought ruin his way. (He didn't have the Bible.) This is the lesson we are to learn from the book of Job, that people wrongly blame God for what the devil does.

Look at this Scripture. In Job 3:25 Job said: "For the thing which I *greatly* feared is come upon me, and that which I was afraid of is come unto me." Now notice, Job said the thing he "greatly feared" is come unto him and that which he was *afraid of* took hold of him, he was *not in rest, nor quiet, yet trouble came*...(v. 26).

Now turn to what the Lord said in Proverbs 1:33, "But whoso(ever) hearkens unto Me, *shall dwell safely* and BE QUIET from fear of evil." (This is directly opposite to Job's experience.)

It is evident then, if Job was filled with tormenting fear it was not from God, for God hath not given us a spirit of fear (2 Tim. 1:7), so then it had to be the devil bringing fearful thoughts to his mind, which we are now taught to cast down (2 Cor.10:3-5). It is also so that Job, moving in fear, *continually* offered sacrifices for his children, because of their partying, for he feared that they may have been cursing God in their hearts. Fear, then was moving him at that time, and not faith, and the two are direct opposites (Mark 5:36; Mark 4:40).

Now we thank God for Job's patient endurance. We realize that he thought God was doing it to him and so he said, "Though He slay me, yet will I trust Him." But yet Job's theology was all wrong as he himself admits in Job 42, where he repented for "Speaking words without knowledge," and uttering things which he "knew not." Another translation reads, "I thoughtlessly obscured the issues: I spoke without intelligence of wonders beyond my ken (beyond my ability to understand)."

Remember, he didn't have the Bible. He had heard about

God and walked in all the light he had at that time which wasn't much, for he didn't have the written Word like we do. First Peter 5:8-9 says, "Be sober, be vigilant, because your adversary the devil, as a roaring lion, walketh about, seeking whom he may devour, *whom resist steadfast in the faith,* knowing that the same afflictions are accomplished in (come against) your brethren that are in the world."

Here, the Scripture tells us what to do. It does not say accept it, because God is permitting it; or that it is God's will for your life, or God sent it to teach you. It says, resist the devil with faith in God. James 4:7 says the same thing. Resist what the devil brings, for nothing he brings comes to work out for your good.

Job knew nothing about the devil, he only had heard about God. So naturally anything that happened, he thought it was God. If you study the Book of Job, you'll see from chapter 3 on, he cursed the day he was born and he began to speak out of the bitterness of his soul.

But the critic wants you to believe Job spoke for God. Not only the critic, but satan also wants you to believe that sickness and disease and calamity are God's will for you, so that you don't resist him, and the critic takes Romans 8:28 out of context and tries to prove that everything that happens is God's will and works out for your good. That's ridiculous theology. How can it work out for people's good when parents die young and their children are left orphaned, or relatives die and go to hell, or men are destroyed for a lack of knowledge, homes destroyed, babies starve to death, and so on. There are multitudes of evil things that happen in the earth in the lives of people, and even to God's people, that are NOT the will of God (Gen.6:5-12). Romans 8:28 cannot therefore be pulled out of context and be used in such a way as the critic uses it. Even his being so critical of faith and men of faith, is not working out for people's good but he is overthrowing the faith of some (2 Tim. 2:18).

The critic in his book, glorifies Job and blames God for his problems when all the time, the divine Word says, "do not err my beloved brethren, every good gift and every perfect gift is from above and cometh down from the Father of lights, *with Whom is no variableness, neither shadow of turning*" (James 1:16-17). He defends erring man, makes excuses for satan and blames God (Rom. 3:3-4).

If God is sending or permitting the devil to attack to purify His saints, and conform them to His will as the critic says, why did He send Jesus to destroy the works of the devil? Would that not be sending someone out to destroy His own will? (Jesus said, "Every kingdom divided against itself cannot stand.") Why does the Word teach that Jesus "went about *doing good, healing* ALL that were oppressed of the devil" (Acts 10:38)? And that Jesus said He came to do the will of His Father (John 6:38; Heb. 10:5-7), and said it was "Kingdom *against* kingdom." Why did Christ heal "all" who came to Him in faith? Surely there would have been at least "one" out of the many multitudes of people that He healed that God wasn't finished with yet, if the critic's theology is correct (Luke 4:40; 6:19; Matt. 15:30). Jesus further said, "if you've seen Me, you've seen the Father." But the critic would rather go back to a few obscure passages in the Old Testament in the Book of Job, back to a time when men had no Bible at all to reveal God's truth to them, and neglect the clearer passages taught by the Lord Himself. Remember, all Scripture must agree, and the obscure passages should be looked at in the light of the clearer revelation of God's Word.

Now it is obvious the Bible commends Job's endurance, but it is silent as to his faith. Yes, he was a good man of God, but could only walk according to the knowledge he had. But the fact is, he did operate in great fear, not great faith, as he, himself, had said in Job 3:25-26: "For the thing which I *greatly feared* is come upon me, and that which I was afraid of is come unto me. I was not in safety, neither had I rest, neither was I quiet, yet trouble came." Why, even medical science knows fear can open the door to many emotional and physical problems. Fear and faith do not mix. They are opposites.

Over and over again, God in Scripture tells His people to fear not, only believe. Let's look at God's revelation on the comparison of faith to fear. The first place we see the manifestation of fear in the human race is after Adam and Eve listened to the devil and disobeyed God. They then hid themselves and WERE AFRAID (Gen. 3:4-10). Fear was the great hinderer of God's people throughout Scripture. On the one hand, Scripture speaks of "the shield of faith." On the other it reveals that fear does open the door to the devil and problems. Cares, worry, fear, anxiety are all hindrances to God's working in a person's life. Jesus said: "The cares of this world choke the Word and it becometh unfruitful" (Mark 4:19). (See also Matt. 6:25-34; Phil. 4:6-8.)

It is just that the critic's understanding of Scripture is so partial and superficial. He has failed to rightly divide the Word and compare scripture with scripture, and then has been used by the adversary to attack in his ignorance, men who are teaching God's truth. As the Word says in Matthew 8:26: "Why are ye so fearful, oh ye of little faith?"

Mark 4:40: "And He, (Jesus), said unto them, (His chosen apostles), 'Why are ye so fearful? How is it that you have no faith?'"

In Luke 8:50, Jesus said, "Fear not, believe only and she shall be made whole."

Like oil and water, fear and faith do not mix. Fear is believing something bad is going to happen; it's believing contrary to God's will (2 Tim. 1:7). And Job's testimony was that he greatly feared not only was he believing the devil, but he was speaking and acting on what the enemy was telling him. This is what put all that he had in the devil's power. God merely acknowledged that this was so (Job 1:12).

Not only that, but much of what Job said in the book of Job were his complaints out of the bitterness of his soul (Job 7:11). In Job 9:17 he said God, "multiplied his wounds without cause" and that God "filled him with bitterness" (Job 10:1).

No, it wasn't God that filled him with bitterness, God says in Scripture, "let all bitterness and wrath" be put away from you, and do not let any "root of bitterness" spring up in any of you and defile you (Heb. 12:15). Certainly then, God wouldn't fill anyone with bitterness. Let's look now at some of the other statements made by Job. Chapter 3:1: "After this, opened Job his mouth and cursed his day." Is that faith? Verse 2: "Let the day perish wherein I was born."

Verse 11: "Why died I not from the womb?"

Job 6:4: "For the arrows of the Almighty are within me. The POISON drinketh up my spirit, the terrors of God do set themselves in array against me."

Let's see his statement here in the light of God's Word. "It is not the arrows of the Almighty, for God instructs us to "Above all take the shield of faith wherewith ye *shall be able* to quench all the fiery darts (*in the Greek, flaming arrows*) *of the WICKED ONE*" (Eph. 6:16). God is not the wicked one, satan our adversary, the devil is. God does not give poison to drink up our spirit as Job said, but the poison that destroys people's lives is from the old serpent the devil, and it is not "the terrors of God" for "God hath not given us the spirit of fear " (2 Tim. 1:7). God is love and perfect love casts out fear.

David said in Psalm 91, that if you make the Lord your refuge, *"thou shalt not be afraid for the terror* by night nor the ARROW that flieth by day. Nor for the pestilence that walketh in darkness, nor for the destruction that wasteth at noonday." Verse 10: "There shall NO EVIL BEFALL THEE, neither shall ANY PLAGUE COME NIGH THY DWELLING."

We encourage you to read the *God inspired words* of David in Psalm 91.

Now let's see more of Job's statements:

Chapter 7:4: "When I lie down, I say when shall I arise, and the night is gone? and I am full of *tossings to and fro unto the dawning of the day.*" (This is the curse. See Deuteronomy 28:67.) Now listen to what God says will happen if we keep sound wisdom and discretion in Proverbs 3:23-24:

"Then shalt thou walk in thy way safely and thy foot shall not stumble. . . . *When thou liest down, thou shalt NOT be afraid*: yea, thou shalt lie down and *thy sleep shall BE SWEET.*"

Again, it's seen Job's idea of things and what he was believing was wrong. . .just as we saw by comparing Job 3:25-26 to Proverbs 1:33, that Job couldn't have been listening to God but satan. . . .him first with thoughts and imaginations and then got him to believe problems were coming (2 Cor. 10:3-5). Job then began speaking and acting on that fear. Faith is the shield, but fear is the open door for satan to work as is clearly revealed throughout Scripture. Not only that, but satan persuaded him that his problems were from God (just as most unsaved people still believe when bad things happen today. For they, too, don't really know about the devil, but we Christians should know better (Acts 10:38). Sad to say most of the critics don't really know what *in the world* is going on. So the devil laughs as he destroys people's lives and then people put the blame on God.

Job said his days are spent without hope (Job 7:6). (Does God take hope away from people?) In Romans 15:13 He is called, "the God of hope" who fills us with hope. In Job 7:11 again Job speaks from the bitterness of his soul and complains. (Are those acts of faith? First Corinthians 10:10 says, "Neither murmur ye, as some of them also murmured, and were destroyed of the destroyer."

In 7:14, he said God "scared him with dreams and terrified him through visions."

In 7:17, he thought God set his heart on him to attack him, but it was satan who did (1:8); (John 10:10).

In 9:22, Job said that God "destroyed the perfect and the wicked."

In 9:23, that God laughs at the trials of the innocent.

In 10:1, again he speaks from the bitterness of his soul (not by inspiration of God).

In 10:3, He says to God, "Is it good unto thee that thou shouldest oppress?"

God is not the oppressor, satan is. (see Acts 10:38-- "oppressed of the devil") It is obvious that he didn't know what was happening to him. He continues on in the next verses to grumble that God is not a man so how can God understand?

In Job 10:7: he says, "thou knowest that I am not wicked. . . ."

In 10:8, he accused God of destroying him. Remember, satan comes to destroy; satan had the power of death (Heb. 2:14), and the curse causeless shall not come (Prov. 26:2).

Now remember when reading the Book of Job, that Job knows nothing of the wicked one, just as most of mankind today. He doesn't have the written Word to explain to him what's happening. He simply interprets what's happening in the light of his limited knowledge. The Book of Job is really written to show how people (even God's people) in their ignorance, complain against and blame God wrongly for the things the devil is doing.

In Job 10:16, Job said, "God hunted me as a fierce lion." Now remember, the Bible reveals in Job 1:7 that it was satan walking up and down the earth. Compare this with what Peter said in 1 Peter 5:8-9: "Be sober, be vigilant; because your adversary the devil, *as a roaring lion, walketh about*, seeking whom he may devour: whom resist steadfast in the faith, knowing that the same afflictions are accomplished in your brethren that are in the world." Who then, is this fierce lion seeking to devour and destroy people's lives? The devil! But Job thought it was God, and the critic agrees with Job and says it's God doing it. Shame on him (2 Tim. 2:15).

The Book of Job is written to show you how people who don't

understand what's really happening accuse God wrongly. They do so because of their ignorance, when really, it's the devil that is their problem. But instead of reading and listening to God's Word, people have sided with Job and still haven't learned this lesson. They search for Scriptures such as Romans 8:28, twist its meaning and try and apply it to all life's circumstances, as though everything, including evil, is working out for people's good. But as we've already shown, this is not the case. But we know that God can turn a situation around and make it work out for a person's good, and give them victory over the devil if they love God. "If ye love Me, keep My commandments." "Whosoever heareth these sayings of Mine, and acts upon them, is like unto a wise man." Only those that know God's Word and do it in the midst of a storm or trial, will have it turn around for their good by God's working. Others can be destroyed by them (1 John 2:14; 1 John 5:4).

So Romans 8:28 cannot be used as though it's an automatic thing. This promise is for those that "love God." And if you love God, Scripture says you'll "keep His Words;" "keep His commandments;" endure, and overcome "temptations." If you love God, you'll not love the world. So, if we do what His Word says to do in the midst of a storm, *then* He will turn it around and make it work out for our good. He can then, watch over His Word to perform it (Jer. 1:12; Mark 16:20; John 15:7). But you cannot put all that happens in one bag and say it's all working together for people's good. To do so is to wrongly divide the Word of truth.

In Job 10:20, he tells God to leave him alone.

In Job 11:6, he says "robbers prosper," they that "provoke God are secure" and that God causes them to have abundance. Is this in agreement with the doctrine and teaching of Christ? Surely God is not inspiring him to say such things, is He?

In 19:6, he says, "God hath overthrown me and hath compassed me with His net," (God doesn't work to overthrow people.) "Thy will be done on earth as it is in Heaven." It was the snare of the fowler he had fallen into (Ps. 91:3).

Then in 19:21: he says, "Have pity upon me, have pity upon me o ye my friends, FOR THE HAND of God hath touched me" (Acts 4:29-30). It wasn't God's hand who touched him to cause all these problems, satan tried to provoke God to do it, but God wouldn't. The Lord simply acknowledged to satan that all he has is in your power (1:9-12). God didn't put him there, he put himself there. Faith is the shield, fear tears down the hedge (Eph. 6:16; Col. 1:13). God had put up a hedge (Job 1:10). "His truth shall be thy shield and buckler" (Ps. 91:4).

But Job opened the door by believing satan's imaginations. Job then wanted a book written, and wanted it to be written down forever, to tell what he went through, so God did it (19:23). God had it written down to show how people ignorantly blame Him for everything that happens in the earth.

Chapter 23: he complains again and says he wants to find God to justify himself. This continues on and on. The one thing commendable about Job, is that he continues to say he will trust God, even though he thinks God is not doing right by him.

Later, God comes in a whirlwind and reveals to Job that he knows very little about what's going on in the world or in creation. Then Job answered the Lord and said, ". . .therefore, have I uttered things that I UNDERSTOOD NOT; things too wonderful (difficult; hard) FOR ME WHICH I KNEW NOT" (Job 42:3).

This is what the critics need to say and do if they really want to be like Job. In verse 6, Job repented in sackcloth and ashes of all he said. God then corrected Job's friends also, and told them that they too needed to repent and speak as Job did, acknowledging that they also said many things that they understood not, nor did they know all about what was happening.

After all this was cleared up, *"the Lord turned the captivity* of Job" and when he realized that God wasn't his problem, that God wasn't the one doing it to him, he got back into faith and prayed for his friends (v. 10), and God gave him twice as much as he had before.

What then, is the purpose of the Book of Job? The Book of Job shows men that there are many things in life they don't understand, and that only God's written Word can teach people the truth (2 Tim. 3:16-17); that people should not blame God falsely for what the devil is doing (John 10:10); that because Job endured and never renounced his faith, nor cursed God. God was very merciful and pitiful after his repentance even though Job spoke in his ignorance, many things about God that weren't correct, that God accepts people as upright when they walk in the light they have, and He will grant mercy to those who are ignorant (1 Tim. 1:11-12). So the Bible does not speak of Job's great faith but only his endurance (James 5:11).

The critic concludes his chapter on Job by referring to someone's experience and how they remained physically handicapped and says it is to the glory of God. Can he not read the New Testament? Where can it be shown in Scripture that anyone ever came to Jesus for healing and was refused, or that Jesus said he had to remain that way for God's glory? The only place Jesus "COULD DO NO MIGHTY WORKS" was in His own hometown and it was because of "THEIR UNBELIEF." "Let God be true and every man a liar."

Get a concordance and look up the words glorified, glorify, and glory, etc., and you will see that God got the glory only when people were delivered from satan's works (Matt. 9:6-8; 15:31; Luke 7:15-16; Acts 3:1-16). To teach otherwise is to teach a "different gospel." We compassionately say these things, not to be critical of anyone who's having a struggle against something that has afflicted them. We love them in Christ, and may the Lord bless them for their patience and love in the midst of their trial, but to help them and others to be free of satan's snares and lies, we must continue to preach the truth (John 8:31-32).

Chapter 7

Do Faith Teachers Deify Man and Teach That We Are "gods" as the Critic States?

By no means! God is the Creator, we are the creature helpless without Him, for we even exist by the breath of God (Ps. 100:3). When people read all the lies, exaggerations and partial quotes the critic stresses, is it any wonder that he has created confusion in the body of Christ and hindered the Lord's people from learning about faith? For he continually implies that the faith message says things it doesn't say. The "Faith Message" simply says, "believe God," in every area of the Word while the critic constantly implies, "Is it really so, what God has said" (Gen. 3:1-2)? Now we don't choose to believe he does it intentionally but ignorantly. But he should heed the warning of James 3:1. May God have mercy on him for the discord he's sown among the brethren in his ignorance (Prov. 6:16-19).

Now then, are we sons of God through the new birth? Yes, for the Scripture testifies of this but not in the same way that Jesus is. 1 John 3:2 says, "Beloved, now are we the sons of God, and it doth not yet appear what we shall be: but we know that when He shall appear, we shall be like Him, for we shall see Him as He is." James wrote, "of His own will *begat He us*, with the Word of Truth."

Again, the thing is that most of these critics spend so much time studying cult and occult material that they speak *from the abundance* of their hearts, and it's clear that they have lost much of the truth of God in the shuffle.

It is obvious to us, that we who were sinners and children of wrath by nature are not equal with, nor ever could be equal with

God or His Son, even though He made man in His own image and likeness. Christians are not divine, but only a partaker of God's divine nature (2 Pet. 1:3-4; Heb. 3:14; 1 Cor. 6:17).

I have heard the Faith Message for more than two decades, and I have only heard a sentence or two a few times, *quoted from Jesus* where Jesus Himself said, "I said ye are gods" (John 10:33-36). "The Jews answered Him saying, for a good work we stone thee not; but for blasphemy; and *because that thou being a man, makest thyself God.* Jesus answered them, is it not written in your law, I said, *Ye are gods? If He (God) called them gods, unto whom the Word of God came, and the Scripture cannot be broken*; say ye of Him, whom the Father hath sanctified, and sent into the world, thou blasphemest; because I said, I am the Son of God?" Now Jesus said that.

Paul, too, called satan the "god of this world" not because satan is equal to God, or by nature the same as God, but because of the position he gained over mankind through his deception. Moses, too, is called by God "a god unto Pharaoh" because of the power of life and death he had given to him (1 Cor. 8:5-6).

Now I realize that a few, (by no means all), who teach the faith message from God's Word, imply or have quoted Jesus and said, "ye are gods" in a way that could be interpreted wrong by those who don't know the Word, but let's also give them the benefit of the doubt as we have the critics since love believes the best of others. They simply say it because Jesus said it. But I've not heard *any of them* say that any Christian is deity or divine. So then, they were not referring to the nature of a man when saying such a thing, but rather the position of authority God had given man in this world. So too, Paul was not talking about satan's nature being the same as a god when he called him the "god of this world," but only the position of authority he gained through Adam's fall. We absolutely know there is only "one true God" (John 17:3), and besides Him, there is no God (Isa. 44:6).

We further fully understand that Jesus as the Son of God is unique, divine and the only Son of God who is divine by nature even though

Scripture calls us "sons of God."

In faith circles it is taught that we are created a spiritual being in God's class. This simply means He is a Spirit and He *created us* in His image and likeness with a spiritual side to our nature so as to fellowship with Him and to worship Him in spirit and in truth. *No where have I ever heard* that faith teachers say we become God or divine. That would be ridiculous, but the critic constantly implies and exaggerates such things. These are no more than exaggerated false accusations similar to how the Pharisees tried to undermine Jesus' authority and credibility.

That man was created by God in such a way as to live by faith, speak by faith like God does, and be imitators of God. The Scriptures do testify, we then reflect God, and have His power in earthen vessels (2 Cor. 4:7), but are not by nature God nor ever could be.

God did make man so much in His image and likeness that His Son could later come to the earth, partake of flesh and blood, and come in "the likeness of men" (Phil. 2:7). He identified Himself with mankind and became the Son of man. He still is and will be eternally called *a man* as recorded in 1 Timothy 2:5: "For there is one God, and one mediator between God and men, *the man* Christ Jesus" (Heb. 10:12; Rev. 1:12-13).

Now He has not lost His unique place of divinity because of this, and is still worshipped as Lord and God (John 20:18), but we only point these things out about man to show that God did create man to actually be in His family (Eph. 3:14-15). Not as His pet, not robots, but *very much* in His own image and likeness. So much so that He could consider us His own children. 2 Cor. 6:18: "And (I) will be a Father unto you, and ye shall be My sons and daughters, saith the Lord Almighty." You, as a human, could not say this about a horse, dog, or anything outside of your own class of being (Acts 17:29-30). And yes, we are created beings, but created by an infinite God (1 John 3:2); His workmanship (Eph. 2:10). Being His workmanship, man is as much like Himself as He could create a living being, although we are presently only operating in a minute portion of man's abilities to come (Heb. 6:5; Phil. 3:21).

The Bible says He came to bring "many sons to glory." He is "not ashamed to call us brethren," and He has made us "joint heirs" with Himself. God further says, we are "partakers of Christ," are "predestined to be conformed to the image of His Son," that His Son is the "firstborn among many brethren" and we are called "to the obtaining of the glory of our Lord Jesus Christ" (2 Thess. 2:14).

Another thing I'd like you to consider, dear reader. You could go to any denomination, or any group of Christians that ever were, including the apostles themselves, and you could take little quotes out of context from the many different preachers and make anything sound like it's totally off the wall. But only the critics, like the Pharisees of old, spend all their time and money to do such things.

If you wonder about someone's doctrine, first ask to see a statement of faith, then you'll know what a person's preaching is really in agreement with, and then also look at the fruit they are producing for Jesus said, "By their fruits ye shall know them." Are people being saved? Is born again being preached? That will settle it, for no cult is telling people that they need to repent of sin, make Jesus Lord of their life, believe He's the only Savior, be born again, and obey God and His written Word as recorded in the Bible. Did God then give man a high position, create him in His likeness and give him dominion in the earth? Yes, and man is called in Scripture, a "coworker together with God" and of "the household of faith." So redeemed man is God's child, but not divine in himself. (Please also read Hebrews 2:5-13.)

What About God?

The critic says the faith message demotes God and implies because faith ministers, like Jesus, teach that "all things whatsoever you ask in prayer believing *ye shall receive*," that "God is a cosmic gofer, a genie waiting for us to rub Aladdin's lamp of faith." Notice the words he uses. The critic doesn't know the difference between faith in God and rubbing a magic lamp. Why listen to such men? Listen to God's Word: 1 John 5:14-15: "And this is the confidence that we have in Him, that if we ask anything according to His will, He heareth us, and if we know that He hear us, whatsoever we ask, *we know that we have the petitions that we desired of Him*."

First John 3:22: "And *whatsoever we ask*, we receive of Him, *because* we keep His commandments and do those things that are pleasing in His sight."

Mark 11:24: "Therefore, I say unto you, *what things soever ye desire*, when ye pray, *believe* that ye receive them, and ye shall have them."

John 16:23-24: "And in that day, ye shall ask Me nothing, verily, verily, I say unto you. *Whatsoever* ye shall ask the Father in My name, *He will give it you*. Hitherto, have ye asked nothing in My name, ask, and ye shall receive, that your joy may be full."

The critic doesn't really believe these Scriptures and doesn't want you to believe them either. He neither enters in himself and hinders those who would want to. Woe to you lawyers, (religious leaders) you have taken away the key of knowledge from God's people (Luke 11:52-54).

Is God Just Formless Spirit or a Spirit?

The critic then says, faith teachers are wrong because they say God is a person seated on a throne. Jesus said, "God is a Spirit" (John 4:24). The critic believes that because it's taught from the Word, that God has a spirit body and is seated on a throne; that faith preachers are trying to make God in the image of man. (See Revelation 5:7 and Daniel 7:9-14.) No, we do not make God in our image, God made us in His image and for this reason we are the way we are.

First John 3:2 says, "Beloved, now are we the sons of God, and it doth not yet appear what we shall be: but we know that, when He shall appear, *we shall be like Him*, for we shall see Him as He is." Jesus is the "express image of the invisible God," while Adam is the image of Jesus (Rom. 5:14). Then Adam had a son in "his own likeness, after his image" (Gen. 5:3). So then Scripture testifies that God sovereignly chose to create man in His own image and likeness—very much like Himself. Jesus saw the Father (John 6:46), and so will we (Matt. 5:8).

The critic rejects God's revelation of Himself and persists that God has no bodily parts, that He's just Spirit. He then is much like many occultists who believe God is some universal mind somewhere. They also don't believe in a real, personal God, seated on a throne and neither does the critic. Nor does the critic believe that the Son is really the only begotten Son of God, who came out from the bosom of the Father (John 1:1, 18), God of God, light of light, true God of true God, begotten not made, and he ridicules anyone who does implying God could not "really" have a Son (Eph. 1:3).

The Faith Message, if it teaches anything, teaches the integrity of God's Word. You can take God's Word at face value. This is what is emphasized. Again, all Word preachers are also individuals and so we don't cling to everything that's said by someone just because they say they are in the faith (Word of God) movement, but all things are compared to the Word of God, to see whether or not these things are so. If someone known as a faith preacher makes a statement that's off, realize he's an individual, and he's not speaking for the thousands of other sincere dedicated men of God who are walking by faith. One man's statement is not necessarily another man's doctrine.

Would it not be wrong to do this with any born-again denomination? Yes, so I hope the critic sees this and understands how wrong he is when he includes all faith ministries in his attacks.

Listen to these revelations from God about Himself and His bodily form. "So God created man in His own image in the image of God created He him, male and female created He them" (Gen.

1:27), and the Bible says, "The Lord God formed man's body of the dust of the ground and BREATHED into man's nostrils, the breath of life and man became a living soul" (Gen. 2:7). And God *saw* everything He had made (Gen. 1:31). Adam and Eve heard the voice of the Lord God, *walking in the garden* in the cool of the day (Gen. 3:8).

God "*came down* and darkness was under *His feet. He rode upon a cherub* and did fly," "the blast of the breath of *His nostrils*" (Ps. 18).

Daniel said, "I behold till the thrones were cast down and the *Ancient of Days did sit, whose garment was white as snow, ant the hair of His head* like the pure wool, *His throne* was like the fiery flame, (Dan. 7:9). "I saw in the night visions and behold one like *the Son of man*, (Jesus), came with the clouds of Heaven and came to the Ancient of Days, and *they brought Him* near *before Him*" (v. 13). (See also Matthew 24:30.)

If you look at the Son of God who's the image of His Father in Revelation 1:12-15, you will see and know then that the Father is as much a person as is the Son who came out of God.

In Revelation 5:7, Jesus went and took the Book *out of the right hand of* Him *that sat* upon the throne. No doubt, the critic, if he was alive during Daniel's time or John's time, would have mocked them also for saying they saw God seated on a throne.

Jesus spoke of God as having a "shape" (John 5:37). Paul said, Christ existed in the "form of God" (Phil. 2:6).

Ezekiel said, "I saw visions of God" (1:1). He said he heard like the noise of great waters, (see Revelation 1:15) as *the voice of the ALMIGHTY* (v. 24). And above the firmament that was over their heads, was the likeness of *a throne*, as the appearance of a sapphire stone, and upon the likeness of the throne WAS *THE LIKENESS AS THE APPEARANCE OF A MAN* ABOVE *UPON IT* (v. 26). He saw Him from *His loins up* and from *the loins down*.

Chapter 2:4 reveals, the One he saw was the *"Lord God."* (But he did not see His face.)

Paul said, man is the "image and glory of God" (1 Cor. 11:7). James said, "men which are made in the similitude of God" (3:9).

The Lord God told Moses, "And it shall come to pass while My glory passeth by, that I will put thee in a cleft of the rock and will cover thee WITH *MY HAND* while I pass by; and I will take away *Mine hand* and thou *shalt see My back* parts but *MY FACE* SHALL NOT BE SEEN (Exod. 33:22-23). No natural man can look upon God's face and live.

The Scriptures further mention God's heart, eyes, ears, lips, head, hair, arms, tongue, fingers and soul, and that He eats, lives in a city on a planet called Heaven; wears clothes, and engages in numerous other activities, just like the creatures He's created. So we are the way we are and exist and live as we do because of Him, not vice versa.

Exodus 24:9-12: "Then went up Moses and Aaron, Nadab and Abihu and seventy of the elders of Israel: and *they saw the God of Israel:* and there was under *his feet*, as it were, a paved work of a sapphire stone, and as it were the body of Heaven in His clearness, and upon the nobles of the children of Israel, he laid not His hand: also *they saw God* and did eat and drink, and the Lord said unto Moses, Come up to Me into the mount, and be there: and I will give thee tables of stone, and a law, and commandments *which I have written*; that thou mayest teach them." Not only that, but the Bible says, "Blessed are the pure in heart for they shall *SEE God*" (Matt. 5:8). We shall see His *"face"* (Rev. 22:4-6). Wow! Think about it! So who's right? God's Word, or the critic who ridicules faith teachers who say man was really created in the image and likeness (similitude) of God? The critic also ridicules the fact that God really has a Son who is God of God and Light of Light. But what does the Scripture teach?

First of all, we do not teach there are three Gods, but one God in three Persons. The Spirit and the Son of God proceeded forth from the Father, out of the very being of God's bosom and so Christ, the Word, really is God and *also was with God* as John wrote in John 1:1, 18.

"In the beginning was the Word, and the Word was *WITH GOD and the Word was God.*" The Father said, "This is My *beloved Son*, hear Him." The demons knew He was Christ, "*the Son* of God." John wrote, "*God sent His only begotten Son* into the world that we might live through Him." Satan, who had been in Heaven, knew also that God had a Son and that the Son of God had creative powers for He said to him, "If thou be *the Son of God*, command these stones that they be made bread." Peter said, "Thou art the Christ, *the Son* of the living God." And Jesus answered and said unto him, "Blessed art thou, Simon Barjona, for flesh and blood hath not revealed it unto thee, but MY FATHER WHICH IS IN Heaven" (Matt. 16:17). Paul spoke of "the God and Father of our Lord Jesus Christ."

Jesus said, "it is also written in your law that the testimony *of two men is true*" (John 8:17-18). "*I am One* that bears witness *and the Father* that sent men beareth witness of Me." This makes two. Jesus said, "For as the Father hath life in Himself, so hath He given to the Son to have life in Himself," so then God really does have a Son (John 3:16). See also John 14:16; John 17:21-22; John 6:38; John 20:17; Acts 2:33; 10:38.

Yes, we will really see the Father and the Son in Heaven, God and His Son (Rev. 22:1, 3, 5). So then, those who do not believe man really was created in the image and likeness of God, are really the ones who don't believe the Scriptures, and those who deny God really has a Son, also deny the clear revelation of God's Word. "But unto the Son, He (the Father) saith, Thy throne, O God, is forever and ever: a scepter of righteousness is the scepter of Thy Kingdom. Thou hast loved righteousness and hated iniquity; therefore God, even thy God, hath anointed thee with the oil of gladness above thy fellows" (Heb. 1:8-9; John 20:17)). Assigning to God, as the Scripture does, form and bodily appearance, takes nothing away from God. He is still Almighty, Omnipotent, Omnipresent, and Omniscient. He is still *El Shaddai*, the God that is more than enough and we know there is *nothing* too difficult for Him.

The marvel is that He made us in His image and likeness, which is probably one reason why satan now hates us so much, for he wanted to be like God (Isaiah 14:12-14). God has an eternal plan to have glorified sons and daughters in His image and likeness which will come to pass, which no devil, angel, demon or man can stop. But for the time now being, in His sovereign choice, He made man, gave man a free will, turned the earth legally over to man, but again, only for a certain time period, and determined that He would only intervene in the lives of free moral agents in proportion to the petitions requested of Him. Although He would allow them to experience the law of sowing and reaping (Gal. 6:7). This does not belittle God. This is His great, marvelous, and wondrous plan. Therefore, we really are free moral agents, God really is God, and it truly is all working according to the scriptures and not according to man's religious ideas about things. Futhermore, we really do have an enemy to conquer.

What About Satan? What Happened at the Fall? Did Satan Gain Any Legal Authority in the World?

Well, the critic is upset because faith teachers say that at the fall, Adam and Eve who were created as children of God (Luke 3:38), became alienated from the life of God (Eph. 4:17-18), became spiritually the children of the devil (1 John 3:8, 10) and that satan became the pseudo god of this world (2 Cor. 4:3-4). All of this happened because of the choice of their wills.

God originally placed man under the government of His Son, but Adam, yielding to satan, fell away from God and became subject to the authority of the devil. Man, at the fall, then came under the influence of satan and his kingdom.

Listen to what John, the apostle writes in his first epistle to the church. "He that committeth (practices) sin is of the devil, for the devil sinneth from the beginning" (Rom. 5:12; 1 John 3:8). "In this the children of God are manifest and *the children of the devil. . .whosoever doeth not righteousness is not of God*, neither he that loveth not his brother. . ." (v. 10), (v. 12). So, natural people are now "by nature children of wrath" (Eph. 2:2-3), and satan is their spiritual stepfather, so to speak, for Jesus said to those in John 8:44, "Ye are of *your father* the devil, and the lusts of *your father* ye will do."

Are we wrong to agree with God's Word? Is not this why we need to be *born again*? "But as many as received Him, (Christ), *to them* gave He power *to BECOME* THE SONS of God" (John 1:10-12). Because of Adam's choice, his seed also became subject to satan. After the fall, Adam and Eve were no longer partakers of God's divine nature (2 Pet. 1:4); (John 15:1-7), but became ruled over by the devil, the prince of the powers of the air. Ephesians 2:2 says, "Wherein in times past, you walked according to the course of this world, according to the prince of the power of the air. *The Spirit that now worketh in the children of disobedience.*"

With man's spirit separated from the life of God, satan began to rule men through the desires of the flesh and of the mind (Eph. 2:3). They did not become satanic beings but fallen human beings now under the influence of the devil and demons (Gen. 6:5), and under his authority (Col. 1:13).

Originally, as we've stated, the earth was delivered to the children of men. "The Heaven, even the heavens are the Lords, but the earth *hath He given* to the children of men" (Ps. 115:16). And God said, "*let them have dominion. . .over all the earth. . .*" (Gen. 1:26-28).

Psalm 8 says, "Thou madest Him (man) to have dominion over all the works of Thy hands." So God, in His sovereign choice, turned the earth over to men to do with as they pleased, and it is evident that this is the case. All we need do is to look around us at this world and see how people live to know that this is so. But God also determined and set a certain time at the end of the world, in which He would judge men great and small for the works they have done in their bodies, in this temporal life (Rev. 20:11-15; 2

Cor. 5:9-11). Although thank God we Christians are delivered from the wrath to come, provided that we continue to abide in Christ (1 Thess. 1:10; 1 John 2:28; Heb. 3:14).

Genesis 2:16-17: "And the Lord God commanded the man, saying, of every tree of the garden thou mayest freely eat: but of the tree of the knowledge of good and evil, *thou shalt not* eat of it: for in the day that thou eatest thereof, thou shalt surely die."

Now, the serpent, (the devil), came into the garden and deceived the woman into thinking they could be as gods like God, if she only disobeyed God, and He told her "she would not surely die."

Genesis 3:6 says: "And when the woman saw that the tree was good for food, and that it was pleasant to the eyes, and a tree to be desired to make one wise, she took of the fruit thereof, and did eat, and gave also unto her husband *with her*; and he did eat." Scripture states, Adam was not deceived (he was not fooled by satan), (1 Tim. 2:14). He chose to do what he did and when he submitted to God's adversary rather than to God, He went under the authority of darkness. This also caused him to go under the power of sin (Gal. 3:22; Col. 1:13). He then became dead in trespasses and sins (Eph. 2:1).

Scripture says, "By one man sin entered the world and DEATH BY SIN" (Rom. 5:12; 1 Cor. 15:26). Death and suffering then, entered this world when man went contrary to the will of God. And the one that had the power of death, who gained entrance and came to kill, steal and destroy God's creation was the devil and his legions (Heb. 2:14; Eph. 6:12; John 10:10). So the devil gained legal entrance being permitted into this world by Adam (Luke 4:6), but this is temporal and will last only for the allotted time period originally given to man. (See Revelation 11:15, 12:12; Matthew 8:29.) God sets the boundaries.

When satan came to Christ on the mount of temptation, the Scripture says, "And the devil, taking Him up into an high mountain, shewed unto Him ALL THE KINGDOMS OF THE

WORLD IN A MOMENT OF TIME. And the devil said unto Him, 'All this power (authority) WILL I GIVE THEE, AND THE GLORY OF THEM, FOR *that is delivered unto me*, and to whomever I WILL, I give it'" (Luke 4:5-8).

Certainly, if he didn't have it to give, at least temporarily, Christ would have known it and it would have been no temptation at all. You cannot be tempted by someone if the one tempting you doesn't possess it. The fact is, he did have it, for Jesus, Himself, said concerning him, "...the prince (ruler) *of this world*, (satan), cometh and hath nothing in me" (John 14:30). Now none of this took God by surprise, but God permitted the serpent (the devil, a free moral agent also) to continue on in his course for the allotted time given him also before the judgment, and to be in the garden to really give man a freedom of choice. Again remember, Adam was not deceived but knew about the serpent. He was therefore responsible for what he did.

Paul, in his letter to the church, called satan the "god of this world" (2 Cor. 4:3-4), while John wrote that the "whole world lieth in the embrace of the wicked one" (1 John 5:19). And all those who have not made the decision to follow God are "walking" according to the course of THIS WORLD, according to the prince of the powers of the air" (Eph. 2:2). Satan's hierarchy is called, *"the rulers of the darkness of this world"* (Eph. 6:12).

Let's quote from Luke 4:5-6 from a few other translations: "Next the devil led Him up and showed Him in a flash, all the kingdoms of the world..." (New English Bible).

Verse 6: "And the devil said unto Him, To Thee will I give all this authority and the glory of them" (American Standard Version). "I will give you all this domain and its glory..." (New American Standard Bible).

"...for it has been handed over to me..." (New American Standard Bible).
"...for it has been put in my hands..." (New English Bible).

. . .for it has been "turned over to me" (Goodspeed's American Translation).

And I give it to whom I will (Revised Standard Version); to anyone I please (Goodspeed's American Translation).

Who gave it to him? Certainly not God. To whom was the earth and its domain originally given? Adam, Who then gave the earth for this time period over to the devil? Adam. How? By willingly submitting to the devil, for again, Scripture tells us that "Adam was not deceived" (1 Tim. 2:14).

". . .and Adam was not beguiled. . ." (New English Bible).

". . .and Adam was not fooled by satan" (Kenneth Taylor's Living Letters).

Contrary to God's will, Adam did eat of the fruit together with Eve (Gen. 3:6).

He absolutely knew God's enemy and God's command. God's will was that he not choose the "tree of knowledge of good and evil" and God made this clear to Adam. This was an act of treason, and through this act the door was opened to satan and his host of unseen invisible powers to legally be here, but again only for as long a time period (lease so to speak), as was originally given to man. And at the end of that time period, satan himself, will be dealt with and cast into the bottomless pit (Rev. 20:1-3). This he knows (Rev. 12:12). And at the end of the time given to men, Christ will come and put down all rebellion in this part of God's creation (1 Cor. 15:26-28). And then at the end of the millennium satan *must be* let loose to give others who are born during that time, the freedom and right to choose between Jesus or satan (Rev. 20:3). Then cometh the end and also the beginning of a new heavens and a new earth.

So even though Scripture calls satan "the god of this world" and reveals he temporarily has a certain right to be here, this, by no means, means that he's an equal and opposite to God, or that

God has failed in the least. God has already foreseen all things, and even showed John the end of the millennium, the end of satan, and the new Heavens and the new earth wherein dwelleth righteousness.

The critic has a hard time with all this, because he leans so much to his intellect and tries to figure things out with his mind instead of accepting God's revelation by faith (Heb. 11:3). But we know God is the eternal Almighty, Omnipotent One who inhabits eternity, while satan is a mere fallen angel created by God (Ezek. 28:15).

So the critic's criticism that says we say satan is equal with God is once again shown to be a lie and a false accusation. And not only in this but he has consistently taken half sentences, twisted things, sarcastically manipulated and interpreted things through his own reasoning and he has refused to say the other things that are taught by faith teachers that *he knows* are right on.

In faith circles, man is neither portrayed as divine or demonic, but human beings created in the image and likeness of God, capable of partaking of either God's divine nature (Heb. 3:14; John 15:1-7; 2 Pet. 1:3-4), or yielding themselves to the prince of the powers of the air and thereby inviting demons to work in and through them (Eph. 2:2).

I realize, there may be a few who have taught some extremes on some of these things, but the critic has taken what some man may have said on one tape, who's intentions may have been completely different from how the critic took it and said that's what all faith ministries are teaching. He has either misunderstood or is lying, for it's obvious he doesn't know. This chapter is written to help you see where the majority of faith teachers are coming from, as I see it.

Another thing the critic says in his attack is that faith teachers say both God and satan are subservient to man in this world. His is a ridiculous statement. Although it may sound repetitious, again here is what is really being said: God created man and sovereignly chose to give man full authority in the earth over a certain time period that man could use all the good things God created according to their free wills, which He gave them.

God also ordained that He would only involve Himself in the affairs of men during this time period in response to their inviting Him to, and according to their faith in Him and His Word. So He tells us to "pray His will be done on earth even as it is in Heaven." "Ye have not, because ye ask not." "*Whatsoever* ye shall bind on earth, shall be bound in Heaven, and *whatsoever* ye shall loose on earth shall be loosed in Heaven;" "If thou *canst believe*, all things are possible to him that believeth;" "ask ye of the Lord rain" in the time of the latter rain. God has consistently revealed all the way through the Bible that He works with, in and through, willing men of faith and that man, during this time period, is a coworker together with God" (1 Cor. 3:9).

There are hundreds of other Scriptures that prove that this is how God set things up. This is what prayer is all about. Let man "have dominion" He said, and so it is. This then by no means makes God subservient to man. It is God's plan. It's how sovereignly He chose things to be. It's not that man controls God, because of the way God created man, man's free will is now the doorway into his life, and by it, he lets God or satan work in his life. As for satan, we do have authority over him as long as we are submitted to God and His Word, for we need God's power to back us up, and His name and authority to enforce this (Luke 10:19; John 15:4-5; James 4:7).

Now because satan gained legal entrance into the earth does not make God a failure at all, for as we've said, God foresaw all things, although He let's free moral agents (satan included) take their own course (Prov. 1:30-33). Only until the day of the Lord when every score shall be settled. In other words, God sets the boundaries. "And hath made of one blood all nations of men for to dwell on all the face of the earth, and hath determined the times before appointed, and the bounds of their habitation" (Acts 17:26). So He neither created Adam nor lucifer a robot, but both beings were created upright. Both of them used their free wills to go contrary to the will of the Creator (Isa. 14:12-14; Rom. 5:12).

We know that God owns the earth by right of creation. "The earth is the Lord's, and the fullness thereof." But this time period of dominion over the earth given to men by God, was legally in the hands of Adam who opened the door to sin, death and satan (Rom. 5:12; 1 Cor. 15:26), all of which is contrary to God's will (1 John 3:8). So satan now has a legal right to be here until the end of this time period (Matt. 8:29; Rev. 12:12), but his kingdom is temporal. God knew this would be the case. The end result of God's plan is that God wins and so does anyone who sides with Him. But in the meantime, because He has chosen to have men as His coworkers, He now "searches for a man to stand in the gap" and tells us to "pray that the Lord of harvest would send out laborers."

Why tell us to pray for these things and many other things if He could just automatically do them without us praying? How come every great revival has come as a result of prayer and men doing what God's Word says to do? But because the critic does not believe what the Bible testifies concerning these things, His whole understanding of what's happening in the earth is clouded by his own carnal, religious reasonings and training. He has believed someone's theological system, rather than God's Word. That's what his faith is really in and this is why he has so much trouble with "the message of faith" as it's revealed in the Bible.

So we say by God's Word, that God owns all things, but gave the earth to be under the dominion of man for a certain set time period. It is evident that there are many things contrary to the will of God happening in the earth. First Peter 5:8 says, "Be sober, be vigilant, because your adversary, the devil, as a roaring lion, walketh about, seeking whom he may devour." Verse 9 says, we are to "resist him steadfast in the faith." And John 10:10 says, "The thief cometh not, but for to steal, and to kill and to destroy: I am come that they might have life, and that they might have it more abundantly." Whatever then is killing, stealing or destroying life and happiness, and hinders people from living Godly lives in the earth, is not of God.

"Love not the world, neither the things that are in the world. If any man love the world, the love of the Father is not in him. *For all that is in the world*, the lust of the flesh, and the lust of the eyes, and the pride of life, *is not of the Father*, but is of the world. And the world passeth away and the lust thereof: but he that doeth the will of God abideth forever" (1 John 2:15-17). If all that's happening in the earth was God's sovereign will, then He's responsible and no man is responsible for any crime. But this is not so, for every man will be judged "according to their works" (Rev. 20:12). John said all the corruption in the world *is not* of the Father (James 1:16-17).

During this time period, God will not go contrary to man's will and satan can't. Satan can, under certain conditions, attack, but he cannot overcome if we fully believe God's Word and boldly and consistently act upon it. It is a constant battle for the will of man. God, on the one hand, brings truth and preachers of truth. Satan brings lies, deceptions, traditions and religion. Now Jesus says, "*If ye abide* in Me and My words abide in you, ye shall ask what YE WILL and it shall be done unto you" (John 15:7). God's will then doesn't automatically happen in a person's life. But only when we believe His words, pray according to His will and act in agreement with truth, or when someone else believes His Word and prays for us. If it were the case, that His will was automatically done, all would be saved, filled with the knowledge of His truth, and we'd have a Heaven like place on earth, for we can tell by His commands what He wills (Gen. 1:31; Matt. 5:10). (See also 2 Peter 3:9; 1 Timothy 2:4.) But Scripture, putting the responsibility on man says, "*Whosoever* shall call on the name of the Lord, shall be saved" (Acts 2:21), and "whosoever *will let him* come."

So then man must use his will to cooperate with God before God's will takes place in the man's life. When Adam exercised his will to yield to satan's enticements, God withdrew, for He accepts the free moral agent's decision (Isa. 59:2). Adam then became dead in trespasses and sins (Eph. 2:1), and was separated from God (Eph. 4:17). We can see on the other side of things, that if a man repents of sin and his ties with satan, and calls out on the name of the Lord to save him, God then responds to Him and gives that man the power to become a child of God (Rev. 22:17; John 1:12; Rom. 10:13) and overcome the devil (James 4:7).

God wouldn't change what was done once He decided and decreed His plan (Gen. 1:26-27), nor did He will to, for man was created free and the way God chose to do it was the best way if man was to retain liberty of will. Scripture says, "with Him is no shadow of turning," He "changes not," He "will not alter what's gone out of His lips," His Word is "forever settled in Heaven."

By foreknowledge He foresaw all things and knew what He'd do to counteract the fall, so there was not the slightest chance of failure on God's part.

What God Can't Do

Now the critic, in not understanding God being righteous and therefore He must keep His own word, gets upset when a preacher says, "God couldn't do" something.

But there are numerous things God cannot do. "It is impossible for God to lie." It's impossible for Him to be unjust, get sick, have respect of persons, be immoral, break His own Word, become hateful, change, go contrary to truth, yield to fear, dabble in the occult, overlook sin, be pleased without faith, and a thousand other things.

Jesus, in His own hometown, "could there do no mighty works" (Mark 6:5-6). Was it God's will that the people be healed? Yes. Did they get healed? Just a few with minor ailments. Why? They wouldn't believe Him. So God cannot just do anything now in the earth because He is God. And He, Himself, in His infinite wisdom, chose to set it up this way. It was the only way if He were to really have free moral agents with Him in Heaven as His "sons and daughters" and not just robots. This doesn't mean God is subservient to man by any means. For what man can order God around?

Now we know God is the judge of all His creation, but God will not go against truth, or righteousness. God is His own Supreme Court and will not alter or break His own Word. So after the fall, God temporarily was on the outside. He could not just change what had happened. He truly did give men free wills. He truly did give them a limited time of legal rights to do what they willed in the earth. It is evident that the masses of people on earth are living contrary to what God wills (See Genesis 6:5), but for those who call on His name and invite Him into their lives He enters once again (Gen. 4:26; Rom. 10:13). Now that He's made man a *FREE* moral agent, He cannot just force Himself past man's will and make a man get saved, even though He wills it (1 Tim. 2:4). If that were the case, again, He'd make everyone get saved for "Jesus tasted death for every man, all nations, all the world, every creature, whosoever will," nor can He keep one saved who later chooses to rejects Him (Heb. 3:14; John 15:6; 1 Tim. 6:12; Col. 1:21-23; Rom. 11:22-23). So then once God has given His Word, He has no legal right to change it and go in a different direction, nor does He need to or will to change it for all He does is perfect and according to His own infinite wisdom and knowledge. It's the way it is because He knew this was the only way it could be if man was to retain his liberty of will and be the way God desired him to be in eternity.

Chapter 8

What About Jesus Christ and the Atonement?

What Did Christ Suffer?

The critic says, "faith teachers demote Christ." He says because a preacher said, "If you stood Jesus and Adam side by side, they would look and sound exactly alike," that the preacher is therefore demoting Christ to the level of a mere mortal. Is this really the case? What saith the Word?

First of all, Paul said that Christ was *"found in fashion as a man;"* "was made in the likeness of men" (Phil. 2:7-8). He took on the seed of Abraham and was made *in all things like His brethren* (Heb. 2:16-17); that *He was made a little lower than the angels for the suffering of death* (Heb. 2:9); He came in the *likeness* of sinful flesh (Rom. 8:3), and "He is not ashamed to call us brethren" (Heb. 2:11). Was Paul demoting Christ? Was Paul saying Jesus was nothing but a mere mortal man lower than the angels? No, of course not. But if you took what Paul said out of context like the critic does with faith teachers, and then not look at the other things Paul wrote, you could say the same things about him.

Jesus, the divine Son of God came here to identify Himself with humanity, and the Bible says, *Adam was the figure*, (the type or image) *of Him who was to come* (Rom. 5:14). He had made man so much in His image and likeness, God's own Son could, Himself, become a man and yet still be the Lord. Now of course, men who are sons of God by the new birth, do not at all compare to the eternal Son of God, for in His nature, He is divinity, He is divine, omnipresent, and omnipotent while we are not (Matt. 28:18). But when He came here as a man and walked on this earth, He limited Himself and was in all points, like you and I until after His High

Priestly work for our redemption was accomplished (Heb. 5:1-9). He hungered, He tired, He thirsted; He cried out to God in prayer (Heb. 5:7), and was in the days of His flesh in all ways like us with all our limitations, but yet by nature He retained His divinity (1 Tim. 3:16). We know He was God the Son, "God with us" and "God manifest in the flesh." But yet He was born into this world as a man and referred many times to Himself as "the Son of man." And Adam, who was created as a son of God (Luke 3:38), looked similar and spoke similar. Does that demote Jesus? Only in the mind of the critic, for the Lord God said, "Let us make man (Adam) in our image after our *LIKENESS*. . ." (Gen. 1:26). *So God created man in His own image* (reflection).

Not only did God create man in His own likeness, but Scripture says, that we are predestined to be conformed to the image of God's Son (Rom. 8:29-32), and that Christ will change our vile bodies to be made like unto His glorious body (Phil. 3:21), and when we see Him, we will be like Him (1 John 3:2-3); and we shall rule and reign with him; be seated with Him; God will dwell with us, and we'll obtain the glory of our Lord Jesus Christ (2 Thess. 2:14; John 17:22). We do not say anymore than God's Word says, but leave it just as it is written.

Are we wrong for believing God's Word? But the critic overthrows the faith of many who are not grounded in God's Word and is used by the enemy to hinder people from hearing God's message of faith.

Now we fully understand that man without Jesus is nothing. But Jesus came down to the earth as a man in order to raise man up that he might be seated with Him. So to Him be all the glory (Eph. 2:6).

Jesus then in His humanity, became, and was, in all points like you and I except He didn't have sinful flesh. His flesh came directly from the Word (Gen. 3:15; Luke 8:11; John 1:14; Heb. 10:5). He had to become man to represent man, so Paul writes the second man is the Lord from Heaven (1 Cor. 15:45-47). And "this man" offered one sacrifice for sins forever (Heb. 10:12). Is He man or isn't He? Scripture says He is (1 Tim. 2:5). But He's also more than man; He also is God's Son (John 10:36): Deity manifest in the flesh, the Christ, the "Son of the living God." (See also Matthew 16:13-17.)

Now I am not claiming that some faith teachers have never made some mistakes, but watch for critics who lump all ministers together and presume what one says, all agree with. I don't think this is so in any Christian circle or denomination. But some of these critics in their ignorance are used as a tool of the devil to attack and try to destroy good, solid works of God. Woe to him that sows discord among the brethren (Prov. 6:16-19). There will be no mercy to him who judges his brother without mercy (Rom. 14:4; 10-13; 1 Cor. 4:3-5; James 2:13; 4:11-12).

Now as God, Jesus could not be tempted for God *cannot be tempted* with evil (James 1:13), but as a man, He *was "tempted in all points like you and I yet without sin"* (Heb. 2:18; 4:15). As God, He doesn't grow weary (Isa. 40:28), but as a man, He did (John 4:6). As God, He could not grow in wisdom but as man He did (Luke 2:52). As much as the critic says he believes Jesus was man, he refuses to allow Him to be a man. Hebrews 5:9 says, "And being made perfect, (in human experience), He became the author of eternal salvation unto all them that obey Him."

Thank God the eternal Son of God through whom the worlds were made, came in the fullness of time to be made of a woman to save sinners (Gal. 4:4).

The Critic Then Says Faith Teachers Say, God Spoke Christ into Existence, Because One Has Said, "The Embryo That Was in Mary's Womb Was Nothing More Than the Word of God."

Again the critic's statement is ridiculous. Let's see now where the critic has missed it. It's not that God spoke the eternal Son of

God into existence some two thousand years ago, for He was the eternally begotten Son of God who came out from God and was with God before there was any creation at all (John 1:3). He is God of God. But what is said in the Word is that God, through the angel, sent His Word to Mary (Acts 7:53); (Luke 1:26-45). The seed that became woman's seed (Gen. 3:15), was the Word of God (Luke 8:11; 1 Pet. 1:23). It was this seed of the Word that Mary received by faith (Luke 1:38), and *the Word became flesh* (John 1:14). *A physical body* was prepared by the Word for the second person of the Godhead (Heb. 10:5). So the faith teacher was speaking of the fleshly body of Christ, coming from the Word, while the critic states that the faith teacher said, God spoke Christ into existence in Mary. I hope you can see there is a world of a difference here. Evidently, the critic can't.

Just as you received the incorruptible seed into your heart (James 1:18; 1 Pet. 1:23), and were born again by the Word and the Spirit and became a partaker of God's divine nature (1 Cor. 6:17), so Jesus in His humanity was conceived of the Word and the Spirit (Matt. 1:18-20), and partook of humanity (Heb. 2:14).

So it is true that the same Word that created all things also was used to produce the flesh body of the Son of God when He partook of humanity.

Also the saying that God painted a picture through the prophets of what His Son would do, and saying a body was brought about by God's Word, does not take away from the pre-existence of Christ. It is obvious that Christ was in the beginning with God (John 1:1-3), and through Him all things were made (Heb. 1:2-3; Col. 1:15-17).

Many things the critic attacks is because he can only feed on milk and not meat. (See 1 Cor. 3:1-3.) So then, Jesus is the eternal Son of God who was with God in the beginning, who, as planned before the foundation of the world came into this world in the fullness of time to seek and save that which was lost and to deliver us from satan's authority (Col. 1:13). He came to reconcile and redeem man by His death, life, shed blood, and resurrection

(Rom. 5:9-10; 3:25). To do so, He became man; He faced and conquered satan as a man and then was declared to be the Son of God, by His resurrection from the dead after sin's penalty had been paid (Rom. 1:1-4; Acts 13:32-33). He is the King of Kings and Lord of Lords, the beginning and the end through whom all things were made; the only Savior of the world, and there's no other name under Heaven other than His name, whereby men can be saved (Acts 4:12). This is what we believe!

What About The Atonement?

What price did Christ pay to redeem man? What happened from the cross to the throne? Did Jesus go to hell? Is Hades (hell) really paradise as the critics teach?

First of all, Jesus remained the Holy Son of God on the cross as He bore our sin in His own body on the tree. He had to have a physical body in order *to experience the consequences of sin in the flesh* (Rom. 8:3), and taste death and all of its sting for us (Heb. 2:14). Sin in the flesh, is what causes the veil (the spiritual separation) between man and God (Gen. 6:2; Rom. 7:18-25; Isa. 59:2; Heb. 10:20; Gal. 5:19-21).

Paul wrote in 1 Cor. 15:55-57: "Oh death, where is thy sting? Oh grave, (in the Greek, Hades or hell), where is thy victory?" *We see Hades and death thought they had the victory over man.* "The sting of death is sin. . . ." Now, where did Paul get this quote from? He got this quote and expounded a little on it, from Hosea 13:14 where the Messiah says, "I will *ransom them* from the power of the grave, I will *redeem them* from death. O death I will be thy plagues, oh grave, *(Hell), I will be thy destruction. . . .*" You will notice throughout the New Testament that death (both spiritual and physical) and hell always go hand in hand: both are the consequences of sin (Eph. 2:1).

There is only one Redeemer who could possibly pay the price and be a ransom for us all, and that person is Jesus. To mockingly say that He did not go to hell when the Bible says He did, is possibly to reject His redemptive work (Acts 2:27, 31). To say He didn't suffer after physical death is to negate the Word of God, for the Bible declares it both by type, (Jonah in the whales belly: Jon. 2 and Matt. 12:40), and also by Peter's preaching, that He was "loosed from the pains of death" when He was raised up from the dead on the third day (Acts 2:24). The fact is, Peter, on the day of Pentecost, quoting the prophesy given out through David by the Spirit of Christ concerning the Messiah, preached that Jesus said, "thou wilt not leave (in the Greek, forsake; abandon) My soul in hell, neither wilt thou suffer thine Holy One to see corruption" (Acts 2:27, 31-32). *In other words, neither death nor hell would have the final victory.*

Man's penalty because of sin is presently a death of trespasses and sins before physical death (a separation from God), and hell after physical death (Heb. 9:27). It's appointed unto men once to die (physically) and *after this* the judgment. Sinners are now incarcerated in hell for satan has legal authority over them. For mankind to be legally delivered from there, someone who's righteous must go and pay the penalty for sin and suffer the consequences of it. Remember, the Messiah said in Hosea 13:14, that He would be death's plagues and hells destruction. Why? To ransom us so that the gates of hell could not prevail against the church (1 Tim. 2:6). He would have to enter death's domain and conquer it for us.

Some people want to change the word hell and make it paradise or Abraham's bosom, but you cannot do that and be honest with God's Word. To do so is to handle God's Word deceitfully (2 Cor. 4:1-2). If Jesus didn't pay the full wage and penalty of sin, then there were things left out that you and I must still pay for. But thank God He paid it all.

These following Scriptures prove that hell (Hades) is a place of torment, and remember, we must let Scripture interpret Scripture, for it's all the same Greek word.

Now we've seen by combining 1 Corinthians 15:55 with Hosea 13:14, that Hades, or hell, grave as it's translated in the KJV, (but the Greek word is Hades), is a place of DESTRUCTION, not a place of comfort. As a matter of fact, there is not even one place in the New Testament where hell (Hades), is described as a place of comfort, but is almost always connected directly with *death* and it is revealed to be a place of suffering. We know death is an enemy (1 Cor. 15:26), and that satan had the power of death (Heb. 2:14), which Christ came to destroy by dying and rising again for us. And we also know He came to get the keys of Hades (hell) so that the gates of hell could not prevail against the church (Rev. 1:17-8). In Luke 16:23, when *the Bible describes the death of the wicked rich man* it says, "And in hell (Hades) he lift up his eyes being in torments." Scripture says, Jesus made His grave with the "wicked" and with the rich *in His death*(s). In Hebrew, the word for death here is plural (Isa. 53:9-10; Acts 2:24, 31). In Luke 16:24, it says the rich man was in torment in the flame. Verse 28 says, Hades (hell) is a place of torment, a place of pain. It is a place where sinners must go as a consequence of their sin and ties with satan because they are under the authority of darkness. Is this not so?

For sin put man under satan's authority (Col. 1:13). Now nowhere does it say that God exercised the authority of death and hell. If that was so, Jesus would not have had to go there to obtain the keys of death and hell (Hades) and God would have already had them. (See Revelation 1:17-18.) Both of these things are revealed as enemies (1 Cor. 15:26; Matt. 16:18). He has though, made Ghenna, which in the Greek means "lake of fire," "the lake of fire" and prepared it "for the devil and his angels" (Matt. 25:41). Furthermore, Jesus said, ". . .I will build My church and the gates of hell (Hades) shall not PREVAIL AGAINST IT" (Matt. 16:18). If God had the authority there, what is that statement about? Is Jesus working against His own Father? Of course not. It is evidently a place where certain demons and satan do have access to torment the sinners that have left their bodies, for the two evil beings named death and hell in Revelation 6:8, will have to give up the dead they've held captive (Rev. 20:13-14), and then *they too* will be cast into the lake of fire (Gehenna). The place prepared for the devil and his angels (Matt. 25:41). On the other hand, Abraham's bosom was where just men went who had faith in God and His Covenant. Angels had access there (Luke 16:22). It would be foolish for Jesus to say, "the gates of paradise or Heaven will not prevail against the church," or, "Thou wilt not abandon or forsake My soul in paradise," or to say that "Jesus was loosed from the pains of paradise," which you must do if you say Jesus was in paradise three days and three nights. Nor was that what He said. He said, "as Jonah was three days and three nights in the whales belly: so shall the Son of man be three days and three nights in the heart (center; core) of the earth" (Matt. 12:40).

Those who serve satan in this life will go to be with him to be tormented in the next life, for the enemy has authority over them because of sin, at least until the time Christ returns, and then satan himself will be cast into the bottomless pit (the deep) and later, the lake of fire. And all who have followed him, will later go there too (Rev. 20:13-15). Until that set time though, sinners who leave this life, are presently held captive by death and hell (Revelation 20:13-14).

Those who choose to serve the Lord, and make Jesus the Lord of their lives now, will now go to be with Jesus and be blessed by Him in the next life. The reason for this is that they are then under His authority and care. If thou shalt confess with *thy mouth*, Jesus as Lord. . .thou shalt be saved (Rom. 10:9). 2 Corinthians 5:8 says concerning Christians, ". . .to be absent from the body is to be present with the Lord." For those who accept Jesus then, the gates of hell have no authority over them, for Scripture says that Christ "delivered us from the authority of darkness" (Col. 1:13).

Now we know that Jesus came first to reconcile us to God and then to conquer death, hell and the grave. He partook of flesh and blood that He might experience all the consequences that came upon us because of sin (Heb. 2:14). Without a body, He could not experience the separation from the Father that sin in the flesh causes (Rom. 6:10). For remember, as He bore our sins *in His own body* on the tree, He cried out, "My God, My God, why hast Thou forsaken (abandoned) Me?" This was a separation between God and His Son because of the veil of sin in the flesh. Next, He died physically and finally. As Jonah was three days and three nights in the whale's belly, (which Jonah described as a type of hell; a place of torment), even so, did the Son of man have to spend three days and three nights in the heart of the earth. One person ridiculously wrote, Christ ascended back up to Heaven when He died physically. Heaven, friend, is not in the heart of the earth and Christ was raised up from the dead. He did not come down from the dead. There was no dead in Heaven at that time. They try and say Hades is paradise because the Bible says Christ's soul went to Hades (hell) (Acts 2:27, 31).

But Jesus said concerning those who refused to repent in Capernaum, that they would be "thrust down to hell" (Hades). Also, there are two evil spirit beings in the Book of Revelation called death and hell (Hades) who rode pale horses and they went out to kill (Rev. 6:8). Death went first and Hades followed him and gathered the prisoners. And at the end of Revelation 20, death and Hades (hell) were cast into the lake of fire. Why would God cast paradise, or good angels, into the lake of fire?

Now we know that Jesus went into the lower parts of the earth (Eph. 4:9-10). One area was the deep–the place where demons did not want to go (Rom. 10:7). As Paul wrote, "who shall descend into the DEEP"? (in the Greek, bottomless pit) that is, *to bring Christ up again from the dead?*" The deep here is the same word as bottomless pit in the Book of Revelation. It is a prison, a place of judgment (Rev. 20:1, 7). We also know, He was in hell. (Hades)

Isaiah 53:8 states, "He was cut out of the land of the living, for the transgression of My people was He stricken. He made his grave with *the wicked* and with the rich in His death (v. 8), (again the word for death in Hebrew is plural). . .see also again, Luke, *the wicked* went to hell.

Isaiah 53:10 says, *His soul* was *made an offering for sin.* Jesus said in John 10, that He would give His life (soul) for the life of the sheep.

In Acts 2 Jesus said, "Thou wilt not leave (abandon) *My soul in hell.*" So after three days and nights, the Spirit of God raised

Him up (Rom. 6:4; 8:11). God loosed Him from the pains of death (Acts 2:24), for it was not possible that He should be held by it. Death then, lost its dominion over Him and all who would accept Him and His saving work. (See Romans 6:9.) After He arose He said, "I am He that liveth and became dead, and behold, I am alive forevermore. Amen, and have *the KEYS* of hell (Hades) and death" (Rev. 1:18).

So then, He got the keys from someone. We know that satan *had* the authority over death and we saw that there is a spirit being called Hades (hell) that worked with the spirit of death, but notice Jesus had conquered death and hell for us so that the gates of hell could not prevail against the church and that death could be destroyed (2 Tim. 1:8-10).

In Revelation 20:13-14 we see at the end of the millennium, death and hell had to give up the dead (spiritually dead people) who were in them (in their prison house), and they were judged every man according to their works. And death and hell (Hades) were themselves cast into the lake of fire (Gehenna). So, as we've stated, they couldn't have been good angels.

Note: There is then a difference between hell (Hades) and the lake of fire (Gehenna). Satan has never had authority in Gehenna.

Christ was the first one ever to come out of hell and was declared to be the Son of God by His resurrection from the dead. The prince of this world had been judged and the power of death was defeated by Christ's resurrection.

Now it was after Jonah spent three days and nights in the whale's belly that he then went and preached to the people in Nineveh. And it was after Christ was loosed from the pains of death, after three days and nights, that He preached to men in the unseen world and then led captivity captive by going by the Spirit across the great gulfs that were fixed between hell, Abraham's bosom and possibly other areas of the underworld (1 Pet. 3:18; Eph. 4:8-10). On one side was where death and hell operated, on the other side angels carried just people who believed and whose bodies died, to Abraham's bosom.

Remember too, when they came to get Christ to crucify Him, He said, "this is your hour and the POWER (authority) OF DARKNESS" (Luke 22:53). It was satan's moment, (his hour), but only for a short period of time (Gen. 3:15). After that Christ broke the bands asunder and rose again, and the serpent's head (power and authority over man) was crushed (Gen. 3:15). Note too, how the Old Testament sin offerings were burned with fire. Fire is the consequence of sin as is clear in Scripture.

Did Christ go to hell? The Bible clearly says He did. Will you, dear reader, listen to the skeptics who seek to water down everything the Lord has done for us, or praise and thank Jesus who paid the ultimate price for you, so that He who found you half dead, could raise you up again and pour in the oil and the wine? Even the ancient creed of the church in order to fight heresy said, "Christ descended into hell. . ."

Some have even thought that when Christ said, "it is finished" on the cross, that He meant the New Covenant was finished; that His saving work was completed. But was He saying that or is that just their interpretation of it? Let us show you from God's Word it could not have yet been complete, as far as the establishing of the New Covenant.

True, the Mosaic Covenant with its ceremonial laws and certain civil laws were finished, the law was until Christ. Christ is the end of the law (Rom. 10:4). The old came to an end. He was the final sacrifice. The veil was rent, signifying the old was finished with its shadows and types, and the reality of the new began with the shedding of His precious holy blood. But Christ's work as High Priest of the New Covenant wasn't finished until after His death; after the three days and three nights in the heart of the earth; after His resurrection (Rom. 4:25), and after His ascension into Heaven, where He brought His Blood into the Heavenly Holy of Holies as great High Priest, to appear in the presence of God *for us* (Heb. 9:24). It was after that, that He sat down on the right hand of the majesty on high, for the work was *then* finished (Heb. 9:11-12).

Now let's see the scriptures. It is obvious He spent three days and nights in the heart of the earth. He said so (Matt. 12:40). So He arose again from the dead on the third day. Death is more than just physical. He conquered it all for us and not just part of the curse that came because of sin.

On the first day of the week, just after His resurrection, Jesus appeared to Mary in the garden (John 20:16-17): "Jesus saith unto her, Mary. She turned herself and saith unto Him, Rabboni, which is to say, Master. Jesus saith unto her, Touch Me not; for *I am not yet ascended* to My Father: but go to My brethren and say unto them, *I ascend* unto My Father and your Father; and to My God and your God."

Notice what He said to her, "I have NOT YET ASCENDED UNTO My Father. . ." (this was three days after His crucifixion). She was not permitted to touch Him until after He, as High Priest, brought His blood into the Heavenly Holy of Holies, "Neither by the blood of goats and calves, but by HIS OWN BLOOD He entered in once unto the Holy Place, having obtained eternal redemption *for us*" (Heb. 9:12). Verse 24: "For Christ is not entered into the Holy Place made with hands, which are the figures of the true, but into *Heaven itself*, now to appear in the presence of God *for us* (Heb. 9:24). Remember, this was three days and nights after He died on the cross. When the holy, precious blood of Christ was brought into Heaven and God accepted it, the power of sin and satan was forever broken. God, through that blood, can now cleanse and bless the unworthy and make them new creatures in Christ. Every drop of Christ's precious blood points to His complete surrender of self-will to His obedience, His death, and all the suffering He endured for us. It's all represented in the blood, and God accepted it. The atonement was made.

When this final act had been accepted by God, and the Covenant was sealed with His blood, Christ, our High Priest, then came back down "the same day" (John 20:19), and they were then permitted to touch Him (John 20). At some point after this, He *sat down* on the right hand of the majesty on high (Heb. 1:3; Mark 16:19). The work of the New Covenant was finished.

So it's obvious they are wrong who say the *New* Covenant had been fully completed at the cross before He died, or that Jesus went back up to the Father immediately after His death, for Jesus said that that was not so. Scripture also says, we were reconciled to God by "the death of His Son." At the time, Christ said, "It is finished," He hadn't even died yet. Look at these Scriptures:

"For when we were yet without strength, in due time Christ died for the ungodly" (Rom. 5:6).

"But God commendeth His love toward us, in that, while we were yet sinners, Christ *died for us*" (Rom. 5:8).

"For I delivered unto you first of all, that which I also received, how that Christ *died for our sins* according to the Scriptures" (1 Cor. 15:3).

"But we see Jesus, who was made a little lower than the angels for *the suffering of death*, crowned with glory and honor, that He, by the grace of God, should *taste death for every man*" (Heb. 2:9).

"For as much then, as the children are partakers of flesh and blood, He also, Himself, likewise, took part of the same; *that through death* He might destroy him that had the power of death, that is, the devil" (Heb. 2:14). He outwitted satan who had the authority of death, when satan killed Him and allowed Him to enter the realm of death and hell. Christ conquered it and destroyed satan's power.

So the New Covenant couldn't have been finished at that time, nor was that what Christ meant. Again when He said, "It is finished" He hadn't even died yet. It was the Old Covenant that was finished. It was the old, with its shadows and types, that He spoke of. He knew that He, the true High Priest was beginning the real priestly work, the New Covenant in His blood. So the veil of the temple was rent from top to bottom, signifying the end of the old earthly sanctuary with its rituals and ceremonial sacrifices.

Furthermore, it says He was raised three days later, "for our justification" (Rom. 4:25). That is, when justification was made available to us (1 Cor. 15:17). He had to die and be raised again so that we too could be raised. *All of our redemption experience is tied up with His experience.* The Bible says we were identified "with Him."

True, the offering of Jesus on the cross sealed satan's doom and defeat for Christ hung there, the just for the unjust, His body torn, His blood shed, as the sacrifice for our sins. Certainly the shedding of His blood was precious to God as He died the death of the cross as the Lamb of God, but He still had to legally defeat satan, death and hell for us (Heb. 2:14). So there are two sides to the same coin, so to speak. Christ went to the cross to satisfy God's broken law (Gal. 3:13), then entered death and hell for us, for sin had sold us into slavery (Rev. 1:17-18); (Col. 1:13; Heb. 2:14).

Had satan known that Jesus was not only the last sacrifice of the Old Covenant, but also going to establish a New Covenant in His own blood, He would "not have crucified the Lord of glory" (1 Cor. 2:8; John 14:30; Luke 22:53; Acts 2:23).

So the old was finished and the new began. The cross was the pivot point—the meeting place—where the middle wall of partition between Jew and Gentile was torn down, (Eph. 2:11-16), and where the devil's doom was sealed, for there was no stopping it now. (Col. 2:14-15). Where the High Priestly work of the New Covenant began; where the final sacrifice (the Lamb) was slain; it's where the blood of God's eternal Son was shed and where the ceremonial law came to an end.

So again in review, let's look at some Scriptural facts, which point to Christ's sufferings:

(1) Jonah's awful experience in the whale's belly, where he said, "I

am cast out of Thy sight." The weeds were wrapped around him; his soul fainted within him; his life was brought up from the pit; the earth, with it's bars, was around him, and Scripture says, he cried out of the belly of hell, and God spoke and the fish vomited Jonah out. This was a type of Christ and His sufferings (Jon. 2:1-10; Matt. 12:40; Ps. 88).

(2) David prophesied that Christ went to hell and Peter preached it (Acts 2:25-31).

Verse 27: the Spirit of Christ said through David's prophecy, "Because Thou wilt not leave. . ." (again the Greek word for leave is the same word as forsake when Christ said, "My God, My God, why hast Thou forsaken Me?") So then, He said, "Thou wilt not leave My soul in hell, "his soul being sin offering" (Isa. 53:10). Again, in verse 31, "He (David) seeing this before, SPOKE OF THE RESURRECTION OF CHRIST, that His soul was not left (abandoned; forsaken) in hell, neither His flesh did see corruption." So His resurrection was out of hell then, and by Christ's own testimony it was AFTER three days and three nights. His resurrection was not out of paradise or Heaven. Would He really say, "You'll not abandon My soul to paradise" as some say? Come on critics, think about it.

(3) Paul said, Christ was raised up from "the deep" not lowered from paradise (Rom. 10:7). The deep is the place where the demons did not want to be consigned to. Were they really saying please don't send us up into paradise? "And they (the devils) besought Him that He would not command them to go out into "the deep" (the pit) (Luke 8:31).

Death and hell (Hades) are always connected in the New Testament, and are never a place of comfort, but rather a place of gates and bars. "The gates of hell (Hades) shall not prevail against the church" (Matt. 16:18). We've seen that it's a place of torment, "And in hell (Hades) he lift up his eyes being in torment (in the flames)," (Luke 16:22-28). It is guarded over by two spirits called Death and Hell (Hades), "and I looked and behold a pale horse; and *his name that sat on him* was death and hell (Hades) followed with him and power was given THEM" (Rev. 6:8). Evidently sinners are held there as prisoners in this place of torment by death and hell (Rev. 20:13), and death and hell will have to let these prisoners go to stand before God at the great white throne judgment and then these spirit beings themselves, will be cast into the lake of fire (Rev. 20:14). So they must be fallen angels (Matt. 25:41).

(4) The word for *deep* (abussos; abyss) that Christ was finally raised from (Rom. 10:7), is the same Greek word as "bottomless pit" where satan will experience incarceration himself. (He will reap what he has sown. Gal. 6:7) It's called a "prison" in Revelation 20.

The word *deep* then, of Romans 10:7 is the Greek word for "abussos; abyss," or in English, "the bottomless pit" (Rev. 9:1-2, 11, 17:8, 20:13). Certainly, the bottomless pit is not where paradise is located as the critic's theology must imply, seeing they say that this is where He went three days and nights, or they say that He went back to the Father; so according to their theory then, the Father lives in the pit. But away with such thoughts. Jesus, we know, had to go into the lower *parts* of the earth (Eph. 4:9-10). On the one hand, to satisfy justice (Rev. 20), and on the other hand, to conquer satan, death, hell and the grave (Acts 2) He had to pay both the penalty for sin and suffer sin's consequences of being under the authority of darkness (Luke 22:53; Rom. 6:9; Gen. 3:15; Heb. 2:14), to fully free man. So He had to deliver man both from the wrath of God and from the authority of darkness (1 Thess. 1:10; Col. 1:13) not just one or the other. Much misunderstanding comes when people see only one of these two things Christ had to accomplish.

(5) There is a fallen angel that has charge at the present time, over the pit (deep) and his name is *Appolyon*, which means "destroyer" (Rev. 9:11).

(6) Jesus entered into death and hell and said in Hosea 13:14, *"I (the Messiah) will 'ransom'* them (sinners) from the power of the grave; *I will redeem* them from death." To *redeem* means "to pay the full price, to recover by paying the ransom, *to clear by full payment"* (has to do with God).

Ransom means "to buy back; to redeem from captivity or slavery by payment; to pay for the release of someone who has been captured by an enemy." (This has to do with satan.)

Both of these words are also used in the New Testament. The law demanded full payment. Sin's wages was death; spiritual and physical. Spiritual death is separation from God. Physical death is the separation of the man from his body, and after this, comes hell.

The Bible says, Christ "gave Himself a ransom for all. . ." (1 Tim. 2:6). Galatians 3:13 says, "Christ hath redeemed us from the curse." We were held prisoners until the entire debt was paid. Jesus came to give Himself in our place. Jesus continues by saying, "O death, I will be thy plagues, O grave (Hades, hell), I will be thy destruction." This is the ransom. See again I Corinthians 15:55. The word *grave* here as we've stated, is "Hades" (hell). The cross reference is in Hosea 13:14 where Christ says, "*I will ransom them from the power of the grave.*" (from the power of hell) Thank God He did it. We need not stay spiritually dead now. We need not go to hell. We too can have resurrection bodies (Phil. 3:21).

(7) Jesus went to "destroy him that had the power of death, that is the devil" (Heb. 2:14), and to obtain the keys of death and hell, (Hades); (Rev. 1:17-18), so that their gates could not hold the redeemed of the Lord and prevail against the church. Women's seed (Christ) had come to crush the serpent's head and destroy satan's hold on mankind.

(8) Christ hath redeemed us from the curse of the law, (Sin is the cause while death and hell are the effect and curse of sin, Christ was made a curse for us. . .Gal. 3:13), for He hung on the cross, bore our sins, experienced a veil (separation), from His Father and so said, "My God, My God, *why hast Thou* forsaken (abandoned) Me?" Then He died and descended into hell as also the ancient creed written to combat heresy declares, to ransom us so we don't have to go there.

(9) When Jesus said, "Father, into Thy hands I commend My Spirit"

He was not saying that at that time, He was going to be with the Father, (as the critics think), for the truth declares that three days later, He told Mary He had "NOT YET ASCENDED" to the Father (John 20:17). But it was a statement of trust in the Father that His Father would not allow "His soul to be abandoned in hell, neither would His flesh see corruption" (Acts 2:26-32; Heb. 5:7-9).

(10) Animal blood could only purify the flesh for they are only flesh (Heb. 9:13).

But Christ went to the cross, spirit, soul and body to redeem man spirit, soul and body, and to taste death and its sting in all three areas that sin affected in the triune nature of man (Heb. 10:12). A full redemption had to cover all three areas of man's nature in order to set men free in all three areas of their nature. Christ had to suffer the full consequences and pay the full penalty that man must pay for sin in order for sin to be put away, and have it done with once and for all. For if He didn't pay for it all, there would still be some of it left over for us to pay.

(11) It was always that the sin offering's blood was shed on the altar, the sacrifice was then killed, the sin offering *burned with fire* and then the blood taken into the Holy of Holies as testimony that the sacrifice had been made. It was after it was accepted that the people were sprinkled with the blood (Heb. 9:19-22). It is called in Scripture, "the blood OF THE SACRIFICE," or "the blood OF THE SIN OFFERING;" "The blood of the Covenant." Now His *soul* was the sin offering as is stated in Isa. 53:10-12. The blood is the blood of the sin offering.

(12) His blood represents all He did in paying the penalty for our sins. Every drop points to His tremendous sacrifice and it has power to wash away all sin. Scripture says, we were "reconciled to God by *the death* of His Son, and He was RAISED FOR OUR JUSTIFICATION" (Rom. 4:25).

Our complete justification was provided for *when He was raised* from among the dead. He then, after His resurrection, brought His Blood into the Heavenly Holy of Holies as the blood of the New Covenant (Heb. 9:11-12), and with this blood of the sin offering, He obtained eternal redemption for us (Eph. 2:4-6; Heb. 9:13). So it wasn't yet finished until after His resurrection and after He ascended and went into the Heavenly Holy of Holies to appear in the presence of God for us. There God accepted His High Priestly work and the blood sealed the covenant.

(13) God had said, the serpent would "bite His heal" but that He would crush the serpent's head (Gen. 3:15). When they came to crucify Him, He said, "This is your hour and *the power (authority) of darkness*" Luke 22:53.

He yielded Himself into the hands of wicked men, who (as Cain was) were moved by the powers of darkness to crucify Him. Peter preached concerning Him that by wicked hands He was crucified and slain (Acts 2:23; 1 John 3:12). It was at that same time He yielded Himself as the last Adam, to him that had the power of death, that is the devil. Satan thought that he had Him (Heb. 2:14), but when Christ arose, He had conquered death, hell and the grave for us. And Paul said,

"death hath NO more (no longer) dominion over Him" (Rom. 6:9). So it must have had dominion during that short time when the power of darkness had its hour, and Christ bore our sins. Here's three more translations: "death has power over Him no longer"--(The Emphasized New Testament by J. B. Rotherham);

"death over Him no more hath Lordship"--(Twentieth Century New Testament);

"death's power to touch Him is finished"--(New Testament in Modern English by J. B. Phillips).

(14) Burnt offerings are a type of God's fiery judgment on sin (Rev. 20:15).

(15) As man, He suffered what men should have suffered. And yet He was declared to be God's Son, when God raised Him from the dead after sin's penalty was paid in full and satan had

been defeated (Heb.2:14). Jesus' whole redemptive work, seeing that all high priests are taken from among men (Heb. 5), was done as a man. He had to do it *all as a man*; and until the time He sat down, His whole life was dependent as a man on the Father. This is why in the days of His flesh, He cried out to the Father who was able to save Him out of death; for once He agreed to go through it, He could not change His Word (Heb. 5:7). It was not just physical death that caused Him to sweat great drops of blood. If so, why didn't the thieves on the cross also sweat blood, for they then would have faced the same thing He did? Was He weaker than mere mortal man? Of course not! He faced much more than just physical death, and He knew that this was the case. Never before in all eternity had such a dreadful event taken place, and to think, church, He did it for us. Wonderful Jesus. Let me inject something here. (We love Jesus our Lord, with all our hearts and would never teach anything that would take any glory from Him, who He is, or His redemptive work. Our purpose is only to stick with His Word and compassionately help His people.)

(16) Jonah preached *after* the three days and nights of being in the whale's stomach. (Jesus preached after being in the belly of hell three days and three nights. . .)

(17) Christ was loosed from the pains (in the Greek, birth pangs) of death (Acts 2:24), and raised from the "deep" (Rom. 10:7), which is a "prison" (Rev. 20:1-3, 7), on the *third* day.

(18) Christ's own testimony was, He became dead, was in hell, and there He seized the keys of death and hell (Revelation 1:17-18).

(19) Jesus abolished death and brought life and immortality to light through the Gospel (2 Tim. 1:10).

(20) Scripture speaks of the pains of hell, (Ps. 116:1-19), and the "*power of death*;" Jesus was loosed from the "pains" of death (Acts 2:24; Ps. 16:10).

(21) The judgment fell on the sinner's substitute. The Lamb's blood

was shed. They died at the altar and were cast into the fire as judgment on sin (Ex. 23:18; 30:10; 24:8; 12:13). The scapegoat was bound by a strongman and had to be sent into the wilderness out of God's sight where the wild beasts were. (See Luke 11:21-22.) (a type of demons and being sent to hell)

(22) The flesh that moves the sinner to sin, must be nailed to the cross and go to the grave; the soul with the will must go to hell (Isa. 53:10); the spirit must be alienated from God (Eph.4:17). This is the consequence of sin, as all Christian's know.

(23) Jesus, the Holy One, had to go through all that sin would have to go through, in order to put away sin by the sacrifice of Himself. So, Paul says, "For He hath made Him to be sin for us, Who knew no sin; that we might be made the righteousness of God in Him" (2 Cor. 5:21).

(24) He gave His flesh for the life of the world (John 6:51). His soul was made an offering for sin (Isa. 53:10; John 10:15). His Spirit was separated from His Father (1 Cor. 6:20; Matt. 27:46; 1 Pet. 2:24; Isa. 59:2), and He then went to hell (Heb. 9:27; Acts 2:23-32).

(25) Jesus never became a sinner, nor took on a satanic nature, but rather, it was the just suffering the consequences of sin for the unjust, but He did truly suffer and face all of the consequences of sin. If not, we would still have some of it to face ourselves.

(26) Sin offerings and burnt offerings go together.

(27) The sin offering was most holy, but it had to be killed and burned (Heb. 10:6; 13:11).

(28) Again, the scapegoat (also a type of Christ) had the sins of Israel pronounced on it, and then it was bound by a strongman and hauled off into the wilderness where the wild beasts were. It was symbolically driven out of God's sight (Jon. 2:4; Lev. 16:21-22; Luke 11:21-22).

(29) Jesus had to have a body in order to suffer all that sinful man was due to suffer. Without a body, He could neither suffer physical death, nor the separation from the Father caused by the sins in the flesh, which is the veil (Heb. 10:20; 1 Pet. 2:24; Isa. 59:2).

(30) Because Christ paid the full penalty to set us free, our spirits can now receive the life of God and our minds can be renewed. We can receive a resurrection body and thank God now no believer has to go to hell. The gates of hell (Hades) shall not prevail against the church. "The forces of death shall never overpower it" (Goodspeed's American Translation). "The power of the underworld shall not overthrow it" (New Testament: A Translation in the Language of the People by C. Williams). "And the might of Hades (hell) shall not triumph over it."

(31) To say that Christ went to hell as the scriptures teach, does not take away from the precious Holy blood of the sin offering, *the blood* of the sacrifice. We believe His blood cleanses, washes away sin, and that we have redemption through His blood (1 John 1:7; Rev. 1:5-6; Eph. 1:7), just as we also believe we were reconciled to God through the death of His Son, and He was raised for our justification. But there could be no redemption without the death, suffering and resurrection of Christ. He had to conquer satan and death also. It all is a part of the whole plan for saving man.

(32) Well-known ministers from Watchman Nee to Andrew Murray; books from the Wycliff Bible Commentary, which represent a wide cross section of American Protestant Christianity, to books written by Martin Luther, say similar things concerning Christ's sufferings.

(33) Spiritual death is a state of existence "forsaken of God" (Eph. 2:12). It is not a nature. It's a separation from God because of the veil that sinful flesh caused (Eph. 4:18). Paul spoke of sin in the flesh (Rom. 8:3; Heb. 10:20). Sin is much like serpent's venom, while Christ's blood is the only antidote. Satan, the old serpent, does have authority over those who are dead in trespasses and sins and does work in them, through the flesh and mind, but they don't become a part of him. But fallen men are considered his children by virtue of their own sins (1 John 3:10; Eph. 2:3), and he

being the father of sin is considered their father (John 8:44), and is the father of all that live lives of sin (1 John 3:8). "But the man whose life is habitually sinful, is spiritually a son of the devil" (New Testament in Modern English by J. B. Phillips).

(34) Christ remained holy on the cross, but suffered what a sinner must need to suffer. Death for awhile had dominion over Him (Rom. 6:9; Gen. 3:15; Luke 22:53; Acts 2:23). He was forsaken of the Father because of our sin which He bore, for God cannot look upon sin (Hab. 1:13).

(35) So Christ experienced this veil between Himself and the Father, but only because *He bore our sin in His own body*. It is not a matter of Him accepting satan's nature, as some may have thought, but a veil caused by our sin caused alienation from the life of God, the Father (John 5:26).

(36) The sin offering was to be holy, without spot or blemish, but the sins of the people were to be placed on it and it suffer the consequences of their sins (Isa. 53:6).

(37) The scripture that Paul wrote, "He who knew no sin was made to be sin for us, that we might be made the righteousness of God in Him" means, He was dealt with as sin needed to be dealt with, that we might be dealt with as righteous. No one could literally become sin, but one could suffer all the awful consequences of sin.

(38) To say that Jesus could not be forsaken of the Father, is to deny Christ's own words, who said He was. That He is God of God, having come out from the bosom (the very Being) of the Father, the real Son of the living God, reveals to us that God does have a Son called "the Word," who has His own will and who said He "came down from Heaven NOT TO DO *My own will* but the will of Him that sent Me" (John 6:38).

"And He that sent Me is *with Me*;" the Father hath not left Me ALONE. . .for *I DO* always those things that please Him (John 8:29).

"It is written in your law that the *testimony of TWO* is true. I am ONE that bears witness of Myself, and the Father that sent Me beareth witness of Me" (John 8:17-18).

"The Word was WITH God and the Word was God. . . ." (John 1:1). "I seek not *Mine own will* but the will of the Father which hath sent Me" (John 5:30).

Jesus prayed that His followers would "be one" even as He and His Father *"are one"* (John 17:21-26). And we could go on and on with dozens and dozens of more scriptures if space permitted, but we will not at this time.

So then, Jesus really is "the Son of the Living God" as the Word teaches, and because He came out of the being and bosom of the Father, He is also God of God, light of light, true God of true God (Heb. 1:8-9). "The express image of the invisible God" (Heb. 1:3). And as we've seen, and the scriptures do testify, He, God's only uniquely, begotten Son, came out from the Father and came into the world (1 Tim. 1:15; 1 John 4:4; Rom. 8:32). He has *His own will*, separate from the Father as He said (John 6:38), and experienced what He dreaded the most; to be separated from, and forsaken of, His Father, because of our sin (Matt.27:46). In all of eternity, never had such a thing occurred. This was the cup He dreaded to drink (Luke 22:42), and what caused Him to sweat blood. We may not understand all this but it is what the scriptures reveal happened.

One critic says, "God cannot be divided" or else God, as revealed by scripture, would cease to exist. But as we've shown you from scripture, God the Father, and His Son, were separated when Christ bore our sins in His own body on the tree. There was an eternal purpose, which He purposed in Christ Jesus our Lord (Eph. 3:11-12).

Will you listen to man's reasoning or the scripture record of what took place? *No where* does the Bible say if God and His Son were ever separated, God would cease to exist. And faith theology does not say that "only" spiritual death would do away with the curse as the critic implies it does, but His body also, was beaten, bled, and was nailed to the cross because of man's sinful flesh, and His soul too was made an offering for sin (Isa. 53:10). Again, He had to have a physical body in order to suffer sin's consequences for without it, He couldn't have suffered and died for man.

(39) Scriptures do speak of Christ being quickened, "made alive" from this state of death (Col. 2:11-13), and that those to whom Paul was writing, were quickened (*made alive*) *"with Him."*

It's obvious that He was not speaking of their physical bodies for none of them to whom He wrote had resurrection bodies yet, so he must have meant they were "made alive" from out of that state of being "dead in trespasses and sins" with Him. This spiritual resurrection out of this state of death, (this separation from the Father), as well as physical resurrection, was provided for by Christ who had come to destroy death in every arena. For us to be raised out of this state of spiritual death by His resurrection power, must be because He entered our condition and was raised by the Father out of it also. For all of our redemptive experience is directly tied up with His experience. God included us "IN CHRIST" and now by faith, what He experienced becomes ours, for it was His resurrection out of death, spiritual and physical, that opened the door of provision for our resurrection out of them (Rom. 6:4).

Spiritual death doesn't mean "cease to exist," or to become a satanic being, but it simply means a separation from God, the Father.

Ephesians 2:5 says, "Even when we were dead (spiritually) in sins, (God) hath quickened (made us alive) *together with Christ.* (in the Greek, Co-jointly together with Christ)." In other words, Paul is saying when He was made alive, we were made alive with Him. And so Jesus, the last Adam, was made a quickening (life giving) spirit" (1 Cor. 15:45).

"And to you who once *were dead* (spiritually) by reason of your sins and your uncircumcised nature; to you God gave life in giving life to Christ! He pardoned all our sins" (Col. 2:13);

(Twentieth Century New Testament translation).

The Bible says we were crucified with Christ (Gal. 2:20); died with Christ (Rom. 6:4-6); we were buried with Him (Col. 2:12); we were quickened together with Him (Eph. 2:4-5; Col. 2:12-13); risen with Him (Col. 3:1), and are seated with Him (Eph. 2:6). And in the future He will "change our vile bodies to be made like unto His glorious body."

What He did, He did for us. He included us. His experience becomes our experience by simple faith. After the penalty was completely paid for, He was raised from the dead by the glory of the Father (Rom. 6:4). He had to bear all the curse so that we could be blessed with "every spiritual blessing in Heavenly places in Christ" (Eph. 1:3).

(40) God spoke and Christ came forth. Do you not believe God could speak and Christ come forth? One critic thinks this is ridiculous. But let's see, "Jesus spoke and Lazarus' spirit came forth" (John 11:43-44). God spoke to the fish and it vomited Jonah out. (type of Christ's suffering-- Jon. 2:10)

Jesus spoke to the dead girl saying, "Maid arise' AND HER SPIRIT CAME AGAIN" and she arose (Luke 8:53-57). Jesus said, "Marvel not at this, for the HOUR IS COMING in the which *ALL that are in the graves* shall *hear His voice* and *SHALL come forth*; they that have done good unto the *resurrection of life*, and *they* that have done evil unto the resurrection of damnation" (John 5:28-29). *All* shall come forth in the same way. . . So why not Christ when He was raised from the dead? John said, He heard a voice talking with Him which *said, "Come up hither. . ."* and immediately, I was in the spirit and behold, a throne was set in Heaven, and One sat on the throne. . ." (Rev. 4:1-2).

It is a mystery to me, how anyone can read the Bible and not see what Christ had to suffer for us. Yes, the cross is important. It is where the great High Priest of the New Covenant offered Himself as the Lamb of God. Yes, the blood is the only thing that can cleanse away sin, it is "the blood of the Covenant," the blood *of* the sacrifice, the blood of the sin offering, and the power of redemption is in the blood. . .but included in, and also a vital part of His redemptive work, is His death, suffering, going to hell and being raised for our justification (Rom. 4:25). He could not have just taken His blood from His veins and cleansed us, it's that His blood represents sin judged and the penalty paid and satan conquered, therefore, it can now cleanse sinners. It can now wash away all sin (Rev. 1:5-6), and enable us to overcome the devil (the death angel); (Rev. 12:11). Christ, our Passover, was sacrificed for us (1 Cor. 5:7). Satan had shed innocent blood and sealed his own doom.

What is born again? It's to have this veil of sin removed and be reunited with the Father God (2 Cor. 3:16); to no longer be alienated from the life of God (Eph. 4:18). It's to receive the life of God, eternal life (Rom. 6:23).

Jesus said, "For as the Father hath life in Himself, *SO HATH He given* to *the Son* to have life in Himself (John 5:26). Christ willingly laid down His life according to the will of His Father (Gal. 1:4), that He might take it up again after paying for our sins (John 10:18).

If born again is having our sins removed, being raised to life by the glory of Father God (Rom. 6:4), and being brought back into fellowship and relationship with the Father because of sin's barrier being removed. In this sense, it is true as the Scripture teaches that Jesus was "the firstborn from the dead," (not first raised for many others were raised from the dead before this) "the firstborn among many brethren." His church is the "church of the firstborn," and He's the first begotten from the dead " (Rom. 8:29; Col. 1:18; Rev. 1:5; Heb. 12:23).

And so He is then, the Head of the church and the New Creation. Christ is it's Source, as well as the source and beginning of everything else in creation (John 1:3). He was willing to go through it all to redeem man and to do so Himself so that as the Scripture says, *"in all things, He might have the preeminence."* No other being in creation, could have the privilege of being the "FIRSTBORN" among many brethren, with all its firstborn privileges, or be the "first fruit" of the coming harvest. This place is His. He is King of all kings, Lord of all lords, Prophet of all prophets, Man above men, Teacher above all teachers, and in this too, He has the preeminence. Paul said, "And we declare unto you glad tidings, how that the promise which was made unto the fathers, God hath fulfilled the same unto us their children, in that He hath raised up Jesus again; as it is also written in the second Psalm, Thou art My Son, this is the day I have begotten Thee" (Acts 13:32-33). He is the "firstborn from the dead," the forerunner; the head of the body, the church, its beginning.

Colossians 1:18 says, "And He is the Head of the body, the church: Who is the beginning, the firstborn from the dead; that in all things He might have the preeminence." (Be first and head over all creation including the New Creation.)

The firstborn from the dead, "He is to the church, the source of its life" (Twentieth Century New Testament).

"It begins with Him, since His was the first birth out of death" (Knox Translation).

"He is its origin, the first to return from the dead" (New English Bible).

"So that He is first in everything" (Kenneth Taylor's Living Letters).

"That He, in all things may stand first" (Twentieth Century New Testament).

If we deny what He did for us in any area then that cannot be applied to us, for "according to *your faith*, it will be done to you." Let us be careful then, not to deny any of His saving work in any area (Heb. 9:28).

God had an eternal purpose which He purposed in Christ Jesus our Lord, His only begotten Son (Eph. 3:9-12). And a part of His plan was to "bring many sons to glory" to form the eternal family of God and household of faith (Eph. 3:11-15).

Hebrews 2:10-18 says, "For it became Him, for whom are all things, and by whom are all things, in bringing many sons unto glory, to make the captain of their salvation perfect through sufferings. For both He that sanctifieth and they who are sanctified are all of one: for which cause He is not ashamed to call them brethren, saying, I will declare thy name unto My brethren, in the midst of the church will I sing praise unto thee, and again, I will put My trust in Him. And again, behold I and the children which God hath given me. Forasmuch then as the children are partakers of flesh and blood, He also Himself likewise, took part of the same; that through death He might destroy him that had the power of death, that is, the devil; and deliver them who through fear of death were all their lifetime, subject to bondage. For verily He took not on Him the nature of angels; but He took on Him the seed of Abraham. Wherefore, in all things it behooved Him to be made like unto His brethren that He might be a merciful and faithful High Priest in things pertaining to God, to make reconciliation for the sins of the people. For in that He Himself, hath suffered being tempted, He is able to succor them that are tempted."

So we see that Jesus is not ashamed to call us brethren. For both He that sanctifieth (Jesus) and they who are sanctified (us) are all of one God. In 2 Corinthians 6:18 God says, "And (I) will be a Father unto you, and ye shall be My sons and daughters, saith the Lord Almighty."

Now we don't go around and worship one another just because the source of our new birth is of God, but we do worship Jesus for He is the Source of creation, and of our "New Creation" together with the Father and the Holy Ghost. He is the eternal Word who was with God and is God. It is just that as wondrous as it may be, He willed to become man and somehow as a man, go through these things for us to reconcile us back to God His Father in order to obtain a help meet for Himself, and He did so of His own free will. This takes nothing away from Him or His divinity, but rather magnifies His grace and greatness, and moves us to worship Him all the more, and to thank Him for His goodness.

We can do nothing without Him and are nothing without Him, but it is He who provided a new birth for us. Paul said, we are now to be joint heirs with Him (Rom. 8:16-17); to have a glorified body like His (Phil. 3:21); to be conformed to Him in every way (Rom. 8:29; 1 John 3:2-3), but it's all Him doing it for His creation. Wonder of wonders. Will you, Mr. Critic, condemn us for believing God's Word? Know this also, we know that the believer is by no means, an incarnation as Jesus was, for He was, and is, God by nature and was manifest in the flesh, and while the believer may have God dwelling in him by His Spirit (2 Cor. 6:16), the believer is not by nature, God as Jesus is, nor will the believer ever be.

Jesus was deity *by nature* who partook of humanity. We are humanity *by nature* and are simply, by God's grace and work, partaking of His divine nature. But according to Scripture, we could stop abiding in Him, have our good fruit wither away and be as a branch broken off that is withered away, and end up being cast into the fire (John 15:6; Jude 12). "For we are made partakers of Christ, if we hold the beginning of our confidence steadfast unto the end" (Heb. 3:14). Certainly then, we know these things and that it's a fearful thing to fall into the hands of the living God, and so we serve Him with reverence and Godly fear (Heb. 12:28-29).

Again, it's obvious also that Jesus remained holy and divine, but there are certain things peculiar to Him as a man, that are not peculiar to Him in His divinity. What saith the Scriptures?

Hebrews 5:7 says, "Who in the days of His flesh, when He had offered up prayers and supplications with strong crying and tears unto Him that was able to save Him from death, and was heard in that He feared." Did He ever do this as God?

Hebrews 2:9 says, "But we see Jesus, Who was made a little lower than the angels for the suffering of death, crowned with glory and honor, that He by the grace of God, should taste death for every man." Could this be so of Jesus as God?

There are also a host of other Scriptures such as Him being tempted (Heb. 2:18; 4:15), but God cannot even be tempted with evil (James 1:13). He grew in wisdom, but God cannot for He is perfect wisdom (Luke 2:52). His knowledge was limited (Mark 13:32). He had to pray to obtain power as a man (Luke 6:12-19), but yet in His divinity He has all power (Matt. 28:18). He was made a little lower than the angels in His humanity, but in His divinity He created the angels (Heb. 2:9). He learned obedience (Heb. 5:9). He grew weary, thirsted, and was hungry. It all clearly shows He really was here as a man in all points like us.

If we cannot comprehend all this, leave it to God (Eph. 3:20). Sufficient it is for us to know that the divine eternal Son of God truly became man for our sakes, for the suffering of death to redeem us. He did, somehow, experience life as a man without losing His divine nature, and He did, somehow, pay the full penalty of man's sin as a man before He brought His blood into the Heavenly Holy of Holies.

Now to say Jesus was never separated from His Father is wrong. To say He didn't go to hell is unscriptural. To say He was not quickened out of this state of death, is to not believe the Bible, which says He was (Eph. 2:5). You may not understand how it all could be, just as you cannot comprehend the other things connected with His humanity, but we must let the Bible speak for Itself. If you choke on meat, go back to milk, but don't get upset with those who eat meat and take God's Word at face value. Jesus is our Lord and Master and before Him we humbly bow.

Chapter 9

Another Look at Prosperity

Paul wrote to the church, "Upon the first day of the week, let *every one of you* lay by him in store, AS GOD HATH PROSPERED HIM."

Does the Lord have pleasure in the prosperity of His servants? (See Psalm 35:27.) Did He make Solomon rich or not? Did Abraham increase in flocks and herds and maidservants and menservants as the Scripture says, because he served God? Was David blessed when he served God? Did Paul write that God would supply all your needs *according to* His riches in glory by Christ Jesus? Did God tell Israel if they'd hearken unto His voice, "all these blessings shall come upon thee and overtake thee. . .?" Thou shalt be "plenteous in goods." Are all the promises of God in the Bible, yes and amen to those who are in Christ as the Scripture says? Will He in truth still "add all these *things*" unto you if you seek first the Kingdom of God and His righteousness? Yes! Amen. If "every good gift and every perfect gift comes down from the Father of lights," and "with Him there's no variableness nor shadow of turning" (James 1:17), it must be that riches and prosperity are good and perfect gifts or God would never have given them to Solomon, David, Abraham, and others. Nor would He have pleasure in the prosperity of His servants.

Now when prosperity is taught, the first place a person should prosper is in their spiritual life. You can own the world but without God it's worthless. "The prosperity of fools shall destroy them" (Prov. 1:32). On the other hand, John said, "I pray above all things that thou mayest prosper and be in health even as thy soul prospers" (3 John 2). Here we see we will prosper in every area of life as our souls prosper. How are our souls to prosper? "Receive with meekness, the engrafted Word," which is able to save your souls." Be doers of the Word and not hearers only." "Be not conformed to this world, but be transformed by the renewing of your mind." "Think on things good, pure, lovely. . . ."

God told Joshua to meditate in His Word, day and night that he might "observe to do according to all that is written therein, for then, (He said), thou shalt make thy way prosperous and then thou shalt have good success" (Josh.1:7-8). Jesus said, "Seek ye first *the Kingdom of God and His righteousness*, and *ALL* these *things* shall be added unto you" (Matt. 6:33). And John wrote, "*whatsoever* we ask, we receive of Him, *because* we keep His commandments, and do those things that are pleasing in His sight" (1 John 3:22).

So in all things, you must be living right in the sight of God, and doing what He said to do in order to prosper scripturally. He said, bring Him all the tithes, and He then promised a certain amount of prosperity and the devourer being rebuked from your goods (Mal. 3:10-12). He said give to the poor and He'd repay you again (Proverbs).

Walk uprightly and He'd not withhold any good thing (Ps. 84:11). Do what's right in His sight, keep His commandments, walk in love towards all your brethren, and He'd give you *whatsoever* you ask (1 John 3:22). Give and it shall be given to you again (Luke 6:38). Whatsoever a man soweth, that shall he also reap (Gal. 6:7). Paul, in speaking of finances said, "He that soweth sparingly shall reap also sparingly, but He that soweth bountifully shall reap also bountifully" (2 Cor. 9:6-11). And we could go on and on with numerous other, clear scriptures about God's will concerning His people prospering.

Now no faith teacher believes everyone's going to be a millionaire in this life, but God does will for you to have life and to have it more abundantly. He does have good news for the poor as well as for people's spirit's, soul's and bodies, because He loves people, and redemption legally releases us from the curse of poverty that came because of sin. "For ye know the grace of our Lord Jesus Christ, that though He was rich, yet for your sakes He became poor, that ye through His poverty might be rich" (2 Cor. 8:9). God's original plan for Adam was not poverty. There is a difference between believing God for a good supply and fleshly coveting to be filthy rich. I've not heard a faith teacher yet say, God wants you filthy rich, but He does want you to have an abundant supply and prosper, so that you can be blessed and be a blessing to others and help the work of God in the earth. Certainly, one can do more for the Kingdom of Heaven if he has more money, just as satan uses money for evil purposes.

One author criticizes the Faith Message and the teaching that God wants you to prosper, but yet he has a house estimated around seven hundred thousand dollars and drives a fine car. And yet he says he's against prosperity. I think it's about time he be temperate in all things and let his moderation be known to all men if he's so concerned about God's people prospering. I wonder who he says prospered him? Check out all those who, in their books, criticize Biblical prosperity. See if they have a small income, old car, and little old house on the poor side of town. If not, why not?

Being poor is no sin, but being poor has no special redeeming qualities in itself, except perhaps, that the person is not trusting uncertain riches. On the other hand, *they could* be envious when they don't have things, or prideful that they are poor. Notice, I said "could be," not "are." If you have an abundant supply, you can help more with Gospel work as well as be blessed yourself, and there is nothing wrong with that. God wants you to be successful. You are His child, but He doesn't want you coveting after riches (I Tim. 6:5-11). Put obedience first and the blessings will follow (Deut. 28:1-14).

I realize people can push a good thing that is in God's Word too far, and they stop being temperate, or moderate and then become a stumbling block. It's obvious, it has been a reproach in times past. Howbeit, Jesus said to His disciples concerning prosperity, that with it, there would come persecutions. Satan by no means, wants God's people to prosper but he doesn't mind if his kids prosper from all kinds of filthy deals. Now the critic criticizes some faith teachers in big ministries who emphasize prosperity, (because God has led them to teach His children this area of the Word), but he refuses to see the hundreds of thousands of dollars sent out by some of these ministries to salvation ministries overseas, or for that matter, the "hundreds of thousands" of people that have come to the Lord through some of these faith ministries. I'm aware of these things, but the critic (like the Pharisees of old), will find only what he's looking for and see only what he wants to see. He will not report on the fact that the larger faith ministries have seen hundreds of thousands and some even millions come to the Lord, through their ministries over the years. How in the world can the critic then say they are not of God? How many have been saved under the critic's ministry?

So then, prosperity in and of itself is not evil. God has streets of gold, mansions, and gates of pearl. He doesn't have some form of false humility that says if you're humble you'll live in a shack. So it can't be that He's against people being blessed. He said He'd make you plenteous in goods, but what He wants first is your heart. "For where your treasure is, there will your heart be also." And, "You cannot SERVE God and money." But it is not the money that is evil, it is the "love of money" that is evil. There are people who don't have a dime and yet covet money and would kill for it. So the problem if there is one is in the heart.

Now typically, unless a person is called of God to be a channel of financial blessing to the church, prosperity will occur step by step over time with a miraculous intervention of God here and there according to God's leading, His opening doors and also a person's faith.

Most faith teachers do not press the issue that God wants you to be rich, but that God does want to, as a good Father, take care of you. Howbeit God did make Abraham rich and we are His seed (Gal. 3:29). It's His good pleasure to give you the Kingdom. He does desire that you have good success (Josh. 1:7-8). I consider myself a faith teacher and teach on Biblical prosperity just a few times a year, but teach on winning souls much more. Perhaps though, I should teach on this area of prosperity more (Deut. 8:18).

Prosperity comes from God's blessing, and through you doing what His Word says to do (James 1:25), and by Him adding things to you as you seek first His Kingdom and His righteousness, but the truth is, it does come. You should have your needs met and things that you desire, that are consistent with a Godly life (Mark 11:24). *He promised that things* would be added to you, promised answered prayer (Matt. 21:22), and redeemed you from the curse, which includes poverty (Gal. 3:13-14).

Scripture further reveals that God desires that you "always having *all sufficiency in all things* may abound to every good work." But your heart must be to abound to good works and to store up treasure in Heaven. You must be working to promote God's Kingdom on earth and you must be willing to let it go if the Lord requests it of you as He did the rich young ruler whose riches had *him*.

Now I don't personally believe Jesus would have worn a Rolex, but there is nothing wrong if someone does. That's up to them, to do with what they have. I believe Jesus could and would, give one to someone who was faithful; someone who didn't covet one, but desired a Rolex. "Delight thyself in the Lord and He shall give thee the desires of thine heart" (Ps. 37:4). Now Jesus did, when He was here as the "Son of man," have all His needs met. He fed over five thousand people lunch. He paid His and Peter's taxes with a coin from a fishes mouth. He took care of numerous disciples who lacked nothing. He filled Peter's fishing boats with fish. So He never came to a place where He couldn't pay a bill or was lacking, but yet He was not extravagant either.

Now don't let the critics talk you out of believing God and trusting His guidance to be blessed. As I said, most of them who write books attacking the Faith Message have big homes, cars, plenty of goods and nice clothes. God is no respecter of persons. If they are blessed and say it's God out of one side of their mouth, while condemning others for trying to help people see God is concerned about this area of their life, out of the other side of their mouth, don't let them stop you. But in all things, use some of your finances to win the lost and promote God's work. This is the only thing that will last forever.

It is evident though, that the Gospel restores to man what was lost at the Fall. When Jesus came "to proclaim the acceptable year of the Lord," He said He came to preach "Good News to the poor." He was saying, "I'm the Jubilee." The fiftieth year was when people would be released from the bondage and oppression of debt and every man could return to His own possessions. We can return to living life as God meant it, for He's prepared a table before us in the presence or our enemies. (See Psalm 23; 1 Peter 2:25.) So financial breakthrough is also in God's plan, but eternal salvation is the more important.

Contrary to what the critic says, the prosperity message does not teach a lifestyle of self-indulgence and selfishness, but rather obedience and faith. If you obey God, do what His Word says to do about finances, bless His work, bless others, believe, and walk uprightly, God will answer your prayers, He will make grace abound toward you, He will open doors according to His own will, and add things unto you. He will, as He did with Joseph, cause His favor and blessing to be on your life, your children and all that you have.

To say that because a person teaches such things from the Word, that they are covetous and selfish, is to say you are "a judge." A position that only God can have. "To His own master He standeth or falleth." Romans 14:12-13 says, "So then every one of us shall give account of himself to God. Let us not therefore, judge one another any more: but judge this rather, that no man put a stumbling block, or an occasion to fall, in his brother's way." If only the critic would heed the Word of the Lord.

What About Preachers on Television or Radio That Tell You to Give?

It's OK for them to teach you to give from God's Word and even to ask for financial support if they've sowed to you spiritual things as Paul also said (1 Cor. 9:11). Now we believe the tithe, (the first 10 percent) belongs to the local church, (the storehouse of the meat of His Word), but offerings then are up to you. We do believe it is wrong though, to promise a specific miracle to everyone and then say, "send the money to me and my ministry." What should be said is pray about it, and if the Lord speaks to your heart, send the money to where God leads you to give, or give it to your church and God will bless you according to His written Word and your conformity to it. Or you can just decide you'd like to help a ministry out that is doing a good work and "whatsoever good thing any man doeth, the same shall he receive from the Lord." But no one should ever force others to give to "their" ministry. Teach them God's Word on prosperity, encourage them to give to God, but after the tithe, where they give to God is up to them. Just make sure you're sowing in good ground where the Word is preached and good fruit is being produced, or you'll not reap a harvest from God and you certainly don't want to sow finances in ministries where faith, prosperity, and God's Word are being ridiculed.

We know there may be certain occasions when the Spirit of God moves on an offering in a supernatural, special way. God told Moses, "Take Me up an offering" to move people to an act of obedience, and truly as people act in faith, God can then "make all grace abound" towards someone so that they "having all sufficiency in all things may abound to every good work" (2 Cor. 9:8). But normally, it's an act of obedience to the written Word itself.

Paul taught, "He that soweth (money) sparingly, shall reap also sparingly, he that soweth bountifully, shall reap also bountifully, every man according as he purposes in his heart, so let him give, for God loveth a cheerful giver."

One thing the critics do is they always spiritualize Jesus' words when they don't agree with them, or they say He was using figurative language. He, (the critic), says, that when Jesus says you shall receive "an hundred fold *now in this time*, houses, brethren, sisters and mothers and children, AND LANDS with persecutions *and in the world* to come eternal life," that Jesus was speaking metaphysically rather than literally, whereas faith teachers take Jesus' words to mean just what Jesus says. Those who have given their lives for the Gospel, have been blessed with multitudes of brothers, sisters and children in the Lord (1 Cor.

4:15; 2 Tim. 1:27; Matt. 10:42; 13:23).

"Then Isaac sowed in that land, and received in the same year an hundredfold: and the Lord blessed him" (Gen. 26:12). If you give up lands for Jesus and the Gospel's sake, the Lord will bless you back abundantly. He literally blessed Peter after He used His boat to preach from. So much so, that they filled two fishing boats with fish and the boats were filled and came to the point of sinking (Luke 5:1-7).

When seven loaves of bread were given to Him and a few little fishes, He literally fed five to ten thousand people and there were seven FULL baskets of food left. (See also John 6:5-13.) Then there is the little woman in the Old Testament who blessed the prophet with her last meal, and God literally multiplied the food for many months during famine.

Since Jesus is the same yesterday, today and forever, He can still perform the same type of miracles and bless and multiply that which is given to Him today. To say He cannot do similar things today is to change the Scriptures. Jesus further taught that if people will keep and do His Word with an honest and good heart, they can bring forth fruit, in some thirty, in some sixty, and *some one hundredfold* results (Mark 4; Luke 8; Matt. 13). This is literal. Results then, can come, even up to a hundredfold. It's all according to the proportion of faith and obedience to His Word. Now some things are rewarded here; others will come at the resurrection of the just, but where Jesus says you can receive a hundredfold and be blessed now, in this life, He means it. You can believe it and expect His Word to come to pass, provided you're living right and doing what He said to do (Rom. 1:16; 1 John 3:22).

The one thing that's taught is that you must give, give, give–to the poor, to God's work, to the church, and that this is how prosperity will come. This is not selfishness. It is faith in God's law of sowing and reaping. But if there's no faith, then neither will one cheerfully sow some of their seed (finances).

Faith teachers teach that you are redeemed, that Christ bore your sins, bore your sickness, bore your poverty (2 Cor. 8:9), and paid the full price to release you from the fall and its effects. But to experience it, you must believe God's Word, obey it, and conform yourself to it. (See 1 Peter 2:24; Matthew 8:17; 2 Corinthians 8:9.) We realize the comprehension of all this takes time. People vary; but faith can grow (2 Thess. 1:3). We are to grow in grace and knowledge, and as we continue on in His Word, the truth eventually penetrates and sets us free.

All of God's promises in Christ are yes and amen (2 Cor. 1:20), which simply means if you are in Christ, God says yes to all of them, provided you meet their simple conditions.

If we are redeemed from sin, we do not have to live in it. If we are redeemed from sickness, we don't have to live in it. If we are redeemed from poverty, we don't have to live in it. Sin, sickness and poverty came as a result of the fall, so the solution for them must be found in the redemption that is in Christ Jesus (Luke 4:18). But everything must be received by faith (Matt. 9:29; Rom. 1:16). You must believe the good news (Heb. 4:2; 3:19).

Now nowhere do faith teachers teach that poverty is a sign of spiritual failure. You can be abundantly blessed spiritually and still be lacking financially, but if you are in poverty there may very well be things you are either doing wrong, or not doing. It is possible to be destroyed financially because of a lack of knowledge, or to have been brought up with a poverty mentality, but nowhere does the Bible imply it's God's will for ANYONE to be in poverty. Remember, prosperity is a gift of God (Eccles. 5:19). Listen to God's Word. ". . .let every one of you lay by him in store as *God hath prospered him. . .*" (1 Cor. 16:2).

"Praise ye the Lord. *Blessed is the man that feareth the Lord*, that delighteth greatly in His commandments. His seed shall be mighty upon earth: the generation of the upright shall be blessed. *Wealth and riches shall be in His house: and His righteousness endureth forever*" (Ps. 112:1-3).

"And *the Lord shall make thee plenteous in goods*, in the fruit of thy body, and in the fruit of thy cattle, and in the fruit of thy ground, in the land which the Lord sware unto thy fathers to give thee" (Deut. 28:11).

"Every man also *to whom God hath given riches and wealth*, and hath given him power to eat thereof, and to take his portion, and to rejoice in his labor: *this is the gift of God*" (Eccles. 5:19; James 1:17).

"Let them shout for joy, and be glad, that favour my righteous cause: yea, let them say continually, let *the Lord be magnified, which hath pleasure in the prosperity of His servant*" (Ps. 35:27).

"*And Abram was very rich* in cattle, in silver, and in gold" (Gen. 13:2).

"And if ye be Christ's, then are ye Abraham's seed, and heirs according to the promise" (Gal. 3:29).

"But thou shalt remember the Lord thy God: for *it is He that giveth thee power to get wealth*, that He may establish (confirm) His Covenant which He sware unto thy fathers, as it is this day" (Deut. 8:18).

"*The blessing of the Lord, it maketh rich*, and He addeth no sorrow with it" (Prov. 10:22).

"But ye shall be named the priests of the Lord: men shall call you the ministers of our God: ye shall eat the riches of the Gentiles, and in their glory shall ye boast yourselves" (Isa. 61:6).

"And God said to Solomon, Because this was in thine heart, and thou hast not asked riches, wealth, or honor, nor the life of thine enemies, neither yet hast asked long life; but hast asked wisdom and knowledge for thyself, that thou mayest judge My people, over whom I have made thee king: wisdom and knowledge is granted unto thee; and *I will give thee riches, and wealth*, and honor, such as none of the kings have had that have been before thee, neither shall there any after thee have the like" (2 Chron.1:11-12).

God said all the silver and gold is His. Even though the ungodly may be carrying it around. *"The wealth of the sinner is laid up for the just."* Need we say more? Realize God gives riches and wealth, and He only gives good and perfect gifts (James 1:16-17). So we conclude that prosperity, God's way, is a gift from God. Who then, mocks this "prosperity message" from God's Word? Satan, for he wants the Christians to stay poor and under the curse, so that they will not promote God's work in the earth.

The Covenant-Keeping God

Scripture calls God the "Faithful Covenant-keeping God." No where, do faith teachers say God is a failure, or prone to make mistakes, as the critic says they do. Really, the critic twists everything that's said, interprets it according to his judgmental spirit, sifts it through his intellectualism, views it in the light of all the cult and occult material he's studied, and comes up with a mixed up conclusion.

So in reality, although he thinks he knows, he doesn't even begin to understand where most faith teachers are coming from. He doesn't know the difference between boldly acting on God's faithful Word and playing, as he said, "Let's make a deal." God doesn't make deals as such, but He does watch over His Word to perform it.

He says faith theology says, "Adam committed cosmic treason by selling his god-hood to satan, for the price of an apple and God was left on the outside, desperately searching for a way back in." No, faith theology does not say that.

Now let's straighten it out according to real faith theology and you'll see exactly how far off the critic's statement is.

God created man in His own image and likeness, and gave man legal authority and responsibility in the earth, for a fixed time period set by God. Adam was not a god, not divine, but created by God to be a son of God (Luke 3:38). He did commit an act of treason, (betrayal; breech of faith), which opened the door for satan to enter the world. God withdrew, because of man's sin, but God made man a promise that a redeemer, (woman's seed), would come and deliver man from the devil and the effects of sin. Now God is Almighty, omnipotent, omniscient, omnipresent, and has foreknowledge and so foresaw what would happen. That's why Jesus was foreordained *before* the foundation of the world. But what He saw by foreknowledge were the decisions men made by choice. He saw that free moral agents using their liberty of will, would use the good things He created, for evil as well as for good and so He determined a day when He would judge the world in righteousness, yet He also chose to provide a redeemer and determined that He would grant mercy, grace and forgiveness to every man who would use their will to repent and chose to believe in, walk with and obey His Son as Lord and Savior. He provided a way in His plan whereby He could blot out their many transgressions and where they could still retain their liberty of will.

God further determined He would not interfere or intervene in the lives of free moral agents, unless they used their wills to call upon Him or act upon His Word (2 Pet. 3:9; Rom. 10:13). Where the critic really misses it though is in not understanding God's dealings with man. He fails to recognize that God really created man a free moral agent and deals with man accordingly. He thinks of man as more of a preprogrammed puppet or robot with God pulling the puppet's strings.

It's not that men can make deals with God, it's that God has given men the opportunity and blessed privilege to use their free wills to believe Him and do what He says to do, and if we'll do so, He will fulfill His part of the Covenant (Isa. 1:19).

Is not a covenant a legal, binding agreement (Gal. 3:15)? Can we not take God for what He says and believe He will fulfill

His promises? After all, this is what has pleased God all the way down through the ages. So let us believe God's Word, His promises, and all He's revealed and let us choose to serve Him reverently with Godly fear (Deut.7:9). Can you now see how once again the critic has misunderstood what's said in this message of faith in God?

Where Does Sickness Come From?

Does God want you to suffer pain, sickness and oppression? The critic doesn't believe God will fulfill His healing promises.

The critic refers to a few whom he has found, who tried to believe God and died, because they didn't seek medical attention and he focuses on them. But what about the *multitudes* that did seek medical help and died? These he doesn't mention. Again, it's six of one and a half dozen of the other. If we were to go to a graveyard and find out the history of those who died, we'd find multitudes that had trusted medical science and died. On the other hand, there are multitudes that have found God faithful to His promise concerning healing (Prov. 4:20-22).

Think about this, if sickness is the will of God, you should never even go to a doctor to try and get it removed, for to do so, would be to try and hinder God's will in your life. Others say God gave us medical science now. Well, that's a poor excuse, because, as we've shown, multitudes die who go to medical science for help, and besides this, we've only had our present technology in this area for perhaps the past thirty years. What about the other 1900+ years? And why would God send sinners out to heal Christians and then charge them tens of thousands of dollars? Is it not supposed to be "freely you have received, freely give"?

Now let's once again see who brings sickness, and we'll go right to God's Word to see it. Acts 10:38 says, "How God anointed Jesus of Nazareth with the Holy Ghost and with power, Who went about doing good and *healing all that were oppressed of the devil,* for God was with Him."

Please notice that the multitudes Christ healed were oppressed by the devil. Matthew 8:16: "When the even was come, they brought unto Him many that were possessed *with devils*, and He cast out the spirits with His Word, and healed all that were sick." Here we see evil spirits were causing sickness.

Luke 4:40-41: "Now when the sun was setting, all they that had any sick with divers diseases, brought them unto Him, and He laid His hands on every one of them, and healed them. And devils also came out of many, crying out, and saying, Thou art Christ, the Son of God. And He, rebuking them, suffered them not to speak, for they knew that He was Christ."

It's clear here that the people brought those who were sick and diseased. When He laid hands on every one of them to heal them, devils came out of many of them. So devils then were the cause.

In Luke 13:10-16, you will see Jesus setting a woman free from a spirit of infirmity and curvature of the spine, and in verse 16 He said that "satan" had her bound. He cast out blind devils, deaf spirits, dumb spirits, spirits of fever, sickness, insanity. We will give many other references as we proceed.

Jesus said in His great commission in Mark 16:17-18: "And these signs shall follow them that believe: In My Name, shall they cast out devils, they shall speak with new tongues, and they shall take up serpents, and if they drink any deadly thing, it shall not hurt them, they shall lay hands on the sick and they shall recover."

James, under inspiration of God, wrote instructions to the church as a whole. James 5:14-15: "Is any sick among you? *Let him call for the elders* of the church, and let them pray over him, anointing him with oil in the name of the Lord, and the prayer of faith shall save the sick, and the Lord shall raise him up, and if he have committed sins, they shall be forgiven him."

But the critics refuse to believe these clear instructions from God's Word, saying healing passed away with the apostles, or God put that disease on you to teach you something. Both of these statements by the critics are cruel and rob people of faith in God's promises.

Every time the New Testament mentions sickness and disease, demons are right in the middle of it. In each commission Jesus gave any of His followers, He also commissioned them to heal the sick and cast out devils. Jesus taught that the "thief cometh not but for to steal and to kill and to destroy" but Jesus came that we "might have life and have it more abundantly" (John 10:10).

The critic says it's cruel to tell people God wants to help them. No. What is cruel is to tell people that disease is God's will for them, or that God won't put on you more than you can bear, or that God's doing it to perfect you, make you humble, or teach you something. Why do bad things happen to good people? Because the devil doesn't like anybody (1 Pet. 5:8-9). You may learn something in it but it wasn't God's will you learn it that way, but rather, through His Word (2 Tim. 3:16-17).

The God of the Bible says, "I am the Lord that healeth thee." The early church prayed that God would "stretch forth His hand *to heal* and that He'd grant that signs and wonders may be done *by the name* of His Holy child, Jesus" (Acts 4:29). Should *we* not do the same (2 Tim. 3:16-17)?

Now, sickness is not always because of someone's specific sin (John 9:1-3), but it can be. After Jesus healed one man He said, "Sin no more lest a worse thing come upon thee."

Romans 5:12 says, "Wherefore, as by one man sin entered into the world, and *death by sin*, and so death passed upon all men, for that all have sinned." So it's obvious sin gives place to the devil (Eph. 4:27). But some people are destroyed for a lack of knowledge, or others have been taught tradition like the critics teach, instead of God's Word, and so accept it as their lot in life

(Rom. 10:17). And there are other reasons in Scripture, but God is never to blame (James 1:16-17).

We thank God for medical science for even in the natural, men have somewhat learned to overcome the works of the devil.

Chapter 10

Do Faith Teachers Teach That Man Is Boss Over God?

Is Man the Boss Over God? One Critic Claims That That's What Faith Teachers Proclaim

But what is truly said? As we have pointed out, the Almighty God through Christ, created billions of miles of universe, created the angels, man and every living creature. He created stars so large that millions of our suns could fit in one; and created the proton so small, it would take twenty five trillion protons, laid side by side, to span a linear inch. Our own Milky Way Galaxy alone is about one hundred thousand light years in diameter. (A light year is the distance light can travel in a year, going the speed of 186,000 miles per second.) Even the smallest one-celled animal, the amoeba is far more complex than man's greatest achievements or super computers.

So could man possibly boss around a God who, through His own power and understanding, created all things visible and invisible? Of course not. So faith teaching could not be as the critic has said. But the fact remains that God, in His sovereign choice in dealing with man as free moral agents, has chosen (during this temporal time period), to work with man as *co*-laborer (1 Cor. 3:6-9; Ps. 8).

Just because we believe and obey God, and use the authority He's given us in Jesus' name, does not mean we are bossing God around, but rather, cooperating with Him in His own plan for man and doing what He, Himself, has told us to do. God's actions are dependent on man's actions only when it comes to individuals and certain things occurring in the earth at this present time, not when it comes to His overall eternal plan.

It's not that man could resist God if God didn't want it to be so from the beginning. But God by His own sovereign choice, chose to make free moral agents and deal with each person individually. He will not alter His Word or plan, for with Him there's no variation, nor shadow of turning.

Now there will come a time when each person will have to give an account of themselves before God and this, no human being can escape. If the Word of Faith movement taught we were equal with God, man could also then resist going to the great white throne judgment, but we all know he can't (Rev. 20:11-15).

It's in this life alone that God has given men the liberty to chart their own course. And "It's appointed unto men once to die, and after this, the judgment" (Heb. 9:27). But for now, they can choose to repent, believe the Gospel and obey God, or they can reject it. To that extent, God, in His sovereignty has given mankind sovereign choice over their own lives and destinies and He will not override their wills even though they go contrary to His will and desire for them (2 Pet. 3:9). He could have created us robots, or computers and programmed in us what to choose, but He didn't. If a man doesn't accept Jesus as Lord before they die, then they lose their soul and their right to choose God over satan. They are then locked into their decision forever (Rev. 22:11). So to say that faith ministers teach that man is boss over God is foolishness on the part of the critic. Father forgive him, he knows not what he thinks he knows.

One Critic Says That Because Faith Ministers Teach That You Need "Knowledge of God's Word to be Set Free, That That is Gnosticism

He implies knowledge of God's Word will not benefit you, and that knowledge of it is not really necessary to be set free.

But what does the Scripture say? Jesus said in John 8:31-32,

"If you continue in My Word, you are My disciples indeed, and ye shall KNOW the truth and the truth shall make you free."

". . .and you shall find out the truth" (Twentieth Century New Testament).

". . .and you will have knowledge of what is true" (New Testament in Basic English).

". . .you will understand the truth" (Moffatt's Translation).

". . .And the truth will set you free. . ." (New Testament: A Translation in the Language of the People).

Peter said in 2 Peter 3:17-18: "Ye therefore, beloved, seeing ye know these things before, beware lest ye also, being led away with the error of the wicked, fall from your own steadfastness. But *grow in grace, and in the knowledge* of our Lord and Savior, Jesus Christ. To Him be glory both now and forever, amen."

"Grace and peace be multiplied unto you through the knowledge of God, and of Jesus our Lord" (2 Pet. 1:2).

The knowledge of God's written Word rightly divided, is what is emphasized by faith ministers (2 Tim. 2:15). The critic says in trying to compare faith teachers with early century Gnostics, that faith teachers emphasize "knowledge" as a means of deliverance. But what he fails to note or tell his readers, is that it's "knowledge of God's truth" that is emphasized, not mere intellectual knowledge or human philosophy. Knowledge of God's Word is necessary for us to grow spiritually (I Pet. 2:2); to be a good workman (2 Tim. 2:15); to be free to serve God (John 8:31-32); to overcome the wicked one (1 John 2:14); to walk by faith (Rom. 10:17).

God told Joshua, "This Book of the Law shall not depart out of thy mouth; but thou shalt meditate therein day and night, that thou mayest observe to do according to all that is written therein; for then thou shalt make thy way prosperous and then thou shalt have good success" (Josh. 1:8).

Now the critic quotes one Bible teacher who said, "It is the amazing fact that there are two kinds of knowledge in the world today, and we have never contrasted them, or compared them. One is knowledge we have obtained through the five senses. The other is revelation from God."

The critic said, "this is pure gnosticism with its distinction between the physical and spiritual worlds." First let me say this. The critic neither understands what the preacher said, nor can his mind grasp even some of the simplest of spiritual truths. Let me explain what was really said.

The preacher simply said that the Bible is truth we've received from God. We could not have obtained the knowledge of the "why" of creation; of how God created; about angels; about God's plan of salvation; the precious Blood of Jesus and it's cleansing power, unless God *revealed it*. Paul said in Galatians 1:11-12: "But I certify you, brethren, that the Gospel which was preached of Me is not after man. For I neither received it of man, neither was I taught it, *but by the revelation* of Jesus Christ." The Bible came also as the Holy Ghost moved upon the prophets to speak (2 Pet. 1:20-21), through dreams, visions, revelations, apostles, angelic visitation and the Lord Himself.

The Bible is given by inspiration of God (2 Tim. 3:16-17), and did not come through the avenue of man's intellectual searching or by the five senses. That is all that's said. The critic, though, makes mountains out of mole hills and tries to lead the reader into believing that the Word of Faith message is saying things it does not say.

The critic then says, "such an artificial distinction leads us to believe that we live in two worlds; a spiritual one and a natural one. . . ." He says this because he doesn't believe you have a spiritual side to your nature. But Paul wrote, "I pray God *your* whole *spirit*, soul and body be preserved blameless" (1 Thess. 5:23).

Was not Jesus dealing with both worlds when He cast out (*of people's bodies*) THE SPIRITS with His Word (Matthew 8:16)? Or when He dealt with the devil who is a spirit (Matthew 4:1-8)? He said His disciples would see "angels ascending and descending upon the Son of man" (John 1:51). He had spiritual power upon Himself (Acts 10:38), and so did His disciples (Luke 9:1; Acts 4:33), and we could go on and on. And all this was happening when He, who existed in spirit form, came and entered a body of flesh and blood and walked here as a man in this natural, physical world. But the critic implies that if we think we are dealing with two realms, spiritual and physical, that that is cultic. Can he not read? Having eyes does he not see? Having ears can he not hear? Has he even been born again of the Spirit (John 3:3)? Is not God a spirit? Was not Jesus with the Father in spirit before He came here and took upon Himself flesh and blood (Heb. 10:5)?

After he criticizes faith teachers for saying, "we need to grow in the knowledge of God" he then says almost the contrary, that faith ministers look down on knowledge, (but we only mean his brand of intellectualism, which reasons away God's Word when one doesn't understand it). He says, "They have substituted the supernatural for the rational quite deliberately, 'as if the two are in opposition.'"

Let me say this. There are times when the rational is opposed to faith. Did you ever hear of walls of a city falling down because people shouted, or fire not harming someone who was cast into it? Did you ever see iron swim, or handkerchiefs bring healing to people, or the shadow of a fisherman bring deliverance to a multitude? Men being led by the Spirit, walking on the water, having children when they were one hundred years old: being translated as Enoch, or carried by the Spirit as Philip and Ezekiel were? We could go on and on and show you in the Bible that there are numerous things that happen in the lives of those who have faith in God and His Word that are beyond the realm of reason and in the realm of the miraculous, but the critic will have none of this. It must all be logical to him. It's OK that it happened in time's past according to him, but God *could not* do those things now, in our day, is his implication. Or perhaps he doesn't really believe any of the supernatural elements of the Bible at all.

Do you know what that is brethren? It's his lack of real faith showing, and he wants everyone else to be in the same state of unbelief that he is in. But let us "let God be true" and stay with the Word.

So then, revealed knowledge is knowledge God has revealed to us in the scriptures. Paul said, "But as it is written, Eye hath not seen, nor ear heard, neither have entered into the heart of man, the things which God hath prepared for them that love Him. But *God hath revealed them unto us by His Spirit*: for the Spirit searcheth all things, yea, the deep things of God. For what man knoweth the things of a man, save *the spirit of man* which is in Him. Even so the things of God knoweth, no man, but the Spirit of God. *Now we have received not the spirit of the world, but the spirit which is of God; that we might know* the things that are freely given to us of God" (1 Cor. 2:9-12).

In Ephesians 3:3, Paul wrote, "How that by revelation *He made known* unto me the mystery; as I wrote afore in few words."

Now we know that everything that we believe that we have received from the Spirit of God, must be first subject to the written Word of God. The Holy Spirit will not contradict Himself—He's the Spirit of truth. It is obvious in the above passage though that the Holy Ghost has *literally* come to teach us and open up the eyes of our understanding by His working in us, and He enables us to see things that we could not see without His assistance (See 1 Corinthians 2:14; John 16:13-14; 14:26.) Paul prayed that the church would receive the Spirit of wisdom and *revelation in the knowledge* of Him; (God) that the eyes of our understanding would be opened (Eph. 1:15-19). Even though they were born again and Spirit-filled, they still needed this to take place in them (Eph. 1:15-19). So revelation knowledge is the written Word of God, and also there is the knowledge of the written Word that the Holy Spirit illumines to a person individually, as the Holy Spirit enables a person to comprehend and understand what *God's intention* was when He inspired men to write a verse (Prov. 1:23). Jesus said concerning the Holy Ghost in John 16:14,15: "He shall glorify Me; for He shall receive of Mine, and shall show (reveal) it unto you. All things that the Father hath are Mine: therefore said I, that He shall take of Mine, and shall show (reveal) it unto you."

" But the Comforter, which is the Holy Ghost, whom the Father will send in My Name, He shall teach you all things and bring all things to your remembrance, whatsoever I have said unto you" (John 14:26). This is literal.

The critic then says that "faith ministers assume that the Scripture is not sufficient in itself for Christian life" and is upset because someone says the "Spirit led me," or "the Spirit told me." Now we realize there are some immature Spirit-filled Christians who, in their zeal and desire to be used by God, have said, the "Spirit said," when the Holy Spirit didn't really "say." To error is human but this does not do away with the Scriptural, Biblical fact that the church, as the Lord established it, was led by the Spirit (Acts 16:6-7), and the Spirit did speak to them (Acts 8:29). "Then *the Spirit said* unto him, Behold, three men seek thee. Arise therefore, and get thee down and go with them, doubting nothing, for I have sent them." The Holy Ghost also had a part in their counsel meetings. Acts 15:28: "For it seemed good to the Holy Ghost, and to us, to lay upon you no greater burden than these necessary things."

It is not that the Bible is not sufficient, but that being led by the Spirit, gifts of the Spirit, tongues, casting out devils, visions from the Holy Spirit (Acts 2:16-18), prophecy, angelic visitations and healing power in Jesus' name are *all a part of what the Bible says belong to the church*, so it is all a part of the "faith that was once delivered to the saints." *It is* all a part of the Word of God; It is Bible. He then, is the one who really does away with parts of God's Word. We say God's Word is sufficient, that it is more than enough and we do believe in the work and ministry of the Holy Spirit as is revealed in the Word. He simply shows he knows nothing about the reality of the Spirit of Truth leading a person. "Howbeit when He, the Spirit of Truth is come, He will guide you into all truth; for He shall not speak of Himself; but whatsoever He shall hear, *that shall He speak*: and He will show you things to come. He shall glorify Me; for He shall receive of Mine, and shall show it unto you. All things that the Father hath are Mine: therefore said I, that He shall take of Mine and shall show it unto you" (John 16:13-15).

Nowhere, have I *ever* heard by any faith teacher, that being led by the Spirit takes the place of the written Word, but only that it has its own purpose as revealed in the written Word. So in this also, the critic greatly errs, not knowing the Scriptures nor the power of God.

The critic is also upset because faith teachers don't preach on or against sin all the time. Let me say this. He really doesn't know because he's not been in every faith filled church. Teachers are set in the church to teach and instruct *believers* how to live and please God. When you preach to an audience of sinners as an evangelist does, then you can consistently preach on sin and then show them they need to be born again. The saint ought to know better than to be living in sin all the time. . .he has become a new creature in Christ and in Christ, is dead to sin. Although there are those in some denominations who have been wrongly taught that they can live like the devil and grace will cover for them whether they repent of sin or not (Titus 2:11-12; Jude 4). What Christians do need to be taught is that they are cleansed; they've been restored; God has given them the gift of righteousness; that they don't need to live a life of sin any longer. They need to be shown from God's Word who they are in Christ, and that sin no longer has dominion over them (Rom. 6:14); that victory is ours in Christ. In this area also "faith is the victory." And yes, we do give instructions concerning living right, for if a person doesn't live right in God's sight then neither would their faith work (1 Tim. 1:19).

The critic, in his book, further continues to label Bible believing, Spirit-filled Christians as the "new Charismatics." Let it be known to the reader that almost every one who has taken the time to write books and attack the Faith Message, is also against the beliefs of all Holy Spirit filled believers who speak in tongues as the Bible teaches, or at least against what they believe about the present-day ministry of the Holy Spirit in the lives of believers. It may help you to know this when reading their critical arguments, to know where *most* of them are coming from. Ask any of them if they have received the Baptism with the Holy Ghost after the new birth, like it was received in the Bible (Acts 8:12-17; 19:2; Eph. 1:13), and have spoken in tongues as the Scriptures teach and you will find, for the most part, that they will either deny the Biblical Scriptural evidence, say they don't speak in tongues, or take I Corinthians 13 out of context, twist it and say it's passed away. So it is they, who through *their* traditions make the Word of God void (Acts 2:4; 10:44-46; 19:2, 5, 6; 1 Cor. 14:2, 39; Jude 20), or they use some other excuse to deny the plain, written Word of God. Here is the real root cause of their lack of understanding the present-day ministry of the Holy Spirit. No one should have really entered the pulpit without the Baptism with the Holy Ghost (Acts 1:4-5; John 16:12-13; 14:21). Those that have done so are, many times, really the ones causing all the division in the body of Christ because of their lack of understanding of God's Word and the present-day reality of the power of God. Who then is really staying with what is written? Faith teachers. Of course ,we realize that there are many other wonderful men of God who are doing a good work for the Lord. Let us all just labor in the area of the vineyard the Master has assigned us and stop the squabbling.

Everything That Happens in Our Lives Whether Good or Bad Before the World Began "For Our Good."

He says, "faith teachers deny this." He then takes Romans 8:28 out of context as his proof text. Yes, we do deny it. Let me ask this: What about the multitudes that die and go to hell? Is that for their good? Did God plan that? How come then, the Scripture says that God is "not willing that any man perish." If God planned it all and He's not willing that any man perish, how come they do?

The critic of the Faith Message says, faith ministers are wrong for saying it is the devil who plans "bad things for our lives." Can he not read? Jesus said in John 10:10: "The thief cometh not, but for to steal, and to kill and to destroy: I am come that they might have life, and that they might have it more abundantly." In Luke 13:16 He said, "And *ought not this woman, being a daughter of Abraham, whom satan hath bound*, lo, these eighteen years, *be loosed* from this bond on the Sabbath day" (Gal. 3:29)?

He says it's all *God's* providence. According to him, there's no use in "resisting the devil steadfast in the faith" (1 Pet. 5:8-9), or in praying to change things. His theology is that man is not a free moral agent, that God planned for multitudes to go to hell in His plan for them, so the critic rejects Christ's redemptive work for every man, and then throws the blame all on God's sovereign providence. But the truth is, he knows much about his theology, but very little about the Bible he professes to defend, or God's sovereignty, but rather he is as the Pharisees of old. But he will probably never come to believe that that is the category he falls under, as they also refused to see. I don't say these things to be mean, but only because there are so many people who have been taught to believe things that are not in the Bible, instead, they've been taught the "commandments of men" and know it not. The reason for writing this book is to help people see God loves them and desires to help them in life, and to clear up things which have caused division in the body of Christ concerning the "Faith Message." This wonderful move of faith in God that our gracious Heavenly Father has given to the church (Matt. 7:11; Rom. 8:31-32).

The Critic Says Faith Teachers Go by Spiritual Laws and Are Therefore Metaphysical

What faith teachers really say is that God's Word is law (the law of life). If we obey it and do what it says, we will be blessed (Deut. 28:1-15). It is called the perfect law of liberty in, James 1:22-25. Paul said that "the Gospel is the power of God unto salvation to everyone that believes it," and spoke of the "law of faith" (Rom. 3:27; 1:16), and that we are free to believe or not believe (Rom. 8:2).

It is our obedience and conformity to God's Gospel that affects our lives, for He watches over His Word to perform it (John 15:7). But the critic says God predestined everything that happens. The killing, rape, child abuse, wars, suffering and misery, pain, poverty, and sickness. No wonder he's against the faith message which teaches Christians to believe God's Word and take a stand against the devil (James 4:7), for he doesn't even believe the devil himself is bad, but rather that God programmed and predestined the devil to do what he does. Fine bearer of Good News he is. He is a follower of a man, who, hundreds of years ago, taught and believed God predestined everything and that no man's will was really free.

One critic goes on in his book to deny the gifts of the Spirit, tongues, the signs that Jesus said would follow believers (Mark 16:17-18), and to deny any kind of scriptural "experience." Can you not now see where some of these critics are coming from?

He further calls Holy Spirit-filled Christianity, a "tongues and healing movement." But it's not a movement; it is the Word of God. It's the real Gospel. One critic that has written against the faith movement also says in his same book, that "Charles Finney rejected every major doctrine of Christianity," that Smith Wigglesworth's Pentecostal gifts were part of a mere movement. He says, "Finney's human centered ideas are in the Word of Faith movement:" saying that Finney (one of the greatest evangelists since the time of the apostles) is wrong for teaching that man has the ability to obey God. Not only that, he speaks out against the Keswich Convention, A. J. Gordon, F. B. Meyer, A. B. Simpson, Andrew Murray, D. L. Moody and R. A. Torrey, implying that they were wrong while he is right. He says that when Kathryn Kuhlman speaks of salvation being a "definite experience" and that you can know you are "saved," the critic acknowledges he doesn't know what she means by this. Does he not have the Spirit bearing witness with His spirit that he is a child of God (Rom. 8:16)? The fact is he later says he does not believe we have a spiritual side to our nature (1 Thess. 5:23; 1 Cor. 2:11).

Does he know the Lord (John 17:3; Heb. 8:11)? Has he been *born again* of the Spirit (John 3:1-8), or is he just religious? This receiving of eternal life into one's self, does cause a change and truly makes one a new creature (2 Cor. 5:17-18). "Therefore if any man be in Christ, *He is* a new creature. . . ." "A new heart also will I give you, and a new spirit will I put within you, and I will take away the stony heart out of your flesh, and I will give you an heart of flesh" (Ezek. 36:26). This is not a mere memory verse; this is reality.

Are There Spiritual Laws?

Let me ask this. Are there natural laws that govern gravity, chemistry, mathematics, and physics? Certainly. And these invisible fixed laws put here by God, govern this natural, physical creation, right? Well, the Bible also speaks of laws of God's Kingdom: the law of faith, the law of love, the law of liberty, and the law of truth. These are laws of His Kingdom. God's laws are not metaphysical as the critic implies. He says those of the faith movement are moved by impersonal laws and not by God. Let me ask the critic this: Does the law of gravity affect him? Could he ignore it and step off a ten story building saying these impersonal laws have no bearing on Christians' lives? Contrary to God's Word He does not believe your words have any effect in your life, even though Jesus Himself said in Mark 11:23, "For verily I say unto you, that whosoever shall say unto this mountain, be thou removed and be thou cast into the sea, and shall not doubt in his heart but shall believe that those things which he saith, shall come to pass, he shall have whatsoever he saith."

And Solomon wrote, "The power of life and death is in the tongue" (Prov. 18:21). Is the critic wiser than Solomon? Greater than Christ? He seems to think so.

So it is not a matter of manipulating God and spiritual laws with faith, but it is obedience by faith to God's laws of prosperity, health and truth as is revealed in the Word of God. It is being a doer of the Word. His Word is the "law of life." Never once in all my years of hearing the Faith Message, have I ever heard a faith teacher call God's laws, "metaphysical laws," as the critics constantly speak of. Perhaps it's they who are involved in an impersonal metaphysical form of godliness and religion with no power. Second Timothy 3:5 says, "Having a form of godliness, but denying the (miraculous) power (of God) thereof: from such, turn away." The word deny here means "refusing; to not know about or recognize; to disown" (Jude 3-4, 12, 16, 19-20).

The critic says men of God such as: Paul Yonggi Cho, the pastor of the world's largest born again, Full Gospel church, (about 700,000 members); Abraham, Jacob, Joseph and others, had to use metaphysical laws to bring about changes in their lives. But Cho has never said any such thing. Cho uses Biblical principles in his teaching, which the critic, (who can only digest milk), chokes on. If you only read the critic's book, you'd conclude that the critic was honest and only reporting what Cho actually said, but this is not the case. The critics always fail to put in the scriptures, that these various men of God actually use in their books and tapes, and then take parts of what they say out of context. Then he adds his own words and interpretations to it to make you think that what's being taught in the Faith Message, is according to what they, (the critic), says is being taught.

So realize that faith teachers teach the Bible and *never ever use the phrase* "metaphysical laws." It is the critics that do such. Out of the abundance of *their* hearts *their mouths speak*. The critic says, "according to Word of Faith teachers, God Himself, is subject to spiritual law and works through it." What is really said is that God does things a certain way according to His own perfect wisdom and understanding and because His way of doing things is perfect, God will not vary, nor is there any shadow of turning with Him. He does it the same way all the time. He's not subject to laws. He is the law of all that live, so He works according to His own perfection. He told us that, "*Man* shall not live by bread alone, but by every word that proceedeth out of the mouth of God" (Matt. 4:3-4). So we are to obey His Word, which governs His creation and thereby, walk in agreement with Him. He is then pleased because of our faith in His Word and watches over it to perform it (Jer.

1:12; John 15:7; 2 Pet. 1:3-4; Deut.28:1-3). Is it wrong to teach God will not go contrary to truth or righteousness; that He cannot lie or break His Word? I think not.

In the Word of Faith, God is all in all. He is the focus of everything. To worship Him, love Him, obey Him and do exactly as His Word says is the goal. We know He is God and we are forever His creation, and that in-between Creator and creation is an impassable gulf (Ps. 17:4). And we will join our faith with His Word and fight the good fight of faith against the enemy of men's souls.

Should We, As Christians, Believe in Miracles and Believe for Miracles From God?

The critic is one of those in unbelief who says no. But little does he realize that every answered prayer is a miracle. And the apostle John wrote in 1 John 5:14-15: "And this *is the confidence that we have in Him, that if we ask anything* according to His will, He heareth us, and if we know that He hear us, whatsoever we ask, *we know that we have* the petitions we desired of Him."

And also, in I John 3:22 John says, "And whatsoever we ask, we receive of Him, because we keep His commandments, and do those things that are pleasing in His sight." John believed you could get all your prayers answered, and so did Jesus.

Jesus said in Matthew 21:22: "And *all things*, whatsoever ye shall ask in prayer believing, ye shall receive."

Is it wrong to teach people God will watch over His Word to perform it, or to teach about answered prayer? Anything that would really help Christians, the critic either denies or implies it passed away or sows his seeds of doubt about it, and yet he thinks he's a preacher. A preacher of what? For whom is he preaching?

He then goes back and quotes men two to three hundred

years after the apostles, who had lost faith in the miraculous gifts of the Holy Spirit, and tries to prove by this that the gifts have ceased. He rejects Iraneus' testimony that the dead were raised, speaking in tongues and healing were still around in 120-202 AD. Iraneus was a disciple of the apostles themselves. It wasn't until the church became lukewarm that these things were lost.

The critic then says, what modern Christianity has forgotten is that "the primitive Christian demonstrated his faith by his virtues" implying that there was no place for miracles. But what saith the Scriptures? All one needs do is look at the Book of Acts and see the primitive Christians in action. Paul said that his preaching was not in enticing words of man's wisdom, but in demonstration of the Spirit and of power; *that men's faith should not stand in the wisdom of men, but in the power of God* (1 Cor. 2:4-5). There's Paul's testimony.

Yes we need obedience, walking in love, and all the fruit of the Spirit, but miracles also have their purpose. John 6:2: "And a great multitude followed Him, because they saw His miracles which He did on them that were diseased."

John 2:23: "Now when He was in Jerusalem at the Passover, in the feast day, many believed in His name, *when they saw the miracles* which He did."

Luke 10:8-9: "And into whatsoever city ye enter, and they receive you, eat such things as are set before you, and *heal the sick* that are therein, *and say unto them*, The Kingdom of God is nigh unto you."

Acts 4:33: "And *with great power gave the apostles witness* of the resurrection of the Lord Jesus, and great grace was upon them all."

Acts 4:29-30: "And now Lord, behold their threatenings and grant unto thy servants, that with all boldness they may speak Thy Word. By stretching forth Thine hand to heal, and that signs and wonders may be done by the name of Thy holy child Jesus." They didn't just demonstrate their Christianity by virtue alone. That would not have won the multitudes to Christ (Acts 2:22). It takes preaching with power (Rom. 15:19).

Acts 5:12-14: "And by the hands of the apostles were many signs and wonders wrought among the people, and they were all with one accord in Solomon's porch. . .and believers were the more added to the Lord, multitudes both of men and women."

Acts 8:6: "And the people with one accord gave heed unto those things which Philip spake, *hearing and seeing the miracles* which he did."

When Jesus raised Lazarus, John 11:45 says, "Then many of the Jews which came to Mary, and had seen the things which Jesus did, believed on Him." The critic refuses to believe miracles have any impact on people because he has NO FAITH in miracles. But Jesus said in Mark 16:17-18, in the Great Commission to His followers, "And *these signs* shall follow them that believe, in My name shall they cast out devils, they shall speak with new tongues, they shall take up serpents and if they drink any deadly thing, it shall not hurt them; they shall lay hands on the sick, and they shall recover." This is the demonstration given by the first Christians and the pattern for all Christians everywhere. No doubt the critic, like other critics before him, wants to erase these Scriptures, but God's Word stands sure. These signs still follow believers! The reason tongues, casting out devils and healing doesn't follow him, is because he doesn't believe Christ's Words.

The critic says instead of miracles, we are to believe Christ's Gospel and obey His written Word. But he doesn't grasp the fact that in Christ's Gospel and commission, Christ told us to preach the Gospel, cast out devils and heal the sick. *This is His Gospel* and it includes miracles and yet he doesn't obey it. As a matter of fact, in every commission Christ EVER gave His disciples, He told them to also heal the sick and cast out devils. Paul said in Romans 15:19: ". . .Through mighty signs and wonders, by the power of the Spirit of God, so that from Jerusalem, and round about unto Illyricum, *I have fully preached the Gospel of Christ.*"

The power gives witness of the resurrection of the Lord Jesus (Acts 4:33). Yes, it is the Gospel that imparts the faith (Rom. 10:17), but miracles open up some, to give heed to what is said. (See Acts 8:6.)

Hebrews 2:4 says, "God also *bearing them witness*, both with signs and wonders, and with divers miracles, and gifts of the Holy Ghost, according to His own will." It is still the same today (1 Cor. 12:28).

In John 14:11-12, Jesus says, *"Believe Me*, that I am in the Father and the Father in Me, *or else believe Me for the very works sake. Verily, verily, I say unto you*, He that believeth on Me, the works that I do shall He do also and greater works than these shall He do, because I go unto My Father."

Miracles in the New Testament didn't just take place through apostles, but also through men such as Philip, the evangelist and Stephen, the deacon (Acts 8:5-6; 6:8). There was also the unknown disciple who did miracles (John 9:38-40), the seventy, Ananias (9:10-17), plus others; for in Christ's commission to His church, the promise of power was given to all believers (Mark 16:17-18; Acts 1:8).

The critic says, Jesus did His miracles just to prove His deity, but let's ask this: If that's the case, then He failed to prove it in His own hometown, where He *could not* do any mighty works because of *their unbelief* (Mark 6:1-6). Now we know Jesus Himself, saw more miraculous results than His followers (John 21:25). The main difference in this area between Jesus and His disciples, is that Christ, in the days of His flesh as the Son of man, never doubted, but prayed, fasted and fully cooperated with the Father and the anointing of the Holy Ghost (John 20:30-31).

But much of the church today is like disciples as recorded in Matthew 17: "And I brought him to Thy disciples and they could not cure him." In Matthew 17:17-20 it says, *"Then Jesus answered and said, O faithless and perverse generation*, how long shall I be with you? How long shall I suffer you? Bring him hither to Me. And Jesus rebuked the devil, and he departed out of him, (proving it is still His will that all be healed even when His disciples fail), and the child was cured from that very hour." "Then came the disciples to Jesus apart, and said, *Why could not we* cast him out? And Jesus said unto them, *because of your unbelief* for verily I say unto you, if ye have faith as a grain of mustard seed, ye shall say unto this mountain, Remove hence to yonder place, and it shall remove, and nothing shall be impossible unto you."

Again, the reason "for failure" was *their unbelief.* The critic fights miracles, fights God's healing power and answered prayer, and implies if there were miracles today, it would take away from the uniqueness of the person and work of Christ. But it does not, for *it is Christ* working through His body, the church, in proportion to their faith. The reason the critic hasn't seen miracles through his life and ministry is *because of his unbelief* in these areas of the Word (Heb. 11:6; Heb. 4:2). Did Peter take away from Christ's uniqueness when multitudes were healed as his shadow overshadowed them (Acts 5:15-16)?

The written Word of God teaches us that God set miracles and healing in the church (1 Cor. 12:1-11, 28-30). It shows us that Christ commissioned the apostles to teach ALL nations and to command them to observe ALL THINGS He commanded them *even unto the end of the age* (Matt. 28:18-20).

Who are we to believe? God's Word or the critic who says that portions of God's Word have passed away? Realize this: Those of us who believe in the Gifts of the Holy Spirit, tongues, healing, casting out devils in Jesus' name are doing and believing simply what the Word of God actually does say. We are "contending for the faith which was *once* delivered to the saints" and we've found out it works. The critics though on the other hand, constantly try to tell you that parts of God's Word, God's Covenant and Gospel have passed away. But this is so only in their circles and in their minds, and the reason is unbelief (Gal. 3:5). See then, he is not contending for *the* faith once delivered to the saints, but for *his beliefs.* Don't let satan steal from you the living Word, through these modern day traditions of men. Naturally, satan would want to stop the Holy Spirit's operation through the church, and he does so, many times, through well meaning but ignorant men. The leaven of religious leaders is still the number one hindrance to Bible faith.

So miracles, as taught by the Word of Faith preachers, are not miracles they do of their own power, but miracles accomplished by the working and anointing of the Holy Spirit's power through the name of Jesus, just as the early Christians did (Acts 3:16; 10:38). Jesus and His Gospel are the same today as they always were. To Jesus then, goes all the glory when people get healed and set free. This certainly does not take away anything from Jesus, for it's His Word, His Spirit, His name, His anointing, His power and He can work through us as He said, "according to our faith" (Matt. 9:29). And He Himself said, "these signs" shall follow "them that believe" (Mark 16:17). How then could this take away from the uniqueness of Jesus? Can you not see all these attacks are only the reasonings of a man?

The critic in his book keeps on saying that God's power, if manifested, is metaphysical. He just can't grasp God's power is spiritual power, which comes from the indwelling Holy Ghost (1 Cor. 6:19). Acts 10:38 states: "How *God anointed Jesus* of Nazareth with the Holy Ghost and *with power,* who went about doing good and healing all that were oppressed of the devil, for God was with Him." The critic says, "The healing revival began with metaphysical cults." No, it began with Jesus. The critic believes he's a Christian; believes he is dedicated and yet he has NO power, so he reasons if others who are Christian have power manifested in their lives and ministry, it must be metaphysical, otherwise he would have it, but he doesn't realize how much unbelief he is in.

The critic tries to imply then that God now heals through doctors. First he says, God puts the sickness on you and then that He heals through doctors, who many times, have to let their patients die and charge their relatives tremendous amounts of money. Again, what then ever happened to God's principle of "freely you have received, freely give?" for this is what He told His disciples to do when He commissioned them to heal the sick (Matt. 10:8). Besides this, there are very few doctors who would ever give God the credit or the glory. Most doctors are sinners. Now do you see the patients of the doctors giving God any credit? So to say God now is healing through doctors, is to say God has sent out sinners to heal the church. Somehow, I think he has gotten things reversed.

He has God making people sick, then sending them to sinners so they can cure them, but they only can do it once in a while and then for large sums of money. And in his mixed up theology, he has made it so that He, (God), never gets the credit, but rather, man (the doctor), gets the credit and the glory. All you have to do to see the average doctor's resistance against God, is to go pray for a patient when the doctor's there. If he's not a Christian, he will be very upset that you're there. This is a fact. Now we do not belittle medical science and their natural fight to help man. We are thankful for the knowledge they've gained, with the brains God has given man. We commend them for that and their dedication to help people, and if a Christian needs to go to a doctor, that's fine. That's between them and God, but the average doctor is no more doing it for God's glory than the dump truck driver picks up garbage for the glory of God. They are doing it mostly for the money, (some though have sincerely dedicated their lives to helping people, which is very commendable).

Again, God's healing is always, "freely you have received, freely give," but this is not the case with medical science, which many times leave the families with hundreds of thousands of dollars in medical bills. The critic's attempt to leave the Gospel and revert back to the natural once again, is futile. He does it in every area. "But the natural man receiveth not the things of the Spirit of God: for they are foolishness unto him: neither can he know them, because they are spiritually discerned" (1 Cor. 2:14). Go to the doctor if you must, there is no condemnation in that, but don't say it's now God's means of healing people. His thinking is that we've gained such ground medically. Yes, but what about the past 1900 years when men had many foolish ideas about curing people medically? Dear critic, explain that. Your theory is shot through with holes.

The critic then goes aimlessly on to say it's superstitious to see a demon as the cause of sickness, but what saith God's Word? Please read these following clear Scriptures from God: "How God anointed Jesus of Nazareth with the Holy Ghost and with power, Who went about doing good, and healing all that were oppressed of *the devil*, for God was with Him" (Acts 10:38).

Luke 13:16: "And ought not this woman, being a daughter of Abraham, *whom satan hath bound*, lo, these eighteen years, be loosed from this bond on the Sabbath day?" The Bible says it was a "spirit of infirmity" (Luke 16:10).

Matthew 8:16: "When the even was come, they brought unto Him, *many* that were *possessed with devils*, and He cast out the spirits with His word and healed all that were sick."

Matthew 12:22: "Then was brought unto Him one *possessed with a devil, blind and dumb*, and He healed him, insomuch that the blind and dumb spake and saw."

Luke 4:40-41: "Now when the sun was setting, all they that had any sick with divers diseases, brought them unto Him and He laid His hands on every one of them, and healed them. And *devils* also *came out of many*, crying out, and saying, Thou art Christ, the Son of God. And He rebuking them, suffered them not to speak, for they knew that He was Christ."

John 10:10: "The thief cometh not, but for to steal, and to kill, and to destroy, I am come that they might have life, and that they might have it more abundantly."

These scriptures are sufficient for any normal thinking human being to know that the devil and demons are behind sickness and disease. The critic says, "if everything bad is from a demon, then it's not my fault if I do wrong, and I do not need to repent." No, you'd still need to repent if you've done evil for yielding to the enticements of the demon with your free will when you should have yielded to God (Rom. 6:16), but let us remember that this same critic has already said, everything good or bad, was predestined by God. And if what *He* said is so, then we need not repent of anything for all is preprogrammed by God and He's to blame. Why then does God, in the Book of Acts, *command men* everywhere to repent? If that's what He wanted, wouldn't He have programmed it so, if what the critic believes is true?

Do you see how contradictory the critic's theology is? Jesus healed people with Holy Ghost power (Acts 10:38); He is the same yesterday, today and forever (Heb. 13:8); and He told His disciples to do likewise (John 14:12; Acts 1:8; Mark 16:17-18). And He taught it was all through faith.

Matthew 9:29: "according to *your* faith. . ."

Matthew 8:13: "*as thou* hast believed. . ."

Mark 9:23: "if *thou* canst believe. . ."

"Daughter *thy faith* hast made thee whole." This is the Word: The Truth. Why believe ye the skeptics? The critic then goes back to the Old Testament where these things are more obscure, to try and prove that God, not the devil, makes people sick. But God Himself told us, "this is My beloved Son, hear Him."

"For Moses truly said unto the fathers, A prophet shall the Lord your God raise up unto you of your brethren, like unto Me, *Him shall ye hear in all things whatsoever He shall say unto you*. And it shall come to pass, that every soul, which will not hear that prophet, shall be destroyed from among the people" (Acts 3:22-23).

Paul said in 1 Timothy 6:3-4: "*If any man teach otherwise*, and consent not to wholesome words, even the words of our Lord Jesus Christ, and to the doctrine which is according to Godliness, He is proud, knowing nothing, but doting about questions and strifes of words, whereof cometh envy, strife, railings, evil surmisings." Jesus clarified everything for us and clearly taught that it was the devil who bound people with sickness (Luke 13:16); that it was the devil who came to kill, to steal and to destroy (John

10:10).

Jesus is the Way, the Truth and the Life. He came to do the will of God (John 6:38), and to speak that which the Father told Him to (John 12:48-49), and was manifested to destroy the works of the devil (1 John 3:8). This is why He healed all who came to Him (Luke 4:40, 6:17; Matt. 8:16). God only told Israel what would happen to them if they gave place to the devil (Eph. 4:27), and that He would now have to permit it because of their actions which were contrary to Him. They, by their sin and rebellion, put God in a position where He'd have to remove His hand of protection from them (Deut. 30:19; 5:29), and let them eat the fruit of their own ways. There was no sense in telling them all about satan and his works at that time for they, as a people, could not cast out devils using the name of Jesus like we can today. If we would listen to Jesus' teaching, look at His ministry, and then look back at the Old Testament, much light would be shed on what was really going on back there. Jesus revealed to us what was happening behind the scenes. But the critic refuses to hear Christ and says very little about the devil having anything to do with sickness or any problems at all, even though Christ's whole ministry was centered around bringing people deliverance from satan's sickness', diseases and torments (Acts 10:38).

He then tries to persuade people that the apostle Paul was sick and God refused to heal him, but realize this, it's this same Paul who had so much of God's healing power manifested through him, that handkerchiefs and aprons were brought from his body and placed on the sick, "and the diseases departed from them and evil spirits went out of them" (Acts 19:11-12). Nowhere in the Bible does it *say* Paul was sick.

He literally fights for the right to be sick and oppressed by the devil, and tries to persuade Christians to accept sickness, even in the face of the fact that Jesus revealed to us that sickness is from the devil. Who then is really preaching "a different gospel?" We are told by the apostles to use our faith and resist the devil (Eph. 6:10-17; 1 Pet. 5:8-9). The critic then goes over to another seemingly proof text of his and quotes Galatians 4:13-14: "Ye know how through infirmity of the flesh I preached the Gospel unto you at the first. And my temptation which was in my flesh, ye despised not, nor rejected, but received me as an angel of God, even as Christ Jesus."

But he fails to realize it was in this region that Paul was stoned and left for dead as is recorded in the Acts of the Apostles. So it was not sickness, but the result of persecution and stoning, that caused this infirmity in his flesh (Acts 14:18-21). Listen to Paul, "Are they ministers of Christ? (I speak as a fool) I am more; in labours more abundant, in stripes above measure, in prisons more frequent, in deaths oft. Of the Jews five times received I forty stripes save one. Thrice was I beaten with rods, once was I stoned, thrice I suffered shipwreck, a night and a day I have been in the deep" (2 Cor. 11:23-25).

The critic goes on to say that according to II Corinthians 12:7-9, the Lord refused to remove Paul's problem. But this is not what was said. The Lord pointed out to Paul that His grace and power that He gave him was sufficient (vs. 9), to overcome this. All he needed to do was believe it, (Rom. 5:2; Eph. 1:19). So Paul rejoiced because when he didn't have the strength in himself against the *messenger of satan* (2 Cor. 12:7), that Christ's power would give him the ability to overcome (vs. 10). Notice that what he suffered was for *Christ's sake*, not for his sake. See verses 23-30 in chapter 11 and you'll see all his sufferings. Not once did he mention sickness or disease.

Now we are not saying you cannot learn something in sickness. David learned not to go astray. But we are saying it is not God's will, nor does God send it; and God has told us to heal the sick and to resist the devil with our faith (1 Pet. 5:8-9). The critic goes on to say, God caused the man in John 9, to be born blind. He says God does these things in order to heal them. What glory is there in that? And what of the Scriptures that teach the devil makes people sick (Acts 10:38)? Peter said, Christ healed "*All* that were oppressed of the devil." This man included. Was Peter wrong? Who then, put the blindness on him? If God specifically sent the devil out to do these things as the critic implies, is He not also party to the acts? And what of innocent babies getting awful diseases? Is that God? "Do not err My beloved brethren. Every good gift and every perfect gift is from above and cometh down from the Father of lights, with whom is no variableness, neither shadow of turning" (James 1:16-17). Jesus said, "Every kingdom divided against itself cannot stand." If God sent sickness and then Jesus came and destroyed sickness, His Kingdom could not stand (See Matthew 12:24-30.) What about animals getting sick and diseased and being born crippled? They have not sinned have they? God didn't just let the devil attack them so He could heal them, did He (James 3:11-12)?

The truth of the matter is, there is really a devil who once was an angel of God named Lucifer, who used his free will to go *contrary* to God's will (Isa. 14:12-15). He really does come to destroy God's creation, the human, as well as the beast. He does walk about as a roaring lion, seeking whom, or what, he may devour (1 Pet. 5:8-9). Sin opened the door to him (Rom. 5:12; Heb. 2:14), and gave him entrance into this world (Luke 4:5-6).

So Jesus was sent as the "Son of man" to destroy the *works* of the devil and to fulfill the will of His Father, and when He had opportunity and people would believe, He healed them *"all."*

Notice the phrases the Lord uses in these following passages: Matthew 4:23-24: "And Jesus went about all Galilee, teaching in their synagogues and preaching the Gospel of the Kingdom and healing *all* manner of sickness and all manner of disease among the people. And His fame went throughout all Syria, and they brought unto Him all sick people that were taken with divers diseases and torments, and those which were possessed with devils, and those which were lunatic, and those that had the palsy, *and He healed them.*"

Notice, *"all manner of sickness* and *all manner of disease."* It was all oppression of the devil.

Acts 10:38: "How God anointed Jesus of Nazareth with the Holy Ghost and with power, Who went about doing good, and *healing all that were oppressed of the devil*, for God was with Him."

In this passage it's pointed out that they brought unto Him "ALL" sick people in that region and *He healed them.* Them who? All who were brought to Him. Another thing to notice is that right in the middle of sickness and disease, as in verse 24, devils are also mentioned. Scripture says, Christ cast out spirits of sickness (Matt. 8:16); Blind and dumb spirits (Matt. 12:22); Spirits of infirmity (Luke 13:10-16); Spirits that caused seizures (Mark 9); Insanity and suicidal devils (Mark 5). As a matter of fact, He cast out almost as many devils from people, as there were people who had diseases or sickness' (Mark 1:32-39). You can further see healing is for all by the following Scriptures. "ALL" (Matt. 8:16); "He healed them" (Matt. 15:29-31); "As many as touched Him were made whole" (Mark 6:56); "*All* they that had any sick with various diseases" were brought to Him and *every one* of them was healed (Luke 4:40-41); And the *whole multitude* sought to touch Him, for there went virtue out of Him and He "*healed them all*" (Luke 6:19); Healed every one (Acts 5:16); *others also* which had diseases in the island came and "*were healed*" (Acts 28:7-9).

Need we quote more? The same words, "all," "as many," and "every one" that are used for salvation, are also used for the healing of people's diseases. Not only so, but there are men of God such as T. L. Osborn, who have preached the full Gospel in the nations of the world to crowds of fifty thousand up to three hundred thousand people, and multitudes have been healed instantly of all manner of sickness and disease from insanity to leprosy right now, in our generation, as the Gospel is preached (Acts 14:7-10). This has caused multitudes to turn to the Lord. But send out a missionary without God's power and he may win a convert here or there, while the multitudes perish. What about this? How did these present-day Bible miracles happen then if they had long passed away? Did the Lord forget His healing power had passed away?

The critic would rather fight God's method of evangelism (Luke 13:14-15) and hold fast to his tradition. He ridicules the real Gospel and labels Christ's Gospel a "health and wealth gospel." Shame on him.

The critic reasons that if Christ died to provide both forgiveness of sins and healing for us, that "the logical conclusion is that if one gets sick, he really has not had his sins forgiven." But this conclusion is unreasonable, for he yet fails to see and understand Christ's teaching on faith and the free moral agency of man. Jesus said, "according to *your faith* be it unto you" (Matt. 9:29). Each area of our redemption though, legally accomplished, is vitally experienced as we "walk by faith" (1 Tim. 4:10; Rom. 5:2; Titus 2:11; Eph. 2:8-9). He further fails to see that the "thief cometh not but for to steal, to kill, and to destroy." And that Christians can be destroyed because of a lack of knowledge of God's Truth (1 Tim. 2:4). Weakness' in the body then can also come because of heredity, overwork, and the lack of right food and exercise. These can weaken the body to where it's more susceptible to an attack. So you can be a good person and still have an evil spirit attack you physically, as in Luke 13:16, or as in the case of Job. Just as good people have had evil men attack them (1 Thess. 3:1-2), and it is no more God's will for an evil spirit to attack you than it is His will for an evil man to attack you.

Also then a person can accept God's Word on forgiveness and be blessed, and at the same time, use their free will as the critic does, to reject healing and it will be unto them, "according to their faith," in proportion to how much they believe God's Word (Rom. 1:16). Shall we say then, if one is saved from sin, they could no longer sin (I John 2:1)?

Must We Have Faith to be Healed?

The critic says, "the answer is an ecstatic NO!" He says that "vaccinations work whether one believes them or not." True, but God is not a vaccination and His Word says, "without faith it is impossible to please Him" (Heb. 11:6). This could not be said about vaccinations. Jesus said, "Daughter, *thy faith* hath made thee whole" (James 1:6-7).

But the critic says *no*, one doesn't need to believe, for if it's God's will, He will just do it. But what does Jesus and God's Word say?

"And Jesus said unto the centurion, Go thy way, and *as thou hast believed*, so be it done unto thee, and his servant was healed in the selfsame hour" (Matt. 8:13). (Not as Jesus believed, but as the centurion believed.)

Matthew 9:2 says, "And behold, they brought to Him a man sick of the palsy, lying on a bed: and *Jesus seeing their faith* said unto the sick of the palsy, Son, be of good cheer, thy sins be forgiven thee."

Matthew 9:22 says, "But Jesus turned him about, and when he saw her, he said, Daughter, be of good comfort, *thy faith* hath made thee whole. And the woman was made whole from that hour."

Matthew 9:28-29 says, "And when He was come into the house, the blind men came to Him and Jesus saith unto them, Believe ye that I am able to do this? They said unto Him, Yea, Lord. Then touched He their eyes, saying, *According to your faith* be it unto you."

Matthew 15:28 says, "Then Jesus answered and said unto her, O woman, great is *thy faith*, be it unto thee, even as thou wilt. And her daughter was made whole from that very hour."

And in Acts 14:7-10 it says, "And there they preached the Gospel. And there sat a certain man at Lystra, impotent in his feet, being a cripple from his mother's womb, who never had walked: the same heard Paul speak: who steadfastly beholding him and *perceiving that he had faith to be healed*, said with a loud voice, Stand upright on thy feet. And he leaped and walked."

Now it is the rule that the free moral agent have faith to be healed himself, but there are exceptions. The elders can pray "the prayer *of faith*" to get the sick one healed (James 5:14-15). A believer can use the name of Jesus in faith for a sick one. "And His name *through faith in His name*, hath made this man strong, whom ye see and know, yea, the faith which is by Him hath given him this perfect soundness in the presence of you all" (Acts 3:16).

In every case though, someone is exercising faith on earth. The critic goes on to give a list of miracles where he feels no faith was exercised because it is not specifically mentioned that faith was exercised. But if you look at each situation, you will see that their actions, or someone else's actions involved reveal that they were exercising faith. He criticizes faith because he believes God predestines everything and really doesn't believe men can choose to believe God. He says, "Even Kathryn Kuhlman had to admit that some people were healed without faith." He then gives an example of a man who was healed in her service who said he didn't have faith.

Well at least here the critic admits there were supernatural healings from God going on in Miss Kuhlman's meetings, but only because, at this point, it is to his advantage (seemingly) to do so. But this is not hard to answer. Miss Kuhlman and thousands of others in those meetings, had faith and were believing in miracles. The man possibly had a relative or friend bring him and that was an act of faith.

Matthew 8:16: "They brought"

Matthew 4:24: "They brought"

Mark 4:32: "They brought"

The very fact that someone brought him there to be healed, or he came to the meeting, could have opened the door for his miracle. Besides this, hours and hours of prayer goes on for the sick and suffering before these meetings. So it is still faith that opens the door for the miracles, one way or another.

"He therefore, that ministereth to you the Spirit, and worketh miracles among you, doeth he it by the works of the law, or by the hearing of faith" (Gal. 3:5)? Certainly he does it in response to faith, as the Scriptures most certainly testify.

The critic goes on to say in Luke 17:12-19, all ten lepers were healed, but only one had faith. Here again, his ignorance shows up, for *all ten of them* acted on Jesus' Word and went to show themselves to the priest before they saw anything. That, my friend, was *"faith."* All were healed but not all were as thankful. In this life which is given to men, we are told, "all things are possible *if thou* canst believe."

The Point of Contact

The critic, in not understanding the simplest things about God's teaching on faith, criticizes some men of God for teaching about a point of contact. What is a point of contact? It is the point when you begin to believe God's promise, the point you release your faith and start believing for your healing or answered prayer. The critic says this is magical and very dangerous. How little he really knows God's Word, for he doesn't know the difference between magic and faith. There is in Scripture, the doctrine of "laying on of hands" (Heb. 6:2).

Jesus laid hands on people to heal them (Luke 4:40). Jairus asked the Lord to come and lay hands on his daughter that she might be healed and live (Mark 5:23). Jesus said believers would "lay hands on the sick and they would recover" (Mark 16:17-18). The Apostles laid hands on people to heal them. Handkerchiefs and aprons were brought from Paul's body and laid on the sick and the sick were healed (Acts 19:11-12). At some point, a person must "believe they receive it," before they can have it (Mark 11:24).

This is all that's meant by the point of contact. Jesus told a man, "Go wash in the pool of Siloam," and the man went and did as Christ said and came seeing.

We could quote other instances also, but these are sufficient to help a person who's open to God's truth to see what preachers mean by a "point of contact." Faith is then released in God and His promise.

Chapter 11

Faith In Faith or Faith In God?

The Critic Says, as Though He's An Authority on the Subject, That "In the Word of Faith Movement, Faith in Faith, Rather Than Faith in God" is What's Promoted

Again, the critic's ignorance of what he is criticizing is showing. For where someone like Reverend Kenneth Hagin writes a book entitled, *Having Faith in Your Faith*, he's not leaving God out, but only trying to encourage the believer that you can pray and believe God's promises and trust God, as well as anyone. You don't always need to run to this one and that one, asking them to pray the prayer of faith for you. Have "faith in your own faith," for God has also dealt to you "the measure of faith" (Rom. 12:3).

If someone were to *honestly* read Brother Hagin's book, you will see it's all directed towards faith in God and His Word, but the critic's view is tainted by his zealousness to prove others wrong who don't see eye to eye with his theology. He then quotes another *non* Spirit-filled believer who says, "If a person is healed merely because he believes he is healed, then the power is in his mind and God is merely a placebo to activate his belief."

But the Word of Faith preachers do not say you will be healed merely because you believe you will be, but rather because you believe God's promise or provision. "Through faith and patience (we) inherit the promises" (Heb. 6:12). There is a world of a difference here, but the critic wants you to view faith teachers through his critical eye and according to his misguided opinion.

The critic says, "faith healers will not tackle organic diseases such as broken bones, filling teeth, kidney stones, hernias." But I, myself, have seen or heard of all these things being healed. It's just that the critic has never heard of such things because of the circles of unbelief he lives in, but I do not believe he would believe even though he heard honest people testify of being healed of these things. For if he believes not the Scriptures in these areas, neither would he believe if one were raised from the dead in front of him (Luke 16:31). So if he does not believe the Scriptures which say these things shall happen, neither would he believe if it happened before his very eyes (John 3:10). He would reason that away also.

Also let me say this, it is healing through faith, not just faith. The "prayer of faith shall save the sick and *the LORD* shall raise him up" (James 5:14-15). "Then Peter said, Silver and gold have I none; but such as I have give I thee: *In the name* of Jesus Christ of Nazareth rise up and walk. And he took him by the right hand and lifted him up: and immediately his feet and ankle bones received strength. And *His name through faith in His name hath made this man strong*, whom ye see and know: yea, the faith which is by Him hath given him this perfect soundness in the presence of you all" (Acts 3:6, 7, 16). And this miracle really upset the religious leaders of their day (Acts 4:1-20).

The prayer of faith is a prayer of trust in God and His Word of promise. It is judging Him faithful as Sarah did (Heb. 11:11). This is not demanding God, but believing God will do what He said He willed to do, and this pleases Him. Now healings can be instantaneous or gradual. Jesus said, "shall recover."

Again we must realize, we cooperate with Him in proportion to our faith (John 14:12; Mark 16:17-18). When there is more anointing and Holy Ghost power operating through an individual who is full of faith, there are greater manifestations of God's healing power demonstrated. "And Stephen, *full of faith* and power, *did great wonders* and miracles among the people" (Acts 6:8). But not all Holy Ghost-filled believers who believed in healing in those days, saw these same results through themselves as Stephen and Philip did.

Also, an individual may receive faith to be healed from the preaching of the Gospel, and an instantaneous miracle can result (Acts 14:7-10). Then there were times when Christ's disciples couldn't get people healed even though it was God's will to heal them. The hindrance was their unbelief (Matt. 17:15-20).

Jesus' promise to believers is that the sick "shall recover" (Mark 16:18); not that it would always be instantaneous. Yes, the Lord's miracles were mostly instantaneous and of great power because He, like Stephen, was full of faith and was a man of constant prayer. He was the most yielded vessel to the Holy Spirit that ever lived, but He left us an example that we should follow in His steps. We now minister in proportion to our faith. It's the same way with evangelists who preach a salvation message. Some are more full of faith and anointing than others and they win more people to the Lord. "For he was a good man, and full of the Holy Ghost and of faith, and much people was added unto the Lord" (Acts 11:24).

Shall we criticize those evangelists that don't get the hard cases saved? Shall we say the new birth isn't for everyone because not all get saved when they hear a preacher of salvation? Shall we say, "if he'd go and deliver instantly the drug addict right before *my eyes* then I'd believe in salvation?" Of course not. Because people vary, and their faith varies, the preachers also vary in ability, but God's Word never varies. But we should thank God for the good that is accomplished through the Gospel. Whether it's people getting saved, filled with the Holy Spirit, or healed, let's thank God and learn more and more how we can cooperate with Him and do His will more fully like Jesus did, who healed them "*all.*"

The very fact that there are so many skeptics writing books and modern-day Pharisees, makes it hard for people to believe. The critic says, "Word of Faith theology makes the healer a hero when miraculous cures are claimed, but always blames the seeker when a healing does not happen. This unbalance does not promote Christian love and charity, but places more guilt on those who are not healed."

Let us answer now, the critic. First of all, *"Word of Faith"* theology has never stated that the one who prays the prayer of faith is a hero, nor does it blame the seeker when a healing does not happen. Jesus though, did tell *His disciples* the demon oppressed boy was not healed because of "their unbelief." Whether we want to accept the responsibility or not, unbelief is the major cause of not receiving from God. For "without faith, it's impossible to please Him" (Heb. 11:6). "So we see, they *could not* enter in because of unbelief" (Heb. 3:19). Was Paul being mean and unkind by saying that? No, he was simply stating a fact. That does not mean when it comes to healing, that we are saying they don't have faith for salvation, but rather, they've probably listened to too many people like the critic. (And I don't mean to sound this way about the critics, but it's so obvious that they are a great hindrance to the Lord's people having faith.) Mark further wrote that *Jesus* could not heal people in His own home town because of "their unbelief" (Mark 6:1-6).

Secondly, he says it does not promote Christian love and charity. Is it wrong to want to help people and try, through God's Word, to raise their faith level to where they can receive from God (Rom. 5:2; James 1:6-8; Matt. 9:29; Mark 9:23)? Are we not to be like Jesus who was moved with compassion to heal the sick, or Paul who was a helper of people's faith (1 Thess. 3:10)? But the critic says, God put the diseases on faithful Christians and then tells them to go to a sinner (doctor), to try and get it off of them. He then proceeds to remove the blame off of the devil and put it on God. Does it promote Christian love to tell people "God took your child," "God caused that car wreck," "God broke your home up" (I John 1:5)?

Mr. Critic, what about those who are not saved when you preach the Gospel to them? Will you be so cruel as to say that they are not saved because of their unbelief? Do you see then that it's not really it being a matter of being cruel by saying their unbelief keeps them blind (2 Cor. 4:3-4)? It's a fact. Our job is to help them through the Word of God to have faith, to open their eyes, and turn them from darkness to light (Acts 26:18). The reason salvation is preached to them is to help them, not hurt them; the same is true with healing. It's preached to help people and give them hope, not to hurt them.

The critic goes on to say that writers from the Old Testament to the New Testament, encouraged taking medicine. His statement is ridiculous. For God's Word says Asa trusted to the physicians and he died. (See also Mark 5:25-26.) We know that the Word of God speaks hundreds of times more about God's supernatural healing power than it ever even hints at natural medicine. We are not saying it's wrong to take a medicine that can help relieve pain, there's no condemnation in that, for healing is here for man not man for healing, but we are saying the Bible does not teach it as the critic implies it does. He rejects God's method and chooses man's. In the Old Testament times on earth, and up until about forty or fifty years ago, there were many foolish ideas that people had about the medical healing of different diseases and it is still made up of many guesses. So we cannot say God gave us medical science for healing. If so, we ask again, what about the past 1950 years, or past 6000 years for that matter? Medical science is simply natural man learning to fight against disease with natural methods.

The critic says, "in others who are healed," through the ministry of faith teachers, "there is a spiritual pride that says, 'Look at me! I had enough faith.'" Here again he admits, people do get healed, then he professes he is a discerner of the thoughts and intents of people's hearts. He says, because someone gets healed by God, that person has spiritual pride. Funny how God didn't know that. Does not Scripture say, "God resists the proud but gives grace to the humble?" He says if some don't go to physicians, the result "may be death." True, just not going to a doctor will not bring healing and is not necessarily faith. It may be works trying to imitate faith or the person may not go because they are frightened of doctors, or because they've listened to someone who wrongly told them, it is a sin to go to a doctor. But going to a physician may also "result in death," as the graveyards can testify.

He does all he can to discourage faith in God and His promises in this area, sows seeds of fear, says miracles have passed away, and says that God makes people sick, and then tells people to trust God first for healing. How ridiculous! After listening to Him, no one could ever believe God for healing. He also will not tell you of the multitudes of Christians that trusted physicians and died. We could go around the world and dig up testimonies about Christians who went to doctors and died; about people who were led to believe they'd be healed and spent all they had and grew nothing better but rather worse (Mark 5:25-26). Now we don't say this to criticize doctors and medicine. But if someone is healed by a doctor's care, is he not the hero? Very few unsaved persons praise God and give God the actual credit when the doctor did a successful operation. But when people are healed through faith in God, God gets all the praise, glory, and honor (Matt. 9:8; 15:30-31; Acts 4:16-21).

The critic says, the Lord never had healing services like we see today. But let's see the Scriptures: "And it came to pass on a certain day, as he was teaching, that there were Pharisees and doctors of the law, sitting by, which were come out of every town of Galilee, and Judaea, and Jerusalem, and the power of the Lord was present to heal them" (Luke 5:17).

Luke 6:17-19: "And He came down with them and stood in the plain, and the company of His disciples, and a great multitude of people out of all Judaea and Jerusalem and from the sea coast of Tyre and Sidon, which came to hear Him, and to be healed of their diseases, and they that were vexed with unclean spirits and they were healed. *And the whole multitude sought to touch Him* for there went virtue out of Him, and 'healed them ALL.'" Picture a multitude rushing upon the preacher to touch him that they might be healed. Quite a healing meeting, wasn't it?

Luke 4:17-22: "And there was delivered unto Him the book of the prophet Esaias. And when He had opened the book, He found the place where it was written, The Spirit of the Lord is upon Me because He has anointed Me to preach the Gospel to the poor, He hath sent Me to heal the broken hearted, to preach deliverance to the captives and recovery of sight to the blind, to set at liberty them that are bruised. And He closed the book and He gave it again to the minister, and sat down and the eyes of all them that were in the synagogue were fastened on Him. And He began to say unto them, This day is this Scripture fulfilled in your ears. And all bare Him witness and wondered at the gracious words which proceeded out of His mouth. . ."

Verse 40: "Now when the sun was setting, all they that had any sick with divers diseases brought them unto Him, and *He laid His hands on every one of them* and healed them." (Here He went about laying hands on sick people to heal them.)

Paul also preached healing as a part of the Gospel (Acts 14:7-10). In every commission Jesus gave, He told His followers to also heal the sick and cast out devils. In Mark 16:18, Christ said, believers "shall lay hands on the sick and they shall recover." He commanded them to preach the Kingdom of God "and heal the sick therein."

How else are you going to minister to the sick, except preach to them the Gospel and line people up and lay hands on them (Mark 16:18)? Paul wrote, "Let everything be done decently and in order," did he not? The critic says, there was nothing too hard for the Lord, that He healed all who came to Him. True, He healed all who came to Him *in faith*. But He could not heal those in His own hometown because of their unbelief (Mark 6). Yes, He is our perfect example. The perfect revelation of the perfect will of God (John 6:38). But it's also true no one ever preached like Jesus, operated as a prophet like Jesus, taught like Jesus, and had multitudes respond to him like Jesus.

Shall we then get rid of all pastors, teachers, and evangelists, because they don't measure up to Jesus' perfection in these areas? This is what the critic implies must be done if he's to remain consistent with His theory about how this all works. He also says, the Lord's healings were "always" permanent. But he fails to heed and listen to the Lord's warning to the man in John 5 who was healed by Christ. . . "Sin no more LEST A *WORSE THING* COME UPON THEE" (John 5:14), and says once a person is delivered from evil spirits, and if he doesn't fill himself up with the things of

God, that the evil spirits can come back with others, "and the last state of *that man* is worse than the first" (Luke 11:23-26).

The critic then says if God wants everybody healthy, why does everyone die? We need to stay right with the Word of the Lord. The Lord has promised the sick that they would recover if they believed, but not that they would not age and the body naturally wear out. Yet you do not have to be diseased to die. This is true for many people. Why must we let the devil kill us with disease in order for us to leave this life (Acts 10:38; John 10:10)? God said, "with long life will *I satisfy you.*"

Why not just breathe our last and go on to be with the Lord? So then God heals because He promised to, but He has not promised to keep these bodies we inherited from Adam alive in their present state forever. They are mortal bodies because they've come from Adam's seed (Rom. 8:11). But thank God He has promised us resurrection bodies like Jesus, the last Adam, in the time to come (Phil. 3:21).

Brethren, faith is the victory (1 John 5:4). If we don't believe what God said in His Word in any area, it shall be to us in those areas as it is to the sinner. The storms of life come to all. Jesus said,

"Therefore, whosoever heareth these sayings of Mine and doeth them, I will liken him unto a wise man which built his house upon a rock. And the rain descended and the floods came and the winds blew and beat upon that house, and it fell not for it was founded upon a rock. And everyone that heareth these sayings of mine and doeth them not, shall be likened unto a foolish man, which built his house upon the sand. And the rain descended and the floods came and the winds blew and beat upon that house and it fell, and great was the fall of it" (Matt. 7:24-27).

Although the battle was legally won by Christ, we must still appropriate it all by faith (Matt. 9:29; Josh. 1:2-3). And we must resist satan steadfast in the faith (1 Pet. 5:7-8). As long as we are here in this present life, we must use our "shield of faith" to resist sin, sickness and satan. This, and this alone, is what makes us face life's circumstances differently than the sinner who knows not God. You cannot just stamp Romans 8:28 on all of life's circumstances and say it's all God, for that is not what that Scripture says.

More On Prosperity

"But seek ye first the Kingdom of God and His righteousness, and all these things shall be added unto you" (Matt. 6:33).

Nowhere do Word of Faith preachers preach a get-rich-quick scheme as the critics imply. But rather, if you obey God you'll be blessed for doing so. In speaking concerning finances, Paul writes in 2 Corinthians 9:6-8: "But this I say, He which soweth sparingly shall reap also sparingly and he which soweth bountifully shall reap also bountifully. Every man according as he purposeth in his heart, so let him give, not grudgingly, or of necessity, for God loveth a cheerful giver. *And God is able to make all grace abound toward you* that ye always having all sufficiency in all things, may abound to every good work." (This is literal.)

Is the farmer wrong for believing there will be a harvest when seed is planted? Does he not have faith enough in nature to believe the earth will bring forth a harvest? Is it wrong then, when the apostle says that if we give to God's work bountifully, we will reap also bountifully? God's requirement is that we give cheerfully in faith. This pleases Him, and He is pleased that we believe His Word works. In Malachi 3:10, the Lord says, "Bring ye all the tithes into the storehouse, that there may be meat in Mine house and prove Me now herewith, saith the Lord of hosts, if I will not open you the windows of Heaven and pour you out a blessing that there shall not be room enough to receive it." Here the Lord says prove Me. Is it wrong then, to teach God will fulfill His Word and fulfill His promises? To believe that God will fulfill His Word is not self-pleasing, but God-pleasing. It is an act of trust in God andHis faithful Word.

We realize that extremes can exist, for they exist anywhere in any group, but any extremes are not in the main flow of the Word of Faith message and should not be taken as what is characteristic of faith ministries, even though the critics will search high and low for extremes and emphasize that as though all who are in the Word of Faith Message preach the extremes. We believe we are to be blessed (Gal. 3:14), but we are also to be temperate in all things and let our moderation be known to all men. Do the critics who criticize prosperity do so? As we've stated before, one of the head men who have attacked the prosperity message from God's Word the most, has himself a seven-hundred-thousand-dollar home. How then did he obtain his prosperity, seeing he says that God doesn't want people to prosper? We further understand that a few people, and ministers of various backgrounds, can go to extremes in their promises to people in this area, or by constantly showing pictures of themselves in supposedly humble positions. Now we don't judge any specific person concerning their hearts, for only God knows that (1 Sam.16:7), but rather we do see that when they do such things, they leave themselves open to be misunderstood, and so should refrain from such practices.

What About Luke 6:38?

"Give and it shall be given unto you, good measure, pressed down, and shaken together, and running over, shall men give into your bosom, for with the same measure that ye mete withal, it shall be measured to you again." The critic says this verse tells us to give without the thought of receiving back. Read it again, and see if it says it will be given unto you. Certainly the Lord says you will receive again, and not just as much given, but rather, good measure, pressed down, shaken together and running over. In Galatians 6:7 the apostle writes, ". . .God is not mocked; for *WHATSOEVER* a man soweth, that shall he also reap." In other words, you will receive back to yourself whatever you give out. Again Paul, in referring this law of God concerning finances says, "But this I say, He which soweth sparingly shall reap also sparingly and he which soweth bountifully, shall reap also bountifully. Every man according as he purposeth in his heart, so let him give, not grudgingly or of necessity for God loveth a cheerful giver. And God is able to make all grace abound toward you that ye always having all sufficiency in all things, may abound to every good work" (2 Cor. 9:6-8).

We understand that the cheerful heart also, has a part to play in it. If the heart's wrong, all is wrong. But yet, if you give cheerfully, trusting in the Word of the Lord, God is pleased and will "*multiply* your seed sown" and "increase the fruits of your righteousness" (vs. 10). Sometimes you will receive it back in this life and some of it, at the resurrection of the just. All of this is in obedience to the Covenant. Did not Jesus come to give us life and life more abundantly? And did not Jesus say it will all be according to your faith?

But the critic ceases not to sow doubts and as sure as God's law of sowing and reaping works, he will raise a harvest of unbelief in the promises of God in those that listen to Him. Woe to those that cause believers to stumble and hinder them from receiving life more abundantly when this is one of the main reasons Christ, being moved by love towards man, came (John 10:10). How little the critic understands the "Good News" of total redemption. He's not sure about experiencing salvation, denies the Holy Ghost Baptism, says miracles and gifts of the Spirit have passed away, tells people God sends them sickness and evil trials, excuses the devil, predestines some to hell, and preaches God wants people poor. What "Good News" is he preaching? Certainly not from the Bible. Is it not he then that preaches "a different Gospel?"

We understand about covetousness and greediness. This is to have no place in the heart of one who operates in God's Word and expects to receive a harvest, for "faith worketh by love" and the apostle John wrote, "And *whatsoever* we ask, *we receive* of Him (from God) *because we keep His commandments* and *do those things* that are PLEASING IN HIS SIGHT (1 John 3:22). John was not greedy for saying this.

What needs to be done is for the child of God to continue to walk by faith, keep doing what God's Word says, trusting God that it will be even as God said. Prosperity God's way, is not a get-rich-quick scheme, but a way of life, a living to give; and if we seek first His Kingdom and His righteousness, "ALL these things" will be added unto us by the Lord Himself (Matt. 6:33). "The blessing of the Lord maketh rich and He addeth no sorrow with it."

Mark 4:26-29: "And He said, So is the Kingdom of God, as if a man should cast seed into the ground, and should sleep and rise night and day, and the seed should spring and grow up, He knoweth not how. For the earth bringeth forth fruit of herself, first the blade, then the ear, after that, the full corn in the ear. But when the fruit is brought forth, immediately he putteth in the sickle, because the harvest is come."

No one should ever feel guilty for their poverty or lack. This does not mean you're not spiritually rich in your relationship and fellowship with God, which is the more important thing. But what should be done, is to be faithful to act on God's Word, keep on doing what God says in this area also (2 Cor. 8:7-9), and the time to reap results will surely come forth—first the blade, then the ear, then the full corn in the ear, and then full harvest time comes (vs. 20). As we've said, some in this life and some at the Resurrection of the just. Much of it has to do with receiving wisdom from God's Word on how to cooperate with God, how to work as unto the Lord heartily, how to give to your employer more than is expected of you; be faithful in tithes and offerings, agreeing with God's Covenant with your words and actions, having a good attitude, following the leading of the Holy Spirit, being diligent in business and getting out of a poverty way of thinking, if that's the kind of environment you were raised in (Rom. 12:2-3). Is God a respecter of persons? No (Acts 10:34). But He cooperates with all men equally on the basis of their conformity to His Gospel (Rom. 1:16). It's how much of His Word we act on by faith that pleases Him (Heb. 11:6), and He rewards those that diligently seek Him. His *reward* is never cancer, poverty, oppression, evil trials, and temptations, for those are not rewards.

So find out what God's Word says about prosperity, obey Him and see if, in time, He will not open up the windows of Heaven and pour you out a blessing you'll not have room enough to contain. Ecclesiastes 5:19 says, *"Every man also, to whom God hath given riches and wealth and hath given him power to eat thereof, and to take his portion and to rejoice in his labor, this is the gift of God."* And remember, according to James 1:16-17, God only gives good and perfect gifts. So then riches and wealth, when coming from the Lord, is a good and perfect gift.

Chapter 12

Positive Confession: Getting Rid of Corrupt Talk

Positive Confession

The critic, in not understanding that God really did create man in His own image and likeness, mockingly says concerning "Word of Faith" preachers, "They actually believe that we can create our own reality or circumstances by what we verbalize aloud." He then calls this a radical belief and metaphysical. Now we would never put it the way he put it. But again, he doesn't know the difference between the occult and God's Word, as we will plainly show you from the Scriptures.

First listen to what Jesus said to His disciples after He *had spoken to a fig tree* and it had withered up from the roots. "For verily I say unto you, that whosoever shall say unto this mountain, Be thou removed and be thou cast into the sea, and shall not doubt in his heart, but shall believe that those things which he saith shall come to pass, he shall have whatsoever he saith" (Mark 11:23). Notice, *Jesus said* that if you do not doubt in your heart, but shall believe that *Those things which you saith*, shall have *whatsoever*." Does Jesus then, "actually believe" your words have an effect on your life? Certainly He does. So then, according to Jesus, whosoever shall have whatsoever he saith, good or bad, if he doubts not in his heart, but believes it will come to pass. This then is the reason for many things that happen in people's lives whether they know it or not. This, along with other scriptures concerning this subject which have come through the apostles, the prophets and other men of God like Solomon in the Old Testament, are all that is taught by Word of Faith preachers. Is what the men of God in Scripture teach about concerning our mouth, our tongue and our words metaphysical? Why listen to the critic who criticizes whatever his intellect cannot grasp, even if it's in the Bible? Anything he cannot understand because he's not yet received the Holy Ghost Baptism, he labels as "metaphysical." Perhaps it is he who is into something metaphysical, for "out of the abundance of the heart, the mouth speaks."

James 3:3-6 says, "Behold, we put bits in the horses mouths, that they may obey us, and we turn about their whole body. Behold also, the ships which though they be so great, and are driven of fierce winds, yet are they turned about with a very small helm, whithersoever the governor listeth. *Even so, the tongue* is a little member, and boasteth great things. Behold, how great a matter a little fire kindleth! And the tongue is a fire, a world of iniquity, so is *the tongue* among our members, that it defileth the whole body and *setteth on fire the course* of nature, and it is set on fire of hell."

It is obvious that James teaches that your *tongue* is like a rudder on a ship, or like a bit in the horses mouth. Whichever way you turn it is the direction your life will go. But the critic will say James is metaphysical for stating such things. He says your words have no such effect on your life. He, in his ignorance, is saying, if people believe what Jesus said in Mark 11:23, that they have "fallen into the lie of satan." He doesn't even begin to understand where Word of Faith teachers come from in regards to this, and yet he sets himself up like judge and jury thinking he's defending truth when really he's fighting it. And forget about his comparisons concerning what Jesus taught about words and metaphysical writers, for satan has gotten them to copy God's way of doing things, not us copying them.

He then says, "The desire to control one's private world, or the world at large, is the essence of the sin of rebellion." How ridiculous of a statement. Does he go to work? Did he choose to have a family? Does he buy things for his home at his discretion? Is he not, to a degree then, controlling his own private world? If what he says is so, he should go and lay down in a field somewhere, and do nothing. But if God, in His Word, has revealed to us that our words and obedience do have an effect in our lives, then let's have enough sense to believe God knows more about it than we do.

"A man's belly shall be satisfied with the fruit of his mouth, and with the increase of his lips, shall he be filled. Death and life are in the power of the tongue, and they that love it shall eat the fruit thereof" (Prov. 18:20-21). "The mouth of a righteous man is a well of life, but violence covereth the mouth of the wicked" (Prov. 10:11). Is obedience to God then as he put it, "the essence of the sin of rebellion?"

Here is one for the critic who has not ceased to destroy the work of other ministries with his words. Proverbs 11:9: "An hypocrite with his mouth destroyeth his neighbor, but through knowledge shall the just be delivered." All you need do, dear reader, is look up in your Strong's Concordance all God says about words, tongue, mouth, confess, speak and you will absolutely see that much of your life is governed by what you say. What you say reveals what's in your heart. "This book of the law shall not depart out of thy mouth, but thou shalt meditate therein, day and night, that thou mayest observe to do according to all that is written therein, for then thou shalt make thy way prosperous and then thou shalt have good success" (Josh. 1:8).

"As for me, this is My covenant with them, saith the Lord, My Spirit that is upon thee, and *My words which I have put in thy mouth*, shall not depart out of thy mouth, nor out of the mouth of thy seed, nor out of the mouth of thy seed's seed, saith the LORD, from henceforth and forever" (Isa. 59:21).

Here you have it. This is all that's taught by Word of Faith preachers. We do it because He said to do it (James 1:22). If He said, "words" affect our lives, and He did (Mark 11:23), then we are smart enough to believe He knows more than us, how He created us to function. But the critic says, "that's magic." Jesus spoke to the winds and waves and they obeyed Him, He spoke to leprosy and it departed, He cast out the spirits with His Word, He said His words were "spirit and life" and He told His disciples they, likewise, could do the same, for that's how *God created them*. Is that magic (Matt. 17:18-20)? John 14:12: "Verily, verily, I say unto you, he that believeth on Me, the works that I do shall he do also, and greater works than these shall he do because I go unto My Father."

The critic then quotes a faith teacher and says he, (the faith teacher), often promotes magic by saying, if we "in faith use the name of Jesus" we shall have anything we want, (within God's will), and nature and demons will obey us. Well, John the apostle said in 1 John 5:14-15: "And *this is the confidence that we have in Him, that if we ask anything according to His will, He heareth us. And if we know that He hears us, whatsoever we ask, we know* that *we have* the petitions that we desired of Him."

Jesus said, "In My name, ye shall cast out devils. . . . " And concerning nature and things, read what Jesus said in Mark 11:23. Now all of this is "according to your faith" in God's Word as far as you believe (Mark 9:23). This is not magical, this is faith in God. Again the critic shows he doesn't know the difference between faith and magic.

Second Cor. 4:13 states: "We, having the same spirit of faith, according as it is written I believed, and therefore have I spoken, we also believe and therefore speak." This is the very essence and spirit of faith, it's what faith is all about. Believing in the heart and speaking with the mouth.

Genesis 1:3: And God said, "Let there be light and there was light."

Romans 10:9-10: "That if thou shalt *confess with thy mouth* the Lord Jesus, and shalt *believe in thine heart* that God hath raised Him from the dead, *thou shalt be saved.* For with the heart man believeth, unto righteousness and with the mouth confession is made unto salvation."

So on the positive side, God "watches over His Word to perform it" (John 15:7). On the negative side, Scripture says in I Corinthians 10:10: "Neither murmur ye, as some of them also murmured and were destroyed of the destroyer." He says faith preachers replace God's moral laws with metaphysical so-called, spiritual laws. Contrary to what he says, we teach unless you put God and obedience to Him first, and love your neighbor as yourself, your faith won't work (Gal. 5:6). We must live by the golden rule if we want God's blessing. "Therefore, all things whatsoever, ye would that men should do to you, do ye even so to them, for *this is the law and the prophets*" (Matt. 7:12). "Jesus said unto him, Thou shalt love the Lord thy God with all thy heart, and with all thy soul, and with all thy mind. This is the first and great commandment. And the second is like unto it. Thou shalt love thy neighbor as thyself. On these two commandments *hang all the law* and the prophets."

Love then, is the fulfilling of God's law. But the critic who is so judgmental and harsh with other Christians, does not even fulfill this, so neither would his faith work, even if he believed he had any. The more I look at his criticism, the more I realize he doesn't know what he's talking about. If he's doing it ignorantly in unbelief, may the Lord have mercy on him (1 Tim. 1:13). But if not, his wrong doing will come before him when he stands before the Lord (Col. 3:25). God told Israel, "as surely as you've spoken in Mine ears that I will do to you. . . ."

The critic says, God "is not manipulated by mere words," but God "looks at our hearts and attitudes." True, God is a discerner of the thoughts and intents of the heart (Heb. 4:13). And we know God cannot be manipulated for He is Omniscient and Omnipotent. But it is also true that what comes out of your mouth, for the most part, *reveals what's in your heart*, and Jesus, in speaking of people's words revealing what's in their hearts said, "Either make the tree good and his fruit good, or else make the tree corrupt and his fruit corrupt, for the tree IS KNOWN BY HIS FRUIT!" (words) "O generation of vipers, *how* can ye, being evil, speak good things? For out of the abundance of the heart, the mouth speaketh. A good man out of the good treasure of the heart, bringeth forth good things and an evil man, out of the evil treasures, bringeth forth evil things. But I say unto you, that every idle word that men shall speak, they shall give account thereof in the day of judgment. For *by thy words thou shalt be justified, and by thy words, thou shalt be condemned*" (Matt. 12:34-37). Notice, it is by "your words" that you will be justified or condemned. Does that sound like God is not concerned with "mere words?"

The critic then goes on to say, "both metaphysical cults and the health and wealth leaders assert that to possess something, you must desire it intensely." In other words (he says) "faith teachers say, covetousness helps." Was Jesus then teaching us to be covetous when He said, "What *things* soever *ye desire* when you pray, believe ye receive them and you shall have them" (Mark 11:24)?

Or David, when he said, "Delight thyself also in the Lord, and He shall give thee *the desires* of thine heart" (Psalm 37:4). *Desire* means, "to wish for the possession and enjoyment of something." This in itself, is not wrong, and it will be in balance if you also are delighting yourself in the Lord. "No good *thing* will He withhold from them that walk uprightly."

Solomon wrote, ". . .the desire of the righteous shall be granted" (Prov. 10:24). "The desires of the righteous is only good" (11:23). "Hope deferred, maketh the heart sick, but when the desire cometh, it is a tree of life" (Prov. 13:12). "The desire accomplished is sweet to the soul. . ." (13:19).

So it is obvious, desire is not necessarily the same as covetousness, as the critic states. He needs to study his Bible more. There are good desires within the will of God that God will bless His children with (Matt. 7:11). Jesus said, "Ask and you shall receive, that *your joy* may be full." It seems as though the critic has not come to know God as "Abba Father" but rather to him, God is only a formless, sovereign judge, whose intimidated by us acting on His Word and then expecting results.

Back to Our Words

The critic says that faith teachers say, "If we speak the right words, we will never have trials." Now in all my years in the faith message, I have *never heard anyone* teach that. What is taught though, is that when you face the storms of life, that you are to act on the Covenant you have with God, to put on the whole armor of God, and *take the sword of the Spirit, which is the Word of God.* (See Eph. 6:10-17; Matt. 7:24-27.) That means to speak God's Word and declare the truth of your covenant in the face of contrary circumstances (John 15:7). We do what Jesus did and say what is "written" (Matt. 4:4). God then, can watch over His Word to confirm it. Remember, He's dealing with free moral agents.

So Paul writes, "Let us hold fast the confession of our faith without wavering, for He is faithful that promised" (Heb. 10:25). In other words, let us keep our words and believing in agreement with what God's Word says, regardless of the changing circumstances and then "faith is the victory that overcometh the world" (1 John 5:4). We do not reject God's truth, just because the devil comes to kill, steal, or destroy, but rather we use God's Word and "resist the devil steadfast in the faith" (1 Pet. 5:8-9). God's truth is our "shield and buckler." And let me add these Scriptures:

"He that keepeth his mouth, keepeth his life, but he that openeth wide his lips, shall have destruction. . . ." "A fool's mouth is his destruction. . . ." "Whoso keepeth his mouth and tongue, keepeth his soul from troubles" (Prov. 10:11; 12:6,14; 13:3; 18:20-21; 21:23).

It is obvious then that people's mouths do get them in a lot of trouble, with other people, with God and with satan. We therefore will not reject God's truth because someone fights it and criticizes God's message of faith.

The critic goes on to say, we could "never be perfect enough to receive anything from Him," implying that Christ's teaching us to pray for specific things is wrong. We, as faith ministers, know it's all by grace through faith and we don't stand in our own righteousness (1 Cor. 1:30), but we know also that according to Matthew 21:22 Jesus said, "And all things, whatsoever ye shall ask in prayer believing, ye shall receive."

In Mark 11:24 He says, "Therefore, I say unto you, what

things soever *ye desire*, when ye pray, believe that ye receive them, and ye shall have them."

John 16:23-24 tells us, "And in that day, ye shall ask Me nothing. Verily, verily I say unto you, *whatsoever* ye shall ask the Father in My name, He will give it you." We are not saying we are perfect and therefore expect to receive, we come on the basis of the blood of Jesus and His Covenant promises (Heb. 10:20), nor are we always teaching on receiving answered prayer as the critic implies. We emphasize these things in this book only because this is where the critic has chosen to attack the Word.

The real difference between Word of Faith teachers and those whom satan is using to counterfeit and copy God's principles concerning *words and their power* is that faith teachers teach people to obey God, agree with God's Word, and take the sword *of the Spirit*, which is the Word of God (Isa.59:19-20). Our dependence then is on the Holy Spirit's working through God's Word to create the fruit of the lips, to work through our words as He did through Jesus. Our faith and dependency then is totally in God (Acts 1:8).

In Matthew 8:16 it tells us, "When the even was come, they brought unto Him many that were possessed with devils, and He cast out the spirits with His word and healed all that were sick."

Matthew 12:28 says, "But if I cast out devils by the Spirit of God, then the Kingdom of God is come unto you." Notice then, it was the Holy Spirit that worked through His Word.

Acts 1:8 says, "But *ye* shall receive power, after that the Holy Ghost is come upon *you*, and ye shall be witnesses unto Me, both in Jerusalem, and in all Judaea and in Samaria, and unto the uttermost part of the earth." It would be the Spirit then working through their words to convict men of their need of Jesus.

Those in cults are basing things on themselves and what they, without God, can do. *We, as Christians, know* that without

Him we can do nothing (John 15:5). We know His Word reveals that words can also give place to God or the devil. "Neither murmur ye, as some of them also murmured, and were destroyed of the destroyer" (1 Cor.10:10).

"That *if thou shalt confess with thy mouth* the Lord Jesus, and shalt believe in thine heart that God hath raised Him from the dead, thou shalt be saved. For with the heart man believeth unto righteousness, and with the mouth confession is made unto salvation" (Rom. 10:9-10).

"For whosoever shall *call* upon the name of the Lord, shall be saved" (Rom. 10:13).

With hundreds of scriptures in the Bible that teach on words, the effects of words, prayer, asking and receiving; holding fast our confession of faith; being judged by our words; our words being like the rudder on a ship; the power of life and death being in the tongue; and so on, you'd think that someone who claims to be a student of the Bible would never say that God is not concerned with "mere words," but they do say it.

All the Faith Message does is put emphasis on this important topic as it's revealed in Scripture. If God's revealed it, shouldn't we believe it, line up with it and act upon it? Who cares if satan tries to copy it? The counterfeit does not do away with the real. He just knows these things work for he's been around a lot longer than those who criticize God's Word in this area. So he tries to use these principles of God's Kingdom to his own advantage. On the other hand, he uses people such as the critic to use his words to attack the real work of God and compare it to the counterfeit to stop believers from cooperating with God. Oh the subtlety of the serpent! The heretics are labeling Bible preachers "heretics." His words are used to destroy faith and then he says words have no effect.

So then, faith teachers come from the angle of believing God's Word, obeying His truth, and faith in God, while the metaphysical cults operate on a humanistic level of faith in self, such as self-effort, self-pleasing, self-righteousness. So the two cannot even be compared as though it's all the same source (1 John 4:5-6).

The critic says, "the prosperity people proclaim that God must grant any prayer request they ask in faith." But this is not taught. It is only things in agreement with His will, which is "all things that pertain to life and Godliness" (2 Pet. 1:3), and it's not that God must, but that He is willing.

First John 5:14-15 says, "And this is the confidence that we have in Him, that *if we ask anything* according to His will, He heareth us, and if we know that He hear us, whatsoever we ask, *we know that we have* the petitions that we desired of Him." Hmmm, seems as though the apostle John taught it also. Was John then one of those "prosperity people?" A "name-it-and-claim-it teacher?" So we don't say he "must," as the critic implies, but rather that our Heavenly Father is fully willing to help His children in this life. If someone is walking with the Lord, they are not going to ask for things that will hinder their relationship with God. John the Apostle also said, "And *whatsoever* we ask, we receive of Him, BECAUSE *we keep* His commandments and *do those things that are pleasing in His sight.*"

We understand you cannot live in rebellion to God's will and moral government and expect answered prayer, nor can you exercise faith in God and be living in known sin, for faith works by love, and as John wrote, "Beloved, if our heart condemn us not, THEN have we confidence before God" (1 John 3:21). And "this is the love of God that we keep His commandments, and His commandments are not grievous" (1 John 5:3).

The critic then foolishly says, "Word of faith leaders DEMAND that God give them the things they want, rather than the things they need." First of all, everyone knows man cannot control or demand that God do anything, so it would be foolish for us or anyone else to do so, for if we did, we'd never get anything anyway. Secondly, God Himself, promised to supply both our needs *and desires* (wants), as long as they pertain to life and Godliness. So we believe He will supply our needs and if we delight ourselves in Him, He also will grant the desires of our heart in His own good time (Ps.37:4). The delighting yourself in Him, controls the desires in your heart. You will not desire evil things while delighting yourself in God (Matt. 7:11). We will continue to believe our Father's words regardless of what the critic says.

The critic will not accept any verse at face value, but tears apart all Scriptures and explains them away, believing because he's been on this earth for a few decades and he knows some Hebrew and Greek, that he understands all that is in the mind of the Creator and that without the help of the Baptism with the Holy Spirit (1 Cor. 2:9-14).

I would like to ask him, how many hours he spends in prayer a day? How much has he personally given in his ministry to help missions? Has he given hundreds of thousands or even millions of dollars to overseas salvation ministries, as some of the larger Word of Faith Ministries have to bring the Gospel of salvation to the other parts of the world? Or would he take apart those scriptures on spreading the Gospel likewise? And the one (critic) we speak of now actually does do it, implying that people's wills are not free but predestined. He not only tears down Word of Faith Ministries, but all Full Gospel, Holy Spirit-filled believers and churches, and casts aside many pages of the New Testament.

Dear reader, please realize these critics who write these books against faith and God's Word, are more like modern day Pharisees than men of faith. They know nothing of the work, leading, or guidance of the Holy Spirit as is revealed in God's written Word. If you listen to some of them, you won't know what's from God or what's from the devil. You'll have no faith in answered prayer and end up confused. Their's is nothing but a human theology about religion, speaking evil of things that they understand not. Let's believe God's Word. If Jesus said in Mark 11:23: "For verily I say unto you, that whosoever shall say unto this mountain, be thou removed and be thou cast into the sea, and shall not doubt in his heart, but shall believe that those things which he saith shall come to pass, he shall have whatsoever he saith." Let's have enough sense to believe it regardless of how the critic tries to negate Jesus' Words and say they don't mean what they say. This so called, "higher criticism" has come and gone, but Jesus' Words live on forever.

The critic assumes, presumes, twists, pulls out of context, irrationally compares Scripture with cultic activities, and "with good words and fair speeches, deceives the hearts of the simple" (Rom.16:17-18). "Beware of the leaven of the Pharisees and the Sadducees." That statement by Christ, was not just for Bible days, but is as much applicable to us today as it ever was. And they all come dressed in their robes of religion, appearing as minister's of righteousness, reasoning in their heart against Christ's Word, and they consider Christ's real followers "ignorant and unlearned men" (Acts 4:13). But it is they, who are ignorant, even though they consider themselves learned and high and lifted up. "In that hour, Jesus rejoiced in spirit and said, I thank Thee O Father, Lord of Heaven and earth, that Thou hast *hid these things from the wise and prudent* and hast revealed them unto babes, even so Father, for so it seemed good in Thy sight" (Luke 10:21). It's not great intellectual abilities that opens men's eyes to these things, it is God.

It is God then who opens people's eyes to see, not their great intellectual capabilities, or puffed up knowledge of Greek and Hebrew (Eph. 1:15-19). It's on your *knees* and not in *degrees* that you gain the knowledge of God. It tells us in Ephesians 1:16-19, "Cease not to give thanks for you, making mention of you in my prayers, that the God of our Lord Jesus Christ, the Father of glory, *may give unto you the spirit of wisdom and revelation in the knowledge of Him, the eyes of your understanding being enlightened*, that ye may know what is the hope of His calling, and what the riches of the glory of His inheritance in the saints, and what is the exceeding greatness of His power to us-ward who believe, according to the working of His mighty power."

But the critic goes on his own, not believing in any such working of God in people. He fights every manifestation and operation of the Holy Ghost and calls it cultic. He needs to be careful lest he attribute the work of the Holy Spirit to a devil and destroy himself and others with him. I say this not as criticism, but as a warning from God's Word (Jude 3). He is, in fact, the heretic in these areas, teaching philosophy and traditions of men, taking away from people "the key of knowledge." He enters not in himself and those who desire to learn more of God's ways as revealed in God's Word, he hinders. Jesus was very forceful and called the Pharisees of His day, "blind guides" who "strain gnats and swallow camels."

The critic claims the Bible is sufficient and then denies much of it. He quotes scriptures to prove his point, but other scriptures that disagree with him he refuses to take at face value. He breaks them down until he twists them to mean what he wants them to and then he goes about to criticize men of God who are doing a work of faith with power. He is one who has the form of Godliness, but *denies the power of God.* He knows not the scriptures, nor the power of God and in this he greatly errs. Christianity is a "head thing" to him. Whatever Scriptures he cannot understand with his mind, he labels metaphysical, or occultic if it's acted on today. He may not realize it, but that's what he does. His Christianity is a product of his own mind and of a Dark Age school of theology. Let's get back to the true Word of the Lord as it is actually recorded in the Bible.

Now Here's Something to Think About

When Jesus was here, He was ministering as a prophet under the Old Covenant (Mark 6:4). The New Covenant had not yet begun. He came to clarify things, to make God's real will known and to reveal to mankind, what the Father was really like. He said, "If you've seen Me, you've seen the Father."

The Scribes and Pharisees had their ideas about God; about how He sovereignly was controlling everything; that He caused the sickness and brought about the poverty (John 9:24). Almost identical to some people's theology today, it was a "Que sera, sera, whatever will be, will be" theology. But when Jesus, who was sent from the Father, came to reveal God's will (John 6:38); it was the religious leaders who could not understand His living faith. Jesus preached in John 10:10: "The thief cometh not, but for to steal, and to kill, and to destroy, I am come that they might have life, and that they might have it more abundantly." But they wouldn't hear it. They reasoned that couldn't be God, because He doesn't line up with our theology so they labeled the work of Christ, "the devil." They had their legalistic, systematic way of doing things, their traditions, their great intellectual schools of theology, but no one was seeing God at work, because there was no faith being taught or exercised. It was a religious system of "do's" and "don't's." Supposedly "the faith." Jesus then, came with a "faith message," preaching and teaching the people to believe, saying, "according to your faith be it unto you" (Matt. 9:29). (See also Mark 9:23; Matthew 8:13.)

He demonstrated that God would answer prayer, heal people, forgive, and bless if they would "only believe." But the Pharisees couldn't stand it because it didn't happen through them or their school's of theology and feared saying, "if we leave him alone, the world will go after him." Because he was outside of their little circle, they refused to acknowledge His miracles as from God, but said it was the devil. They couldn't believe someone was saying that words had power. They refused His miracles. They said, He being a man makes Himself God, and *many such like* things.

We want you to notice the parallel. It is precise. Jesus said, "If they (religion) have persecuted Me, they will also persecute you." The critics, like the Pharisees of old, don't realize what side of the fence they are on. That if they were there in Jesus' day, they would have responded to Him the same way they respond to men of faith today, and they don't even know it. They would not have been in the group of disciples who healed the sick and cast out devils, but with the Pharisees who said, "That's the devil;" "that's occultic;" "that's not God." "God gave us doctors."

Think about it, church. The Pharisees had no power with God and there was no response from the Holy Spirit in their religious ministries. All they had was their theology and great intellectual arguments through which they persuaded people to believe them rather than God's Word (1 Thess. 1:5; 1 Cor. 4:19,20). And so, today, there are those who do not believe that God *is* today, just as much God as He *was* then. That He can do now, what He could do then and in their ignorance, they strive to make you a child of unbelief like themselves. You must weigh the evidence and see who really lines up with God's Word and choose between faith or unbelief, health or sickness, Jesus or satan. Will you be like Joshua and Caleb who had a spirit of faith and entered into the Promised Land, or be like the ten who came back with an evil report saying, "we can't," "we saw," "we were afraid." The multitude is not always right, nor are the leaders of religion always correct just because many follow them, as the Word of God also proves.

The critics, like the Pharisees, want you to accept everything as from the hand of God, but Scripture says Jesus Christ was manifest "to destroy the works of the devil." He showed us what God was like. He is the perfect revelation of the will of God (1 John 6:38; Heb. 10:5-7). He corrected people's wrong thinking about God, and the common people heard Him gladly. Everyone that is, except the Pharisees, for they clung to their theology, regardless of what Christ did or taught.

It is no different today, now that a strong Faith Message in the integrity of God's Word is once again being taught. Religious leaders must again find excuses as to why they don't have faith to pray for the sick, cast out devils and speak in tongues like Jesus said we should (Mark 16:17-18). They must again find excuses for their ministers being powerless. So they conveniently say to their followers, "it passed away," or "it's the devil healing people." This they teach people, rather than teach them God's Word and because there is no response from the Holy Spirit because of their lack of faith, they say, "the gifts of the Holy Spirit passed away;" "He doesn't lead people anymore;" "the things the Bible said He'd do, He doesn't do now. They reason and say all we need now is the Bible and at the same time, they deny the very things the Bible says will happen in this dispensation of grace and age of the Holy Spirit, who is the Miracle Worker (1 Cor.12:1-11). God is not the author of all that confusion.

What About the Bible? Is the Bible Enough?

One critic says that because Full Gospel preachers teach that the Spirit of God, who indwells us, can speak to us or lead us from within (John 16:13), that we are implying that the Bible is not enough (1 John 2:26-27). Because he has denied the Biblical experience of receiving the Baptism with the Holy Spirit after salvation, he also cannot understand this area of the Word of God, and God's instructions in it concerning the Holy Spirit and His ministry in the life of a believer. Being led by the Spirit of God, is something that's *in the Word*, not a separate thing that the Bible never speaks of (Rom. 8:14). It is obvious that if we are filled with the Holy Spirit, He is within us. First Corinthians 6:19 asks us, "What? Know ye not that your body is the temple of the Holy Ghost *which is in you*, which ye have of God, and ye are not your own?" And in John 14:17, it says, "Even the Spirit of truth, whom the world cannot receive, because it seeth Him not, neither knoweth Him, but ye know Him, for He dwelleth with you, and *shall be in you*."

The *Bible* also says that the Holy Spirit will teach us (1 Cor. 2:13); God will reveal things to us by His Spirit (1 Cor. 2:7-10): Not things beyond His written Word, but what He's saying in His Word (1 Cor. 2:14). He will *guide us* into all truth; He will speak (John 16:13); He will take the things of Jesus and reveal them unto us (John 16:14); He would bring things to our remembrance (John 14:26).

The Spirit spoke to Philip (Acts 8:29). He also spoke to Peter (Acts 10:19). The Spirit also bears witness with our spirits, that we are God's children (Rom. 8:16). "There is a spirit in man and the inspiration of the Almighty giveth them understanding" (Job 32:8). "The spirit of man is the candle of the Lord" (Prov. 20:27). (In other words, that's where He makes His will known.)

"And immediately when Jesus perceived *in His spirit*, that they so reasoned within themselves, He said unto them, "Why reason ye these things in your hearts" (Mark 2:8)? Paul said, "I *perceive* that this voyage will be with hurt" (Acts 27:10), and it was. This perception did not come from his mind, but his spirit. But the critic says in his book that "bypassing the mind is like the occult's spirit guides." In saying this, he also accuses Jesus and the apostles of occultic activity. Paul also said, "If I pray in an unknown tongue, *my spirit prayeth*, but my understanding (mind) is unfruitful" (1 Cor. 14:14). But the critic has no clue as to what is said.

Again, because he leans so much to his intellect, and his own understanding rather than God's Word, he can't see that satan, who's been around a long time, knows how man is created to function and simply counterfeits the real. But as we've shown from the Scriptures, the real remains (Prov. 3:5-6). Yet he thinks because satan is counterfeiting, that there cannot possibly be the real leading of the Holy Spirit. The critic then says, "God, however, is always rational" in His dealings with man.

This once again shows how little he knows about the life of faith. God led Israel to the Red Sea with Pharaoh's army behind, mountains on both sides and the Red Sea in front of them. According to natural reasoning, that was not a rational move, but through faith, the Red Sea was opened and the victory won. God had Joshua march around the walls of Jericho and then shout, and the walls came tumbling down. Is that logical? How about telling a blind man to wash in the pool of Siloam to receive His sight; or Paul's handkerchiefs bringing healing to people; walking on water; Peter's shadow passing by and people being healed; iron swimming; blood on doorposts to protect the Israelites from an unseen angel of death; people being thrown into fire but not being burned; Noah being told to build an ark on dry ground; and we could go on and on.

The critic would not believe that God spoke to any of these men of God if he lived during their time. He would have been outside the ark saying, "God is too rational to tell any of these men such things." He says that Word of Faith teachers say that if they have a vision or if they say, "Jesus told me," that they are infallible.

But this is not the case. For if you listen, you will hear that all true Word of Faith teachers say everything including all manifestations of the gifts of the Spirit are all subject to the written Word of God. The Spirit of God doesn't make mistakes but people can. We well know that the Bible is the infallible Word of God and in so believing, we also believe what it says about the Spirit of Truth guiding us into truth, speaking to us, revealing the things of Christ to us (John 16:13-15); leading us (Rom. 8:14); His intervention (Acts 16:6-7); His manifestations (1 Cor. 12). His teaching us (1 Cor. 2:12-13); His anointing us (Acts 1:8; 1 John 2:26-27); His bringing things to our remembrance (John 14:26), and His giving us supernatural utterance (Acts 2:4; 10:44-46; 1 Cor. 14:2; Jude 20). These are sufficient to show that the Spirit of God actually does speak, lead, guide, teach, reveal, manifest, anoint, give utterance. Sufficient, that is, *if you believe the Bible* (Acts 2:17).

So, let us not add to or *take away* anything from God's written Word by saying that the Holy Spirit will not do what the Bible says HE WILL DO. No true Word of Faith teacher says that a revelation he gets, adds to the written Word of God, for the Bible is complete. The revelation given by the Spirit is an unveiling by the Spirit of what was in the heart of God when He inspired men to write something in His Word. First Corinthians 2:9-16 tells us,

"But as it is written, eye hath not seen, nor ear heard, neither have entered into the heart of man, the things which God hath prepared for them that love Him. But God hath revealed them unto us by His Spirit, for the Spirit searcheth all things, yea, the deep things of God. *For what man knoweth the things of a man, save the spirit of man which is in Him? Even so, the things of God knoweth no man, but the Spirit of God. Now we have received not the spirit of the world, but the Spirit which is of God, that we might know* the things that are freely given to us of God. Which things also we speak, not in the words which man's wisdom teacheth, but which the Holy Ghost teacheth, comparing spiritual things with spiritual. But the natural man receiveth not the things of the Spirit of God, for they are foolishness unto Him, neither can he know them, because they are spiritually discerned. But he that is spiritual judgeth all things, yet he, himself, is judged of no man.

For who hath known the mind of the Lord, that He may instruct him? But we have the mind of Christ."

Furthermore, the Bible reveals that the Spirit of God can lead an individual in decisions of ministry and also in personal decisions that will affect their lives (Prov. 3:5-6; Rom. 8:14; Acts 16:6-7).

The critic, in further trying to deny the Holy Spirit's present work says, Jesus was the "final prophet," implying there were no more prophets after Christ. But he has failed to read the rest of the New Testament, which speaks of numerous other prophets after Jesus was here. All one needs do is to read the Book of Acts to see that this is so. (See Acts 13:1-3.) Ephesians 4:10-13 says, "He that descended is the same also, that ascended up, far above all heavens, that He might fill all things. And He gave (after His ascension), some apostles, *and some prophets*; and some evangelists; and some pastors and teachers; for the perfecting of the saints, for the work of the ministry, for the edifying of the body of Christ, *till we all come in the unity of the faith*, and of the knowledge of the Son of God, unto a perfect man, unto the measure of the stature of the fullness of Christ." Till when? Till *we all* come in the unity of the faith.

First Corinthians 12:28 says, "And God hath set some *in the church*, first apostles, *secondarily prophets*, thirdly teachers, after that miracles, then gifts of healings, helps, governments, diversities of tongues." Set where? In the church. The critic ignorantly goes on to say, "to promote the idea that there would be more prophets after Him, is to say that he revealed God and His will incompletely and thus imperfectly, so that we need more." But this is not the real case. True, Jesus is the Prophet of all prophets. He was infallible. We also know that New Testament prophets *in the church* are to have what they say judged by other prophets showing there is the possibility of human error (1 Cor. 14:28-32), but this does not do away with their God given purpose in the church. According to the New Testament, we know they do not hold the same place of authority as the Old Testament prophets, the Lord Jesus or the New Testament apostles which have given us the written Word of God.

So during this Church Age, no New Testament prophet has any authority to add to or take away from Scripture. But no critic has the right to take away from Scripture things which he cannot understand and say there are no more prophets. The Word of God stands sure. God set prophets *in the church* (1 Cor. 12:28). So there had to have been prophets after Christ, yet not of the same caliber. None of this diminishes Jesus, for He's the one, together with God the Father, who set them in the church. Who then shall we believe? The Bible or the critic? Now we realize that there are extremes with a few that say they are prophets, and either try to control the lives of others, or say people cannot understand God's mind without them. But we must stay with the written Word, regardless of these extremists. They who do such things, are not in the Word of Faith.

The critic says that ministers who teach on "how to be led by the Holy Spirit," are saying that the Bible is insufficient. No, they are teaching what the Bible reveals about the Holy Spirit's ministry in the life of a believer. So it is not the faith teacher that says the Bible is insufficient, but rather the critic. The critic proceeds to go back to the Old Testament and speak of false prophets, but he himself, needs to read Peter's epistle, that just as there were false prophets among the people then, there shall also be false teachers among us today.

Now we realize we are to try those who say that they are prophets (1 John 4:1-3), but we also need to make sure they who call themselves teachers do not teach any part of the New Testament has passed away, and must judge also what they say by the written Word, not by their theological intellectual reasonings or because they are over a big church or organization or have a radio or television facility. What it all boils down to is that the critic, on the one hand, does a little good in pointing out some extremes that are not in the real flow of the "Word of Faith," but on the other hand he falls short, and is being used by the enemy to destroy faith in people's lives and cause division in the body of Christ, because of not having received the Holy Spirit as the Bible teaches (Acts 2:4). Because of this, he has no awareness of the real, living presence and working of the Holy Spirit in the life of a Spirit-filled believer. This is usually the real root cause of most of these critics' confusion in these matters.

The critic even goes on to say, "to summarize, the witness is *indirect*. The Holy Spirit and the Christian uses the Word and THE MORAL PROGRESS in one's life, *to draw the common conclusion* that one is a child of God." This statement makes me wonder about the critic. Is he a Christian or just religious? What Bible verse is that? The Bible says, "He that believeth on the Son of God HATH THE WITNESS IN HIMSELF" (1 John 5:10). "The *Spirit bears witness with our spirits*, that we are the children of God" (Rom. 8:16). "And *this is eternal life* that they may KNOW THEE, THE ONLY TRUE God and Jesus Christ, whom Thou hast sent" (John 17:3). "And they shall not teach every man his neighbor and every man his brother saying, KNOW the Lord; for *ALL SHALL KNOW ME* from the least to the greatest" (Heb. 8:11). And *"we know"* we have passed from death to life because we love the brethren (1 John 3:14).

It is the critic who will say you can't take these scriptures for what they say but to the child of God, they make perfect sense just as they are; they mean what they say and say what they mean. The critic has a peculiar way of twisting things to make it look as though those who take God's Word for what it says are wrong and that his rationalization is right. He cannot even see that he is the one who denies the Bible in many areas, conveniently saying anything he doesn't agree with, has passed away.

So it is the Word of Faith teachers then, that teach that the Bible is the infallible Word of God, and that we need all that the Bible reveals belongs to us, as New Testament believers. We are to "contend for the faith, which *was ONCE* delivered to the saints" (Jude 3). The critic is upset, because we believe that we can accept all of the New Testament as being valid for today. He speaks and says, "Everywhere, someone is proclaiming that some truth that was lost for hundreds of years, and is now being restored." But yet he who is obviously an avid follower of Calvin believes that lost truth was restored during Calvin's time, putting himself in the same category of those he criticizes. He says, the Bible denies the Spirit speaking to people apart from Scripture. But yet, all through the Bible, God has sent angels to speak to people: The Holy Spirit spoke to people like Philip the Evangelist to go into the desert (Acts 8), or Peter concerning some men who came to his house (Acts 10). These specific things which could not possibly be addressed in the Bible, can be addressed by the Holy Spirit and were, throughout the Scriptures. If He did it in someone once, He can do it again (Acts 2:4). And as we've stated, the Holy Spirit, in His leading, will never guide one contrary to the written Word of God (2 Pet. 1:20-21). So let's believe what the Bible actually does say about these things (Matt. 9:29).

Chapter 13

Another Look at God and His Sovereignty

The critic says, "All heresies stem from a defective view of God." Finally, he says something correct. And this is exactly the root of his misunderstanding of God's working in the earth. He has misunderstood the free will of man; what predestination in God's plan means and includes, and what faith in God is all about. The critic goes on under this heading to say, God "does not have a body." Where does he get this from? Jesus spoke of seeing God, and He further told the Jews, "Ye have neither heard His voice at any time NOR SEEN HIS SHAPE" (John 5:37). We know the pure in heart shall SEE GOD" (Matt. 5:8). John saw Jesus receive a book "OUT OF THE RIGHT HAND of Him that SAT upon the throne " and Daniel saw the "Son of MAN" go stand before the Ancient of Days (Dan. 7:9-13). Now we could go on and on here, but we've addressed this in another part of this book.

Now, God is God alone—Almighty, Omnipotent, Omniscient, Omnipresent, and Eternal. We understand this. We are created beings. It is He that hath made us and not we ourselves. So then, can man "limit the Holy One of Israel?" Yes. Why? If the critic could understand this one thing about God's plan, many other things would clear up for him. God, in His sovereign choice, gave the earth for a certain time period to mankind, and gave to men a free will. And He determined He would deal with mankind according to their free wills. So during this time period given to man, God tells us to "be doers of His Word," so that we would be blessed. He tells us to choose to obey, to pray, call upon His name, plus numerous other things which are man's responsibility.

Because God Himself gave man authority in the earth and made man free in will, does this mean that God is subject to man?

By no means, for it was God Himself who designed it to be this way but only for a certain time period which He determined in the counsel of His own will. When this time period is up, all men—small and great—will have to give an account of their lives to God. There is coming a "day of wrath" when God will judge the secrets of men. So God is in ultimate and final control. But the critic fails to tell people that this is what Word of Faith preachers really believe, and tries to make it look as though faith teachers say "we can control God."

The critic persists in not really believing in man's free will. He says God only saves who He wills, taking a scripture out of context, and denying the words of Christ, which declare the Gospel is for "all the world; every creature; every man; whosoever; and all nations," and yet he says his predestination theory gives security. What if then, God predestined you to be another Judas and destined you to fall away in the last moments of your life? What security is there in that? He goes on to pull another Scripture out of context to try and prove that everything that happens to people, happens for their good and was determined by God. What about the rape, divorce, robbery, murder, hatred, bitterness, fighting, and perversity! Where do these men find these doctrines? Certainly not in the Bible for God commands us not to do these things. "Do not err My beloved brethren. Every good gift and every perfect gift is from above, and cometh down from the Father of lights, with whom is no variableness, neither any shadow of turning" (James 1:16-17).

He goes on to say, only God is sovereign. Sure, God is the only One Almighty, and everything ends up as He planned it. But again, in His plan, He determined to create free moral agents and gave them the freedom to choose or reject God. The critic fails to see that being a free moral agent, does not mean we are equal opposites to God. It simply means our will is free and for the time now being, we can do as we will, but a court date is set. If we accept Christ, He gives power to become a child of God (John 1:12). If we refuse, we will be cast into the lake of fire (Matt. 25:41). Does this sound like we are saying man is equal to God as the critic implies?

Listen to this. The critic condemns people for being led by the Holy Spirit and then says, "even the dice thrown by gamblers is ordained by Him." Is God into gambling? The critic goes on to do away with prayer, faith, gifts of the Holy Spirit. He does away with most of the New Testament so he himself then, is the one who conjures up a "different gospel." He then erroneously goes on to say that faith teachers teach a faith without submission to God. But this has never been taught. WE teach that the faith which was imparted to us by God (Rom. 12:3) only works when we walk in love (Gal. 5:6) and are obedient to God, and that we can make shipwreck of faith if we put away a clear conscience (1 Tim. 1:19).

It is faith in God and His Word that is taught. Total submission to a wonderful, loving Heavenly Father. That's it! The Word, the whole Word and nothing but the Word (Matthew 4:4). We fully agree that God does as He pleases, and it pleased Him to create man in His image and make man a living soul. He determined that if men prayed or called upon His name, or believed and acted on His Word, He would intervene in their lives (Rom. 1:16; 10:13; Heb. 11:6; James 1:22). Thousands of times in Scripture, God has told men to choose and obey. But the critic contrary to God says, man can't because man controls nothing.

Now we know, for the most part, God sustains and keeps in motion the part of creation that doesn't have a will, and this continues to go on according to His will (Heb. 1:3). But it is obvious also that men have corrupted the earth and filled it with violence and many things contrary to God's will (Gen. 6:5-12), "And God saw that the wickedness of man was great in the earth and that every imagination of the thoughts of his heart was only evil continually, and *it repented the Lord that He had made man on the earth and grieved Him at His heart*" (Gen. 6:5). Men have polluted things, killed one another, raped, robbed and destroyed. They have done numerous evils to one another which will be judged, and none of that is the will of God. Satan also, the prince of the power of the air, works contrary to the will of God. He sent a tornado against Job's son's house, brings sickness and disease; he has affected the animal and plant kingdom and constantly works to corrupt and destroy God's creation (John 10:10; 1 John 3:8). But the critic goes on to say, "God controls sin," and "He controls evil in some way," as though God is pulling the strings on everything that happens. *shame on him*! The Bible never teaches such things.

    We need to rightly divide the Word of God. It is written in such a way that if you think evil of God, you will see everything in that light, (or rather darkness). But if you determine God is completely good, wants His will to be done on earth even as it is in Heaven, that satan and men do evil, but God will override it when men believe Him, and that He can overthrow the wicked with their own schemes, you will then see things in the true light. Let us not believe any accusation against God, regardless of what obscure Old Testament passages may be implied by the critic. Jesus said, "If you've seen Me, you've seen the Father." He is the revelation of God to man. Interpret the scriptures then, through Jesus. He is the "way, *the truth* and the life" (John 14:6; 8:12).

    The reason the critic cannot understand faith, prayer and the authority God gave to man, is because he doesn't believe man's will is free, and he thinks God ultimately controls and pulls the strings on all the good and all the evil. He has believed the lies and accusations of the adversary who deceived Eve by accusing God (Gen. 3:5-6).

    The critic goes on to say, "The new Charismatics promote satan as lord now." First realize that he acknowledges he does not believe in the Baptism with the Holy Spirit, which is received after salvation as the Scriptures declare. So he does not include himself with Pentecostal, full Gospel, Charismatic, Word of Faith, or other Holy Spirit filled groups. The word *Charismatic* comes from the Biblical Greek word charisma, which means "anointing, unction and endowment" of the Holy Spirit. Nothing wrong with that. Call me Charismatic if you will, I'll accept that. He implies that because we quote Paul when Paul calls satan the "god of this world" (2 Cor. 4:3-4), that we are saying satan is "king of kings." These are the ridiculous kind of statements that come from these critics, for we say no such thing.

Jesus called satan, "the prince of this world" (John 14:30). Was he then, exalting satan? Was He calling him king of kings? Of course not. Satan's forces are called, *"the rulers of the darkness of this world"* (Eph. 6:12). He is the spirit that is now at work in disobedient people (Eph. 2:2-3). Far from promoting satan as some great being, to the contrary we say that *Jesus, God's Son, came as a man and defeated satan* and his forces; He disarmed them and made a show of them openly (Col. 2:15). Satan is behind the mystery of iniquity and when he is finally locked away, wars cease, pain ends, sickness disappears, animals are friendly again and things are once again restored back to the perfect will of God (Isa. 11:1-9; Rev. 20:10; 21:1-7). Would God that the critics would learn to believe the Bible.

As far as the believer is concerned, we've already been legally delivered from the authority of darkness (Col. 1:13), but the world is still "without God and without hope" (Eph. 2:12) and ruled over by the prince of the power of the air (Eph. 2:2-3). But the moment they use their free wills (Rev. 22:17) and accept Jesus as Lord (Rom. 10:9-10), satan's legal authority over them ends. But what still needs to be done is to find out what are the "works of the devil" and then to resist him "steadfast in the faith" (1 Pet. 5:8-9), for as the apostle John wrote, *"This is the victory* that overcometh the world, EVEN OUR FAITH" (1 John 5:4). (See also 1 John 2:14.) So as far as Jesus is concerned, satan was defeated almost two thousand years ago but as far as the church is concerned, it will be unto us according to our stand of faith as we stand our ground believing God's Word of Truth.

"Finally My brethren, be strong in the Lord and in the power of His might. Put on the whole armor of God, that ye may be able to stand against the wiles of the devil. For we wrestle not against flesh and blood, but against principalities, against powers, against the rulers of the darkness of this world, against spiritual wickedness in high places. Wherefore, take unto you the whole armor of God, that ye may be able to withstand in the evil day and having done all to stand, stand therefore, having your loins girt about with truth and having on the breastplate of righteousness; and your feet shod with the preparation of the Gospel of peace;

Above all, taking the shield of faith, wherewith ye shall be able to quench all the fiery darts of the wicked. And take the helmet of salvation, and the sword of the Spirit, which is the Word of God" (Eph. 6:10-17).

Why would we still have to put on God's armor if it was, as the critic said, that Jesus controls everything now? We are told by the Lord to "overcome." All you need do is look at each of Christ's orders to the seven churches and you'll see that He said it was up to them to "repent and overcome." That part is man's responsibility. Christ provided the necessary grace, weapons, redemption and victory, but man's part is to believe God's Word, obey it and stand against the wiles of the devil (James 4:7).

The critic is upset because Kenneth Hagin said, "The world is presided over by satan." He said this idea came from a man named E. W. Kenyon who stated that "The whole human race lives today under the cruel Emperor satan." The critic doesn't know his Bible. Let me state this: Kenyon evidently got this directly from John the Apostle, who said, "We know that we are of God and the whole world lieth in wickedness" (King James Version). Let's look at it from a few other translations.

"We realize that we have come from God, while the world is under the influence of the evil one" (Twentieth Century New Testament).

It is..."in the power of the evil one" (Weymouth Translation in Modern Speech). "We know (positively) that we are of God and the whole world (around us) is under the power of the evil one" (Amplified).

"We know that we ourselves are children of God and we also know that the world around us is under the power of the evil one" (Phillips).

"We know that we are of God's family while the whole godless world lies in the power of the evil one" (New English Bible).

Would God that the critic could accept all the words of the Bible and believe it as it is written, rather than according to his theological training. It should be obvious to the reader by now that the critics of the "Word of Faith" (Rom. 10:8), do not understand any of the Biblical teaching of the Word as to what's really happening.

So then, it is John, under inspiration of the Holy Spirit that revealed, "the whole world is under the power of the wicked one." (See also Ephesians 2:2.) But as the scriptures reveal, this is temporary, for God will, in His own set time, send an angel to bind satan and cast him in the pit. God revealing by this, that satan's doom is ultimately sealed (Rev. 20:1-3), and even satan knows this (Rev. 12:12). But for now, we must exercise the authority that the Lord's given us (Luke 10:19), and cast out devils (Mark 16:17); resist him (1 Pet. 5:8-9); overcome him by the Word (1 John 2:14), and put on the armor of God (Eph. 6:10-17). So what he's doing then, cannot be the will of God.

Satan as in the days of Christ, is STILL THE ONE who is killing, stealing and destroying here on the earth (John 10:10), contrary to the will of God. But the time will come and is set, when he will reap what he has sown. We clearly know God has an ultimate plan, which will come to pass and no devil, angel, or man can stop it, for the mouth of the Lord hath spoken it. But we also believe what God said about our present responsibilities as the body of Christ in the earth. So we will believe, act, obey, speak and exercise the authority He gave us through His name. So then to say that we can believe and obey what God said, does not take away from the sovereignty of God. It shows submission to God and what He said in His Word (James 4:7).

Brethren, God is not the cause of the evil in this world. He has not commissioned the devil to kill, steal and destroy; He sent His Son to destroy the devil's works and to regain authority for us over the devil's works (Matt. 28:18; Mark 16:15-18). If you listen to the critic, you will become like him a doormat for the devil and then you'll thank God for what the devil is doing. Away with such unscriptural thoughts. So it is seen again that we say no more than what is actually written. Satan is a mere fallen angel (Isa. 14:12).

Why Did God Create Man?

The critic is upset because faith teachers have taught that because God is love, He created man in His image and likeness to have a family. What saith the Word?

"For this cause I bow my knees unto the Father of our Lord Jesus Christ, of whom *the whole family* in Heaven and earth is named" (Eph. 3:14-15).

"Wherefore, come out from among them and be ye separate, saith the Lord, and touch not the unclean thing, and I will receive you, and will be a Father unto you and ye shall be *My sons and daughters, saith the Lord Almighty*" (2 Cor. 6:17-18).

"For it became Him, for whom are all things and by whom are all things, in *bringing many sons unto glory,* to make the captain of their salvation perfect through sufferings" (Heb. 2:10).

These, plus numerous other scriptures show that God, who is love, has desired and planned a family composed of free moral agents, with whom He would dwell forever. "That in the ages to come, He might show the exceeding riches of His grace in His kindness toward us through Christ Jesus" (Eph. 2:7).

"And I heard a great voice out of Heaven saying, Behold, *the tabernacle of God is with men, and He will dwell with them and they shall be His people*, and God Himself, shall be with them, and be their God. And God shall wipe away all tears from their eyes, and there shall be no more death, neither sorrow, nor crying, neither shall there be any more pain, for the former things are passed away" (Rev. 21:3-4).

We do not say God "needed" man, but God, who is love, desired to create man in His image and willed to have a family.

I John 3:1 says, "Behold, what manner of love the Father hath bestowed upon us, that we should be called the sons of God, therefore, the world knoweth us not, because it knew Him not."

Revelation 4:11 tells us, "Thou art worthy, O Lord, to receive glory and honor and power, for Thou hast created all things and *for Thy pleasure* they are and were created."

The critic who feels God is an impersonal being needing nothing says, "the idea of a Father God who wanted children sounds ominously like Mormonism with its 'Father God' having children." The critic has forgotten that Jesus revealed God as "Father" numerous times, and that God said, I "will be a Father unto you and ye shall be My sons and daughters." Plus many other scriptures that reveal God designed man to be His sons and daughters. If the critic cannot accept the plain Word of God, then no argument would be good enough for him. Again he now shows he doesn't know the difference between Mormonism and Christianity. Mormonism simply counterfeited and then twisted what was revealed in God's Word, but their explanations of a Father God and family are very different from the Bible view.

The critic then takes a quote from Reverend Hagin, when he said, "He, (God), can't get along without you any more than you can get along without Him." But certainly Brother Hagin was speaking of a whole different topic when the statement was made, but the critic, again taking it completely out of context in his manipulative style, won't tell you that. It should be obvious then, that the critic has not been honest nor even begun to understand God's message of faith, God's plan, or that God created man with a free will. The critic goes on to say, "God controls everything that happens, even the roll of the gamblers dice, that all that happens, good or bad, is the will of God." And then he attacks the Word of faith preachers saying, "One can only imagine the lives that are being wrecked by this (Word of Faith) teaching." He has no logic at all to his own reasonings, but contradicts himself continuously. He attacks others and then says, "It is a great encouragement for the Christian to know that EVERYTHING that happens to him must first be filtered through God's sovereign will."

Is this a great encouragement for those whose lives have been crushed, had their families broken up, children abused or stolen, are dying of cancer, in an insane asylum, and a million other evils? What kind of a message are these so-called preachers, bringing to people? They cease not to blame God, excuse satan, and tell people to accept every evil that comes as their lot in life, completely ignoring the Covenant God has given to us. It is amazing to me that the longsuffering of God waits while all these false accusations against Him are made. First he implies God turns people over to the wicked one and then he says, God "will keep us from the evil one." To me, brethren, this makes no sense.

What About the Local Church?

Let me say this. All Word of Faith preachers teach that every person should attend a local, Bible-believing church and support it with their tithes, prayers, and their regular attendance. God has given the five-fold ministry for the perfecting of the saints. "Wherefore He saith, When He ascended up on high, He led captivity captive, and gave gifts unto men. Now that He ascended, what is it but that He also descended first into the lower parts of the earth? He that descended is the same also that ascended up far above all Heavens, that He might fill all things, and He gave some apostles and some prophets and some evangelists and some pastors and teachers. For the perfecting of the saints, for the work of the ministry, for the edifying of the body of Christ, till we all come in the unity of the faith, and of the knowledge of the Son of God, unto a perfect man, unto the measure of the stature of the fullness of Christ" (Eph. 4:8-13). Notice, these will remain until "we ALL come into the unity of the faith."

Now the critic acknowledges in his book that he does not believe in the supernatural call of God as Paul and the other ministries of the New Testament did. He feels men just choose it as their vocation. But Paul in Galatians 1:1 wrote: *"Paul, an apostle, not of men, neither by man, but by Jesus Christ, and God the Father*, who raised Him from the dead."

Acts 13:2-4: "As they ministered to the Lord and fasted, *the Holy Ghost said, Separate Me Barnabas and Saul for the work whereunto I have called them*, and when they had fasted and prayed, and laid their hands on them, they sent them away. So they, being sent forth by the Holy Ghost, departed unto Seleucia, and from thence they sailed to Cyprus."

First Corinthians 12:18, 28: "But now *hath God set* the members every one of them, in the body, as it hath pleased Him." Verse 28: "And *God hath set* some *in the church, first apostles, secondarily prophets, thirdly teachers*, after that miracles, then gifts of healings, helps, governments, diversities of tongues."

The critic believes that men ordain men. But Jesus told His ministers, "I have chosen you *and ordained you,* that you should go and bring forth fruit. . ." (John 15:16). Perhaps the critic has usurped the office of a teacher and never was called by God and that this is the reason for his confused teachings (1 Cor. 12:3-7).

He constantly says, God is sovereign and in control of *everything*. Then contradicting himself he constantly speaks of things we should do and are accountable for. The critic goes on to say, "the health and wealth" people, virtually never speak of these things (speaking of the local church, worship). This simply goes to show he has not gone to a local church that believes in God's message of faith. For if he did, he would see people "excited about Jesus," worshipping God and reaching out to the lost. He would hear solid teaching from God's Word and see the Spirit of God touch lives.

But more than likely, he would not acknowledge anything that the Holy Spirit was doing there, because he has God in his own theological box, which he believes God cannot jump out of. But let us continue to worship God, believe all His Word and obey all of His Gospel.

Jesus–His Person and Word

First of all, let us speak boldly and say we believe Jesus is God of God, the second Person of the Godhead, through whom all things were made. He is the divine Son of the living God, King of Kings and Lord of Lords. God's only uniquely begotten, who became man for the sake of our redemption. He (divinity) partook of flesh and blood (Heb. 2:14), and is the Shepherd and Bishop of our souls.

Now, Word of Faith teachers always admit Jesus was God manifest in the flesh on the earth (1 Tim. 3:16). He was who He was and is who He is. The "Son of the living God," found in fashion as a man. "But made Himself of no reputation, and took upon Him, the form of a servant and was made in the likeness of men, and being found in fashion as a man, He humbled Himself and became obedient unto death, even the death of the cross" (Phil. 2:7-8). He became in all points like a man, "Wherefore, *in all things* it behooved Him to be made like unto His brethren, that He might be a merciful and faithful high priest in things pertaining to God, to make reconciliation for the sins of the people" (Heb. 2:17); and He was here in the likeness of sinful flesh. "For what the law could not do, in that it was weak through the flesh, God sending His own Son in the likeness of sinful flesh and for sin, condemned sin in the flesh" (Rom. 8:3). While He was here, He hungered, He thirsted, He prayed, He cried out with strong cryings and tears to God. "Who in the days of His flesh, when He had offered up prayers and supplications with strong crying and tears unto Him that was able to save Him from death, and was heard in that He feared, *though He were a Son, yet learned He obedience* by the things which He suffered" (Heb. 5:7-8). He grew in wisdom and stature. "And Jesus increased in wisdom and stature, and in favor with God and man" (Luke 2:52). He was limited in knowledge (Mark 13:32); made a little lower than the angels (Heb. 2:9); and was tempted (Heb. 4:16). All the miracles that He did were by the power of the Holy Spirit (Acts 10:38), and He did nothing of Himself (John 5:19). There were numerous other limitations He willingly experienced while He was here on the earth as a man, representing man, but

He never ceased being who He was, deity manifest in the flesh. He was 100 percent God and 100 percent man, the God-man. Some say He was not limited on earth, but those who say this are not backed up by the scriptures that clearly reveal He was.

Jesus did operate supernaturally as a man, a prophet (Mark 6:4), who saw things by the Holy Spirit's anointing (John 5:19-20). He was the most completely yielded vessel to the Holy Spirit, who ever walked the earth. (See 2 Kings 6:5-20.) He knew who He was and what His mission was, but this does not mean He didn't experience all the natural limitations of a man, for the scriptures reveal He did. To say He grew in wisdom; was made lower than the angels; grew tired; prayed for the Father's intervention and numerous other things, is not heretical but Scriptural. But the critic will say, those who say such things are heretics! Is Paul? Are the writers of the Gospels heretics? Nowhere does the Bible say He functioned as God on the earth. But it does say, *"in all things* it behooved Him to be made like unto His brethren" (Heb. 2:17).

Now Jesus could have done miracles of His own accord if He had not laid aside these privileges for the sake of man's redemption (Phil. 2:7), for even the devil recognized that God's Son had the power to do so, but Jesus wouldn't (Matt. 4:3-4), for He was here to overcome as a man, for man, and He responded to satan's enticement to do so saying, "It is written, MAN shall not live by bread alone, but by every word that proceedeth out of the mouth of God." He had the ability to function as God, but came here and limited Himself to what's available to man through faith, prayer, doing the Word and obeying His Father's will, and He said everyone that is perfect shall be as his master (that is, in his humanity). In this way, He left us an example that we should follow in His steps. Yes, Jesus was both God and man.

To say He did not truly walk as a man, is to deny Him His place in the plan of Redemption. What He did for us, He did as "the last Adam" and "the second man" (1 Cor. 15:45-47). He, the offended one, limited Himself *as man*, lived a perfectly righteous life *as a man*, and then went to the cross *as a man* to represent man and to pay for mankind's sins.

Now this does not mean that because He became man, that we are in the same class as He is, as far as His deity goes. He's the Creator and we are forever the creature. We, in ourselves, are not divine. Yes, we have God dwelling in us (Eph. 2:22; 1 John 4:4; 2 Cor. 6:16), but we can depart from God. Some have come to the place that they have even denied Him (Heb. 3:12) and walk no more with Him, but He cannot deny Himself. So we cannot be God or divine, but Jesus, in Himself, is God's divine Son; He is God of God, true light of true light, who came forth from the bosom of the Father (John 1:18); came into this world (John 16:28) and again He left the world and went back to the Father, and all the time, He was God the Son–Emmanuel. (God with us)

In some things, according to God's infinite wisdom and righteousness, Jesus operated as a man to fulfill all righteousness for us. In things pertaining to men, He was in all points like us, but yet it was still the blood of God that was shed for the remission of our sins (Acts 20:28).

Spirit, Soul and Body

The critic doesn't believe that we are a spirit, or for that matter, he doesn't even believe we have a spirit. His belief is similar to Jehovah Witnesses here. But listen to the apostle, "For what man knows the things of a man, save the *spirit of man*, which is in him" (1 Cor. 2:11)? "The *spirits of just men* made perfect" (Heb. 12:22-23). We know that Jesus is a Spirit, who partook of flesh and blood (Heb. 2:14). A body was prepared for Him. Hebrews 10:5 says, "Wherefore, when He cometh into the world, He saith, Sacrifice and offering Thou wouldest not, but a body hast Thou prepared Me." We also, are spirits who have souls and live in a physical body. "Forasmuch then as the children are partakers of flesh and blood, He also, Himself, likewise, took part of the same; that through death He might destroy him that had the power of death, that is, the devil" (Heb. 2:14). First Thessalonians 5:23 says, "And the very God of peace sanctify you wholly, and I pray God your whole *spirit* and *soul* and *body* be preserved blameless unto the coming of our Lord Jesus Christ."

In Hebrews 12:9, God is called "the Father of spirits." and Paul said, to be "absent from the body is to be present with the Lord" (2 Cor. 5:8). Paul knew people could be in or out of their body and still be themselves.

In 2 Corinthians 12:1-4 He says, "It is not expedient for Me doubtless to glory. I will come to visions and revelations of the Lord. I knew a man in Christ about fourteen years ago, (*whether in the body, I cannot tell, or whether out of the body, I cannot tell: God knoweth*), such an one caught up to the third Heaven. And I knew such a man, (whether in the body, or out of the body, I cannot tell: God knoweth), how that he was caught up into paradise, and heard unspeakable words which it is not lawful for a man to utter."

In or out of the body the man exists. For man is a spirit, who lives in a physical body. Jesus also knew this. He said, "There was a certain rich man, which was clothed in purple and fine linen, and fared sumptuously every day, and there was a certain beggar named Lazarus, which was laid at his gate, full of sores, and desiring to be fed with the crumbs which fell from the rich man's table, moreover the dogs came and licked his sores. And it came to pass that the beggar died, (physically), *and was carried by the angels into Abraham's bosom, the rich man also died,* (physically), *and was buried. And in hell he lift up his eyes, being in torment, and seeth Abraham afar off*, and Lazarus in his bosom. *And he cried and said, Father Abraham, have mercy on me, and send Lazarus that he may dip the tip of his finger in water, and cool my tongue,* for I am tormented in this flame. But Abraham said, Son, remember that thou in thy lifetime receivedst thy good things and likewise, Lazarus evil things, but now he is comforted, and thou art tormented. And beside all this, between us and you there is a great gulf fixed, so that they which would pass from hence to you cannot, neither can they pass to us, that would come from thence. Then he said, I pray thee, therefore father, that thou wouldest send him to my father's house, for I have five brethren, that he may testify unto them, lest they also come into this place of torment. Abraham saith unto him, they have Moses and the prophets, let them hear them. And he said, Nay, father Abraham, but if one went unto them, from the dead, they will repent. And he said unto him, If they hear not Moses and the prophets, neither will they be persuaded though one rose from the dead" (Luke 16:19-31). (Their natural bodies were buried, but their spirit bodies and souls lived on in the spiritual realm.)

The critic refuses to believe what Paul and Jesus revealed and says we are not a spirit, nor are there three parts to our nature, but we are simply "soul and body." Hebrews 4:12 says, "For the Word of God is quick and powerful and sharper than any two edged sword, piercing even to the dividing asunder of soul and spirit, and of the joints and marrow, and is a discerner of the thoughts and intents of the heart." If they can be divided, then they are separate parts of our nature. So man is triune: spirit, soul and body, as the divine Word also states. It is true then, as Jesus said, "what is born of Spirit IS spirit. . . ." "The Spirit itself beareth witness *with our spirit*, that we are the children of God" (Rom. 8:16). This is the part of us that's regenerated at the new birth and what causes us to come alive to the spiritual things of God (1 Cor. 2:14). Paul further said in 2 Corinthians 5:8: "We are confident, I say, and willing rather *to be absent from the body and to be present with the Lord*." "For I am in a strait betwixt two, having a desire to depart and to be with Christ; which is far better: Nevertheless to abide in the flesh is more needful for you" (Phil. 1:23-24). We say no more than what God's written Word says.

The Virgin Birth

The critic here once again either intentionally twists what is taught in most Word of Faith circles, or else he, again, does not comprehend what was said. Word of Faith teachers for the most part, teach that Jesus' human birth came about by the power of God's Word and Spirit. ". . .that which is conceived in her is of the Holy Ghost" (Matt. 1:20). We do not say Jesus was created by God's Word as the critic says we do, but *rather that a body* was prepared for Him by the "Word of God."

Jesus said in Luke's Gospel, "the seed is the Word of God" (Luke 8:11). God's Word is the original seed of everything.

Before there was even a man or seed in man or any living thing, there was only the Word. The Word of God brought all things and all seeds into existence (Gen. 1:1-31). God used His Word of promise to give Abraham and Sarah, a miracle child, which came to pass BECAUSE THEY BELIEVED HIS WORD (Rom. 4:17-21). Hebrews 11:11 says, "Through faith also Sara herself received strength to conceive seed, and was delivered of a child when she was past age, because she judged him faithful who had promised." It was the same with Mary. The angel brought to her, God's Word of promise. Mary said, "Behold, the handmaiden of the Lord, be it unto me according to Thy Word." And because God's Word was believed, He watched over it and performed it. The prophetic word about woman's seed (Gen. 3:15) was then fulfilled and the Word became flesh and dwelt amongst us (John 1:14). In this way, a "body" was prepared for the Son of God (Heb. 10:5), and He partook of flesh and blood.

Elizabeth later prophesied by the Holy Ghost and said, "And blessed is she that believed, for there shall be a performance of those things which were told her from the Lord" (Luke 1:45). The critic says, "if this were possible, why could this not happen again?" He says this because "he thinks" Word of Faith preachers say Mary brought this to pass, "by visualizing it with her mind." That's how far off he is in understanding the real Word of Faith message.

What happened was that God spoke *to her*, *His promise, His Word*. She believed it and God then, brought it to pass (Isa. 55:10-11). But the critic calls this operation of God, "metaphysical" and once again it shows he does not know the difference between what's metaphysical and what's Biblical.

Jesus then came in "the likeness of sinful flesh." The same Word that formed man's flesh in the beginning, brought to pass in Mary, a body of flesh, for the Son of God. Mary's lineage stems from Abraham and David and it was she who believed God.

The critic then writes outright lies and says that the faith movement says that each man has "a spark of the divine within." Nowhere, in almost twenty years of hearing the Faith Message have I *ever* heard that. The critic works much like the secular media or the Pharisees of old, who brought many false accusations against Christ. Times have changed nothing.

And never have I ever heard anyone teach that Jesus had a sinful nature in faith teaching as the critic implies it does, for we know that the Bible plainly states that Jesus was "holy, harmless, undefiled and separate from sinners; and made higher than the Heavens" (Heb. 7:26). But in his manipulative style, he tries to compare "faith teachers" with those in cults and if he cannot find how to do so, he simply, with the stroke of his pen, says that they believe these things (which we do not believe). He implies numerous other false accusations, also many of which are not even worthy to say or to take time on, for they are outright lies, conceived probably by the devil himself to stop people from hearing God's real Gospel (1 Tim. 4:1).

Oh, people of God, why don't you go hear or read for yourself, what is taught by men of God in the Word of Faith, rather than hear the lopsided false accusations of those who know not God's Word nor His power; but rather try to impress you with their intellectual theology, born of the reasoning minds of men? All we ask is that you read a scripture and believe what's actually written and look at the obscure scriptures in the light of the clearer passages. Is this too much to ask?

Now let me again state something we have stated elsewhere. We do not believe Jesus EVER became a sinner as faith teachers are sometimes accused of teaching. Neither in His earthly life, nor on the cross, nor during the three days and three nights He was in the heart of the earth, nor was He ever a sinner. He was the just, dying for the unjust. We do believe that as He "bore our sins in His own body on the tree," and a veil caused by our sin, came between Him and the Father (Heb. 10:20), and He cried out, "My God, My God, why hast Thou forsaken Me?" He was dealt with the way sin would be dealt with. "He who knew no sin was made to be sin for us, that we might be made the righteousness of God in Christ" (2 Cor. 5:21). But yet He was still the holy Son of God. It was in His body that He took upon Himself our sin as the

Lord God laid upon Him, the sin of us all (1 Pet. 2:24).

`Isaiah 53:6 says, "All we like sheep have gone astray, we have turned every one to his own way, and the Lord hath laid on Him the iniquity of us all." He had come to condemn sin in the flesh (Rom. 8:3), and to remove the veil between God and man caused by the sins and works of the flesh (Isa. 59:2). He had come to suffer the wrath for us, to deliver us from the wrath to come (1 Thess. 1:10), and also to deliver us from the authority of darkness (Col. 1:13).

So Jesus offered Himself without spot to God as the spotless lamb of God, *and then* our sin was placed on Him. His soul was made an offering for sin (Isa. 53:10; John 10). From that point He suffered the awful consequences of man's sin (Heb. 2:9). And if He did not suffer all that a man who's a sinner would suffer, then there are still things we need to suffer for our sins. The ransom price had to be paid in full in order to release us from all of sin's slavery. How dare anyone say He didn't pay it all (Gal. 3:13)!

He suffered all of the awful consequences of man's sin (Heb. 2:9). It was after this penalty was paid, that Jesus was raised by the Spirit of God (Rom. 8:11). His soul was not left (forsaken; abandoned) in hell (Acts 2:27-31), but He was raised from the dead, loosed from death pains, and when He was quickened, (made alive) (Col. 2:13), Paul said we were made alive *with Him*.

"And you *hath* (past tense) He quickened, who were dead in trespasses and sins" (Eph.2:1). "Even when we were dead in sins, *hath quickened us together with Christ*, by grace ye are saved" (Eph. 2:5). How were we made alive when we were born again? Was it physically? No, we were quickened spiritually. For we were dead *in trespasses and sins*, and yet, we were physically alive. He experienced the veil removed from between Him and the Father (Heb. 10:20), and so do we when we accept His finished work (2 Cor. 3:16-18; John 20:17; Acts 13:32-33). This is a fact.

Is it then wrong to say we were "made alive" together with Him, just as Paul stated? When were we made alive? Obviously when we were born again (Rom. 6:10-11). What was that? It was being reconciled to God and an impartation of His life into our spirits (Eph. 4:17; Rom. 6:23). When this happened, we were quickened out of our state of death; (See 1 John 3:14.) Now the Bible calls Jesus, the "firstborn from the dead," the "first begotten of the dead," and it calls His church "the church of the firstborn." He came down, tasted death, which was caused by sin and experienced this for us to redeem us that we might live again, and so that in all things, He might have the preeminence (Col. 1:16-18). He was the firstborn of all creation and He willed to be the "firstborn from the dead," *that in all things* He might have the preeminence—be the beginning of all things. No other single man could be the beginning of the church, or the start of the new creation. He is the firstborn of all creation with all its rights and privileges and the firstborn of the church with all its rights and privileges (Rev. 1:5; Rom. 8:29; Heb. 12:23; Col. 1:18). Argue with it if you will, but it is what the scriptures teach. Still we are not saying that He was a sinner, nor did He take into His spirit satan's nature, but rather that He, the Holy One, bore our sin, suffered the real consequences of sin, and paid its total debt for us. He, who was and is holy, tasted death in all its forms for us and then overcame it for us for it was not possible that death could hold Him, for He is the resurrection and this gives to us the keys of victory over these things. "To you God gave life in giving life to Christ" (Colossians 2:13, Twentieth Century New Testament).

"But thanks be to God, which giveth us the victory through our Lord Jesus Christ" (1 Cor. 15:57).

"And when I saw Him, I fell at His feet as dead. And He laid His right hand upon Me, saying unto me, Fear not, I am the first and the last. *I am He that liveth, and was dead; and, behold, I am alive for evermore*, amen. And have the keys of hell and of death" (Rev. 1:17-18).

None of this takes away from Christ's divinity, only that He experienced as He, Himself said, a separation somehow, from the Father (Matt. 27:46). And through the prophetic Spirit said His soul would not be abandoned forever in hell (Acts 2:26-32);

(Isa. 53:10). He was, the Bible states, quickened from this state of death (Col. 2:12-13), made alive and then raised again physically in a resurrection body. And so we are first quickened spiritually, as Paul put it, we have been "made alive together with Him," and are "risen with Him," then later he said we will receive a resurrection body (Phil. 3:21). Adam first died spiritually (was separated from God) on the day he ate of the tree and then later died physically. The process is now reversed by Jesus Christ, the last Adam, who is a life giving Spirit (1 Cor. 15:45).

This doesn't take away from the greatness of our Lord and Savior, but magnifies His grace and mercy and willingness to pay the utmost for us, that we might live unto God once again (Rom. 6:9-10). We,therefore, are not wrong for saying He bore our sin, was forsaken of God, went to hell, was made alive, loosed from the pains of death, received a glorified body and that He is the first begotten from the dead. We say no more than what the Bible actually says. Those who deny what He suffered are the ones who deny what He paid. If we would only believe every Scripture, then we'd have a complete picture. The Scriptures do not contradict themselves. So Word of Faith teachers teach that Jesus was fully God and fully man on earth. That as God the Son, He really did come out of the bosom of the Father and in bodily presence, left His Father and came into this world. "For I came down from Heaven, not to do Mine own will, but the will of Him that sent Me" (John 6:38).

"*I came forth from* the Father and am come into the world, again, *I leave the world, and go to the Father*" (John 16:28).

"And we have seen and do testify that the Father sent the Son to be the Savior of the world" (1 John 4:14). Others such as Lazarus, were raised from the dead before Christ was, but Christ is called the "first begotten" from the dead (Rev. 1:5).

We believe that God's Son really was separated from His Father as He said, and that He truly did taste death and all its workings for every man (Heb. 2:9). We agree with the fact that He arose as the Head of the "new creation," the "firstborn (first begotten) from the dead," the "second man" who came as a quickening spirit to give life to others (John 12:23-24). Because He lives, we can now live also (Rev. 1:17-18). That God could have a Son who is God of God, the Word, and that they could somehow be separated, is revealed in Scripture. If you can't understand it, at least believe God told the truth in the record He gave concerning His Son. If we don't believe it, John said we call God a liar (1 John 5:9-10). To me, it's simple to understand (Heb. 11:3).

Now we are created beings. We could never be the same as Jesus by nature, or substance. He is deity we are not. We are only privileged to be partakers of Christ the true vine, as long as we abide in Him (John 15:1-7; Heb. 3:14). But if we do not continue in His goodness, His Word says we also will be cut off (John 15:6; Rom. 11:22; Heb. 3:14). Jesus had the Father dwelling in Him (John 14:10-11), but He, Himself also, is God's own eternal Son (Rom. 8:31), who came out of the very bosom of God (John 1:18). So Jesus is unique in His own divine nature, but walked as a man on this earth and was an example to us in His humanity. Christ said, "the works that I do shall ye do also" (John 14:12). "As the Father hath sent Me out into the world, even so send I you out into the world."

So in some things, as a man He truly is an example to us and in other things He is uniquely the Holy Son of God. We can never be God, divine, or cease being a created being, while Jesus always was and ever will be, God of God (Heb. 1:8-10).

Did Jesus Empty Himself Of His Divinity?

Now we know that He did not cease being who He was. He did not cease being deity when He was here. He simply, according to Philippians 2:7-8, limited Himself and the use of His Godhead powers, and was found in fashion as a man in all points like you and I (Heb. 2:17).

We many not understand all the *SON* of God went through for us, but we must, by faith, accept God's revelation of what happened. Even though the critic implies it, I have never heard a

Word of Faith minister say Jesus was not God, or the Son of God, while He was here on the earth, or that He gave up His deity. Only that in order to perfectly represent man, the Son of God limited Himself in all points, as a man, and many times He referred to Himself as the "Son of man."

Jesus fulfilled all of God's law for us perfectly as a man, and died as our substitute. In so doing, He redeemed us from the curse of the law (Gal. 3:13-14), and opened the door for men to once again be reconciled back to God, and now through faith in His great redemptive work, we can be freed from all of the curse that came because of sin (John 8:31-32).

Romans 8:31-32 says, "What shall we then say to these things? If God be for us, who can be against us? He that spared not His own Son, but delivered Him up for us all, how shall He not with Him also freely give us all things?" To say He did not make provision for us in every area of life when God's Word says He did, is to nullify the work of Christ and reject what Christ offers (Eph. 1:3; 2 Pet. 1:3-4). It was all paid at the same time. He became the whole curse and all it includes with its effects and consequences that came in because of sin. But now sin has been put away by the work of Christ and so legally, the Father God can now qualify us who have accepted Christ and His finished work, to share in the inheritance of the saints in light (Col. 1:12-13), and thank God, because of Jesus and His saving work, we are also now delivered from the authority of darkness.

Let us again state (so that no one misunderstands) that Jesus, the divine Son of God, partook of flesh and blood. He was God and man. He never ceased being divine by nature, but He limited Himself as a man while He walked here on the earth (Matt. 4:3-4). As a man, He lived a perfect human life, never committing a sin and was the only One who could pay the full penalty for sinners. The just for the unjust.

"But not as the offense, so also is the free gift. For if through the offense of one many be dead, much more the grace of God and the gift by grace, *which is by one man, Jesus Christ*, hath abounded unto many" (Rom. 5:15).

"For as by one man's disobedience, many were made sinners so by the obedience of one shall many be made righteous" (Rom. 5:19).

First Corinthians 15:21 says, *"For since by man came death, by man came also the resurrection of the dead."* (See also verses 22, 45-47.)

Christ's Saving Work

Forgive me for being repetitious, but for the sake of those who have never been taught these things from the Word of God, let's go over it again, one more time.

God, for a certain allotted time period, turned the earth over to man (Ps. 115:16). Adam knowingly sinned and yielded himself to satan; by one man then, sin entered the world and death by sin (Rom. 5:12). Satan gained a legal right to be here. God had allowed free moral agents, both satan (lucifer) and Adam, to choose their own course (Prov. 1:29-31). But God determined and set a day of judgment for both (Rev. 20). For the meantime though, through Adam's sin, satan became "the god of this world" (2 Cor. 4:3-4). Not a god by nature, but only called that because men choose to follow and worship him by their lifestyles rather than the only "true and living God," (Isa. 44:6); and men became subject to the devil, (Col. 1:13; Eph. 2:2; 1 John 5:19; John 8:44), and are children of wrath by nature (Eph. 2:3). They were without God and without hope in this world (Eph. 2:12), and because of sin, they are considered children of the devil (1 John 3:8, 10). Fallen men are alienated from the life of God and their understanding is darkened (Eph. 4:17). God having chosen to create man a free moral agent, would not interfere with the lives of free moral agents unless they used their wills to call upon Him, or others prayed for them, calling on God (Rom. 10:13).

The earth is still the Lord's by right of creation, but temporarily it's in the hands of man and satan. This is the reason for the pain, crime, suffering and destruction. And when God's will is completely done again here on earth, even as it is in Heaven, there will be no more curse, pain, sorrow, crying, death, poverty, disease, and even the animals will get along. God said these "former things" will have then have passed away (Rev. 21:1-7).

Almost two thousand years ago, the Father sent the Son to be the Savior of the world. He came here as the Son of man in the likeness of sinful flesh (Rom. 8:3). When He was here, He was divinity, but yet He laid aside His supernatural Godhead powers and all that would hinder Him from truly being a man with all the limitations that go with it. He said His miracles were not done by Himself (John 5:19), but by the power of the Holy Spirit (Luke 4:17-18; Matt. 12:28; Acts 10:38).

He also said, "that we, if we'd believe, could do the same works He did (John 14:12), which we do see done by men in the Book of Acts and by some men of God today (Mark 16:17-18). He allowed Himself to be crucified for us and bore our sin in His own body on the tree, and when He said, "It is finished," He meant the Old Covenant and its law. That's why the veil was rent, signifying the end of that Covenant and earthly priesthood. The New Covenant was not yet complete, for at the time He said, "It is finished," He hadn't yet died. Yet the Bible says, "We were reconciled to God by the death of His Son" (Rom. 5:10), and that He was raised for our justification (Rom. 4:25). So after His death, He still had to spend three days and three nights in the heart of the earth (Matt. 12:40); go to hell (Acts 2:27-31); be quickened, (made alive) rise again from the dead; enter His body and then afterwards, ascend to the Father (John 20:17), and then finally bring His blood into the Heavenly Holy of Holies, and obtain eternal Redemption for us (Heb. 9:11-12).

This all was a part of the work of establishing the New Covenant in His blood. Jesus then, *did not* say *the New Covenant* was finished when He said, "It is finished," but the *Old* Covenant. So the critics are again shown to be wrong when they imply that, "It was all finished at the cross before He died." So He was the just suffering for the unjust. *He had to suffer all* the various consequences and effects of sin (Heb. 9:27), *so that we could* have the gift of righteousness and *be blessed with all* the spiritual blessings of righteousness (Eph. 1:3). He had to go to hell (Acts 2:27-31), to bring us to Heaven (John 14:6). For hell is where sinners must now presently go (2 Cor.5:21). After the penalty and consequences of sin was paid in full, Jesus was raised up from the deep, (in the Greek, the abyss; the pit-Rom. 10:7), the dead, by the glory of the Father (Rom. 6:4), no longer forsaken of the Father because of baring our sin, He was the first one quickened made alive, (Col. 2:13), and is called the "first begotten of the dead" (Rev. 1:5). Then He entered once again into His body and it became a glorified body of flesh and bone (Luke 24:39). He had satisfied God's justice, conquered satan, disarmed the principalities and powers, and obtained the keys of hell and death (Rev. 1:17-18). He had made the new birth available to men (Heb. 12:23; 11:39-40). The "spirits of just men" could now be made perfect (Heb. 12:23). When a person now confesses Jesus as his Lord, and believes in his heart in Christ's resurrection, God's power that quickened and raised Christ, quickens that person and saves him from his lost condition, (Col. 2:13; Eph. 2:5). They are then joined one spirit with the Lord (1 Cor. 6:17), and become bone of His bone and flesh of His flesh (Eph. 5:30). They then have *"the life"* (1 John 5:11-12).

Christ had both satisfied the claims of justice on the one hand and also delivered man from satan's authority on the other. "Who hath delivered us from the power of darkness, and hath translated us into the Kingdom of His dear Son" (Col. 1:13).

"For as much then as the children are partakers of flesh and blood, He also Himself, likewise, took part of the same, *that through death He might destroy him that had the power of death, that is, the devil."* Now that He's raised, "death hath no more dominion over Him" (Rom. 6:9). This, friend, is not a "different gospel." This is "the Gospel" as it's recorded in God's Word.

So, who then is really preaching "another Gospel?" It is the critics themselves. *"But though we, or an angel from Heaven, preach any other Gospel, unto you than that which we have preached unto you, let him be accursed"* (Gal.1:8-9).

The critics of the Faith Message have said, God predestines some to Heaven, some to hell; that He controls the roll of the gambler's dice; He makes people sick; sends evil trials; will not respond to faith; they mock the Holy Spirit's power and gifts calling it metaphysical; they reject Christ's teaching on words; mock answered prayer; saying "name it and claim it;" deny the full suffering of Christ, and cease not to reject the clear teaching of the Word in numerous areas. How in the world people can continue to believe these men, I don't know.

Dear Brethren, I am not saying these things so straightforward to be mean, but rather to do just as Jude did and "contend for the faith which was once delivered to the saints." We do not want the devil to steal God's precious Word from anybody. "And He said unto them, Know ye not this parable and how then will ye know all parables? The sower soweth the Word. And these are they by the wayside, where the Word is sown; but when they have heard, satan cometh immediately and taketh away the Word that was sown in their hearts. And these are they which are sown on good ground; such as hear the Word, and receive it, and bring forth fruit, some thirtyfold, some sixty, and some an hundred" (Mark 4:13-15, 20). All we desire is that everyone get back to exactly what is written. Just read the New Testament with an open heart and for awhile, just forget everything else you've ever heard through men and "only believe" God's Word. Take it exactly for what it says.

Chapter 14

"A Different Gospel"

Can you not see what has happened? The Lord left us the New Covenant and the blueprint of the Book of Acts to go by, so that we would build His church according to the pattern shown (Heb. 8:5). But instead, the church did the same thing as the Pharisees of old did, and made much of the Word of God void through religious tradition. History has repeated itself. It's not new truth we need; it's not a watered down Gospel with all of the power taken out of it; not the traditions of men that say this or that passed away, but rather the Word, the whole Word, and nothing but the Word. A restoration of the Book of Acts "type" of Christianity.

Ephesians 6:16 says, "ABOVE ALL, TAKING THE SHIELD OF FAITH, wherewith YE SHALL BE ABLE TO QUENCH ALL the fiery darts of the WICKED ONE."

First Peter 5:8-9 says, that we are to resist the DEVIL, "STEADFAST IN THE FAITH." Jesus said that if we would believe we too could cast out devils (Mark 16:17).

Oh the subtlety of the serpent! No wonder the devil hates faith teachers and faith so much. It not only exposes his works, but faith can also demonstrate satan's defeat. Satan has worked hard through religion over the centuries, to keep people blind to the real Gospel. He has religious leaders once again teaching traditions and telling the people that the power of God and the gifts of the Holy Spirit are no longer for us; that the beautiful supernatural prayer language of tongues that God "set in the church," He has now taken out. And yes, satan attacks everything that would stop, hurt, or hinder his kingdom. Satan has once again gotten religious men to deny the "power" of God and the Bible still tells us, "from such (men) turn away" (2 Tim. 3:5).

In Galatians 1:8 the apostle Paul wrote, "But though we, or an angel from Heaven, PREACH ANY OTHER GOSPEL unto you than that which we HAVE PREACHED UNTO YOU, LET HIM BE ACCURSED." In verse 9 he says that if ANY MAN preach another gospel unto you, (anything different from what they preached), let him be accursed! In other words, the Gospel that *we preach now* is to be the same Gospel *exactly* that *they preached then*. There was to be no change in the Gospel, no passing away of tongues, healing, casting out devils, no loss of power or gifts of the Holy Spirit. Do you get it? *No different Gospel!*

Jude, knowing that men who weren't really teachers would creep into the church unawares and change things, showed us that we are to "EARNESTLY CONTEND FOR THE FAITH THAT WAS ONCE DELIVERED TO THE SAINTS." Jesus, in some of His last instructions to His disciples before He went back to Heaven said, that they were to "TEACH ALL NATIONS." "Teaching them to observe (do) ALL THINGS WHATSOEVER I have commanded you." How long? "EVEN UNTO THE END OF THE WORLD" (Matt. 28:18-20). And the Bible reveals that when the church started out, "they continued STEADFASTLY IN THE APOSTLE'S DOCTRINE" (Acts 2:42). But, sad to say, nowadays people continue in this group's doctrine, or that denomination's theology and will fight for their church's tradition. All we ask, dear reader, is that you check up on yourself as to whether or not it's the apostle's doctrine you're continuing in, or some modern group's theory about the Gospel.

Let us now look at the *real Gospel, as it's recorded in God's Word*. All you need then, is to compare what you've been taught with what's actually written and you will then clearly see if you've been hearing *the Gospel*, or a "different gospel." For what is actually written in the Bible, is the *only true Gospel*.

A Different Gospel Says:
"God put that disease on you to teach you something or to perfect you." "Whatever happens in life, is the will of God." "To think that our problems are caused by the devil is archaic." "It's all working for your good you know, so just submit to it."

The Real Gospel Says:
"How God anointed Jesus of Nazareth with the Holy Ghost and power who went about doing good, healing all that were oppressed of *THE DEVIL*" (Acts 10:38). "Be sober, be vigilant, because your adversary the devil, as a roaring lion, walketh about, seeking whom he may devour: *whom resist* steadfast in the faith" (1 Pet. 5:8-9). "For this purpose the Son of God was manifest, that He might *destroy the WORKS OF THE DEVIL.*" Jesus said, "I came down from Heaven not to do Mine own will, but the will of Him who sent Me" (John 6:38). He said in John 10:10, "The thief (satan) cometh not but for to steal, and to kill and to destroy: I am come that they might have life and that they might have it more abundantly." In Hosea 4:6 God reveals, "My people are destroyed for a lack of knowledge."

A Different Gospel Says:
"Don't get involved with that faith bunch and that confession doctrine." "God doesn't answer every prayer you know, so don't get your hopes up too high."

The Real Gospel Says:
"What things soever ye desire when ye pray, believe that ye receive them and ye shall have them" (Mark 11:23). "Hold fast your confession of faith without wavering, for He is faithful that promised" (Heb. 10:23). "And all things WHATSOEVER ye shall ask in prayer believing, ye shall receive" (Matt. 21:22). "And whatsoever we ask, we receive of Him because we keep His commandments and do those things that are pleasing in His sight" (1 John 3:22).

A Different Gospel Says:
"Speaking in tongues is of the devil." "We don't want any of that tongues stuff around here. If no man can understand it, what good is it?" "We forbid you to speak in tongues." "Tongues was only for preaching."

The Real Gospel Says:
"And they were all filled with the HOLY SPIRIT and began to speak with other tongues as the Spirit gave them utterance" (Acts

2:4). "For he that speaketh in an unknown tongue, speaketh not unto men, but unto God: for NO MAN understandeth him; howbeit in the spirit he speaketh mysteries" (1 Cor. 14:2). "What is it then? I will PRAY WITH THE SPIRIT and I will pray with the understanding also. For if I pray in an unknown tongue, MY SPIRIT PRAYETH, but my understanding is unfruitful" (1 Cor. 14:14-15). "I would that you all spake with tongues" (vs. 5). "Forbid not to speak with tongues" (vs. 30). Jesus said, "These signs shall follow *them that believe*. In My name. . .they shall speak with new tongues. . ." (Mark 16:17).

A Different Gospel Says:
"God doesn't need your faith to do something in your life." "All that faith business is of the devil." "Don't hang around those faith people. . . ."

The Real Gospel Says:
"Be followers of them who through faith and patience inherit the promises" (Heb. 6:12). "Without faith it is impossible to please Him (God), for He that cometh to God, must believe" (Heb. 11:6). "According to *your faith* be it unto you" (Matt. 9:29). "Daughter, *thy faith* hath made thee whole" (Mark 5:34). "*If thou canst believe all things are possible to Him that believeth*" (Mark 9:23). "Jesus seeing *their faith*, said to the sick of the palsy, son be of good cheer" (Matt. 9:2). ". . .O woman great is *thy faith*; be it unto thee even as thou wilt." (Matt. 15:28). "And Jesus said unto the centurion, Go thy way; and *as thou hast believed, so be it done unto thee*" (Matt. 8:13).

A Different Gospel Says:
"God put that sickness on you to teach you. If people are getting healed at that meeting, it's the devil." "We don't believe in all that healing stuff." "Don't blame everything on the devil."

The Real Gospel Says:
"Ought not this woman being a daughter of Abraham, *whom satan hath bound* lo these eighteen years, be loosed from this bond on the Sabbath day" (Luke 13:16)? "Then was brought unto Him one POSSESSED WITH A DEVIL, BLIND AND DUMB, and He (Jesus)

healed him" (Matt. 12:22). "And *these signs* shall follow them that believe. In My name. . .they shall lay hands on the sick and they shall recover" (Mark 16:17-18). "Is any sick among you? *Let him call for the elders of the church* and let them pray over him, anointing him with oil in the name of the Lord: and the prayer of faith shall save the sick, and the Lord shall raise him up; and if he have committed sins, they shall be forgiven him" (James 5:14-15).

A Different Gospel Says:
"You received the Holy Ghost when you believed, so you don't need to ask God for the Holy Spirit." "If you are water baptized, you have the Holy Spirit." "We don't believe in the laying on of hands for people to receive the Holy Spirit, and we don't want any of our people involved in that tongues movement."

The Real Gospel Says:
"Have you received the Holy Spirit *since* ye believed" (Acts 19:2)? To these same Ephesians Paul wrote and said, ". . .*after* that ye believed ye were sealed with the Holy Spirit of promise" (Eph. 1:13). Before you became a Christian by accepting Christ, you were by nature a child of wrath (Eph. 2:3). "But as many as received Him (Christ) *to them*, gave He power TO BECOME THE SONS OF GOD" (John 1:12). Sinners cannot receive the Holy Spirit. "Even the Spirit of Truth, whom the world cannot receive" (John 14:17). The gift is only for children of God. "How much more shall *your Heavenly Father* give the Holy Spirit to them that ask" (Luke 11:13; Acts 2:38-39). In Acts 8:12-17, the people of Samaria, "believed Philip preaching the things concerning the Kingdom of God and the name of Jesus Christ, THEY WERE BAPTIZED BOTH MEN AND WOMEN." Now when the apostles which were at Jerusalem heard that Samaria *had received the Word of God,* then sent unto them Peter and John; who when they were come down, prayed for them that *they might receive the Holy Ghost,* for as yet He was fallen upon NONE OF THEM; only they (they only) were baptized in the name of the Lord Jesus. Then *laid they their hands on them, and they received the Holy Ghost."* (So believing, accepting the Gospel, believing on Christ and being water baptized meant they were saved [Mark 16:16] and had eternal life [John 5:24], but it didn't mean that they were automatically filled with the Holy

Spirit). Acts 19:6: "And when Paul *LAID HIS HANDS* UPON THEM, THE Holy Ghost came on them; AND THEY SPAKE WITH TONGUES. . . ." (See also Acts 2:4; 10:44-46.)

A Different Gospel Says:
"People who say the Holy Spirit spoke to them are into occult activity." "There are no such things as gifts of the Spirit today so any manifestation of power must be the devil." "To say the Holy Spirit will speak to us is unscriptural."

The Real Gospel Says:
"Howbeit, when He the Spirit of Truth is come, *He will guide you into all truth*; for He shall not speak of Himself; but whatsoever He shall hear THAT SHALL HE SPEAK: and He will *show you* THINGS TO COME" (John 16:13). "For as many as are led by the Spirit of God THEY ARE THE SONS OF GOD" (Rom. 8:14). *The Holy Ghost said*, "Separate me Barnabas and Saul for the work whereunto I HAVE CALLED THEM" (Acts 13:2). "Then the Spirit said unto Philip, Go near and join thyself to this chariot" (Acts 8:29). "While Peter thought on the vision, *the Spirit said unto him*, Behold three men seek thee" (Acts 10:19). Surely if our body is the temple of the Holy Ghost (1 Cor. 6:19), He can still speak. "And God hath set some IN THE CHURCH. . .miracles. . .gifts of healing. . .diversities (different kinds of) tongues" (1 Cor. 12:28). "But the *manifestation* of the Spirit is given to EVERY MAN (in the church) to profit withal. For TO ONE IS GIVEN BY THE SPIRIT, the word of wisdom; to another the word of knowledge *BY THE SAME SPIRIT*. . . to another faith. . .gifts of healing. . .working of miracles. . .prophesy. . .discerning of spirits. . .tongues and interpretation of tongues. . . . But all these worketh that one and the *selfsame Spirit*, dividing to every man severally as He will" (1 Cor. 12:7-11). Certainly if the same Holy Ghost is in us, He can do the same things He did in other people if He so wills. "But ye shall receive (dunamis, in the Greek) (miraculous) power after that the Holy Ghost is come upon you" (Acts 1:8). "That *your faith should not stand in the wisdom of men* but in THE POWER OF GOD" (1 Cor. 2:5).

A Different Gospel Says:
I know Greek and Hebrew. I don't need that Holy Ghost Baptism to understand the Bible. I have a theological degree and I'm thereby qualified. I went to seminary."

The Real Gospel Says:
"I have yet many things to say unto you, but *ye cannot* bear (understand) them now. Howbeit when He, the Spirit of truth is come, He will guide you into all truth: for He shall not speak of Himself; but whatsoever He shall hear, that shall He speak: and He will show you things to come. *He shall* glorify Me: for He shall receive of Mine, and *shall show it unto you*. All things that the Father hath are Mine: therefore said I, that He shall take of Mine, and shall show it unto you" (John 16:12-15). "But the Comforter which is the Holy Ghost, whom the Father will send in My name, *He shall teach you all things*, and bring all things to your remembrance, whatsoever I have said unto you" (John 14:26). "Now we have received not the spirit of the world, but the Spirit which is of God; *that we might know the things* that are freely given to us of God. Which things also we speak, not in the words which man's wisdom teacheth, but *which the Holy Ghost teacheth*; comparing spiritual things with spiritual" (1 Cor. 2:12-13). Without their receiving the Holy Ghost Baptism, there are many things in Scripture and many operations of the Holy Spirit that a man *cannot* understand regardless of what degrees he has.

A Different Gospel Says:
"Once saved, always saved,' regardless of how you live afterwards." "It makes no difference if you repent or not once you've made Jesus, Lord; you can't be lost."

The Real Gospel Says:
"*Why* call Me Lord, Lord and do not the things which I say" (Luke 6:46)? "Not everyone that *SAITH unto Me Lord, Lord*, shall enter into the Kingdom of Heaven; *but He that doeth* the will of My Father which is in Heaven" (Matt. 7:21). "For *if after* they have escaped the pollution's of the world through the knowledge of the Lord and Savior Jesus Christ, *they are again entangled* therein, *and*

overcome, the latter end is worse with them than the beginning. *For it had been better for them not to have known the way of righteousness, than after they have known it, to turn from the holy commandment delivered unto them"* (2 Pet.2:20-21). "Behold therefore the goodness and severity of God; on them which fell severity; but toward thee, goodness, *IF thou continue in His goodness; otherwise thou also shalt be cut off" (Romans 11:22)*. "In flaming fire taking vengeance on them that know not God and *that obey not the Gospel* of our Lord Jesus Christ" (2 Thess. 1:8). *"Take heed brethren*, lest there be in any of you an evil heart of unbelief, in departing from the living God. For we are made partakers of Christ, *if* we hold the beginning of our confidence steadfast unto the end" (Heb. 3:12, 14). *"He that overcometh, the same* shall be clothed in white raiment; and I will not blot out his name, out of the book of life, but I will confess his name before My Father, and before His angels" (Rev. 3:5). *"IF we confess* our sins, He is faithful and just to forgive us our sins, and to cleanse us from all unrighteousness" (1 John 1:9).

A Different Gospel Says:
"Man's will is not really free. God is sovereign, He has predestined everything. He doesn't have to abide by His own Word. If He did, He wouldn't be sovereign. If we can hinder His working, He's not God."

The Real Gospel Says:
"I call Heaven and earth to record this day against you, that *I have set before you* life and death, blessing and cursing, therefore *choose life*, that both thou and thy seed may live" (Deut. 30:19). "And whosoever *will, let him* take of the water of life freely" (Rev. 22:17). "My Covenant will I not break, *nor alter* the thing that is gone out of My lips" (Ps. 89:34). ". . .it is impossible for God to lie" (Heb. 6:18). "Thy Word O Lord is forever settled in Heaven" (Ps. 119:89). ". . .the Father of lights with whom is no variableness, neither any shadow of turning" (James 1:17). "If you abide in Me and My Words abide in you, ask what ye will and it *shall be* done unto you" (John 15:7). "And He could there (in His own hometown) do no mighty works. . .And He marveled because of their unbelief" (Mark 6:5-6). "Yea, they turned back and tempted God and *limited*

the Holy One of Israel" (Ps. 78:41). This can presently happen because God created man with a free will and because He did so, God will not change it even if a man does go contrary to God's will, and hinders His desire for them. "The Lord is not slack concerning His promise, as some men count slackness; but is longsuffering to us-ward, not willing that any should perish, but that all should come to repentance" (2 Pet. 3:9). But yet people are perishing every day contrary to His will for them. (See also John 3:16; 1 Timothy 2:4; 4:10; 1 John 2:2)

A Different Gospel Says:
"Man has no authority in the earth. God controls everything. God does what He wants, whether you pray or not. Everything that happens is from God."

The Real Gospel Says:
"And God said, *Let us make man* in our image, after our likeness: and *let them have dominion* over the fish of the sea, and over the fowl of the air, and over the cattle, and *over all the earth*, and over every creeping thing that creepeth upon the earth" (Gen. 1:26). "*Behold, I give unto you power* to tread on serpents and scorpions, and *over all the power of the enemy*: and nothing shall by any means hurt you" (Luke 10:19). "*Thou madest Him to have dominion over all the works of Thy hands*; Thou hast put all things under His feet" (Ps. 8:6). "Then saith He unto His disciples, The harvest truly is plenteous, but the laborers are few: *Pray ye therefore the Lord of the harvest, that He will send forth laborers into His harvest*" (Matt. 9:37-38). "Be sober, be vigilant; because *your adversary the devil*, as a roaring lion, walketh about, seeking whom he may devour: *Whom resist* steadfast in the faith, knowing that the same afflictions are accomplished in your brethren that are in the world" (1 Pet. 5:8-9). "And all things, whatsoever ye shall ask in prayer, believing, ye shall receive" (Matt. 21:22). "And these signs shall follow them that believe; In My name shall they cast out devils; they shall speak with new tongues" (Mark 16:17). ". . .ye have not because ye ask not" (James 4:2).

A Different Gospel Says:
"Jesus only suffered physical death and then went up to be with

the Father during the three days and nights."

The Real Gospel Says:
Jesus said, "For as Jonah was three days and nights in the whale's belly; so shall the Son of man be three days and three nights *in the heart of the earth*" (Matt. 12:40). "Therefore did My heart rejoice and My tongue was glad; moreover also My flesh shall rest in hope; because Thou wilt not leave (in the Greek, abandon; forsake), My soul *in hell*; neither wilt Thou suffer Thine Holy One to see corruption" (Acts 2:26-27). "He (David as a prophet), seeing this before, spake of the resurrection of Christ, that *His soul* was not left (forsaken) *in hell*, neither His flesh did see corruption" (Acts 2:31). "Who shall *descend* into the deep (in the Greek, the abyss; the pit) that is to bring *up* Christ again from the dead" (Rom. 10:7). "Whom God hath *raised up*, having loosed *the pains* of death: because it was not possible that He should be holden of it" (Acts 2:24). Death is an enemy (1 Cor. 15:26); Death is of satan (Heb. 2:14); Death temporarily had power over Christ (Rom. 6:9). But it was impossible that death and hell could hold Him. "And when I saw Him, I fell at His feet as dead. And He laid His right hand upon me, saying unto me, Fear not; I am the first and the last: I am He that liveth, and was dead; and behold, I am alive forevermore, amen; and have the keys of hell and of death" (Rev. 1:17-18). "And I say also unto thee, That thou art Peter, and upon this rock I will build My church; and the gates of hell shall not prevail against it" (Matt. 16:18). Physical death alone is not the reason He sweat great drops of blood. If so, everyone would before they died.

A Different Gospel Says:
"The devil is not to blame for the sickness and problems of today." "That was just to explain things to people of that day who were superstitious. Demons don't really tempt people, people just do things."

The Real Gospel Says:
"For *we wrestle* not against flesh and blood, but against principalities, *against powers, against the rulers of the darkness of this world, against spiritual wickedness in high places*" (Eph. 6:12). "Be sober, be vigilant;

because *your adversary the devil*, as a roaring lion, walketh about, seeking whom he may devour: *Whom resist* steadfast "in the faith," knowing that the same afflictions are accomplished in your brethren that are in the world" (1 Pet. 5:8-9). "Submit yourselves therefore to God. *Resist the devil*, and he will flee from you" (James 4:7). "And *when the tempter came to Him*, he said, If Thou be the Son of God, command that these stones be made bread" (Matt. 4:3). "But Peter said, Ananias, *why hath satan filled thine heart* to lie to the Holy Ghost, and to keep back part of the price of the land" (Acts 5:3)? "For this purpose the Son of God was manifest to destroy the works of the devil" (1 John 3:8).

A Different Gospel Says:
"Those who say mere words affect your lives are into metaphysics."

The Real Gospel Says:
"A man's belly shall be satisfied with the fruit of his mouth; and with the increase of his lips shall he be filled. Death and life are in the power of the tongue: and they that love it shall eat the fruit thereof" (Prov. 18:20-21). "For verily I say unto you, That *whosoever shall say* unto this mountain, Be thou removed, and be thou cast into the sea; and shall not doubt in his heart, but shall believe that those things which he saith shall come to pass; *he shall have whatsoever he saith*" (Mark 11:23). "If any man among you seem to be religious and bridleth not his tongue, but deceiveth his own heart, this man's religion is vain" (James 1:26). "But I say unto you, That every idle word that men shall speak, they shall give account thereof in the day of judgment. For by thy words thou shalt be condemned" (Matt. 12:36-37). "Whoso keepeth his mouth and his tongue keepeth his soul from troubles" (Prov. 21:23). "Let us hold fast the profession of our faith without wavering; (for He is faithful that promised)" (Heb. 10:23). "That if thou shalt confess with thy mouth the Lord Jesus, and shalt believe in thine heart that God hath raised Him from the dead, thou shalt be saved. For with the heart man believeth unto righteousness; and with the mouth confession is made unto salvation" (Rom. 10:9-10). "Neither murmur ye, as some of them also murmured, and were destroyed of the destroyer" (1 Cor. 10:10).

A Different Gospel Says:
"God predestines some to Heaven and some to hell."

The Real Gospel Says:
"The Lord is not slack concerning His promise, as some men count slackness; but is longsuffering to us-ward, *not willing that any should perish*, but that all should come to repentance" (2 Pet. 3:9). "And He said unto them, Go ye into *all the world*, and preach the Gospel to *every creature*" (Mark 16:15). "But we see Jesus, who was made a little lower than the angels for the suffering of death, crowned with glory and honor; that He by the grace of God should *taste death for every man*" (Heb. 2:9). "And He is the propitiation for our sins: and *not for ours only, but also for the sins of the whole world*" (1 John 2:2). "Who will have all men to be saved, and to come unto the knowledge of the truth" (1 Tim. 2:4).

A Different Gospel Says:
"It's gnosticism to believe that knowledge will set you free."

The Real Gospel Says:
"Grace and peace be multiplied unto you *through the knowledge of God, and of Jesus our Lord*, according as His divine power hath given unto us all things that pertain unto life and godliness, *through the knowledge of Him* that hath called us to glory and virtue" (2 Pet. 1:2-3). "Then said Jesus to those Jews which believed on Him, If ye continue in My Word, then are ye My disciples indeed; and ye shall know the truth, and the truth shall make you free" (John 8:31-32).

A Different Gospel Says:
"God sends problems to teach you, guide you and correct you."

The Real Gospel Says:
"All *Scripture is given by inspiration of God, and is profitable for doctrine, for reproof, for correction, for instruction in righteousness: That the man of God may be perfect*, thoroughly furnished unto all good works" (2 Tim. 3:16-17). "*And He gave* some, apostles; and some, prophets; and some, evangelists; and some, pastors and teachers; *For the perfecting of the saints*, for the work

of the ministry, for the edifying of the body of Christ" (Eph. 4:11-12). "Howbeit when He, the Spirit of Truth is come, *He will guide you* into all truth; for He shall not speak of Himself, but whatsoever He shall hear, that shall He speak: and *He will show you* things to come" (John 16:13). "But the Comforter, which is the Holy Ghost, whom the Father will send in My name, *He shall teach you all things*, and bring all things to your remembrance, whatsoever I have said unto you" (John 14:26). "But the anointing which ye have received of Him abideth in you, and ye need not that any man teach you: but as *the same anointing teacheth you of all things, and is truth*, and is no lie, *and even as it hath taught you, ye shall abide in Him*" (1 John 2:27).

A Different Gospel Says:
"Salvation is not something you know or experience, you just see moral progress in your life. No one can know they have eternal life."

The Real Gospel Says:
"The Spirit itself beareth witness with our spirit, that we are the children of God" (Rom. 8:16). "Therefore if any man be in Christ, *he is* a new creature: old things are passed away; behold, all things are become new" (2 Cor. 5:17). "And *because you are* sons, God hath sent forth the Spirit of His Son into your hearts, crying, Abba Father" (Gal. 4:6). "We know we have passed from death unto life, because we love the brethren" (1 John 3:14). "*Who are kept by the power of God* through faith unto salvation ready to be revealed in the last time" (1 Pet. 1:5).

A Different Gospel Says:
"The power of God is not for us today. Any supernatural power today is the devil."

The Real Gospel Says:
"But ye shall receive *power,* after that the Holy Ghost is come upon you: and ye shall be witnesses unto Me both in Jerusalem, and in all Judaea, and in Samaria, and unto the uttermost part of the earth" (Acts 1:8). "But I will come to you shortly, if the Lord will, and will know, not the speech of them which are puffed up, but the

power. For the Kingdom of God is not in word, but in power" (1 Cor. 4:19-20). Those "Having a form of godliness, but DENYING THE POWER (dunamis—power of God); from such (men) turn away" (2 Tim. 3:5). "And Stephen, full of faith and power, did great wonders and miracles among the people" (Acts 6:8). "Verily, verily I say unto you, He that believeth on Me, the works that I do shall He do also; and greater works than these shall he do; because I go unto My Father" (John 14:12). "For the promise is unto you, and to your children, and to all that are afar off, even as many as the Lord our God shall call" (Acts 2:39). "That your faith should not stand in the wisdom of men, but in the power of God" (1 Cor. 2:5). "*Who are kept by the power of God* through faith unto salvation ready to be revealed in the last time" (1 Pet. 1:5).

A Different Gospel Says:
"We should not believe that God wants us to prosper but just accept your poverty as your lot in life."

The Real Gospel Says:
"Beloved, I wish above all things that thou mayest prosper and be in health, even as thy soul prospereth" (3 John 2). "Upon the first day of the week let every one of you lay by Him in store, *as God hath prospered him*, that there be no gatherings when I come" (1 Cor. 16:2). "But my God shall supply all your need according to His riches in glory by Christ Jesus" (Phil. 4:19). "Every man also *to whom God hath given* riches and wealth, and hath given him power to eat thereof, and to take his portion, and to rejoice in his labor; *this is the gift of God*" (Eccles. 5:19). "The Spirit of the Lord is upon me, because He hath anointed me to preach the Gospel to the poor" (Luke 4:18).

A different Gospel not found in the Bible further says:
God wants you sick, He breaks up homes, sends troubles, OK's temptations, predestines the evil and the good. A different Gospel says that you can be saved by baby baptism; you can become a Christian without repenting of a life of sin; that you can never reject the gift of eternal life once you've accepted it; that you can live for the devil in this life and then go to be with Jesus in the next; tongues have ceased; their denomination can save you; that

God can go contrary to His own word of truth. It says God can just do anything because He's God; you don't need to be born again; if you are born again, you've already been filled with the Holy Ghost, and so on.

We must stick right with the Bible for only it contains the real Gospel (Jude 3). The Bible is the only real and true record we have of what the Christian faith is and anything contrary to it is a counterfeit.

Dear Brethren, we could go on and on and on concerning many other Bible topics as well. Who then really is preaching a different gospel? It is the critics of the faith message themselves. So it is we who say with Paul, "I marvel that ye are so soon removed from Him that called you into the grace of Christ unto another gospel: Which is not another; but there be some that trouble you, and would pervert the Gospel of Christ. But though we, or an angel from Heaven, *preach any other gospel* unto you, than that which we have preached unto you, let him be accursed. As we said before, so say I now again, If *any man* preach any other gospel unto you than that ye have received, let him be accursed" (Gal. 1:6-9).

If you say you believe "The Gospel," then you must believe it all or you're not really believing the Gospel of God and the "faith that was once delivered to the saints." You are instead believing a watered-down imitation version of the Gospel. Have you continued in the "Apostle's Doctrine" or your church group's doctrine? It is up to you now, to "prove all things and hold fast to that which is good." Jesus said in John 12:48-49, "He that rejecteth Me, and receiveth not *My words*, hath one that judgeth him: the word that I have spoken, the same shall judge him in the last day. For I have not spoken of Myself; but the Father which sent Me, He gave Me a commandment, what I should say, and what I should speak."

Peter said, "For all flesh is as grass, and all the glory of man as the flower of grass. The grass withereth and the flower thereof falleth away, *but the Word of the Lord endureth forever, and this is the Word which by the Gospel is preached unto you.*" We would like to encourage you to go on and read God's Word and just believe each statement made by the apostles in the Epistles, and don't let anyone regardless of what label he may have, talk you out of believing everything in the "Apostle's Doctrine." Now let's look at one more statement made by Paul about Jesus and then we'll take some Gospel quotes from Christ, Himself.

Paul wrote in 1 Timothy 6:3-4: *"If any man teach otherwise, and consent not to wholesome words, even the words of our Lord Jesus Christ, and to the doctrine which is according to Godliness; He is proud, knowing nothing*, but doting about questions and strifes of words, whereof cometh envy, strife, railings, evil surmisings." So Paul, in his Gospel message which he preached said we are to consent to all of what Jesus taught and the doctrine that says you must live a life of godliness (Titus 2:11-12). Paul's message never contradicted Jesus' message. He said we are to listen to Christ, and as a matter of fact, he said that what he wrote in his Gospel message, was from the Lord. "If any man think himself to be a prophet, or spiritual, let him acknowledge that the things that I write unto you are the commandments of the Lord" (1 Cor. 14:37). Then he wrote verse 38: "But if any man be ignorant, let him be ignorant." There is only "one Lord" and "one faith" and Jesus is the author and the finisher of our faith.

So it's all one message from the same Lord. Now let's go back and hear the Gospel of Christ and you determine if it's what you have been taught. Some of his final words to His disciples before He ascended on high in Matthew 28, was to go into all nations "Teaching them to observe all things whatsoever I have commanded you alway, even unto the end of the world. Amen." So then, we are to observe all things He commanded them, *even unto the end* of the age. No one then, has a right to change even one Scripture or one instruction, and say it's not for us today; to do so is to preach, *"a different gospel."*

Have you been instructed concerning all these things that are in the Gospel? That all that He instructed them to obey, we also are to preach, even unto the end of the age? Let's look at the Gospel according to Mark. "And He preached in their synagogues throughout all Galilee, and cast out devils" (Mark 1:39). Have you been told the Gospel says that we are to cast out devils? That devils cause many of people's problems? In Mark 16:17, Jesus said, "And these signs shall follow them that believe; In My name they shall cast out devils; they shall speak with new tongues."

Have you been instructed in these things? "And these are they by the wayside, where the Word is sown; but when they have heard, satan cometh immediately, and taketh away the Word that was sown in their hearts." Here Christ's teaching in the Gospel according to Mark is that satan really does come to steal the Word. Look at how He speaks of the power of words. "For verily I say unto you, That whosoever shall say unto this mountain, Be thou removed and be thou cast into the sea; and shall not doubt in his heart, but shall believe that those things which he saith shall come to pass; he shall have whatsoever he saith" (Mark 11:23). Have you been instructed concerning this? Do you see what I mean? The apostle Paul said, "And what shall I more say? For the time would fail me to tell of Gideon and of Barak and of Samson and of Jephthae; of David also, and Samuel, and of the prophets: *Who through faith* subdued kingdoms, wrought righteousness, obtained promises, stopped the mouths of lions, quenched the violence of fire, escaped the edge of the sword, out of weakness were made strong, waxed valiant in fight, turned to flight the armies of the aliens" (Heb. 11:32-34).

These Scriptures are given with the intent to show you *the whole* New Testament contains *the* Gospel which we are to preach. *None* of the Gospel has passed away, and yet men have once again, through their tradition, made the Word of God of none effect by teaching and saying to the people, "this isn't for today." "God won't do that, this or that was only for the apostles." And when they say such things to God's people, they are preaching not the Gospel of Jesus Christ, but the gospel according to their religion, which is, in truth, a different gospel. So in conclusion here, "Who then is really preaching a *'different gospel?'*" It's the critics themselves. Let us stay right with the Word (See Rom. 2:1-2; 3:3-4; John 12:48-49).

Do you know Jesus as your personal Lord and Savior? If not, you can come to Him right now. He said "him that cometh to Me I will in no wise cast out." The apostle John wrote in John 1:12, "But as many as received Him, to them gave He power *to become the sons of God, even to them that believe on His name.*"

The apostle Paul wrote, "That if thou shalt confess with thy mouth the Lord Jesus, and shalt believe in thine heart that God hath raised Him from the dead, thou shalt be saved" (Rom. 10:9).

You must be willing to repent of a life that's been displeasing to Him and invite Him into your life through a simple prayer.

If you are willing to accept Him now, then pray this prayer sincerely, aloud to Him.

Dear God, I realize that without Jesus, I'm lost and dead in sin. But I believe that Jesus Christ is Your Son, that He died on the cross for my sins, and bore all of my punishment so I could be free. I ask You, right now, to forgive me of all of my past. I accept Your forgiveness Lord, and I now confess that You, Jesus, are the Lord of my life. I receive You into my heart as Savior. I thank You that from this moment on, I belong to You and You are in my life. In Jesus' name, amen.

Chapter 15

The Holy Spirit Baptism

"*Have you received* the Holy Ghost *since ye believed*" (Acts 19:1-2)? Well, have you? These words were spoken by the apostle Paul to a certain group of disciples in Ephesus. The question is clear. The apostle knew that people could believe and yet not have received the Holy Ghost, for it was so in his own experience, as we shall see. A short while later He laid His hands upon these disciples and the "the Holy Ghost came on them: and they spake with tongues and prophesied" (vs. 6), "and all the men were about twelve." This was the beginning of a wonderful work of God in Ephesus. Paul later wrote to the church at Ephesus and said to them in his epistle, "In whom you also trusted after that ye heard *the Word of Truth; the Gospel of your salvation* (1 Pet. 1:23; James 1:18; 1 Cor. 4:16), in whom also AFTER THAT YE *believed, ye were sealed with the Holy Spirit of promise*" (Eph. 1:13). Notice he said that *after that they believed* they received the Holy Spirit of promise, not *when* they believed (Acts 19:2). This is not a small issue. It is possibly the main reason why there is so much division in the body of Christ. For it is this Biblical experience that opens people's hearts and minds to the same type of Spirit-filled, supernatural Christianity as is recorded in the book of Acts and the Epistles.

In this book, we will clearly point out to you from the Bible concerning the receiving of this "Baptism with the Holy Spirit," and show you, absolutely, that there is a difference between being born again by believing God's Word and calling on Jesus' name, which gives to a believer *eternal life* (John 5:24), and the receiving of the Holy Spirit, which empowers the believer's life. All that we ask is that you just believe the Bible for exactly what it says; don't add to it or take away from it (Deut. 4:2). A key word we'll look at in this study is the word "*receive*." So pay close attention to it and it will help you to clearly see what we are talking about. Jesus said, "And I will pray the Father, and He shall give you *another* Comforter, that He may abide with you for ever; even the Spirit of truth; whom *the world (sinners) cannot receive, because it seeth Him not, neither knoweth Him: but ye know Him; for He dwelleth with you and shall be in you"* (John 14:16-17). Notice Christ said, "the world (sinners or the unregenerate) *CANNOT* RECEIVE the Holy Spirit." Why? Because they are children of the devil and children of wrath by nature (1 John 3:10; Eph. 2:3). They first need to become sons of God by being born again. So they are not yet ready to receive the Holy Spirit of promise, which is only for those who have already repented and had their sins washed away. It is God's gift to *His children.*

"Then Peter said unto them, Repent and be baptized every one of you in the name of Jesus Christ for the remission of sins, and (then) ye shall *receive the gift of the Holy Ghost*" (Acts 2:4; 2:38).

The first thing people need to do is to repent of sin and believe the Gospel, and have their sins washed away by the Blood of Jesus (Rev. 1:5-6). When they do this, they then become a new creature in Christ (2 Cor. 5:17-18); a child of God (John 1:12), and *then* after that, they can receive the gift of the Holy Ghost by *asking* their Heavenly Father specifically for this.

Jesus said in Luke 11:13, "If ye then, being evil, know how to give good gifts unto your children: how much more shall your Heavenly Father give the Holy Spirit *to them that ask Him?*" So God's gift to the sinner is eternal life, and God's gift to His children is the Holy Ghost. So it is only after you believe and receive Christ, that God becomes your Heavenly Father, for before that, Paul wrote, we were "all by nature children of wrath, *even as* others" (Eph. 2:3). Only children of God then, will ask for the Holy Spirit to permanently dwell in them. So it is seen that He becomes *your* Heavenly Father after you receive Christ. "He (Christ) was in *the world*, and the world was made by Him, and *the world* knew Him not. He came unto His own, and His own received Him not. *But as many as received Him, to them gave He power to "become" the sons of God*, even to them that believe on His name" (John 1:10-12). Notice here that *the world* (sinners) *can receive* Christ and when they do, they become sons of God. It is a birth; a regeneration of their own human spirit. They then have eternal life. Having received Christ, they then have also the Spirit of Christ, and are partakers of Christ, joined one Spirit with the Lord (1 Cor. 6:17; Rom. 8:9; Heb. 3:14). (John called Christ, eternal life in 1 John 1:2.) Basically what happens is, they are "born again" of Jesus Christ, "the last Adam" (1 Cor. 15:45-49), and become sons of God (1 John 3:2). Jesus said in John 5:24, "Verily, verily, I say unto you, He that heareth My Word and believeth on Him that sent Me, *hath everlasting life*, and shall not come into condemnation; but is passed from death unto life." Notice, it does not say, is passed from death to the Holy Ghost.

John 3:16 says, "For God so loved the world, that He gave His only begotten Son, that *whosoever believeth in Him* should not perish but *have everlasting life*." Again, it does not say that they have the Holy Ghost Baptism. Yes, the New Birth is accomplished by the Spirit's work through the Word and eternal life is imparted to the believer, but that's it. It is a divine person giving *you* a new birth. It's *you* receiving a new heart and a new spirit and being regenerated. It is *you* becoming a new creature, and *you* being born again. It's the *spirit's of just men* being made perfect (Heb. 12:23). "For the wages of sin is death; but the gift of God (to the sinner) is eternal life through Jesus Christ our Lord" (Rom. 6:23).

To receive eternal life then, is to receive Christ, for they are one and the same. Speaking of Christ, John wrote, "For *the life* was manifested and we have seen it, and bear witness and show unto you that *eternal life*, which was with the Father, and was manifested unto us" (1 John 1:2). When you receive this life from the Son of God, you also then become a son of God. "And because ye are sons, God hath sent forth the Spirit *of His Son* into your hearts, crying, Abba Father" (Gal. 4:6), and he that hath the Son, hath the life and has a Christ-like spirit. "And this is the record, that God hath given to us eternal life, and this life is in His Son. He that hath the Son hath life; and he that hath not the Son of God hath not life" (1 John 5:11-12). Now from that point on, because you're a child of God, the Spirit of God is "with you," He has done a creative work in you (Eph. 2:10). He can bear witness "with" your spirit that you are a child of God (Rom. 8:16) and through this new birth you do "know the Lord." True, the Holy Spirit is with you then, waiting for you to invite Him into you in all His fullness.

Personally I knew the Lord after calling upon His name about six months or so before I received the Baptism with the Holy Ghost. I realize that there are variations of this explanation in Full Gospel Christianity. Some are saying you have a measure of the Spirit when born again, and then you later receive a baptism (some say you first receive Christ, and become a child of God by this and then receive the Holy Ghost later). But let's all, like sensible men, like compassionate brethren in Christ, look at the Word and believe it and not fuss among ourselves over terminology. The important thing that we desire others to know is that this Baptism with the Holy Spirit is a separate experience from salvation. This is what we want you to see. It is received *after* the new birth, after salvation.

"And this is life eternal, that they might know Thee the only true God, and Jesus Christ, whom Thou hast sent" (John 17:3). "For I will be merciful to their unrighteousness, and their sins and their iniquities will I remember no more" (Heb. 8:12). Notice He said, "*This is* eternal life." Not, "this is the Holy Ghost Baptism." Let's read John 14:16-17 again, "And I will pray the Father, and He shall give you another Comforter, that He may abide with you for ever; even the Spirit of truth; whom the world cannot receive, because it seeth Him not, neither knoweth Him: *but ye know Him; for He dwelleth with you and shall be in you.*"

First of all, notice He is "another" Comforter and note too that it's possible for Him to dwell with people, *and them to know Him* and His presence and yet the Holy Ghost not be *in them* to empower them, and to open up their understanding (John 16:12-13). "Jesus answered and said unto him, If a man love Me, he will keep My words: and My Father will love him, and *we will come* unto him and make *our* abode (dwelling place) with him" (vs. 23).

In John 14:21 He says, "He that *hath My commandments,*

and keepeth them, He it is that loveth Me." So, He said, if we keep His words and do as He commands, they will make their abode with us.

Let's now look at His command concerning the Holy Ghost. "And being assembled together with them, *commanded them that they* should not depart from Jerusalem, but *wait for the promise of the Father* which saith He, ye have heard of Me, for John truly baptized with water, *but ye shall be baptized with the Holy Ghost not many days hence*. But *ye shall receive power*, after that the Holy Ghost is come upon you; and ye shall be witnesses unto Me both in Jerusalem and in all Judaea, and in Samaria and unto the uttermost part of the earth" (Acts 1:4-5, 8). The Greek word for power here is, "dunamis." It means "miraculous, working power." So those who have received the Holy Ghost have received this "power." How then could anyone say or teach that the power is passed away and yet say they've received the Holy Ghost? Perhaps then the reason they say the power is passed away is because they haven't yet received the Holy Ghost baptism, the source of this power into them, so they know nothing about it.

But concerning the early disciples, "These all continued with one accord in prayer and supplication with the women, and Mary the mother of Jesus, and with His brethren. . .And they were *all filled with the Holy Ghost* and began to speak with other tongues, as the Spirit gave them utterance" (Acts 1:14; 2:4). In Acts 5:32 the Bible says, God gives the Holy Ghost to "them that obey Him." So now they were filled, now the Spirit was *in them*. So there was a difference between the Spirit being *"with them"* and *"in them."* When He came into them and filled them, they spoke as the Holy Spirit gave utterance.

Now go back to John 14:15-17: "If ye love Me, keep My commandments, and I will pray the Father, and He shall give you another Comforter, that He may abide with you for ever; even *the Spirit of truth; whom the world cannot receive*, because it seeth Him not, neither knoweth Him: but ye know Him; for He *dwelleth with you and shall be in you.*" Here again we see in this passage that the world (sinners) *cannot receive the Spirit of truth* (the Holy

Ghost), but we've seen that they can receive Christ (John 1:12). I want you to also see again from this passage that it is possible for people to be acquainted with the Holy Ghost and His *presence before* He is *in them*. Notice what Jesus said, ". . .but ye *know* Him; for He *dwelleth with you* and shall be *IN YOU.*" With you--in you. Two totally different things.

It was the Holy Spirit who led you to Jesus and brought to you the reality of sin, righteousness and judgment *before* you were saved (John 16:8). Even in the Old Testament it said, "The spirit of man is the candle of the Lord, searching all the inward parts of the belly" (Prov. 20:27). And in Job 32:8 it says, "But there is a spirit in man: and the inspiration of the Almighty giveth them understanding." Elijah heard the still small voice, but didn't yet have the Spirit permanently dwelling in him. The disciples preached under the Holy Spirit's influence and even healed the sick, and Peter got a "revelation" that flesh and blood did not reveal to him. So all these Scriptural experiences are possible without the Holy Spirit's indwelling. It was Jesus, the last Adam, who imparted to you through the Holy Ghost, life at the new birth, which springs up in you as a well of living water. "Jesus answered and said unto her, If thou knewest the gift of God, and who it is that saith to thee, Give me to drink; thou wouldest have asked of Him, and He would have given thee living water. . .Jesus answered and said unto her, Whosoever drinketh of this water shall thirst again: but whosoever drinketh of the water that I shall give him shall never thirst; but the water that I shall give him shall be in him *a well of water* springing up into *everlasting life*" (John 4:10, 13-14).

Hebrews 7:25 says, "Wherefore He is able also *to save* them to the uttermost that come unto God by Him, seeing He ever liveth to make intercession for them." "For whosoever shall call upon the name of the Lord *shall be saved*" (Rom. 10:13). Being *saved*, is a person being saved from their lost condition. Being filled with the Holy Spirit is another thing altogether. Scripture says, Christ is a life-giving Spirit, He is the second man and the last Adam, who came to give us a new birth. We were born of the first Adam, but are now born again of the last Adam. "And so it is written, The first man Adam was made a living soul; the last Adam was made a quickening (life-giving) spirit. Howbeit that was not first which is spiritual, but that which is natural; and afterward that which is spiritual. The first man is of the earth, earthy: the second man is the Lord from Heaven" (1 Cor. 15:45-47). And so when we are born again, we are born again of Jesus Christ, the last Adam. *"Being born again*, not of corruptible seed, but of incorruptible, *by the Word of God* which liveth and abideth forever" (1 Pet. 1:23). And what is Jesus called in Scripture? The Word! "In the beginning was the Word, and the Word was with God, and the Word was God" (John 1:1). He has the words of eternal life. "Then Simon Peter answered Him, Lord, to whom shall we go? Thou hast the words of eternal life" (John 6:68).

Now notice what Paul said in 1 Corinthians 4:15: "For though ye have ten thousand instructors in Christ, yet have ye not many fathers: for in Christ Jesus *I have begotten you* through the Gospel." Paul brought Christ's seed (the Word of life) and sowed it into their hearts. They believed, received Christ's word and were born again of Jesus Christ the last Adam. They were begotten of the Word. So Jesus says, "Verily, verily, I say unto you, He that heareth My Word and believeth on Him that sent Me, *hath everlasting life* and shall not come into condemnation; but is passed from death unto life" (John 5:24). Let's see this again in Acts 8. "Then Philip went down to the city of Samaria and preached Christ unto them, and the people with one accord gave heed unto those things which Philip spake, hearing and seeing the miracles which He did. . .And there was great joy in that city" (Acts 8:5-6 ,8). Verse 12 says, "But when *they believed* Philip preaching the things concerning the Kingdom of God, and the name of Jesus Christ, *they were baptized*, both men and women." Jesus said "he that believeth and is baptized shall be saved" (Mark 16:16). All would agree then that they were saved at this point. To be saved *is to be born again* of incorruptible seed *by the Word of God* which liveth and abideth forever" (1 Pet. 1:23). James wrote, "Of His own will begat He us with the Word of Truth, that we should be a kind of first fruits of His creatures" (James 1:18). They were Christians then, born again by the Word of God and they had eternal life (Rom. 6:23).

Now let's read on. Verse 14 says, "Now when the apostles which were at Jerusalem heard that Samaria *had received the Word of God*, they sent unto them Peter and John." Why? To pray for them. Notice what it says: they heard they had received. They heard they received the "Word of God." It did not say they heard; they "received" the Holy Ghost. Now knowing that once a person is born again of the Word, they become a child of God and God becomes their Heavenly Father, they sent Peter and John down there. Why? "Who, when they were come down, prayed for them, *that they might receive the Holy Ghost*: For as yet He was fallen upon none of them: only they were baptized in the name of the Lord Jesus" (vs. 15-16). So then water baptism, repentance, and believing in Christ and the Kingdom of God, does not automatically mean that a person has received the Holy Spirit's indwelling. "Then laid they their hands on them, and they received the Holy Ghost" (vs. 17). Here the Holy Ghost was imparted through the laying on of hands by other Holy Spirit filled believers. "And when *Simon saw* that *through* laying on of the apostles' hands *the Holy Ghost was given*, he offered them money" (vs. 18). Simon *"saw"* something. You cannot actually see the Holy Ghost, for He's like the wind (Acts 2:1-2). He saw that through the laying on of hands the Holy Ghost was given and the manifestation he *"saw"* was "speaking in tongues" as we will clearly point out (Acts 2:4; Mark 16:17). Notice that none of the Samaritans had received the Holy Ghost even though they were believers and were water baptized, not until other believers ministered to them.

When the Holy Ghost comes to fill and take up residence in these temples of our bodies that *have been* cleansed by the blood of Jesus, He also, at the same time, enables us to speak in a Heavenly language (1 Cor. 14:2). More about this later. Just stay open to the Word.

Let's go now to John 7:37-39. "In the last day, that great day of the feast, Jesus stood and cried, saying, If any man thirst, let him come unto Me and drink. He that believeth on Me, as the Scripture hath said, out of His belly, shall flow rivers of living water. But this spake He of the Spirit which they that believe on Him *should receive*: for the Holy Ghost was not yet given; because that

Jesus was not yet glorified."

When He spoke of eternal life He spoke of it as being a well *in you*, (a well is for your own backyard) when He speaks of the receiving of the Holy Spirit He says, out of your belly will flow *rivers* of living water. Rivers generate power and are for many people. "But ye shall receive power, after that the Holy Ghost is come upon you; and ye shall be witnesses unto Me both in Jerusalem, and in all Judaea and in Samaria and unto the uttermost part of the earth" (Acts 1:8). Then it's not just something imparted as a well of life in your own back yard for you personally, but rather a river, the source of blessing and life is then in you to bless others. This is equipment for service and ministry. "But this spake He of the Spirit, which *they that believe on Him should receive*: for the Holy Ghost was not yet given; because that Jesus was not yet glorified" (John 7:39). Notice Jesus said, they that believe on Him *"should"* receive, not *would* receive as some modernistic translators have changed it to fit their theology.

Once you believe, you *then should* take the next step and receive the Holy Ghost. No wonder Paul said, "Have ye received the Holy Ghost *since* ye believed? And they said unto him, We have not so much as heard whether there be any Holy Ghost" (Acts 19:2). This was the norm. Paul himself received the Holy Ghost three days after he had believed on the Lord. Look to the Word: "And Saul, yet breathing out threatenings and slaughter against the disciples of the Lord, went unto the high priest, and desired of him letters to Damascus to the synagogues, that if he found any of this way, whether they were men or women, he might bring them bound unto Jerusalem. And as he journeyed, he came near Damascus: and suddenly there shined round about him a light from Heaven. And he fell to the earth, and heard a voice saying unto him, Saul, Saul, why persecutest thou me? And he said, Who art thou, Lord? And the Lord said, I am Jesus whom thou persecutest: it is hard for thee to kick against the pricks. *And he trembling and astonished said, Lord*, what wilt Thou have me to do? And the Lord said unto him, Arise and go into the city and it shall be told thee what thou must do. And the men which journeyed with him stood speechless, hearing a voice, but seeing no man.

And Saul arose from the earth; and when his eyes were opened, he saw no man: but they led him by the hand, and brought him into Damascus, and he was three days without sight, and neither did eat nor drink. And there was a certain disciple at Damascus, named Ananias; and to him said the Lord in a vision, Ananias, And he said, Behold, I am here, Lord. And the Lord said unto him, arise, and go into the street which is called Straight, and inquire in the house of Judas for one called Saul of Tarsus; for behold, he prayeth. And hath seen in a vision a man named Ananias coming in, and putting his hand on him, that he might receive his sight. Then Ananias answered, Lord, I have heard by many of this man, how much evil he hath done to thy saints at Jerusalem: and here he hath authority from the chief priests to bind all that call on Thy name. But the Lord said unto him, Go thy way: for he is a chosen vessel unto Me, to bear My name before the Gentiles, and kings, and the children of Israel. For I will show him how great things he must suffer for My name's sake. And Ananias went his way and entered into the house; and *putting his hands on him said, Brother Saul, the Lord*, even Jesus, that appeared unto thee in the way as thou camest, *hath sent me, that thou mightest* receive thy sight, and *be filled with the Holy Ghost*" (Acts 9:1-17).

Let's notice some things here. In verse 6 Saul believed and called Jesus Lord. He was thereby saved. Paul later wrote, "That if thou shalt confess with thy mouth the Lord Jesus, and shalt believe in thine heart that God hath raised Him from the dead, thou shalt be saved" (Rom. 10:9). This Paul did on the road to Damascus.

In verses 10-16, the Lord instructs a disciple named Ananias to go lay hands upon Saul (Paul) that he might be filled with the Holy Ghost and receive his sight. "And Ananias went his way and entered into the house; and *putting his hands on him said, Brother Saul, the Lord*, even Jesus, that appeared unto thee in the way as thou camest, *hath sent me, that thou mightest* receive thy sight, and *be filled with the Holy Ghost*" (Acts 9:17). Notice again he was called "Brother Saul" before he received the Holy Ghost. Before he was saved he was a blasphemer, a persecutor, and a child of the devil, not a "brother" (Eph. 2:3).

"Who was before a blasphemer, and a persecutor, and injurious: but I obtained mercy, because I did it ignorantly in unbelief" (1 Tim. 1:13). But when he believed in Jesus and His resurrection, he became a new creature. He was born again and became a child of God (John 1:12). That is why Ananias called him "Brother" Saul *before* he received the Holy Ghost and why Saul could *now* receive the Holy Ghost. "If ye then, being evil, know how to give good gifts unto your children; how much more shall your Heavenly Father give the Holy Spirit to them that ask Him" (Luke 11:13)? This gift of the Holy Ghost Baptism then, is only for those who are already children of God.

We see a similar type of thing in the life of Christ. In His humanity He was "born of the Word and Spirit." "Now the birth of Jesus Christ was on this wise: When as His mother Mary was espoused to Joseph, before they came together, she was found with child of the Holy Ghost" (Matt. 1:18). ". . .that which was conceived in her is of the Holy Ghost" (Matt. 1:20).

The Spirit worked through the Word and brought about His human birth (Gen. 3:15; Luke 8:11; Heb. 10:5), but it wasn't until thirty years later when He was ready to enter into the ministry that He was filled with the Spirit and empowered for service. "Now when all the people were baptized, it came to pass, that Jesus also being baptized, and praying, the Heaven was opened, and *the Holy Ghost descended* in a bodily shape like a dove *upon Him*, and a voice came from Heaven, which said, Thou art My beloved Son; in Thee I am well pleased. And Jesus Himself began to be about thirty years of age, being as was supposed, the son of Joseph, which was the son of Heli. . ." (Luke 3:21-23).

"*And Jesus being full of the Holy Ghost* returned from Jordan, and was *led by the Spirit. . .And Jesus returned in the power of the Spirit* into Galilee; and there went out a fame of Him through all the region round about. . .And there was delivered unto Him the book of the prophet Esaias, and when He had opened the book, He found the place where it was written, *The Spirit of the Lord is upon Me because He hath anointed Me to preach* the Gospel to the poor; *He hath sent Me to heal* the brokenhearted, to preach *deliverance to the captives* and recovering of sight to the blind, *to set at liberty* them that are bruised" (Luke 4:1, 14, 17-18). Here we see He was the Son of God for thirty years before He received the Holy Spirit to empower Him for service. The reason the critics cannot understand supernatural Holy Ghost ministry, is because they have not yet received the Baptism with the Holy Spirit, so they are not yet empowered. Here lies the reason for many of their misunderstandings and why they think miracles have passed away and tongues are not for today. But Jesus told His disciples to go out into all the world and preach the Gospel to every creature, "Teaching them to observe all things whatsoever I have commanded you: and, lo, I am with you alway, even unto the end of the world. Amen" (Matt. 28:20). Notice we were to observe *everything* He taught them, even unto the end of the church age, and this includes the Holy Spirit Baptism and speaking in other tongues (Mark 16:17; Acts 2:4).

Satan has worked to stop multitudes of Christians from receiving the Holy Ghost Baptism and he has done it through religious traditions, telling people they received the Holy Ghost Baptism when they believed. If so, what about Paul's question then in Acts 19:2, and what about all these other passages? Can you give two or three clear passages that say, all who believe automatically receive the Holy Ghost? No, you cannot. Scripture says in the mouth of two or three witnesses let every word be established.

One might say, yes, but I know the Holy Ghost is with me. True, if you are a believer He is *with you*. The twelve apostles also knew Him and even preached and prayed for the sick under His influence, but yet He wasn't *in them*, until they asked (Luke 11:13), and in their case they couldn't receive His indwelling until after Jesus had been glorified (John 7:39). In your case, He enters to live in you when you, as a free moral agent, ask Him to, and only *after* you have received remission of sins (Acts 2:38). So when a person receives Christ, he is born again of His incorruptible seed by the Word of God, and the Spirit of Christ also called the Spirit of God's Son (eternal life) (Gal. 4:6), is in his heart. Christ dwells *in the hearts* by faith, and gives life. Then when the Spirit of God comes into these bodies of ours, quickening them, He gives us victory over the flesh (Rom. 8:11-13). "What? Know ye not that *your body* is the temple of the Holy Ghost which is in you, which ye have of God, and ye are not your own" (1 Cor. 6:19)? Listen to this Scripture: "A new heart also will I give you, and a new (Christ-like) spirit will I put within you: (born again) and I will take away the stony heart out of your flesh, and I will give you an heart of flesh, and (in addition to that) I will put *My Spirit within you*, (the Holy Ghost), *and cause you* to walk in My statutes, and ye shall keep My judgments, and do them" (Ezek. 36:26-27). Two things promised. "And" means, in addition to the first thing provided. Notice, the first thing is "a new heart, a new spirit," and then afterwards, people need to invite God's Spirit into them to empower them and open up their understanding.

"Therefore if any man be in Christ, *he is* a new creature; old things are passed away; behold, all things are become new, and all things are of God, who hath reconciled us to Himself by Jesus Christ, and hath given to us the ministry of reconciliation" (2 Cor. 5:17-18). When a person is born again, this is what Scripture calls, the spirits of just men being made perfect (Heb. 12:23). Now after this, the Holy Ghost can come in and fill your whole being (Acts 2:4). Jesus said, you cannot pour new wine, (the Holy Ghost) into old bottles, (sinners) or the bottles would burst. But new wine must be poured into new wine skins. That is, new creatures with new hearts and new spirits (Acts 2:13; 15-17). First Cor. 12:13 says, "For by one Spirit are we all baptized into one body, whether we be Jews or Gentiles, whether we be bond or free; (salvation) and (in addition to that) have been all made to drink into one Spirit." Notice, "and," which means in addition to the first step, and these to whom He wrote all spake with tongues for they had all drunk into the Spirit (1 Cor. 14). So they were not only given a birth by the Word and the Spirit, and brought into the body of Christ by His power, but also they had taken the next step and had drunk *into the Spirit,* which means they drank until they were full and then immersed in the Spirit (John 7:37-39).

So the Spirit takes you out of Adam and baptizes you into Christ when you're born again. This change takes place in your own spirit. The next step is to "drink into the Spirit." But ye are not in the flesh, but in the Spirit, *if so be that the Spirit of God "dwell in you."* Now if any man have not the Spirit of Christ, he is none of His. (BORN AGAIN) And *if Christ be in* you, the body is dead because of sin; but your spirit is full of life because of righteousness (Mon. translation). But (on the other hand) *if the Spirit of Him* that raised up Jesus from the dead dwell in you, *He that raised up Christ* from the dead shall also quicken your mortal bodies *by His Spirit that dwelleth in you"* (Rom. 8:9-11). If you've partaken of Christ, you belong to Him (John 1:12). If you have the Holy Spirit living in you, you're in the Spirit and can understand spiritual things and supernatural ministries (1 Cor. 2:9-14; 12:1-11). This reminds us of Jesus' words in John 7:37-39, that those who believe on Him *"should"* take the next step and receive the Holy Ghost. The reason for much of the controversy in the body of Christ and most of the division is because some Christians have not been taught this Biblical truth. Nowhere does it say you receive part of the Holy Ghost when you're born again, and then after that you must receive more. No, it says, "Have you received the Holy Ghost since ye believed" (Acts 19:2)? And "after ye believed ye were sealed with that Holy Spirit of promise" (Eph. 1:13). And yes, we understand that different degrees of His anointing and power are released in a Spirit-filled Christian's life depending on their faith and consecration.

The new birth is called the "washing of regeneration and renewing of the Holy Ghost" (Titus 3:5). This is called a "washing," and the same water that washes something can later fill it. The Holy Spirit is referred to as water in the scriptures. He washes us in the new birth and later fills us when we ask.

So once you believe on Him, you have eternal life and are a son. But the next step is to ask for the Holy Spirit. "He that believeth on the Son hath everlasting life: and he that believeth not the Son shall not see life; but the wrath of God abideth on him" (John 3:36). Concerning the Holy Ghost, "Ye have not because ye ask not" (James 4:2; Luke 11:13). Many have been taught not to ask and have allowed men to persuade them that either it's not for today or that they already received when they got born again. But we have shown you Scripturally that this is not the case.

So again, the Holy Spirit will not make His permanent abode in a person who is still a child of the devil. He does not enter in and fill a person until *after that* person becomes a son of God, a new creature in Christ. So it is only *after* that ye believed, that ye are sealed with that Holy Spirit of promise" (Eph. 1:13). (See also Acts 8:12, 14-17; 19:2, 6; John 14:17; 1:12.) Should anyone neglect this seal?

So every person who has repented of a life of sin and believed on Jesus has everlasting life. They are justified and are a child of God, partaking of Christ (Heb. 3:14), and they are born of the Spirit. But not all have invited the Holy Spirit, the Spirit of God, to dwell in them in His fullness. Remember, Jesus said, "we" will come and make our abode in you. So you may have invited Christ into your life, but not the Holy Ghost, which is *another* Comforter. It's when we invite Him in, in His fullness, that He can effectively teach us, guide us, more clearly speak to us, bring back things to our remembrance and empower us (John 16:12-15; 14:26; Acts 1:8; Luke 4:11-14).

"This only would I learn of you, received ye the Spirit by the works of the law, or by the hearing of faith?. . .Have ye suffered so many things in vain? If it be yet in vain" (Gal. 3:2, 4). By this question we can see that the Galatians *knew* specifically when they received the Holy Spirit, and that it was through faith. "That the blessing of Abraham might come on the Gentiles through Jesus Christ; that we might receive the promise of the Spirit through faith" (Gal. 3:14). "He (Paul) said unto them, Have ye received the Holy Ghost since ye believed?" Well, have you (Acts 19:2)? If so, when? Scripturally, how do you know?

We've seen in this chapter that:

—The world (sinners) *cannot receive* the Holy Ghost (John 14:17; John 8:44).
—The world can *receive Christ* and when they do, they "become" sons of God and have eternal life (Rom. 6:23).

–Jesus then said those who believe on Him *"should"* receive the Holy Ghost (Luke 11:13).

–In Acts 8 people had repented, believed in Christ, and were water baptized *but none of them had yet received* the Holy Ghost.

– Hands were laid on them *to receive* the Holy Ghost.

– People call upon the name of the Lord to be saved.

– People have hands laid on them *to receive* the Holy Ghost.

– Being born again of incorruptible seed and being filled with the Holy Spirit are two separate Scriptural experiences.

– He commanded those who love Him to receive the Holy Ghost (Acts 1:4-5).

Christ said to His followers "how much more will your heavenly Father give the Holy Spirit *to them that ask Him?*" (Luke 11:13).

All we ask is that you stay with what is written. It's my prayer that you can at least see the Biblical foundation for this perspective. We simply trust that Luke and Paul knew what they were speaking about. The main point that we make is that the Baptism with the Holy Spirit is a separate Scriptural experience from salvation. Let us go on.

Chapter 16

The Biblical Evidence of the Baptism With the Holy Spirit

How Will You Know?

It should be obvious to you by now that if you've been open to God's Word, that we all, as Christians, need the Baptism with the Holy Ghost in order to understand many things about Christianity to really have power to witness and to truly live the Spirit-filled Christian life.

Let's now take a look at what is not the evidence of the Holy Ghost Baptism. It is not forsaking all and following Jesus for the disciples did that before Pentecost (Mark 1:17-20). It is not joy, for they also had this before Pentecost (Luke 24:52), as did the Samaritans before they received the Holy Ghost (Acts 8:5, 8). It is not zeal for God, for even the Jews had that as did Saul before his conversion (Rom. 10:1-3; Phil. 3:6). They preached the Gospel before the Holy Ghost was in them (John 14:17; Luke 9:2). They had a revelation from God that Jesus was the Christ before they received the Spirit's indwelling (Matt. 16:16-17). Cornelius feared God, prayed always, gave alms and had a vision and wasn't even saved so this couldn't be proof (Acts 10). Apollos taught and was mighty in the Word but not filled (Acts 18:24-26). The Old Testament prophets heard His "still small voice" and spoke as He moved them, but this was not the Holy Ghost Baptism (2 Pet. 2:20-21).

They walked on water, healed the sick, cast out devils and were not baptized with the Holy Ghost. They knew and were acquainted with the Holy Ghost before He was in them (John 14:17). Great faith was exercised before the reception of the Holy

Ghost so that can't be the evidence (Matt. 8:8-10). They sang hymns, were water baptized and had communion but that wasn't the Baptism with the Holy Ghost. Their names were written in Heaven and they were clean through the Word but had not yet received the Holy Spirit. They had peace with God before Pentecost and their minds were opened to a certain degree, but that wasn't it either (John 20:19; Luke 24:45, 49). We see then that *none of these things* could be claimed as proof that the Holy Spirit had come into them and filled them. It is good to do these things, to work for the Lord and have zeal, but the Bible gives its own evidence. "And they were all filled with the Holy Ghost, and began to speak with other tongues, as the Spirit gave them utterance" (Acts 2:4).

In Mark 16:17, Jesus said concerning this church age, "and *these signs shall follow* them that BELIEVE; in My Name shall they cast out devils; they shall SPEAK WITH NEW TONGUES: they shall take up serpents and IF they drink any deadly thing, it shall not hurt them. They shall lay their hands on the sick and they shall recover." All these signs are supernatural. Here was a new sign, a sign directly connected with the incoming of the Holy Spirit into the lives of believers. And it was reserved for this age of the Holy Ghost. Many modernists try and tear out of the Bible these last verses of Mark's Gospel because they do not fit into their theology. But God has seen to it that the Bible was preserved intact just the way He wanted it. In this passage of Scripture, Jesus pinpointed believers by signs—markers that point to something—in this case, to what Jesus calls believers.

One of the signs we'll look at is "they shall speak with new tongues" and see, without twisting, bending, or forcing Scripture to say something it doesn't, whether or not this could be our answer to the evidence of the Holy Spirit's indwelling and fullness. It has been argued that if these signs are to follow, why don't you go around picking up serpents? This question is equivalent to satan's temptation brought to Christ in Luke 4:9-12. Jesus said in these cases, "thou shalt NOT tempt the Lord, thy God," and besides this, we see no Biblical example of early disciples handling venomous snakes as some today foolishly try to do. Remember, "in the mouth of two or three witnesses let every word be established." We MUST let Scripture interpret Scripture and then it speaks for itself. The answer is found in Acts 28:3-6, where Paul accidentally put his hand where a venomous serpent was and was bitten, but he was not harmed. This should clarify this passage for any honest person. Concerning drinking deadly things He says, IF, not WHEN, for again, "thou shalt NOT tempt the Lord, thy God."

Evidently venomous and poisonous things came about somehow at the fall and since Christ redeemed us, we need not fear these things if something were to happen by accident, as long as we believe His words and accept His provision. The other two signs of casting out devils and healing the sick are taking place where God's Word is believed and it is happening according to the proportion of the faith of His followers.

During the forty days following His resurrection, Jesus spoke to His disciples various things concerning the Kingdom of God. In these passages He revealed the important things He wanted the church to know during this Church Age. What He wanted us to know then from those conversations that He had with His disciples is recorded at the end of Matthew, Mark, Luke, and John and also in the Book of Acts. After His resurrection, He spoke of preaching repentance and remission of sins in His name and teaching the Gospel to all nations, He commanded them to proclaim *all of these things* to every creature, even unto the end of the world. He spoke of being baptized with the Holy Ghost and receiving power, casting out devils, speaking in tongues and healing the sick. These then, are the tremendously important truths He wanted impressed upon His church throughout all the age, for this is what is actually written. But, sad to say, many today do not heed the words of Jesus but heed some human teachers that say parts of Christ's great commission have passed away. And what's more, they even fight the manifestations of God's Holy Spirit, which the early church prayed for and exercised. Shame on them. Jesus said, for "whosoever shall be ashamed of Me and My words in this adulterous and sinful generation, of him shall the Son of man be ashamed." Let us never dare to weaken anything that Christ has said by our opinions or manmade theology.

We want to show you now from the scriptures that although you cannot see the Holy Spirit, the receiving of the Holy Ghost is something that can be "SEEN AND HEARD." Look at Acts 2:4, "and they were all filled with the Holy Ghost and *began to speak with other "tongues" as the Spirit gave them utterance.*" The Scripture says that when they were filled, the "multitude HEARD THEM." What Jesus said, had come to pass in the lives of these 120 believers. They spoke in new tongues, which is the New Testament sign of the Holy Spirit's permanent incoming and fullness as we shall see. All the other gifts of the Spirit were temporarily given at times in the Old Testament, but God has reserved tongues for the Church Age to be the sign of His coming into the temple of men's bodies.

Three Manifestations of Tongues

There are three kinds of tongues mentioned in New Testament Scripture. First Corinthians 13:1 mentions people given the ability to speak in tongues of *men* and of *angels*. First Corinthians 14:2 mentions the *unknown* tongue. In the latter, NO MAN UNDERSTANDS what is being said, but God only. In all cases, the one who is speaking did not know what they were saying, for it wasn't by their mind that they were speaking, but as the Holy Spirit was giving them utterance (Acts 2:4). With the incoming of the Holy Spirit into their lives, there came also a visible manifestation of the Holy Spirit's presence. Scriptural evidence as we shall clearly see, of being baptized and filled with the Holy Ghost. Peter said on the day of Pentecost about Christ, "This Jesus hath God raised up, whereof we all are witnesses. Therefore being by the right hand of God exalted, *and having received of the Father the promise of the Holy Ghost, He hath shed forth this, which ye now see and hear*" (Acts 2:32-33).

Note: it is an experience that can be seen and heard. Let's turn for a moment over to Acts 10:44-46. In this passage we see that the Jews "which believed, were astonished as many as came with Peter, because that on the Gentiles also, was poured out the gift of the Holy Ghost," for they at that time, didn't yet believe that the Gentiles could be saved or receive the Holy Ghost. "FOR THEY *HEARD* THEM SPEAK WITH TONGUES AND MAGNIFY GOD." What they heard was evidence enough. These Jewish believers and Peter knew that the Gentiles had received the gift of the Holy Ghost because of their speaking in tongues, as verse 47 clearly shows. Give all the explanations that you can to explain it away but the Scripture stands there in all of its revealing power and simplicity.

If we look at Acts 11:15-17, we see that Peter told the leaders in Jerusalem that the Holy Ghost fell on them AS ON US at the beginning, referring to the time they were filled with the Holy Ghost and began SPEAKING IN TONGUES (Acts 2:4). Did He fall on you like this? This is the Gospel pattern. Let's return to Acts chapter 2.

In this chapter, these unlearned and ignorant men that had received the Holy Spirit were speaking in the languages of the world; languages they had never learned. Now, to them, it was just speaking as the Spirit gave them utterance, but to the many; who came from around the world who understood what these 120 were speaking, it was languages. "And they were all amazed and marveled, saying one to another, Behold, are not all these which speak Galilaeans? And how hear we every man in our own tongue, wherein we were born" (Acts 2:7-8)? Yet to those who only knew the common Jewish language, it was foolishness and babbling. Others mocking said, "these men are full of NEW WINE" (Acts 2:13). But Peter said, "this is that which was spoken by the prophet Joel." Paul, in I Corinthians 14:10,11 said that, "there are, it may be, so many kinds of voices in the world. *none of them* is without signification. Therefore IF I KNOW NOT the meaning of the voice I shall be unto him that speaketh a barbarian and he that speaketh shall be a barbarian unto me." So it was not that the utterances given were not words as the mockers who only knew the common Jewish language thought, but rather, to these many who COULDN'T understand what was being said, as was the case on the day of Pentecost, *to them* it was just babblings or utterances and syllables, just as it would be if you tried to talk with someone of another land. Many of the crowd thought the 120 to be drunk because they couldn't understand that which was said, which is why Peter had to address the issue. Peter then preached to the multitude in a common Jewish language that all could understand, for the Scripture does not say that they preached the Gospel in tongues, but that they spoke as the Spirit gave them utterance, the wonderful works of God. Listen then to what Peter says concerning the speaking in tongues which "many" thought were just drunken babblings or emotionalism. "We are not drunken AS YE SUPPOSE, seeing that it is but the third hour of the day--*BUT THIS IS THAT* which was spoken by the prophet Joel! And *IT SHALL COME TO PASS IN THE LAST DAYS*, saith God, *I will pour out of My Spirit* upon all flesh and your sons and your daughters shall prophesy and your young men shall see visions and your old men shall dream dreams." Are we in the last days or not? If so, then Joel's prophecy is still for us, and this speaking in tongues "is that" which Joel spoke of.

In his sermon to them on this day, he said, "this Jesus hath God raised up, whereof we all are witnesses, therefore, being by the right hand of God exalted and having received of the Father, THE PROMISE OF THE HOLY GHOST, He that shed forth this which YOU NOW "*SEE*" AND "*HEAR*" (Acts 2:32-33).

The outpouring of the Holy Spirit on these believers then, was something that could be *seen* and *heard*. Peter went on to tell them they also could receive the gift of the Holy Ghost if they too, repented and believed and we can be sure he didn't say, we received the Holy Spirit like this, but you have to accept it all without any evidence. *NO!* for Jesus said believers would speak in new tongues and Peter already told them it was something that could be seen and heard. And this "speaking in tongues" was also absolute proof to Peter and the other believers in Acts 10 that the Gentiles had received the Holy Ghost. It wiped out all of their skepticism. It is clear then, if you don't reason against the scriptures, that they, also, in Acts 2:38-39, received the Holy Ghost the same way. There is no further need to mention that they also spoke in tongues. It is obvious it occurred within minutes or shortly after the Acts 2:4 experience.

Acts 8:5-14 reveals the way they ministered the Holy Ghost to these people, and again, we'll see that the receiving of the Holy Ghost was something that could be "seen" and "heard." It is also seen to be a definite experience and is always *after* repentance and believing, and either before, or after, water baptism. Let's see, also, that it came in definite answer to prayer and was a part of the early church's program, along with the fact that a special service was held for the people to receive the Holy Ghost through the laying on of hands. (Read Acts 8:5-20.) In this passage we see Philip, a true New Testament evangelist, preaching the Gospel with signs following. In verse 12 again we see that many of the people of the city *repented, believed the Gospel, were born again*, of the Word (James 1:18; 1 Pet. 1:23), *and water baptized*. In other words, they were saved. Their sins were washed away (Acts 2:38). In verse 14, we see the apostles receiving news of this revival in Jerusalem. Scripture says, *they had heard* that Samaria, "had RECEIVED THE WORD OF GOD," and were begotten through the Gospel (1 Pet. 1:23; James 1:18; 1 Cor. 4:15), and so they sent Peter and John unto them to hold another service, that these saved people "MIGHT RECEIVE THE HOLY GHOST," for up to that time, He had fallen upon NONE OF THEM (v. 16).

Now, if it was non-experiential as some school's of thought say today, how would they know whether or not they had received the Holy Ghost? But the Biblical evidence is clear; they knew that they had repented, believed the Gospel and were water baptized, but "they also knew" that they hadn't yet received the Holy Ghost for none of them had yet spoken in tongues. So they were sent to pray for them that they also might receive the Holy Ghost, for being God's children, they could now receive the promise. In verse 17 it says, "THEN LAID THEY THEIR HANDS ON THEM (the Samaritans) AND THEY RECEIVED THE HOLY GHOST." How did they know? How could they be sure? Remember, Jesus said, "In My Name they (that believe) SHALL SPEAK IN NEW TONGUES," and this is everywhere connected with the Baptism with the Holy Ghost in the Scriptures. Verse 18 says, "And when Simon *SAW* that through the laying on of hands THE HOLY GHOST WAS GIVEN, he offered them money...." How did they know? How did Simon know? What moved dishonest Simon to want to offer them money? What did he see? The same thing they *saw* on the day of Pentecost is the obvious answer, for in Acts 10 we clearly saw how Peter and the Jews with him unquestionably knew the Gentiles had received the gift of the Holy Ghost. Remember, Acts 10:44-47 reveals how they knew beyond any shadow of a doubt, "for they *HEARD* THEM SPEAK WITH TONGUES AND MAGNIFY GOD."

Today, many say that everyone who repents, believes and is water baptized, has this Holy Ghost Baptism. What proof have they from Scripture in the light of all the Word of God, that shows it is a separate experience from the New Birth? You may ask, did Paul speak in tongues when he was filled with the Holy Ghost in Acts 9? Let's take the words right out of his mouth from I Corinthians 14:18, "I THANK MY GOD I SPEAK WITH TONGUES MORE THAN YE ALL." Do you? Paul received the Holy Ghost three days after he was converted on the road to Damascus (Acts 9:6; 9-17). Notice in verse 17 of Acts 9, Ananias, in obedience to the Lord, came to Saul and called him "Brother Saul" and said, the Lord sent him to lay hands on him that he might be filled with the Holy Ghost.

Paul was a believer—casting out devils, healing the sick and speaking in tongues followed him, just as Jesus said. Paul knew the Biblical evidence of the Baptism with the Holy Ghost. In Acts 19:1-6, he said to those whom he perceived to be believers in Jesus, "Have ye RECEIVED THE HOLY GHOST *SINCE* YE BELIEVED?" They hadn't, so Paul told them that this great promise could now be received and in verse 6 when Paul *"laid his hands upon them, the Holy Ghost came on them: and they spake with tongues and prophesied,"* (by the indwelling Spirit of God) "and all the men were about twelve." No where in Scripture does it say that just some of them who received the Holy Ghost spoke in tongues, but rather they were *ALL* filled with the Holy Ghost and they *ALL* BEGAN TO SPEAK IN OTHER TONGUES as the Spirit gave them utterance."

The Scriptures state, "in the mouth of two or three witnesses, let every word be established." We've given six. God does not need to emphasize it any more than that. Add to this, the apostle's statement, "I would that ye ALL spake in tongues and forbid not to speak in tongues," and the testimonies of millions of Christians in our day who have received the Holy Ghost just like in the Bible, and the evidence is overwhelming. So much so, that only the traditions of men could blind people to this wonderful truth, for much of the modern church spends its time and effort opposing that which the early church prayed for. It is not good theology to make theology out of things the Bible doesn't say, as in the case of those who do their best to explain away these Scriptures and read between the lines, rather than just read the lines. So this is not only how the Holy Ghost was received in the early church, but it is still the same way this experience is received today, as millions of honest, Bible-believing Christians testify. It is a vindication of the absolute truthfulness of God's Word, "them that believe. . .shall speak in new tongues." This then is how to receive the Holy Ghost like they did in the Bible. This Baptism with the Holy Ghost is for all children of God for God is no respecter of persons (Acts 10:34). It comes in answer to prayer. It is the great promise of the New Testament. The typical Biblical way to receive this is to have a Holy Spirit-filled believer lay hands on you. It is so definite an experience that someone should know whether or not, and when, they received it, and it is always accompanied with tongues when people are instructed properly from the Word.

All experience is to be based on the clear Scriptures but the Scriptures are given to be experienced if we believe. In all cases, a person has to repent and believe in his heart in Jesus Christ and His resurrection before he can receive the Holy Ghost. It may be a moment later or it may be months or years later, but we only receive what we appropriate by faith, even if something is legally ours in Christ. These are offered gifts and so must be received by faith.

The Necessity of the Holy Spirit Baptism

This Holy Spirit Baptism is necessary for a Christian to really understand much of Christianity (John 16:12-13). It is deeper than intellectually believing a doctrine; Christianity is doctrine translated into experience by the indwelling Holy Ghost. It is the inworking of the Holy Spirit that accomplishes this in a person's life, and it is for all Christians because all Christians need to have doctrine translated into experience, and it is the fullness of the Holy Ghost that does it. This is why what is called a fundamentalist church, knows very little about the real experiential workings of the Spirit. They typically know little or nothing about miracles, signs, the voice of the Spirit, the manifestations of the Spirit or His gifts as is recorded in the New Testament. And because they disagree with the Word in this area, they will never experience much of the true working of the Spirit as is revealed in the Bible (especially in the book of Acts), unless there comes a change of heart and doctrine concerning this.

Now the Lord will never change anyone's doctrine, be it right or be it wrong, but as free moral agents, men can believe what they choose to believe. So only those who are open in spirit to God's Word, will be able to see it--as it is with salvation, so it is with this. But the sad part of it is, multitudes are being led wrongly concerning this, because of wrong teaching by men whose good intentions and zeal without true knowledge in this area, have promoted a wall and mental block against the Holy Ghost, so that the Spirit of God cannot work in the lives of many of God's people the way redemption was designed. As it was in the Old Testament, "My people are destroyed because of a lack of knowledge," so it is today. The priests (leaders) of the people where the Pharisees of old have taught what they thought rather than let the Word of the Lord say what it says. For this, they must give an account (James 3:1). Traditions begin by men saying what the Bible doesn't say, rather than saying what it does say. They are formed by men reading too much *between* the lines and not enough of *reading the lines*. Scripture reveals that the infilling of the Spirit is accomplished when a Christian receives the Baptism with the Spirit. Up to that point when they are born again, they are converted children—God's sons, born of the Spirit, partaking of Christ, but still they cannot grasp many of the supernatural, divine realities of Christianity although intellectually they may agree to some of them as doctrine.

First Corinthians 12:13 explains the Spirit's work in placing a person in the Body of Christ. It reveals how He does it. It also is through a baptism, but this, as we have clearly seen, is a separate experience from being Baptized and filled with the Holy Spirit. There is, in Scripture, the New Testament doctrine of baptisms (Heb. 6:2), and each baptism must be clearly seen and its purpose made clear. They are revealed in the Word but it must be determined which one produces which result. One is for salvation (1 Cor. 12:13), one is for confirmation (like circumcision) of a person's salvation, this is water baptism (Acts 8:12), and one is for manifestation (Acts 1:4; 5-8).

The Holy Spirit Baptism is for manifestation and what is needed is more manifestation, for without the Spirit's manifestation, religion becomes dry and formal and is regulated by the minds of men. They may be intelligent or able to build and run big structures and organizations, but the breath of life is not in it. What comes with the Holy Spirit Baptism is the breath of life in all that's done. There is then life rather than death. Not only does the letter kill, but the very organizations that refuse the supernatural work of the Holy Spirit, kill much of the work of God, so to speak, by stopping the work of the Holy Spirit (2 Tim. 3:5).

The Holy Spirit is working to produce manifestation based on Christ's doctrine. He is here to take the Word of God and make it a divine reality, a living experience in the lives of God's people. Those who say there need be no experience, are those who are basing their beliefs only on their mere intellect. They say this because without the indwelling fullness of the Holy Spirit, they have not received the Baptism that produces manifestations and the unveiling of present spiritual, supernatural realities, for the Spirit of God is the only one who can open up men's minds to these truths (1 Cor. 2:9-14). Christianity is a revealed relationship; it is revealed by the Spirit of God (John 16:13-15), it is not merely an intellectual study, although the intellect needs to see the Scriptures and rightly divide them. Yet the rightly dividing of God's Word can only come from the mind of the one who inspired it in the first place (2 Pet. 1:20-21). The Pharisees, in many ways, were legalists and knew the letter of the Word, and yet they couldn't grasp the spirit of the Word as Jesus Christ taught it; they were blinded by their own reasoning and without the Baptism with the Spirit a person is to a great degree, left up to mere intellectual study. He may know Greek or Hebrew but yet he's blind to most spiritual realities. So it is possible for a person to *think they see* and yet be blind (Rev. 3:14-22). Intellectual study is fine up to a point, but when the scriptures step out into the supernatural, the unassisted mind of man cannot grasp it. So he struggles with it and then finally tries to explain it away. According to his mind, this is the only logical thing to do seeing that he may be a leader or a minister and if he can't understand it, how could anyone else--he thinks. When others say they do understand it because they have been baptized with the Holy Spirit, the intellectual man raises his defenses, he thinks how can they say they understand when I don't? Remember that even though Jesus' disciples were working by the anointing of the Holy Spirit and saw many wonderful things take place, yet Jesus said there were many things they couldn't understand yet until they were filled with the Holy Ghost (John 16:12-13). Jesus told them, "He dwelleth *with you* and shall be *in you*" (John 14:17). As seen, there is a difference between Him dwelling with someone and in someone. It is so vitally important to focus on the Holy Spirit Baptism, for, as stated earlier, this is the way that Christianity is unveiled and this is how the minds and spirits of God's people are opened up fully to understand the scriptures, and again, let it be known that the Holy Spirit will never lead a person contrary to God's written Word.

Tongues, being a part of the experience of the baptism with the Holy Spirit, is also essential in that it is a form of communication between the believer and God, and communication with the author opens up a person's understanding of His Book (1 Cor. 14:2). Here is the problem. What cannot be grasped by the reasoning mind of some, is often rejected as heresy. Christ Himself was rejected as a heretic by the religious leaders of His day, not because He was but because their minds were closed to what He had to say; after all they reasoned, He never learned letters (theology) from them or their schools (John 7:14-17)! He taught some things they couldn't comprehend. And so on goes the conflict between the religious intellectual mind and faith in the heart of others. The mind is ever reasoning but the heart is the receiver and in order to receive this experience and enter into the Spirit-filled life, one's heart must be like that of a little child, believing only God's Word.

With the Holy Spirit Baptism comes instantly a new belief in miracles, healings, gifts of the Spirit and deliverance, just as was in the early church. There comes a deeper consecration to God and a deeper worship of God. It is the Holy Spirit's work to help believers grasp these realities of the Spirit (John 16:12-15; 1 Cor. 2:8-14). That is why there are two camps—those who believe in the Baptism with the Spirit and tongues also believe in being led by the Spirit, gifts of the Spirit, the workings of God, miracles, raising of holy hands and spiritual warfare, for instantly their thinking is transformed. The instant one receives, he can grasp Scriptural truths that he couldn't possibly grasp before, because before a person receives the Baptism with the Holy Ghost they are limited to a great degree, to their own intellect. Those then who refuse this Scriptural experience, are, for the most part, opposed to miracles, signs and wonders being for today, not thinking that every answered prayer is a miracle, but yet they would never deny prayer. They also say other such contradictory things such as sickness is from God but then run to the doctor as soon as possible to get it off them. (See Acts 10:38.) They cannot grasp the supernatural of the Scriptures as something present. The reason is that without the Holy Spirit Baptism there can be no real comprehension of these spiritual realities as revealed in the Word and so with the intellect unassisted and unable to grasp these things, they must try to explain why it couldn't possibly be this way. We see then the old worn out theories such as tongues have passed away with apostles, or they twist 1 Corinthians 13 and say it has already ceased. Or they come up with their own tradition that the Bible is come and we don't need the manifestations of the Holy Ghost today, but these things are not stated by Scripture but only by men's reasoning minds. The heart may be sincere, but the understanding of Scripture in this area is all wrong.

As we have shown from the plain, simple Word of God, the

Holy Spirit Baptism is received after conversion. It is another definite step in the life of a disciple. It may happen a moment after belief, but it always comes AFTER a person has accepted Christ as Savior for the Holy Spirit is given as a gift not to the world, but to the child of God, not for salvation but for power. Tongues are a sign of a believer; there is no Scriptural reason for anyone doubting the validity of speaking in tongues for the Bible clearly teaches it and God said that He set it in the church. It is not a divisive thing for the division comes not from the tongues or the experience, but from those who will not accept the validity of this Biblical experience, and who choose to stick with their tradition instead. Yes, tongues can be misused and spoken out in an assembly at times it shouldn't be (1 Cor. 14), just as anything meant for good can be misused, but that doesn't mean it is not valid. The Bible itself can also be misused as we've seen those who don't believe in this experience have done, but that doesn't mean the Bible itself is not valid.

UPROOTING TARES

"But He (Jesus) answered and said, Every plant (teaching) which My Heavenly Father hath not planted shall be rooted up" (Matt. 15:13).

Let us now address some of the reasonings of men that are not taken from Scripture, but from their school of thought. Some say, "tongues could be of the devil." *Nowhere* in Scripture, do you find a statement like that. In all cases where tongues are mentioned in Scripture, they are always connected with the gift of the Holy Spirit. First of all, we see there is no scriptural proof for any such statement, is there? If so, point it out from the scriptures! Some go around planting fear in God's people rather than preaching the Word. Tongues is taught by Jesus and the other New Testament writers. To receive this experience, a person must first repent of sin and believe what the Holy Scriptures say concerning it and be a child of God. They cannot have unforgiveness in their lives and receive. Jesus said that if a child of God sincerely comes to God, their Heavenly Father, and asks for the Holy Spirit, that they couldn't possibly get a devil. Can we not trust God (Luke 11:9-13)?

Others say: "It is just emotionalism or ecstatic babbling." This is equivalent to what *the doubters* said on the day of Pentecost, "others mocking said, these men are full of new wine." Even those under the influence of unbelief in Jesus' day said that Jesus was mad and had a devil. Festus said Paul was beside himself and mad. . .those mockers on the day of Pentecost said that Christ's disciples were drunk men. Emotionalism? Fanaticism? No, the Bible says in Acts 2:4, "and they were all filled with the Holy Ghost and began to speak in other tongues as the Spirit gave them utterance." It is no more emotionalism today than it was on the day of Pentecost. Yes, the Holy Ghost baptism gives a person more reality, freedom, and boldness in their Christianity—old dead formalism leaves—and some also rejoice and are excited when they receive, just as some are emotional when they experience any good thing in their lives. But that depends on the individual. Some of the same ones who say Pentecostal people are too emotional, will sit in front of their TV and scream at the players of a football game, who can't even hear them, and think nothing of it (Jude 17-20). Even the label "Pentecostal" should not be a divisive thing. This simply means a Christian who believes that the Biblical experience which happened on Pentecost in Acts 2, is for us today. And it is! So a "Pentecostal" or "Charismatic" is just a Christian who has believed in this Biblical experience. After the receiving of this wonderful Biblical experience, a person also has much more freedom to praise the Lord and say "Jesus is Lord" (1 Cor. 12:3). Before this baptism, many pray in Christ's name, but Christ is His title, "the anointed," it's not His name. Note the freedom and reality in worship in those that have received. There is a tremendous difference, for then God is *worshipped* in Spirit and truth.

Another excuse is, "I heard of someone who said he was baptized with the Holy Ghost and now he is backslidden." We could answer this by saying there are many who have been born again who are backslidden and not living for God; should we stop preaching salvation? Man is a free moral agent; God won't *make* a person obey; the person still has a free choice or Paul wouldn't have addressed sin so often and taught on living right in his letters. The people were baptized with the Holy Ghost and spoke in tongues and had gifts of the Spirit but they still needed correcting and teaching on how to live right just as in any church. The baptism doesn't make you morally better or worse than others without your will or cooperation, but what it does offer is a new and deeper dimension of communion with God, richer worship, power to witness, clearer understanding of Scriptures and a new reality in Christianity that was not experienced before, and so we must live our lives by the Bible and not be moved by human failure. Demas forsook Paul, but Paul went on with the Lord; he didn't let that stop him. Judas betrayed Jesus, but the Gospel message was still valid and the apostles continued afterward to perform the same kinds of miracles that they did when Judas was with them. Should we then reject the other apostles because of Judas? God forbid! So don't let that old, worn out excuse stop you from going on with the Lord and receiving this wonderful experience.

Some modern theologians say, "tongues have ceased." Where does it say that in the Word? They take the liberty to inject their opinions into a secluded passage of scripture found in 1 Corinthians 13. They then conveniently change the meaning of the passage and put it in the past tense as though it has already happened. To do so is equivalent to saying we have already been caught up to meet the Lord in the air. If you can do it to one scripture, what prevents us from doing it to all Scriptures that say "shall." If we can say one thing has passed away without the clear witness of two or three scriptures, what could prevent us from saying salvation has also passed away using the same method? Let's put away the reasonings of men and believe the Word. The Bible makes it abundantly clear that God set tongues in the church; that it is prayer (1 Cor. 14:14-15), and it is for the edifying of the believer (vs. 4); and that it is for us till the end of the church age (Matt. 28:20). So that some do not think we are trying to avoid 1 Corinthians 13, let us see what the Word of God really says without twisting it to fit our theology: READ 1 CORINTHIANS 13:8-13. Verse 8: have prophecies failed? No, not the real ones; they are still coming to pass. (The Book of Daniel is prophetic and is still coming to pass.) The testimony of Jesus is the spirit of prophecy. Are we still supposed to witness? God has two witnesses who will yet prophesy (Rev. 11:3). So it has not ceased. God said, in the last days your sons and daughters would prophesy (Acts 2:16-17). Are we in the last days? Paul told the church to desire to prophesy, for through it, the church receives edifying (1 Cor. 14:1, 3-5). Does the church still need to be edified? Prophecy then hasn't yet vanished. Let's quote now verses 9-10, "for we know in part and we prophesy in part, but when that which is perfect is come *then that which is in part shall be done away."*

Has perfect come? Some who like to make theology out of their reasonings say that Paul was talking of the Bible here. Was he? The New Testament wasn't put together as a book until long after Paul had died. Has knowledge as we know it, vanished away? Daniel said prophetically that KNOWLEDGE would be INCREASED in the last days (Dan. 12:4). Look around you; is it increasing or has it vanished away?

Paul, himself, only knew in part but he said THEN (WHEN PERFECT COMES) SHALL I KNOW EVEN AS I am known. NOW we see through a glass darkly; BUT THEN (WHEN PERFECT COMES) FACE TO FACE. The scriptures reveal we do not yet see face to face (1 Pet. 1:8; 1 John 3:2; Rev. 22:3-4), but we shall see face to face when Christ comes back to restore all things (Acts 3:20-21). He will then change our vile bodies to be made perfect like His glorious body (Phil. 3:21), and He will put down all rebellion in the universe (1 Cor. 15:28). Finally, God will make a new heavens and a new earth and there will be no more curse, death, pain or sickness (Rev. 21:1-5). So then when Christ returns for us, we will no longer have need of these gifts of the Spirit and tongues, but until that time, God has set them in the church for good purpose just as long as teachers and pastors are in the church (1 Cor. 12:28-30).

And 1 Corinthians 13:13 doesn't say, "now abideth *'ONLY'*" faith, hope and charity as some manage to say. Paul was simply revealing in this chapter that love will endure forever, but when the perfect age comes, we will not need tongues, for we will speak to God face to face. We won't need the gifts of healings for there will be no sickness. We won't need the word of knowledge he mentioned in 1 Corinthians 12 then, for we will know even as we are known. So He emphasized to them that love will go on through eternity while the gifts of the Spirit will not be needed when Perfect comes. He was saying also that love seeks to build others up and is not selfish, so they should not be like children in their understanding, but that they should seek the supernatural gifts that will edify and benefit the body of Christ most (1 Cor. 14:1-2). Add to this, hundreds of thousands, or even millions of fundamental Bible believing, born again, committed Christians in this day and hour, who will take the witness stand and testify of this scriptural experience and how it has deepened their commitment and relationship to Jesus Christ and the evidence, both scripturally and through personal testimony, is overwhelming.

But those who oppose it, will look for one here or there who never really received but thought they spoke in tongues because someone pressured them to at one time and they listen to their bad experience and write about that rather than believing God's Word and the testimonies of the teeming hundreds of thousands of other sincere Christians who will say how much of a benefit it is and how it deepened their relationship with God. God is the one who gives this experience and He is not the author of confusion. So then all confusion and division concerning this Scriptural experience comes from those who won't believe what God said about it. To say you don't need the "Holy Ghost" is equivalent to saying, "do we really need Jesus?"

Some say, "we don't need the miraculous today. We don't need gifts, tongues and the power of the Holy Spirit," or they say, "the age of miracles is passed away" (2 Tim. 3:5). The devil would like to stop the working of the Holy Spirit and to present to the world, a lifeless church, an organization like any other organization; but what he fears is a church which believes the Bible just as it is written; a church where God's Word is preached and the Holy Spirit is moving in power; where the signs of a believer are occurring (Mark 16:17-18). Nowhere in Scripture, does it talk of an age of miracles, for God is God and there is only ONE FAITH (Eph. 4; Jude 3), and ONE CHURCH as manifested in the Book of

Acts; not an early and a latter church (Col. 1:18), but there will always be some who speculate, theorize and make up man made doctrines about why the church shouldn't be the same as the early church. They don't have any Scripture to make these bold, confident statements on, only a school of thought they were trained up in, and because of this, many are following these opinions of men rather than God's Word. This is the reason that the church as a whole, is in the condition that it is in. The Book of Acts reveals the church when it was alive. This was THE CHURCH as the Lord established it. Look at it and you'll see what the Biblical church of today is supposed to be like. What else can we look at? Only a lack of faith or the traditions of men can keep people blind to it.

Our preaching, teaching and practice should be what the early church preached, taught and practiced when in its Spirit-filled period, rather than in this present lifeless, lukewarm period. If we want to see the real work of the Holy Spirit in the New Testament, let us see how He worked in the lives of those in the Book of Acts, for the Scriptures are the blueprint by which He does His work (John 17:17; John 16:13). And let us believe the "Apostle's Doctrine" over modernistic views.

We see that today a large part of the Christian world opposes that which the Christian church of the Book of Acts proclaimed. Let's not do what the religious leaders did to Judaism and make void the Word of God through OUR TRADITIONS (Mark 7:9, 13). How can any intelligent man say miracles are passed away and then ask people to pray about something? Every answered prayer is a miracle. And how can any professing Bible teacher come up with the confused idea that the age of the miracle worker (the Holy Spirit) is the *only age* in God's dealings with man and that miracles are not to be done? From Acts 2 on, all the chapters that reveal Christ's church demonstrate that the supernatural is a part of our Christian heritage, so let's stay with God's Word for our Christian faith is unchangeable. The reason they say these things is they've not yet invited the miracle worker, the Holy Ghost, into their lives in all His fullness.

Some say Paul didn't think too much concerning tongues.

They say it was unnecessary and it was mentioned last of all. Let's hear Paul's own words, "I thank MY GOD I SPEAK IN TONGUES MORE THAN YE ALL." Love is mentioned after faith and hope, but he said it was the greatest. So these reasonings also are not valid.

Another excuse is, "I don't believe tongues is for everyone," in so saying, at least this excuse admits it is for some. (Is God a respecter of persons?) (Acts 10:34) Is the Gospel just for some? Didn't Jesus say it would follow all believers (Mark 16:17)? As we have pointed out earlier in this chapter, all spoke in tongues when they received the Holy Ghost and the promise is for you, your children and ALL that are afar off, as many as the Lord our God shall call (Acts 2).

The question arises from a passage in 1 Corinthians 12. If not rightly divided, it can cause doubts. Paul in 1 Corinthians 12:28-31, is talking about a manifestation of tongues that only some have, as we shall see when we compare this manifestation which all don't receive, and the prayer language of tongues, which all may receive.

Let's look at this categorically:

Devotional Tongues Prayer Language	Tongues as a Ministry in the Church
Devotional tongues; a language that ALL may receive (1 Cor. 14:2) All (Acts 2:4; 19:6-7)	Tongues as one of the 9 gifts (1 Cor. 12:10) of the Spirit which is only for some NOT ALL (1 Cor. 12:30)
I "will" pray (when I desire) (1 Cor. 14:14)	As the Spirit "wills" (it happens) (1 Cor. 12:10-11)
Speak "not unto men" but unto God Devotional Tongues	Speaks to men to edify the church Tongues as a Ministry in the Church

Prayer Language

(1 Cor. 14:2)	(1 Cor. 14:5; 12:7; 14:27).
Edifies the believer (1 Cor. 14:4)	Edifies the church (1 Cor. 14:5)
Is for ALL believers (1 Cor. 14:23)	Is for "some" in the church (1 Cor. 12:28)
Don't speak out loud in church (1 Cor. 14:6)	Speak out loud in church if there is an interpreter (1 Cor. 12:2-7, 28)
For prayer (1 Cor. 14:14, Jude 20)	To edify, exhort and comfort the church (1 Cor. 14:5)

We see in 1 Corinthians 14:23 that they did all speak in tongues for they all were baptized with the Holy Ghost and Paul said, "I would that you all spake in tongues, and I thank my God I speak in tongues more than you all. Yet in the church I had rather speak five words with my understanding, that by my voice I might teach others also, than ten thousand words in an unknown tongue." He is not belittling speaking in tongues, but is glad that they *"ALL"* did speak in tongues, but in the church (in a public gathering) everything must be done decently and in order, for there may be people who come in to see and they won't understand a word you are saying, so if you all speak in tongues out of order, they'll think you are mad (vs. 23). Yes, you are speaking to God and giving thanks well, but others are not edified for to them it is just utterances (1 Corinthians 14:2; 6-11; 16-17). This too proves that their speaking in tongues was not in known languages for it needed an interpreter and if there was none there, then neither could anyone understand what was being said, but God only.

So, Paul was just pointing out the difference in this chapter between tongues as prayer, worship and giving thanks to God which is for private devotion and edification; and a different manifestation of the Holy Spirit, which is tongues and interpretation which should be manifest in a public gathering, two or three at the most (vs. 27). He is simply saying, the only way a public gathering can benefit is to speak in known languages–but this doesn't, at all, belittle the individual's private prayer language received (1 Cor. 12:28). Paul thanked God for his ability to speak in unknown tongues and furthermore, 1 Corinthians 13 and 14 proves that the tongues received was not typically in known languages, but could be the tongues of men or of angels or unknown.

In all cases, the speaker didn't know what he was saying unless there was an interpretation given by the Spirit (1 Cor. 14:14). Paul then was explaining that tongues and interpretation is for the public gathering but the unknown tongue, (prayer language) is for the individual to be edified privately (1 Cor. 14:4; Jude 20). So not all are to speak in tongues in the church gathering. What had happened was that they, (the Corinthians) had gotten tongues (prayer) mixed up with the gift of the Spirit for public assembly, just as much of the church is doing today. Now, every believer can lay hands on the sick and believe that they will recover (Mark 16:18), but not all have the gifts of healings (1 Cor. 12:30); and all believers can cast out devils (Mark 16:17), but not all have discerning of spirits (1 Cor. 12:10); and ALL can preach the Gospel (Acts 9:1-3), but not all are evangelists (Eph. 4:11). Even so with tongues–all believers can speak with tongues (prayer), (1 Cor. 14:5), but not all have the gift of tongues, for manifestation in an assembly or church (1 Cor. 12:10). There was real, valid tongues being spoken in the church, but no one understood what was being said. It was not a known language, it was not for the purpose of speaking in church; yet there was also a manifestation of tongues and interpretation set in the church as Paul points out, for the benefit of the hearers. In his conclusion to instructing them concerning these things, he said in 1 Corinthians 14:39-40: "Wherefore brethren, covet to prophesy AND FORBID NOT TO SPEAK IN TONGUES. Let all things be done decently and in order."

What Is the Purpose of Speaking in Tongues?

The first mention in the New Testament about speaking in new tongues was by Jesus Christ Himself, "These signs shall follow THEM THAT BELIEVE in MY name. . .THEY SHALL SPEAK WITH NEW TONGUES." Tongues then, are one of the signs that Christ said identifies a true believer and follower of Christ. This new tongues, as Scripture testifies, is a manifestation of God's Holy Spirit in the life of a believer (Acts 2:4), and the language is earthly, angelic or unknown (1 Cor. 13:1; 14:2). Jesus DID NOT SAY tongues would follow only the early church or just apostles, but He said it would follow "THEM THAT BELIEVE."

TONGUES IS SPEAKING TO God—it is prayer from the heart or spirit of man (1 Cor. 14:14). Tongues is the spirit of man speaking directly to God who is a spirit (John 4:24), as Paul said, "my spirit prayeth." This is not typically in a known language for Scripture says, "For he that speaketh in an UNKNOWN TONGUE speaketh not UNTO MEN, BUT UNTO GOD: for NO MAN understandeth him; howbeit in the spirit he speaketh mysteries" (things beyond the natural human mind's ability to comprehend at this time) (1 Cor. 14:2). But, this language is known to God, and after all, we are not praying to men but to God, so there is no reason why men would have to understand it. This prayer language given to us by the indwelling Holy Spirit is not something learned, nor does it originate in any sense from the mind of man. Paul said in the Amplified version of 1 Cor. 14:14, "If I pray in an unknown tongue, my spirit 'by the Holy Spirit' within me prays, but my understanding (mind) is unfruitful" (doesn't know what is being said). You may ask, if you don't know what you are saying, what good does it do? Let me answer by stating this: First of all, we know it is prayer and speaking to God, as Scriptures teach. Why then would God give it to us? Because He knew there would be many things concerning His plan, purpose and will for our lives that we, in our own understanding, know nothing of. (As Paul also said in Romans 8:26, "we know not what we should pray for as we ought" and the Bible says, "you have not because you ask not.")

You are a free moral agent. God cannot just make His will happen in your life without your cooperation. You must "pray His will be done on earth" for it to get done. We can further see that things are not happening automatically according to His will, for in II Peter 3:9 Scripture says, "He's NOT WILLING THAT ANY SHOULD PERISH. . . ," but yet people are perishing every day. His will then, as stated, is not just automatically being carried out.

Also, in the Old Testament it says He sought for an intercessor to stand in the gap but found none. Through this wonderful prayer language, however, His people can pray His will and stand in the gap for things even when their mind knows nothing of what's happening. It is still the person praying and they are praying the will of God for they are praying by the direct influence of the Holy Spirit. Therefore, these Spirit-led prayers can be answered. This then takes the limits off of God during this time He gave to man in the earth. In this way God can move in answer to these Holy Spirit inspired prayers of His people. So now His plans and purposes can be released into our lives, even when our minds don't know what to pray for. A big part of the Holy Spirit's ministry in the life of a believer is to help them in his prayer life. Prayer that is in full agreement with the will of God--wonderful prayer! What a magnificent gift!

No wonder the devil has fought so hard to explain it away and to say it has ceased. The old serpent is constantly working to steal it from believers (John 10:10).

Tongues Can Enable You to Tap Into THE MYSTERIES OF God

"For he that speaketh in an unknown tongue speaketh not unto men, but unto God: for no man understandeth him; howbeit in the spirit he speaketh mysteries" (1 Cor. 14:2). These mysteries you are praying about then, are not for God's benefit, but yours. God answers and an area of the Word is illuminated to you, or there comes an intervention of some kind from God. They also are a means of edification, rest, and refreshing for the believer (Isa. 28:11-12). To edify means to strengthen, uplift, fortify, add joy, and to build up, as Jude also said, "But ye beloved BUILDING UP YOURSELVES ON YOUR MOST HOLY FAITH PRAYING IN THE HOLY GHOST." Which of these doesn't the Christian need? We can see how foolish then it is to say it was just for the early church; for Christians of all generations need to pray, be refreshed and be strengthened in their faith. According to these passages, tongues is also a spiritual exercise which builds up the spiritual part of man (Jude 20).

It is giving thanks well (praise and worship). Why would God want to stop this form of spiritual worship from the heart of man? Any honest person will agree that it doesn't make sense to say tongues have ceased in the light of all that the Scriptures say about it (1 Cor. 14:17).

Tongues then is spiritual prayer, spiritual worship, giving thanks well. It's a spiritual rest and refreshing, and is given so that the believer may be wonderfully enriched and edified in his walk with the Lord. Furthermore according to Christ it is a sign that follows a believer. It is by the operation of the Holy Ghost who comes into the spirit, soul and body of a man, and enables that man to speak in the tongues of men, angels and unknown languages. The spirit of man that has been held captive within since the fall, is once again released to express itself to its Creator— Wonder of Wonders! *"For he that speaketh in an unknown tongue* speaketh not unto men, but *unto God*: for no man understandeth him; howbeit in the spirit he speaketh mysteries" (1 Cor. 14:2).

Other Benefits to Receiving the Baptism in the Holy Spirit

First of all, everything God has planned for us in redemption is important; none of it was an afterthought with God, but was planned from before the foundation of the world. The Holy Spirit is the secret code revealer, so to speak, of the Word of God. First Cor. 2:7-14: "But we speak the *wisdom of God* in a mystery even the *hidden wisdom*, which God ordained *before the world* unto our glory, which none of the princes of this world knew; for had they known it, they wouldn't have crucified the Lord of glory." But as it is written, "Eye has not seen, nor ear heard, neither have entered into the heart of man, the things which God hath prepared for them that love Him, *But God hath revealed them unto us (how?) by His Spirit*." Read also Verses 11-14. Paul said, "We have access by one Spirit to the Father" (Eph. 2:18). This gives us access to His heart and the wisdom hidden in Him. It is His Spirit who is sent to teach us, to reveal truth to us, and to guide us. In John 16:12, Jesus said to His disciples that there were *many things they couldn't understand without this gift of the Holy Spirit*, which leads us to know that some things they could understand. We can see in books written by religious groups who aren't even born again that "intellectually" they can dig out many real truths from God's Word. They can put "2 + 2" together, compare certain Scriptures and come up with some answers, just like some fundamental churches. But they also do not have the Holy Spirit Baptism and so whenever present, supernatural truths are revealed in the Word, their unassisted mind cannot grasp them. They, like those who reject the Holy Ghost Baptism, also reject other Scriptural things like tongues, being led by God's Spirit, the Holy Spirit speaking, miracles. It is beyond their intellectual reach. We don't really blame them. They just cannot understand without this Baptism with the Holy Ghost.

The Spirit of God is the great revealer. He is the one who unfolds the Word of God to God's people (John 16:13; 17:17). He doesn't do it through the mind, but through the spirit of man (Prov. 20:27). The Word of God is hidden manna, but it is not hidden from God's people, but for God's people (Luke 10:17-21). The Holy Spirit is the one who will take the things of Jesus and reveal them to the body of Christ (John 16:12-15). All things are revealed in God's Word that are necessary for life and Godliness, but all that is revealed, cannot be grasped with mind or intellect, much of it "CANNOT" be found out by natural man's searching and intellectual study, for it is the Spirit of God that searches out the things of God and reveals them to men (1 Cor. 2:14).

The Spirit of God then, is the only one who can guide men into the deep but yet simple truths of God's Word, and it is only through teaching what the Spirit has taught, that the truth will really set people free (1 Cor. 2:13), for the Spirit teaches on a spiritual level. Man's mind teaches on an intellectual level. The Word of God is not directed only to the intellect, but also to man's spirit. Its aim is the heart of man (1 Pet. 3:4; Rom. 10:9-10). The Word is life; it has power when REVEALED BY THE Spirit, but it is dead letter, when men just try to explain it by their intellects (1 Cor. 2:13). So man's mind unassisted, cannot grasp many of the real, present supernatural spiritual truths of God's revelation; in many ways it is too simple and the intellect is too complicated (2 Cor. 11:3).

Men have tried to figure out God, His ways and His Word with their intellect only; they've gotten their degrees and studied their Greek or Hebrew, instead of letting the Holy Spirit reveal God. But man's intellect can never figure it all out without the help of the Holy Spirit. Yes, a smart, intellectual man with a Ph.D. can figure and reason many things out. He can come out with many good sounding speeches and sermons that can really help people to a degree, but at the same time, deny much of what the Bible clearly teaches and even call much Holy Spirit inspired teaching heresy. It is the Holy Spirit who guides the spirit of man into the light (John 16:13; Prov. 20:27). Study of Greek and Hebrew is fine as long as you don't forget who the teacher really is.

When the Holy Spirit gives light to a man, he can relay spiritual truths to others and set them free by God's power (1 Cor. 2:13). Because of this, God, not man, gets the glory (1 Cor. 1:25-31). Those who pridefully say they know more and are better teachers because of their great knowledge of Greek or Hebrew, exalt themselves. The words of the prophets were words of the Spirit, their intellects did not reveal it to them, but rather, the Holy Spirit spoke through them (2 Pet. 2:20-21). As God's Spirit was in them at times, temporarily to speak His words, even so in this great Church Age, we can now receive the Holy Spirit to reveal God's words (Prov. 1:25), and it is all revealed and received by faith (Heb. 11:6). This is how the life that is in the Word is unveiled.

Let's look at 1 Corinthians 2:1-14. Verse 14: The natural man is bound to his five senses. He has no other place to get his information from. But God's children are to be guided by the indwelling Holy Spirit. This is not just a doctrinal statement; this is a living experience based on Scripture, for the indwelling Holy Spirit translates Scripture into life's experience in the life of the believer. The Holy Spirit knows the mind of Christ and the heart of God, and by the baptism with the Holy Spirit, the child of God has access to the heart of God, and that which is hidden in God can now be revealed as God wills. The natural man has no avenue whereby he can get spiritual revelation so he is limited to his five senses and his intellectual searching.

Verse 15: the spiritual man is the man filled with the Spirit. Those who don't have the Spirit are to a great degree sensual (ruled by their five senses). They cannot discern or discover most of the things of the Spirit. The present supernatural, spiritual truths are foolishness to them. They are limited to their own abilities. For it is not the mind so much that grasps the invisible truths of God's Word, but the heart, the spirit of man, and this with the help of the Holy Spirit. Because many of God's people have chosen the way of natural man to acquire knowledge and have rejected the Holy Spirit baptism, they have chosen the world's way rather than the way of faith and have, in many instances, become blind to many of the things of God. Now we know that all things must be clearly backed up with Scripture and based on the doctrine of Christ, but it is necessary that God's people receive the baptism with the Holy Spirit, which is revealed in Scripture, to understand many of the present day supernatural truths and realities of God's Word. This is why Jesus, after His resurrection, COMMANDED His disciples to wait and not go anywhere, until they were Baptized with the Holy Ghost (Acts 1:3-4).

Besides the great benefit of the mind and spirit being opened up by the Holy Spirit to receive present Scriptural, supernatural truths, a person also receives an anointing of power to witness (Acts 1:8; 1 Pet. 1:12). It is equipment for service. It gives a person the God-given ability to cast out devils and also to operate in the gifts of the Holy Spirit (1 Cor. 12:1-11). You see practically zero operation or manifestation of the spiritual gifts that God has given to the church as recorded in Scripture in churches where they don't believe in speaking in tongues. This area of the Gospel also they try to explain away, because their minds cannot grasp the realities without the help of the indwelling Holy Spirit. Again, we see the real church as it was manifest in the Book of Acts; this is His church: to change the picture at all is to exchange the truth of God for a lie. To say that the church should not be just like the church of Acts, is to proclaim a different church and a different gospel. No one has the right to paint a different picture of it.

It is necessary that the Christian receive all the equipment God has provided. To ignore or reject what the Scriptures clearly teach is to willingly enter dangerous ground, for Jesus said that if you love Him you'll keep His commandments (John 14:15-16). Sad to say, many things religious men do is labor in vain. Scripture says, "Except the Lord build the house, they labor in vain that build it: except the Lord keep the city, the watchman waketh but in vain" (Ps. 127:1). Some spend their whole life laboring in religion, but teaching contrary to the Word and whatever is contrary to the Word will not be rewarded but rather be judged. Notice they religiously labored, they even built a building but it was in vain.

Now Christ, in the days of His flesh, never did do one miracle until after He (as a man) received the fullness of the Holy Ghost (Luke 4:1). He is our example, the church of Acts is our pattern, the Bible is our creed, and His way is the only way; all else are imitations. Jesus was in the days of His flesh, first conceived of the Holy Spirit (Luke 1:35; Matt. 1:18-21), and thirty years later, that same Holy Spirit came down upon Him and filled Him (Luke 3:21-23; 4:1). From that point on there were miracles and manifestations of the power of the Spirit (Luke 4), and following the same pattern, it was after the disciples had received the Holy Ghost, that they saw visions, dreamed dreams, preached by His power, cast out devils, healed the sick, were translated, were led by the Spirit. The Holy Spirit spoke through the gifts of the Spirit in public assembly, gave discerning of spirits, filled them with joy, gave them the ability to speak in tongues, prophesy, and raise the dead. By the Holy Spirit, Peter fell into a trance and saw a vision, Stephen looked up into Heaven, angels came and brought deliverance.

This then, is *the church* as God established it. To say it is different now, is to reject God's blueprint and build your own structure; it is taking away the words of His Book. Notice again unless the Lord build the house they labor in vain that build it. And notice again, they did build but their labor was in vain. So we must leave all things as written for as Jesus said, "The Word will judge us in the last day," and as Peter plainly pointed out, these things would occur in the last days. "And it shall come to pass IN THE LAST DAYS SAITH GOD, I will pour out of My Spirit upon all flesh; and your sons and daughters shall PROPHESY and your young men shall SEE VISIONS and you old men shall DREAM DREAMS." Add to this the signs Jesus said would follow believers in this church age and we can clearly see that the church in the Book of Acts is the model church.

Let's follow the Bible rather than schools of thought, or the worn out reasonings of men and let's press on in the things of God *as recorded in His Word*. Let's stop our childish reasoning why areas of the Bible aren't for today and use Scriptural reasoning why it is for today, or we may be found to be even fighting against God (Acts 5:39).

To those who claimed to follow Him, He said, "If you love Me, keep My commandments, and I will pray the Father, and He shall give you another Comforter, that He may abide with you forever; even the Spirit of truth. . ." (John 14:15-17, 23). In Acts 1:4-5, 8; *He commanded them* not to go anywhere (to neither preach nor teach) until they had received the promise of the Father and were baptized with the Holy Ghost. It was this gift that would give them both power to work and the ability to understand. If the church of the Lord Jesus Christ would have observed this commandment of the Lord, there would not be the division that there is in the body of Christ, "all" would believe in the supernatural faith, as recorded in the Book of Acts; all would believe in the Holy Spirit Baptism and speaking in tongues; all would believe in praying for the sick and casting out devils (Mark 16:15-29); and most of the world would have been won to the Lord. It is a fact that Holy Spirit-filled ministries and churches are some of the fastest growing churches and ministries in the world. This Baptism with the Holy Ghost was His last and final commission to His followers; this was His order; to deny it is to change His words (Matt. 28:18-20). We are to observe all things He commanded them even until the end of the world. Amen.

Now, you have a choice. Will you believe and obey Jesus' words, or will you follow after modernistic theology conjured up by the reasoning minds of men?

If you have believed God's Word thus far, there waits for you blessing from God, for the promise of the gift of the Holy Ghost is for ALL children, it is unto you and to your children, and to all that are afar off, even as many as the Lord, our God, shall call. This is the faith that was once delivered to the saints (Jude 3; Acts 2:38; 5:29-32).

How To Receive the Baptism with the Holy Spirit

We will now share with you some simple scriptural facts concerning the Baptism with the Holy Ghost and how to receive this blessed gift from the Lord. If you will be open in your heart, believe God's Word and cooperate with God's simple instructions, you also will be baptized with the Holy Ghost and receive that wonderful prayer language that we've written about in this part of the book.

First of all, realize that it is for everyone who is a believer; God is not respecter of persons. Jesus said everyone that asketh, receiveth, and this also is connected with the child of God, who is to "ask" the Heavenly Father for the gift of the Holy Ghost (Luke 11:13). Peter said, the promise is to you and your children and ALL that are afar off. All who are believers in Jesus Christ, then can receive this blessed experience (John 7:39). Next, understand that the Holy

Spirit is a gift. You cannot earn or merit this gift. No one deserves to receive it; but the Holy Spirit baptism is God's gift to you, the believer. Don't look at your past track record and faults. You may have fallen many times; this is one of the reasons you need the Holy Spirit. God offers the gift, a gift is something given free of charge. Your part is to receive the gift. It is God's will for you to receive.

Third, Jesus said, "when you stand praying FORGIVE if you have OUGHT AGAINST ANY." Unforgiveness is contrary to the law of love, so all known unforgiveness and sin must be confessed to God, then the blood of Jesus Christ will cleanse you from all unrighteousness. Now, you are on receiving ground.

Fourth, ask for the gift of the Holy Ghost. The Bible says, "You have not because you ask not." You are a free moral agent; God will not force anything upon anyone. Jesus said, "everyone THAT ASKETH receiveth" and again, "How much more will your Heavenly Father GIVE THE HOLY GHOST TO THEM THAT ASK HIM?" We've seen already that the gift of the Holy Ghost is given in response to prayer. John said, "if we ask anything according to His will, He heareth us and if we know that He HEARS us, whatsoever we ASK, we know that we have the petitions desired of Him." So it is necessary for you to pray. If there are Holy Ghost baptized believers whom you know, ask them to come and lay hands upon you like the Bible says. This also is a wonderful way to receive (Acts 19:6-7). If not, you can pray and ask God for yourself.

Fifth, after asking, you must, by faith drink in of the Spirit (John 7:37-38). Your simple act of faith is to take a deep breath in and drink in then believe regardless of feelings, that you are at that moment, being filled and baptized with, and in, the Holy Spirit. The Holy Spirit is given as breath. Jesus breathed on the disciples and said, "receive ye the Holy Ghost." In Job it says, "The Spirit of God hath made me and the BREATH OF THE ALMIGHTY has given me life." So you need to drink in of the Spirit simply by taking a deep breath in and receiving by faith. "Therefore I say unto you, what things soever ye desire when ye pray, believe that ye receive them, and ye shall have them" (Mark 11:24). It's a simple act of faith.

Sixth, after doing the above things in God's Word, you need to know you then have the ability to speak in tongues. To you it may just sound like syllables. Paul said, "If I pray in an unknown tongue, my spirit prayeth but my understanding is unfruitful." It does not come from your mind but from your spirit. Jesus said, "out of your belly shall flow rivers of living water." So, don't try to think up things to say, for that won't help anymore than it would have helped Peter to think up how he could walk on water. He had to take the step of faith and get out of the boat; then when he took the first step and cooperated with the Lord, God then did the miracle. Likewise, in this, if you have believed you received, then take the first step and begin to speak out of your heart, (your spirit), the syllables the Holy ghost gives. Don't wait until something comes to your mind. Speak out (not in your native tongue) for you only have one tongue. Give the indwelling Holy Spirit something to work with, for it is not Him that speaks in tongues, but it is you who speaks (Acts 10:46), as the Spirit gives utterance. Just as you put forth the effort to speak in English, or your native tongue, so now you must step out and speak in tongues. You take the first step and begin speaking; He will supply the utterance. The miracle will take place. That is your corresponding action. If you say you believe God heard your prayer and that the Holy Spirit has come in, then you also have now supernatural ability to speak in tongues. You may, or may not experience feelings. Don't go by feelings. Paul said, "we walk by faith." So then, speak out the utterances whether it be little or flowing like a river. Jesus said, "these signs shall follow them that believe. In My name. . .THEY SHALL SPEAK WITH NEW TONGUES. . . ."

Seventh, be a doer of the Word. In order for you to receive, you must do as the Scriptures have said. God is watching over His Word to perform it; Jesus is ready to baptize you with the Holy Ghost. Are you ready? You need not fear; for God's Word guarantees that if you ask Him for the Holy Ghost, He Himself, will make sure you receive the a deep breath in and receiving by faith. "Therefore I say unto you, what things soever ye desire when ye pray, believe that ye receive them, and ye shall have them" (Mark 11:24). It's a simple act of faith.

You are about to receive this wonderful gift from God. I will lead you in a simple scriptural prayer that is according to God's Word and will, and by the time we are finished, you will have received the gift of the Holy Ghost. Are you ready? God is! "Now is the accepted time."

OK, here we go.
Pray this prayer aloud:

Heavenly Father, and Lord Jesus, I thank You that I am a Christian and Jesus is my Lord. You said in Your Word that You would give me the gift of the Holy Spirit if I would ask. So right now in Jesus' Name, I ask You to fill me; baptize me with the Holy Ghost. I receive, right now, at this moment into myself, the Holy Spirit in all His fullness, by faith, in Jesus' name. Amen.

Now, take a deep breath in and by faith, drink in of the Spirit. NOW!! Without hesitation, begin to speak out syllables and utterances from your belly, your spirit. It is that simple. Continue to speak in tongues and your prayer language will become more fluent. If you need anyone to pray with you, find a Holy Ghost-filled church and ask for any further prayer as needed.

If you have received help, faith and understanding of the Baptism with the Holy Ghost through this book, it would be a real encouragement to this ministry to have you drop us a line and let us know. We would greatly appreciate it. All correspondence can be sent to:

New Creation Christian Fellowship
4400 North Mayfair Road
Wauwatosa, WI 53225
(414) 461-8770

(Please call for meeting times)

It is our heart's desire that this book bring blessing and help to the body of Christ. Our desire is for everyone to believe all of the New Covenant just as it's written that they also might be blessed, and let us all move on with Jesus, our precious Lord and Savior.

If you'd like any special Holy Ghost services at your church or ministry with Bible Teacher Ted Rouse, you may contact us at: (414) 461-8770, or write us. You can also write for a tape and book list.

May the grace of the Lord Jesus Christ, and the love of God and the communion of the Holy Ghost, be with you all. Amen.

About the Author

Ted Rouse has been married over twenty-seven years and has been in full-time ministry since 1981. Having had a life-changing experience with Jesus Christ when calling on the name of the Lord in his bedroom in the mid seventies, Ted went on to receive the Baptism with the Holy Spirit after reading a book called, *This Awakening Generation* by former Baptist minister, John Osteen.

Ted has written a number of books and booklets such as, *Dear Mr. Evolutionist, Please Answer Me This; A Two Step Journey Back to God; What Hell Is Like, Who Must Go There and Why;* and *The Importance of Continuing in the Faith.*

Having had a supernatural call to the ministry after being filled with the Holy Spirit, the Lord then led Pastor Ted Rouse into the wonderful message of faith in God's Word that has revolutionized his life. It is this learning about the absolute integrity of God's written Word upon which his ministry is founded.

Ted has traveled overseas on various occasions and has seen hundreds filled with the Holy Ghost, just like the meetings in the book of Acts.

Presently, Pastor/Bible Teacher Ted Rouse is pastor of a lively faith-filled church in the Milwaukee, Wisconsin area called New Creation Christian Fellowship. He has four children, and together with his wife, Doreen, are all serving and walking with the Lord.

Pastor Rouse has the following life-changing books and tape messages available. To order any of the following, please contact us at: 414-461-8770

Books:

What Is Hell Like? Who Must Go There and Why?

Continuing On in the Faith

A Two Step Journey Back to God

The Key to the Mystery of Life

Have You Received the Holy Ghost Since You Believed?

Dear Mr. Evoluntionist, Please Answer Me This

Contemporary Christian Music, Where's the Controversy?

Witnesses to the Truth

The One Thing You Must Do to Enter Into Heaven (tract)

Tape Sets:

The Creator and His Word

Fresh Nuggets From God's Word

Grace Is Given

Freedom From Satan and His Works

The Will of Man and the Will of God

Predestination, Foreknowledge, Election and the Free Will of Man